Knowledge Management in Organizations

A Critical Introduction

FOURTH EDITION

Donald Hislop,

Rachelle Bosua, and

Remko Helms

OXFORD

UNIVERSITY PRESS

OXFORD
UNIVERSITY PRESS

Great Clarendon Street, Oxford, OX2 6DP,
United Kingdom

Oxford University Press is a department of the University of Oxford.
It furthers the University's objective of excellence in research, scholarship,
and education by publishing worldwide. Oxford is a registered trade mark of
Oxford University Press in the UK and in certain other countries

First edition 2005
Second edition 2009
Third edition 2013

Impression: 1

Published in the United States of America by Oxford University Press
198 Madison Avenue, New York, NY 10016, United States of America

British Library Cataloguing in Publication Data
Data available

Library of Congress Control Number: 2018931540

ISBN 978-0-19-872401-8

Printed in Great Britain by
Bell & Bain Ltd., Glasgow

Knowledge Management in Organizations

Donald: in memory of my beautiful sister Lesley
Rachelle: for my family
Remko: for my loved ones

Brief Contents

Detailed Contents   ix

Figures   xvii

Tables   xviii

Guide to the Book   xx

Guide to the Online Resources   xxii

1   The Contemporary Importance of Knowledge and Knowledge Management   1

PART 1 **Epistemologies of Knowledge in the Knowledge Management Literature**
....

2   The Objectivist Perspective on Knowledge   15

3   The Practice-Based Perspective on Knowledge   30

PART 2 **An Introduction to Key Concepts**
....

4   What is Knowledge Management?   49

5   Knowledge-Intensive Firms and Knowledge Workers   68

PART 3 **Innovation, Knowledge Creation, and Unlearning**
....

6   Learning and Knowledge Management   91

7   Innovation and Knowledge Processes   110

8   Unlearning, Knowledge Loss, and the Protection of Knowledge   126

PART 4 **Introduction to ICTs and Knowledge Management**
....

9   Objectivist Perspectives on ICTs and Knowledge Management   151

10 Practice-Based Perspectives on ICT-Enabled Knowledge Management   163

PART 5 **Socio-cultural Issues Related to Managing and Sharing Knowledge**
....

**11 The Influence of Socio-cultural Factors in Motivating Workers
      to Participate in Knowledge Management Initiatives**   177

12   Communities of Practice   195

**13   Boundary-Spanning Knowledge Processes in
      Heterogeneous Collaborations**   216

14   Power, Politics, Conflict, and Knowledge Processes   235

PART 6 **The Management of Knowledge Work (and Workers)**

**15   Facilitating Knowledge Management via
      the Use of Human Resource Management Practices**   255

**16   Leadership, Organization Culture Management,
      and Knowledge Management**   271

References   287
Index   315

Detailed Contents

Figures		xvii
Tables		xviii
Guide to the Book		xx
Guide to the Online Resources		xxii

1 The Contemporary Importance of Knowledge and Knowledge Management — **1**

Introduction	1
Key assumptions in the knowledge management literature	2
The knowledge society concept and its links to Bell's post-industrial society concept	3
A critical evaluation of the knowledge society concept	6
Aims, philosophy, and structure	8
Review and Discussion Questions	12
Suggestions for Further Reading	12

PART 1 Epistemologies of Knowledge in the Knowledge Management Literature

2 The Objectivist Perspective on Knowledge — **15**

Introduction	15
Objectivist perspectives on knowledge	15
The knowledge-based theory of the firm	17
Typologies of knowledge	18
Tacit and explicit knowledge	19
Individual–group knowledge	20
An objectivist perspective on the sharing and management of knowledge	23
Conduit model of knowledge sharing	24
Knowledge management processes	25
Conclusion	27
Case study Factors shaping the successful transfer of knowledge within an MNC: an objectivist analysis	27
Review and Discussion Questions	29
Suggestions for Further Reading	29

3   The Practice-Based Perspective on Knowledge   30

Introduction   30

Features of a practice-based perspective on knowledge   31

    The embeddedness of knowledge in practice   31

    Knowledge as multidimensional and non-dichotomous   33

    Knowledge is embodied   35

    The socially constructed and culturally embedded nature of knowledge   37

    The contestable nature of knowledge   39

A practice-based perspective on the management and sharing of knowledge   40

Conclusion   43

Case study The collective knowledgeability of care: a case study of an Italian care home   43

Review and Discussion Questions   44

Suggestions for Further Reading   45

PART 2 **An Introduction to Key Concepts**

4   What is Knowledge Management?   49

Introduction   49

What is knowledge management?   49

Factors influencing organizational approaches to knowledge management   53

Conceptualizing the diversity of knowledge management approaches   58

Knowledge strategy frameworks   58

    Von Krogh et al. (2001): leveraging, expanding, appropriating, and probing   58

    Kim et al. (2014): internal and external codification, internal
and external personalization   60

Knowledge management strategy frameworks   60

    Hansen et al.'s (1999) codification versus personalization framework   60

    Alvesson and Kärreman's (2001) four knowledge management approaches   63

Conclusion   64

Case study Centralizing knowledge management: McKinsey's Knowledge Network   65

Review and Discussion Questions   67

Suggestions for Further Reading   67

5   Knowledge-Intensive Firms and Knowledge Workers   68

Introduction   68

The knowledge economy and the growing importance of knowledge-intensive
firms and knowledge workers   69

Defining and characterizing knowledge-intensive firms   70

Defining knowledge workers: the professional knowledge work perspective   72

Defining knowledge workers: the 'all work is knowledge work' perspective   74

Knowledge work and ambiguity   76

Knowledge and knowledge processes in knowledge-intensive firms   78

    Knowledge workers, intellectual capital, and innovation   78

    Knowledge creation   79

    Knowledge integration/application   79

    Social capital, knowledge workers, and knowledge-intensive firms   81

The willingness of knowledge workers to participate in knowledge processes: contrasting perspectives   82

    Knowledge workers: the ideal employee?   82

    Factors inhibiting knowledge workers' work efforts and knowledge management activities   83

Conclusion   84

Case study The linkages between learning orientation, knowledge assets, and HR practices in professional service firms   85

Review and Discussion Questions   86

Suggestions for Further Reading   86

PART 3 Innovation, Knowledge Creation, and Unlearning

6   Learning and Knowledge Management   91

Introduction   91

The heterogeneity of learning   92

    Characterizing learning in organizations   92

    Learning mechanisms and processes   92

The dynamics of organizational learning   94

The learning organization: emancipation or exploitation?   96

    The learning organization: the advocates' vision   97

    The learning organization: the pessimists' or sceptics' perspective   100

Conclusion   106

Case study The role of time and discontinuities in shaping the complex dynamics of organizational learning   107

Review and Discussion Questions   109

Suggestions for Further Reading   109

7   Innovation and Knowledge Processes   110

Introduction   110

The scope and evolution of Nonaka's knowledge creation theory   111

The epistemology of knowledge creation theory   112

SECI and knowledge creation/conversion 113

Ba 116

The critique of Nonaka's knowledge creation theory 116

Innovation, knowledge processes, and absorptive capacity 120

Conclusion 123

Case study Knowledge creation, absorptive capacity, and product innovativeness 124

Review and Discussion Questions 125

Suggestions for Further Reading 125

8   Unlearning, Knowledge Loss, and the Protection of Knowledge   126

Introduction 126

Unlearning and forgetting in organizational contexts 128

Unlearning as a type of deliberate forgetting 128

Unlearning, learning, and change 131

Antecedents of unlearning 133

Individual-level antecedents of unlearning 134

Organizational-level antecedents of unlearning 135

Knowledge leakage 137

Leakage from tacit and explicit knowledge perspectives 138

Knowledge protection 140

Conclusion 143

Case study The impact of team reflexivity and stress on unlearning and innovation in new product development teams 143

Review and Discussion Questions 144

Suggestions for Further Reading 145

PART 4 **Introduction to ICTs and Knowledge Management**

Inseparability of knowledge management and computer-based technology 148

Linking knowledge management and ICTs 148

9   Objectivist Perspectives on ICTs and Knowledge Management   151

Introduction 151

Objectivist perspective on ICT-enabled knowledge management 151

Epistemological assumptions and ICTs 152

Three ICT-enabled knowledge management approaches based on the objectivist perspective 152

Repository-based approach to ICT-based knowledge management 152

Process and domain knowledge model approach to ICT-based knowledge management 155

Sensor-based approach to ICT-based knowledge management 157

Critical reflection of objectivist approaches on ICTs and knowledge
management   159

Conclusion   159

Case study Wiki as tool to share knowledge in an SME   160

Review and Discussion Questions   161

Suggestions for Further Reading   162

10   Practice-Based Perspectives on ICT-Enabled Knowledge Management   163

Introduction   163

Epistemological assumptions and ICTs   163

Practice-based perspectives on knowledge and the three roles for
ICTs in knowledge management   164

 Network-based approach to ICT-based knowledge management   164

 Collaboration tools to facilitate ICT-based communication
 and knowledge sharing   166

 Crowd-based approach to ICT-based knowledge management   169

Conclusion   171

Case study Yammer at Deloitte Australia   171

Review and Discussion Questions   172

Suggestions for Further Reading   173

PART 5 Socio-cultural Issues Related to Managing and Sharing Knowledge

**11   The Influence of Socio-cultural Factors in Motivating
        Workers to Participate in Knowledge Management Initiatives   177**

Introduction   177

The share/hoard dilemma   178

The context of the employment relationship: employer–employee
relations in business organizations   180

The ubiquity of conflict in business organizations and its impact on
knowledge processes   182

Inter-personal trust   184

Group identity   187

National culture   188

Personality   190

Conclusion   191

Case study ParcelCo: a case study of factors inhibiting knowledge sharing   192

Review and Discussion Questions   193

Suggestions for Further Reading   194

12 Communities of Practice   **195**

Introduction   195

Defining communities of practice   196

Communities of practice: origins, features, and dynamics   197

Communities of practice and intra-community knowledge processes   200

Types of communities of practice   200

Online communities   203

Managing communities of practice   204

Visualizing and analysing communities of practice: social network analysis   207

Critical perspectives on communities of practice   209

    Power, conflict, and the internal dynamics of communities   210

    Blinkered and inward-looking communities   211

Conclusion   212

Case study Communities of practice as means to implement agile
software development at Ericsson   213

Review and Discussion Questions   214

Suggestions for Further Reading   214

**13 Boundary-Spanning Knowledge Processes in
Heterogeneous Collaborations**   **216**

Introduction   216

The significance of boundary-spanning collaboration   218

Characterizing boundary-spanning knowledge processes   220

    Identity   220

    Knowledge   222

Identity, knowledge, trust, and social relations   224

A classification of boundary types   226

Facilitating/managing knowledge between communities   227

    Relationship management   228

    Boundary objects   229

Conclusion   231

Case study Cross-functional knowledge sharing in R&D via
co-location: the case of Novartis   232

Review and Discussion Questions   233

Suggestions for Further Reading   234

14 Power, Politics, Conflict, and Knowledge Processes   **235**

Introduction   235

Two perspectives on power and the power/knowledge relationship   236

Power as a resource and the critical discourse on knowledge management   238

    Theorizing power and power/knowledge relations   238

Linking power and knowledge to conflict and politics 240

The critical discourse on knowledge management and the inevitability
of power and conflict in business organizations 243

Power/knowledge and the dialogical discourse on knowledge management 244

Conceptualizing power/knowledge 245

Discourse, power/knowledge, and the legitimation of truth claims 246

Power/knowledge and conflict across organizational boundaries 246

Conclusion 248

Case study Power matters: the importance of Foucault's power/knowledge
in knowledge management research 249

Review and Discussion Questions 250

Suggestions for Further Reading 250

PART 6 The Management of Knowledge Work (and Workers)

15   Facilitating Knowledge Management via
the Use of Human Resource Management Practices 255

Introduction 255

Why HRM practices are important to knowledge management 256

HRM practices and knowledge management 258

Recruitment and selection 259

Job design 260

Training 261

Coaching and mentoring 262

Reward and performance appraisal 263

HRM, staff retention, and knowledge management 265

Conclusion 267

Case study Rethinking the role of HRM practices in facilitating knowledge
exchange: a case study of CERN, a knowledge-intensive organization 268

Review and Discussion Questions 269

Suggestions for Further Reading 269

16   Leadership, Organization Culture Management, and Knowledge
Management 271

Introduction 271

The impact of organizational culture on knowledge management activities 273

Creating and managing an organizational culture to support
knowledge management activities 277

The conceptualization of leadership in the academic business
and management literature 278

Knowledge management and leadership   281

Conclusion   284

Case study   The impact of organizational culture on knowledge
sharing: the case of Danisco   284

Review and Discussion Questions   286

Suggestions for Further Reading   286

References   287

Index   315

Figures

1.1   Characteristics of a Post-Industrial Society   4

1.2   Schultze and Stabell's (2004) Four Discourses on Knowledge Management   9

2.1   The Conduit Model of Knowledge Sharing   24

4.1   Von Krogh's Knowledge Management Typology   59

4.2   Alvesson and Kärreman's Knowledge Management Approaches   64

6.1   The Modified Crossan et al. Model   95

6.2   Linking Power and Politics to Learning   103

7.1   The SECI Model of Knowledge Creation   113

7.2   Crossan and Apaydin's Determinants of Organizational Innovation   121

8.1   Typology of Organizational Forgetting   130

12.1 How Communities of Practice Underpin Knowledge Processes   201

12.2 Verburg and Andriessen's (2011) Types of Community of Practice   202

12.3 Example of the Visualization of a Knowledge Sharing Network   207

13.1 Easterby-Smith et al.'s (2008) Model of Factors Shaping Inter-organizational
          Knowledge Transfer   217

14.1 Linking Power, Politics, and Conflict   241

16.1 Cameron and Quinn's Organizational Culture Typology   275

Tables

Part 1

2.1	The Objectivist Character of Knowledge	16
2.2	The Characteristics of Tacit and Explicit Knowledge	19
2.3	Generic Knowledge Types	21
2.4	Hecker's (2012) Three Types of Collective Knowledge	22
2.5	An Objectivist Perspective on Knowledge Management	25
3.1	Practice-Based Characteristics of Knowledge	31
3.2	Challenging Objectivist Dichotomies	34
3.3	A Practice-Based Perspective on Knowledge Management	41

Part 2

4.1	Theoretical Foundations of Knowledge Management Theories	52
4.2	Massingham's (2004) Model of Knowledge-Based Strategy-Making Processes	54
4.3	Codification and Personalization Knowledge Strategies	61
5.1	Von Nordenflycht's (2010) Taxonomy of Knowledge-Intensive Firms	71
5.2	Frenkel et al.'s Three Dimensional Conceptualization of Work	73
5.3	The Knowledge, Skills, and Creativity Involved in Office Equipment Service Engineering	76
5.4	The Ambiguities Inherent to Knowledge Work	77
5.5	The Three Dimensions of Social Capital	81

Part 3

6.1	Typologies of Learning	93
6.2	Characteristics of Learning Processes in the Crossan/Zietsma Model	96
6.3	The Learning Company Framework of Pedler et al. (1997)	98
6.4	Factors Affecting Learning in Organizations	107
7.1	Nonaka's Four Modes of Knowledge Conversion	114
7.2	Assumptions and Cultural Values Underpinning Knowledge Conversion Modes	119
8.1	Types of Unlearning	133
8.2	Tacit and Explicit Knowledge Protection Activities and Example Mechanisms	142

Part 4

I	Divergent Approaches to ICT-Enabled Knowledge Management	149
II	ICT Support for Knowledge Management Processes	150

Part 5

11.1	The Potential Advantages and Disadvantages to Workers of Sharing their Knowledge	179
11.2	McAllister's Two Types of Trust	187
11.3	Characteristics of the Traits in the Five-Factor Personality Model	190
12.1	Difference between a Community of Practice and Formal Work Groups	196
12.2	Building Blocks of Communities of Practice	199
13.1	Factors Making Boundary-Spanning Knowledge Processes Difficult	220
13.2	Carlile's (2002, 2004) Boundary Types and their Characteristics	227
13.3	Carlile's Boundary Object Types	230
13.4	Carlile's Boundary Types and Appropriate Boundary Objects	230
14.1	Mapping of Two Perspectives of Power onto Critical and Dialogic Perspectives on Knowledge Management Research	237
14.2	Properties of Power Resources which Make Them Influential	238
14.3	Types of Power	239

Part 6

15.1	Attitudes and Behaviours Relevant to Knowledge Management Initiatives	256
15.2	Types of Loyalty and Strategies for Developing Them	267
16.1	Linking Knowledge Management Initiatives to Organizational Culture	278
16.2	Historical Overview of Diverse Perspectives on Leadership	279
16.3	Distinguishing Leadership from (Micro-)Management	280

Guide to the Book

Definitions

Definition boxes accompany the discussion of essential concepts, helping you to understand key terms.

Time to reflect boxes

Pause and reflect on the material being discussed with these provocative questions, discussion points, and exercises, which are written to develop your critical thinking skills and deepen your understanding of the theory and practices of knowledge management.

Illustrations

Contemporary, varied illustrations from research and the business world, with accompanying questions, illustrate the concepts discussed in the chapter and prompt you to analyse the knowledge management practices of a range of organizations.

Case studies

Longer, more integrative case studies at the end of chapters provide a further opportunity for you to apply what you have learnt from the chapter to practical knowledge management research or a real-life business example. Accompanying case study questions facilitate reflection and discussion.

Review and discussion questions

Review and Discussion Questions

1. What is your position on the knowledge society debate? Do you believe that the economy and society in the country you live in have the characteristics of a knowledge society? What evidence supports and undermines your argument?

2. Why do you think academic interest in the topic of knowledge management has been sustained since it first became a topic of interest?

3. The dissensus-based discourses in Schultze and Stabell's model (see Figure 1.2) raise the idea that knowledge management initiatives may not always be in the best interests of everyone working in an organization. To what extent do knowledge management initiatives create conflicts of interest between senior managers and workers in business organizations?

4. Establishing a link between investment in knowledge management activities and business value/performance raises questions regarding what aspect of business value/performance is examined (such as profit levels, market share, innovation levels, productivity levels, etc.), as well as how it is

Reinforce your learning, aid your revision, and share ideas with these end-of-chapter review and discussion questions, which cover the main themes and issues raised in the chapter.

Suggestions for Further Reading

Suggestions for Further Reading

P. Heisig et al. (2016). 'Knowledge Management and Business Performance: Global Experts' Views on Future Research Needs', *Journal of Knowledge Management*, 20/6: 1169–98.
Considers the challenges involved in identifying the extent to which investments in knowledge management create business value.

U. Schultze and C. Stabell (2004). 'Knowing What You Don't Know: Discourses and Contradictions in Knowledge Management Research', *Journal of Management Studies*, 41: 549–73.
A useful analysis which provides a way to categorize the diverse range of work published on knowledge management.

S. Walby (2011). 'Is the Knowledge Society Gendered?', *Gender, Work and Organization*, 18: 1–29.
Not only examines how issues of gender link to knowledge work and the knowledge society, but also presents different definitions of what constitutes the knowledge economy.

An annotated list of seminal books and journal articles that have contributed to the field of knowledge management are provided at the end of chapters. Use these lists to guide your reading around a particular topic, broaden your understanding, and provide useful leads for coursework and assignments.

Guide to the Online Resources

This book is accompanied by free online teaching and learning resources for both students and lecturers. Students can benefit from web links and additional case studies, while lecturers can make use of exam, essay, and coursework questions, and seminar activities.

Visit www.oup.com/uk/hislop4e/ to find out more.

The Contemporary Importance of Knowledge and Knowledge Management

Introduction

> Some think the 'knowledge turn' a matter of macro-historical change; citing Drucker, Bell, Arrow, Reich or Winter, they assert we have moved into an Information Age wherein knowledge has become the organization's principal asset.
>
> (Spender and Scherer 2007: 6)

> The physical toil of manufacturing is being replaced by a world where we work more with our heads than our hands.
>
> (Sewell 2005: 685–6)

> A firm's competitive advantage depends more than anything on its knowledge: on what it knows—how it uses what it knows—and how fast it can know something new.
>
> (*HR Magazine* 2009: 1)

In a textbook on knowledge management it is important to put the subject in context, as this helps explain the interest in it. The explosion of interest in knowledge management among academics, public policy makers, consultants, and business people began as recently as the mid-1990s. The level of interest in knowledge management since then is visible in a number of ways. First, the knowledge society/economy rhetoric is utilized by a wide range of governments and non-governmental organizations (Fleming et al. 2004; Warhurst and Thompson 2006; Mandelson 2009; Halme et al. 2014). While it is impossible to accurately quantify the number of business organizations which have attempted to develop and implement knowledge management systems, various surveys suggest that a significant number of organizations have undertaken such initiatives (KPMG 2000, 2003; Coakes et al. 2010; Griffiths and Moon 2011). Finally, a search of any search engine such as Google or Google Scholar using the key term 'knowledge management' reveals the vast number of articles, books, and reports that have been written on the topic.

The late 1990s also witnessed an exponential increase in the number of academic articles and books published on the topic of knowledge management. Thus, surveys by both Scarbrough and Swan (2001) and Wilson (2002) revealed that prior to the mid-1990s interest in the topic was virtually non-existent, but from about 1996 onwards, the number of publications on knowledge management grew exponentially. Both these articles, however, suggested that there was a risk that knowledge management was a passing fad (Wilson is particularly scathing and talks of knowledge management as a bandwagon 'without wheels'), and predicted that there was likely to be an 'impending decline' of interest in the topic (Scarbrough and Swan 2001: 56). However, contemporary analysis suggests such a decline has not occurred, and that the early years of the twenty-first century saw a sustained interest in the topic (Ragab and Arisha 2013; Serenko and Bontis 2013). For example, Hislop (2010) found that between 2000 and 2008 the number of academic publications on the topic of knowledge management increased quite significantly.

The ongoing academic interest in knowledge management is also visible in a number of other ways, such as in the emergence of a number of conferences on the topic which have become regular annual events, as well as the topic of learning and knowledge now becoming regular themes at many long-standing management and organization conferences. Finally, there has also been the birth of a number of journals specifically concerned with issues of learning and knowledge management. Serenko et al. (2010) suggest that there are at least twenty peer-reviewed academic journals in this field.

Key assumptions in the knowledge management literature

The central idea uniting and underpinning the vast majority of the knowledge management literature, that it is important for organizations to manage their workforce's knowledge, flows from a number of key assumptions embodied in the three quotations which open the chapter. First, Spender and Scherer's quotation illustrates the assumption that the end of the twentieth century witnessed an enormous social and economic transformation which resulted in knowledge becoming the key asset for organizations to manage. A second key assumption, flowing from the first one, and illustrated by Sewell's quotation, is that the nature of work has also changed significantly, with the importance of intellectual work increasing significantly. The third, related key assumption, illustrated by the third quotation, is that the effective management by an organization of its knowledge base is likely to provide a source of competitive advantage (see also Swart 2011; Andreeva and Kianto 2012; Mehra et al. 2014). See Illustration 1.1 for reflections on this.

 Illustration 1.1 Knowledge management and the link to business performance

Heisig et al. (2016) examined the views of knowledge management academics on the link between knowledge management activities and business performance. The main conclusion was that, despite a number of claims being made about a positive linkage existing between investment in knowledge management activities and business performance, further research is necessary on this complex topic. More specifically, it was concluded that research into the link between knowledge management and organizational decision-making processes, organizational learning, innovation levels, and productivity levels as well as business strategy were some key areas for investigation.

Question

What challenges are likely to exist in attempting to establish a causal relationship between an investment in knowledge management and improved business performance?

While the growth of interest in knowledge management only took off during the mid-1990s the theoretical foundation for the assumptions it makes resonate with, and to some extent flow from Daniel Bell's (1973) post-industrial society concept. Thus it is useful to examine his work in a little detail.

The knowledge society concept and its links to Bell's post-industrial society concept

The knowledge management literature is typically based on an analysis which suggests that since approximately the mid-1970s, economies and society in general have become more information and knowledge intensive, with information-/knowledge-intensive industries replacing manufacturing industry as the key wealth generators (see, for example, Neef 1999; DeFillippi et al. 2006). Arguably, the main source of inspiration for this vision was, and is, Daniel Bell's seminal book *The Coming of Post-Industrial Society*, which was first published in 1973. While earlier writers, notably von Hayek (1945) and one of his pupils, Machlup (1962), developed a similar analysis, Bell's work has provided the main inspiration for contemporary writers in the area of knowledge management. As a consequence, Bell's post-industrial society (see Definition) and contemporary conceptualizations of knowledge society bear more than a passing resemblance to each other. Further, Bell himself has, over time, used the terms knowledge and information societies interchangeably with the post-industrial society concept (Webster 1996).

Bell's analysis is based on a typology of societies characterized by their predominant mode of employment (Webster 1996). Thus, an industrial society is characterized by an emphasis on manufacturing and fabrication: the building of things. In a post-industrial society, however, which is argued to evolve out of an industrial society, the service sector has replaced the manufacturing sector as the biggest source of employment (see Figure 1.1). Another crucial characteristic of Bell's post-industrial society is that knowledge and information play a much more significant role in economic and social life than during industrial society, as work in the service sector is argued to be significantly more information and knowledge intensive than industrial work.

Finally, Bell suggests that not only has there been a quantitative increase in the role and importance of knowledge and information, but there has also been a qualitative change in the type of knowledge that is most important. In a post-industrial society, theoretical knowledge

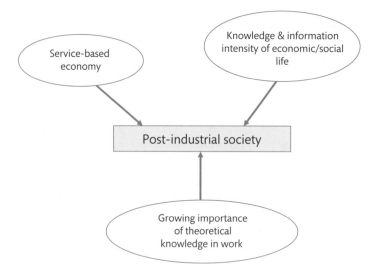

Figure 1.1 Characteristics of a Post-Industrial Society

has become the most important type of knowledge. Theoretical knowledge represents abstract knowledge and principles, which can be codified, or at least embedded in systems of rules and frameworks for action. This is to a large extent because for Bell, in post-industrial societies professional service work is of central importance, and this type of work typically involves the development, use, and application of abstract, theoretical knowledge more than manual work ever did. This relates not just to technical knowledge, such as may be used in research and development (R&D) processes, but also encompasses a large and growing diversity of jobs which increasingly require the application and use of such knowledge—for example, formulation of government policy, architecture, medicine, software design, etc. This topic is returned to and elaborated in Chapter 5, when the debates regarding how to define knowledge work, and knowledge-intensive firms, are examined.

DEFINITION **Post-industrial society**

A society where the service sector is dominant and knowledge-based goods/services have replaced industrial, manufactured goods as the main wealth generators.

An important element of Bell's analysis is that post-industrial societies represent an advancement on industrial societies, as in general more wealth will be generated, and workers individually will have better, more fulfilling jobs. In fact, there is a tendency towards utopianism in aspects of Bell's vision (Vogt 2016), as he argues that: unpleasant, repetitive jobs will decline in number significantly; social inequality will reduce; (all) individuals will have increased amounts of disposable income to spend on personal services; society will be able to better plan for itself; and social relations will become less individualistic and provide greater scope for community development and collective support.

In order to empirically test and substantiate such claims, statistical evidence is typically mobilized to show the increasing importance of service work, and the simultaneous decline of manufacturing employment (see Illustration 1.2). Thus, statistics on the US economy in the mid-1970s were argued to show that 46 per cent of its economic output was from the information sector, and 47 per cent of the total workforce was employed in this sector (Kumar 1995). Castells (1998), in articulating his vision of a network/information society, mobilized an impressive amount of evidence from a wide range of economies which showed the long-term, historical shift from industry to services, and from goods handling to information handling work.

Some empirical evidence on the growing skill intensity of much work also supports Bell's thesis. For example, Zuboff (1988) suggested that advances in computer technology had the potential to make work more knowledge and skill intensive, through the potential for problem solving and abstraction these technologies provide workers. This perspective is supported by research conducted by Gallie et al. (1998) in the UK in the mid-1990s, where almost 65 per cent of workers surveyed reported experiencing an increase in the skill levels of their jobs. Further evidence also reinforces these conclusions (Felstead et al. 2000; NSTF 2000).

 Illustration 1.2 Employment, gender, and definitions of the knowledge economy

Walby's (2011) central focus is on how issues of gender relate to the knowledge economy/society. One element in her paper relates to how the gender composition of employment varies dependent upon how the knowledge economy is defined. Walby utilizes three separate definitions of the knowledge economy. One definition focuses on high-technology manufacturing work, which includes industries such as computers, office machinery, and consumable electronic goods. The second definition of the knowledge economy used by Walby focuses on information and communication technologies (ICTs)-related industries which includes sectors such as publishing, mass media, telecommunications, computer and related activities such as software development. Both of these definitions focus heavily on technology-intensive sectors/industries. The third and final definition of the knowledge economy utilized by Walby is knowledge-intensive services, which includes a wide range of sectors such as air transport, telecommunications, financial services, computers, and R&D. Walby presents data which shows that in the UK in 2005, 1 per cent of employment was in high-technology manufacturing, 4 per cent was in the information technology (IT) sector, and 42 per cent was in knowledge-intensive services. The proportions of employment in each area reflect the specificities of the UK economy, and are likely to vary significantly between countries.

Arguably, the knowledge economy could be defined as the aggregate total of these separate definitions/sectors. However, by disaggregating the knowledge economy Walby is able to highlight gender-related differences in each of the three sub-sectors. In examining the gender composition of employment in the knowledge economy, Walby again focuses solely on the UK, and utilizes data from the UK government's Labour Force Survey. This data shows that the gender composition of employment varies significantly in each sub-sector, with high-technology manufacturing industries being particularly male-dominated with only 32 per cent of jobs in these industries being done by women. While the information sector is also male-dominated in employment terms (36 per cent female employment), knowledge-intensive services are female dominated (61 per cent female employment). Walby's conclusion is that the more centred definitions of the knowledge economy are on technology and manufacturing, the more male-dominated the knowledge economy is, and the more definitions focus on services, the more female-dominated the knowledge economy becomes.

Question

Which of Walby's definitions of a knowledge economy do you regard as the most useful, and why?

Overall therefore, aggregate statistical evidence appears to support the knowledge society/post-industrial society thesis. However, Bell's thesis has been the subject of a sustained, and not insignificant, critique, much of which has relevance to the knowledge society vision developed by contemporary writers on knowledge management. Further, the extent to which work is increasingly knowledge-based has also been challenged by alternative statistics and analysis. The following section changes focus to consider these criticisms.

A critical evaluation of the knowledge society concept

One of the main criticisms of the arguments made by knowledge society or post-industrial society theorists, is that they typically conflate knowledge work with service sector jobs. Thus, as outlined, aggregate statistics on the size of service sector employment is usually used to indicate the transition to a knowledge society (see Time to reflect). However, not all service sector work can be classified as knowledge work, as the service sector is a residual employment category for all types of work which are not either manufacturing or agricultural. Thus the service sector encompasses an enormously heterogeneous range of job types, including consultants and cleaners as well as scientists and security guards. As such, the service sector does not represent a coherent and uniform category of employment. While some service sector work such as consultancy, research, etc., can be classified as being knowledge intensive, other types of service work, such as security, office cleaning, and fast food restaurant work, is low-skilled, repetitive, and routine (Thompson et al. 2001). Therefore to suggest that all service sector employment is knowledge-intensive work does not acknowledge the reality of much service sector work.

 Time to reflect   Call centres and knowledge-intensive work

While customer service work in call centres is typically highly controlled, routine, and repetitive it also involves the use of computers and a significant amount of interaction with customers. To what extent can such work be regarded as more skilled and knowledge intensive than skilled or semi-skilled factory work?

The transition from an industrial to a post-industrial knowledge economy should produce an increase in the proportion of jobs that are knowledge intensive, and a more general increase in the knowledge intensity of work. There is some evidence for this, as statistical analyses typically show that managerial and professional work, which is typically regarded as knowledge intensive, has been one of the fastest growing occupational groups since the 1980s (Elias and Gregory 1994; Fleming et al. 2004). However, focusing on this trajectory alone provides a partial and over-simplistic overview of the way work has been changing. Vogt (2016) argues that there has been a shift in the use of Bell's post-industrial society concept from Bell's original utopianism (making hopeful speculation about the future) towards a more ideological contemporary use, where the concept is used in a blinkered way to emphasize and celebrate certain aspects of change, while obscuring and ignoring others. The aspects of contemporary social change that are often ignored by those advocating the emergence of a knowledge society are now considered.

Simultaneous to the growth in professional and managerial work there has been an equally significant growth in low-skilled, service work (Thompson et al. 2001). This is leading to what Mansell and Steinmueller (2000: 403) suggest is 'a growing polarization of the labour market between highly skilled, highly paid jobs, and low skilled, lower paid jobs . . .', a conclusion reached by a growing number of writers (Littler and Innes 2003; Fleming et al. 2004; Warhurst and Thompson 2006; Alvesson 2014; Alvesson and Spicer 2016). Thus, rather than there being a single trajectory in the direction of upskilling and increasing knowledge intensity, there are two, simultaneous trends, moving in opposite directions. A detailed statistical analysis of employment statistics in Australia conducted by Fleming et al. (2004) provides empirical support for this 'polarization thesis'. Thus while such analyses provide some support for the knowledge society thesis, they also suggest that the idea that there is a universal increase in the knowledge intensity of work in general is simplistic and a little misleading.

Questions have also been raised regarding the way knowledge was conceptualized by Bell. His conception of theoretical knowledge as codifiable and objective draws on classical images of scientific knowledge. However, much contemporary analysis views knowledge as having substantially different characteristics, being partial, tacit, subjective, and context-dependent (see Chapters 2 and 3 for these debates).

While aspects of the analytical frameworks developed by post-industrial society and knowledge society theorists can be criticized and challenged, this does not mean that society and economies have remained unchanged, or that every aspect of these analyses is unfounded. Thus, it is undeniable that the last quarter of the twentieth century was a period of profound change. For the advanced, industrial economies there was not only a significant change in the type of products and services produced, and the nature of work itself, but the role of information and knowledge, in many aspects of social and economic life, also increased substantially. However, it is arguably going too far to suggest that these changes represent a fundamental rupture, witnessing the birth of a new type of society. This is because while much change has occurred, there have also been significant elements of continuity: organizations remain driven by the same imperatives of accumulation, and the general social relations of capitalism remain unchanged.

Such a conclusion is made by McKinlay (2005: 242), who suggests that one of the key drivers for knowledge-intensive firms, such as those in the pharmaceutical industry, to develop knowledge management systems is 'new competitive pressures within capitalism for perpetual innovation in products, services and organization by leveraging the tacit knowledge of their employees.' Thus to challenge Bell's conceptualization of a post-industrial society as representing a fundamental rupture with existing social and economic structures is not to suggest that there has been no change. Equally, such critiques cannot be used to conclude that knowledge is not important to contemporary business organizations.

Aims, philosophy, and structure

The final objective of this chapter is to articulate the general aims and philosophy of this book, as well as outlining the themes and issues examined in each chapter. A useful way to articulate the aims and philosophy of this textbook is to sketch out an overview of the various perspectives on knowledge and knowledge management that exist in the academic literature and locate the perspective adopted here within this framework. As will be seen, one of the features of this academic literature is the diversity of quite different perspectives that exist. However, despite the heterogeneity of the literature on knowledge management, a number of broad perspectives can be identified.

A useful framework that helps to characterize the knowledge management literature, and simultaneously highlight issues which are typically neglected in it, was developed by Schultze and Stabell (2004), which is itself based on Burrell and Morgan's (1979) sociological para-digms framework. As with Burrell and Morgan's (1979) work on sociological paradigms, they articulate a two dimensional framework which produces four distinctive knowledge manage-ment discourses. Due to the different perspectives on epistemology in the knowledge man-agement literature, this is one of the dimensions in Schultze and Stabell's framework. What is here labelled the objectivist perspective, Schultze and Stabell label the epistemology of dualism, and what is here referred to as the practice-based perspective, Schultze and Stabell label the epistemology of duality.

The second dimension in their framework relates to social order, with differences existing in the extent to which existing social relations are regarded as consensual and unproblematic. In relation to the social order dimensions Schulze and Stabell suggest two distinct perspec-tives dominate. The consensus perspective is where existing social relations are regarded as unproblematic and where challenging them is not considered. The dissensus perspective, by contrast, assumes that existing social relations are problematic and rife with conflict and that they typically reinforce power differentials that result in exploitation. The four discourses on knowledge management that emerge when these dimensions are put together are illustrated in Figure 1.2.

What this analysis reveals, and one of the key insights flowing from Schultze and Stabell's framework, is the extent to which the consensus-based perspective on social order predomi-nates in the knowledge management literature. Thus most literature on the topic regards the management of organizational knowledge as being positive and progressive, and un-questioningly benefiting all organizational members, which consequently results in issues of conflict, power, and disagreement being marginalized, if not ignored.

Further, of the four discourses outlined by Schultze and Stabell the neo-functionalist one is by far the most dominant in the knowledge management literature (a conclusion also made by Goles and Hirscheim 2000). This literature not only assumes that the management of knowledge is positive and has potential benefits for all organizational members, but also that the object-like status of knowledge in organizations makes it a resource amenable to managerial control.

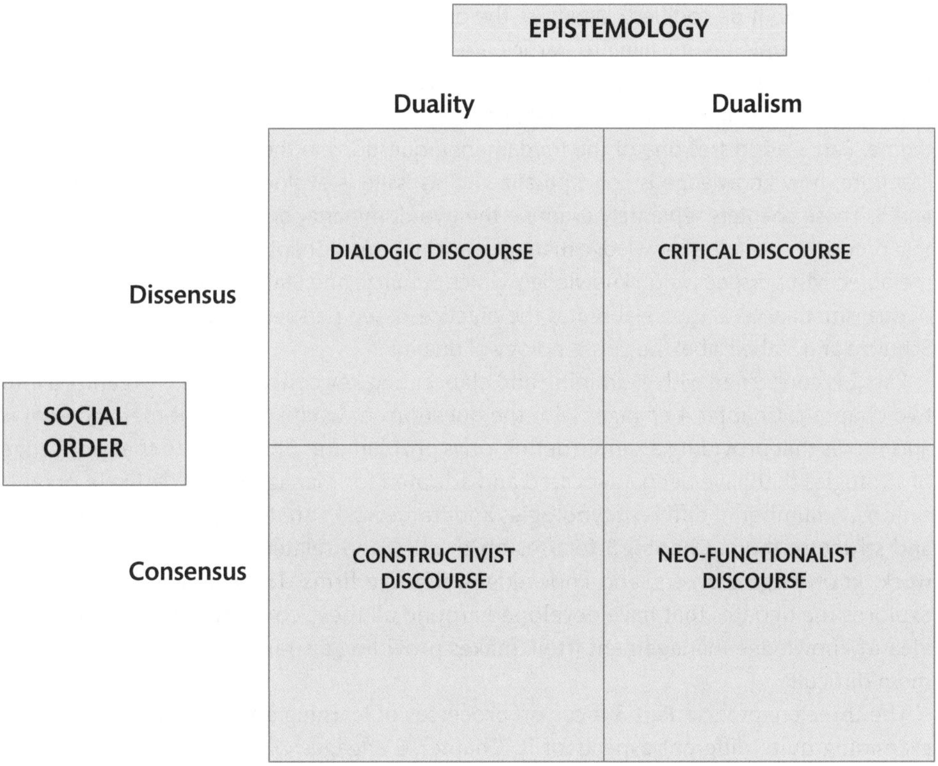

EPISTEMOLOGY

	Duality	Dualism
Dissensus	DIALOGIC DISCOURSE	CRITICAL DISCOURSE
Consensus	CONSTRUCTIVIST DISCOURSE	NEO-FUNCTIONALIST DISCOURSE

SOCIAL ORDER

Figure 1.2 Schultze and Stabell's (2004) Four Discourses on Knowledge Management

Source: Schultze and Stabell (2004).

This book, while it does describe the neo-functionalist discourse on knowledge management (see Chapter 2 in particular), is concerned with giving voice to and drawing on work from the other three knowledge management discourses. Thus, its primary purpose is to provide readers with a rich understanding of the debates and diversity of perspectives that exist within the knowledge management literature through drilling down below the surface assumptions that typically go unquestioned in the mainstream knowledge management literature (regarding both the manageability of knowledge and the extent to which knowledge management involves conflict, power, and politics). This necessarily means utilizing perspectives other than that which Schultze and Stabell label the neo-functionalist discourse. This will allow an in-depth exploration of the issues underlying the theme of knowledge management and provide students with an insight into the debates and disagreements that continue to characterize the knowledge management literature, which would remain invisible if the focus was narrowly on the neo-functionalist perspective.

Thus, the book provides a critical introduction to knowledge management through examining ideas and assumptions that typically are not questioned in the mainstream knowledge management literature. Undertaking such an analysis reveals fundamental and important questions which are likely to be of perennial interest, such as what is knowledge? Can it be controlled? Can it be codified? What are the difficulties involved in sharing or codifying it? Why might people be unwilling to participate in knowledge management initiatives? How these issues are structured in the book is now described.

The book is organized into six separate parts, each of which is focused around a particular theme. Part 1 addresses one of the fundamental questions in the knowledge management literature, how knowledge is conceptualized. This issue is explored in detail in Chapters 2 and 3. These chapters separately examine the two dominant perspectives on epistemology that predominate in the knowledge management literature. Chapter 2 focuses on elaborating the objectivist perspective on knowledge, which Schultze and Stabell label the epistemology of dualism. Chapter 3 then elaborates the practice-based perspective on knowledge, which Schultze and Stabell label the epistemology of duality.

Part 2 is concerned with examining and elaborating key concepts and is organized into two chapters. Chapter 4 engages with the questions of what knowledge management is and shows that providing a simple definition is problematic. This is due to the wide range of strategies that have been advocated and adopted for managing knowledge in organizations. A number of different typologies and frameworks are then utilized to categorize and structure them. Chapter 5 focuses on the key and related concepts of knowledge work, knowledge workers, and knowledge-intensive firms. The chapter examines and explores the debates that have developed around all these concepts, which, as with the idea of knowledge management itself, makes providing a straightforward definition for them difficult.

The three chapters in Part 3 focus on processes of learning and innovation, with each examining quite different aspects of it. Chapter 6 engages with the topic of organizational learning and the learning organization, exploring how the concepts and practices of learning and knowledge management in organizations are closely related. The chapter also examines the contrasting viewpoints on the learning organization that have emerged, specifically engaging with the debate on whether the learning organization increases opportunities for self-development or simply represents a new method of control and exploitation of workers. Chapter 7 examines innovation through the creation and use of new knowledge. The central focus of this chapter is on Nonaka and his various collaborators, whose work on knowledge creation is arguably the most well-known and used of all writing on knowledge management. The chapter will provide a critical evaluation of his work highlighting a number of ways in which it has been criticized. The chapter also briefly considers other perspectives on innovation, emphasizing the extent to which innovation processes involves inter-organizational collaboration between partners, the bringing together of diverse bodies of knowledge, and the roles of absorptive capacity in facilitating such processes.

Chapter 8 examines an equally important aspect of organizational innovation processes, though one which is often neglected in the knowledge management literature, the process of unlearning or giving up knowledge which may be perceived as not having contemporary relevance.

Part 4 examines the role of ICTs in supporting and facilitating the management of knowledge. This part consists of two chapters. The first, Chapter 9, focuses on how those adopting an objectivist view on knowledge see the role of ICTs in knowledge management activities, which is centrally focused around the sharing of codified knowledge. The second chapter,

Chapter 10, examines the role for ICTs in supporting knowledge management activities advocated by those adopting a practice-based perspective on knowledge, which is primarily concerned with using ICTs to facilitate communication and relationship building between people who are geographically dispersed.

Part 5 of the book examines a diverse range of human and social issues related to managing knowledge in organizations, all of which have emerged as being important to organizational attempts at knowledge management. Part 5 begins with Chapter 11 which examines the question of how knowledge processes in organizations are intimately linked to the topic of motivation. The chapter challenges the assumption that people are likely to be willing to share their knowledge, and explores why this is the case. This chapter utilizes the now copious literature that argues for a greater sensitivity to human and social factors.

Chapters 12 and 13 look at the dynamics of knowledge sharing and knowledge generation in two distinctive types of group situation. These chapters both illustrate different aspects of the collective and shared nature of much organizational knowledge. Chapter 12 uses the community of practice concept to consider the dynamics of knowledge sharing and knowledge production in a homogenous group context, where the people working together have well-established social relations, a significant degree of common knowledge, and a sense of collective identity. It closes by examining the potential dark side of communities of practice, which has been relatively unexplored in the communities of practice literature. Chapter 13 considers knowledge processes in more heterogeneous group contexts, where there are limited social relations, a limited degree of common knowledge, and a limited sense of collective identity (for example, in international project teams). This chapter shows how the dynamics of knowledge sharing and production in such a context are significantly different from those that are typical within communities of practice.

Chapter 14 builds from some of the issues touched on in Chapter 13: how knowledge processes are shaped by the conflict and politics that are an inherent part of organizational life. In general, the chapter considers how and why knowledge and power are inextricably linked, and specifically examines how conflicts in the development and use of knowledge can also be linked to the fundamental character of the employment relationship. The chapter examines the contrasting perspectives on knowledge and power developed within what Schultze and Stabell label the critical and discursive discourses on knowledge management.

Finally, the book finishes with Part 6, which is focused on the ways in which management in organizations can manage and facilitate knowledge management activities. This part is organized into two separate chapters. Chapter 15 examines the way that organizations have attempted, and can attempt to shape the knowledge behaviours of their staff through utilizing specific human resource management (HRM) policies and practices such as recruitment, reward, and training. Chapter 16, the final chapter in Part 6, examines the topics of leadership and organizational culture. These topics are considered together due to the significant role that organizational leaders can play in shaping the culture within an organization. The chapter considers the role that senior management in organizations can play in facilitating and inhibiting knowledge management processes, and also how organizational culture can shape workers' attitudes towards the management of their knowledge.

Review and Discussion Questions

1. What is your position on the knowledge society debate? Do you believe that the economy and society in the country you live in have the characteristics of a knowledge society? What evidence supports and undermines your argument?

2. Why do you think academic interest in the topic of knowledge management has been sustained since it first became a topic of interest?

3. The dissensus-based discourses in Schultze and Stabell's model (see Figure 1.2) raise the idea that knowledge management initiatives may not always be in the best interests of everyone working in an organization. To what extent do knowledge management initiatives create conflicts of interest between senior managers and workers in business organizations?

4. Establishing a link between investment in knowledge management activities and business value/performance raises questions regarding what aspect of business value/performance is examined (such as profit levels, market share, innovation levels, productivity levels, etc.), as well as how it is measured. What area (or areas) of business performance is spending on knowledge management likely to facilitate?

 ## Suggestions for Further Reading

P. Heisig et al. (2016). 'Knowledge Management and Business Performance: Global Experts' Views on Future Research Needs'. *Journal of Knowledge Management*, 20/6: 1169–98.
Considers the challenges involved in identifying the extent to which investments in knowledge management create business value.

U. Schultze and C. Stabell (2004). 'Knowing What You Don't Know: Discourses and Contradictions in Knowledge Management Research', *Journal of Management Studies*, 41: 549–73.
A useful analysis which provides a way to categorize the diverse range of work published on knowledge management.

S. Walby (2011). 'Is the Knowledge Society Gendered?', *Gender, Work and Organization*, 18: 1–29.
Not only examines how issues of gender link to knowledge work and the knowledge society, but also presents different definitions of what constitutes the knowledge economy.

 To further your understanding of knowledge management in organizations explore the book's accompanying online resources at **www.oup.com/uk/hislop4e/**

PART 1

Epistemologies of Knowledge in the Knowledge Management Literature

Chapter 1 has introduced the idea that increasingly knowledge is seen as representing the most important asset organizations possess, and that society has witnessed a significant increase in the number of both knowledge workers and knowledge-intensive organizations. This begs a number of questions, not least of which is, what is knowledge? This represents one of the most fundamental questions that humanity has grappled with, and it has occupied the minds of philosophers for centuries. Furthermore, even in contemporary times, interest in the topic of knowledge stems from more than the growth of interest in knowledge management. For example, postmodern philosophy has raised questions about the assumed objectivity of knowledge, and in the process has sparked an enormous debate. Therefore, in engaging with the question of the fundamental character of knowledge it is tempting to look beyond the knowledge management literature and engage with the wider historical and philosophical literature on the topic. However, this temptation is resisted here, for two primary reasons.

First, it is way beyond the scope of this book to attempt to provide any kind of adequate review, however brief, of the debates regarding the nature of knowledge (such as what distinguishes knowledge from belief, opinion, etc.), or to describe, compare, and contrast the different perspectives on knowledge that have been developed by different writers (from Plato and Aristotle to nineteenth-century philosophers such as Hume, Kant, and Nietzsche to twentieth-century writers such as Merly-Ponteau,

Ryle, or Polanyi[1]). The second reason for not engaging with such issues and writers here is that few writers on knowledge management do so. Styhre (2003) suggests two reasons for this. First, writers on knowledge management appear less interested in knowledge per se, instead having a narrow focus on knowledge in workplaces that has practical utility and can contribute to an organization's competitive advantage. Further, he also suggests that writers on knowledge management appear unwilling to embrace the idea that knowledge is not ultimately amenable to management control. However, where knowledge management writers do engage directly with such issues and philosophers, such as the use of Polanyi's work in discussions of tacit knowledge or Foucault's (1980) concept of power/knowledge, reference will be made to the relevant philosophers.

Thus, this section of the book deliberately chooses to focus narrowly on how knowledge is conceptualized in the knowledge management literature. Even with this restricted focus, addressing the question of the nature of knowledge is by no means simple. This is to a large extent because in the contemporary literature on knowledge management there are an enormous range of definitions, and from the way knowledge is described by different writers it is obvious that it is conceptualized in hugely divergent ways. Thus, rather than suggest that there is one single 'true' definition of what knowledge is, the book reflects the fragmented nature of the contemporary debate on this topic and presents the differing definitions and descriptions. As will be seen, the competing conceptualizations examined are based on fundamentally different epistemologies (see Definition).

DEFINITION **Epistemology**

Philosophy addressing the nature of knowledge. Concerned with questions such as: is knowledge objective and measurable? Can knowledge be acquired or is it experienced? What is regarded as valid knowledge, and why?

As outlined in Chapter 1, Schultze and Stabell (2004), drawing on Burrell and Morgan's (1979) analysis of sociological paradigms, suggested that two distinctive epistemologies exist in the knowledge management literature. This is a similar conclusion to that reached by a number of other writers who label their epistemologies differently from Schultze and Stabell (Scarbrough 1998; McAdam and McCreedy 2000; Werr and Stjernberg 2003). This part of the book is structured to reflect these findings, with a separate chapter being devoted to each epistemology, with Chapter 2 examining what is here labelled the objectivist perspective, and Chapter 3 examining what is here labelled the practice-based perspective.

These chapters examine not only how knowledge is conceptualized within each perspective, but also how the management and sharing of knowledge is characterized, based on their different assumptions about knowledge. Therefore, to best understand these competing perspectives, and to allow an effective comparison of their differences, it is useful to read these chapters in parallel, and consider them as being two halves of a debate.

While the objectivist epistemology represents the dominant perspective in the knowledge management literature (Schultze and Stabell 2004), as will be seen in Chapter 3 the popularity of the practice-based perspective has grown over time. These represent probably the most difficult chapters to read, as they are dealing with relatively abstract ideas. However, they provide a useful foundation to the issues addressed in the remainder of the book. Therefore a thorough grasp of these issues should facilitate a deeper understanding of what follows.

---

[1] Anyone interested in developing an understanding of such issues should find and read one/some of the many books which provide an introduction to, and overview of, the philosophy and theory of knowledge.

The Objectivist Perspective on Knowledge

Introduction

The purpose of this chapter is to fully articulate the objectivist perspective on knowledge. In this book the term 'objectivist' perspective is used because this label embodies and highlights what are here regarded as two of this perspective's foundational assumptions: first, that much organizational knowledge is typically considered as being objective in character; and, second, that such knowledge can be separated from people via codification into the form of an object, or entity (explicit knowledge).

This chapter is structured as follows. First, it begins by outlining the key assumptions and characteristics of the objectivist perspective on knowledge. The characteristics of this perspective are further elaborated in the second section which examines and gives examples of work utilizing the knowledge-based theory of the firm, which, as outlined, is one of the most important and well-known theories associated with the objectivist perspective on knowledge. The third section of the chapter examines the development of knowledge typologies that highlight and differentiate between distinctive categories of knowledge (the most well-known being tacit and explicit knowledge). The final section of the chapter concludes by considering how those adopting an objectivist perspective on knowledge typically conceptualize the sharing and management of organizational knowledge.

Objectivist perspectives on knowledge

The primary aim of this section is to describe the principles and characteristics of the objectivist epistemology of knowledge outlining the way it characterizes knowledge, which can be summarized as having four distinctive features (see Table 2.1). Cook and Brown (1999) refer to this perspective as the 'epistemology of possession' as knowledge is regarded as an entity that people or groups possess.

Within the objectivist perspective the entitative character of knowledge represents its primary characteristic. Knowledge is regarded as a (cognitive) entity/commodity that people possess, but which can exist independently of people, in a codifiable form. For example,

Table 2.1 The Objectivist Character of Knowledge

Character of Knowledge from an Objectivist Epistemology
Knowledge is an entity/object that can be separated from those who possess it
Based on a positivistic philosophy: knowledge can be objective
Explicit knowledge (objective) privileged over tacit knowledge (subjective)
Knowledge is a cognitive entity

Hartmann and Dorée (2015: 342) suggest that from this perspective knowledge is considered to be an 'objectifiable transferrable commodity'. Thus, knowledge can be codified, made explicit, and separated from the person who creates, develops, and/or utilizes it. Such knowledge can exist in a number of forms including documents, diagrams, computer systems, or embedded in physical artifacts such as machinery or tools. Thus, for example, a text-based manual of computer operating procedures, whether in the form of a document, compact disc (CD), or web page, represents a form of explicit knowledge. King and Marks Jr (2008) illustrate this assumption through talking about how information technology (IT) -based knowledge management systems 'capture' (p. 131) people's individual knowledge.

A further assumption about the nature of knowledge is that objective knowledge can be produced. The assumption is thus that it is possible to develop a type of knowledge and understanding that is free from individual subjectivity. This represents what McAdam and McCreedy (2000) described as the 'knowledge is truth' perspective, where explicit knowledge is seen as equivalent to a canonical body of scientific facts and laws which are consistent across cultures and time. The idea that explicit knowledge can exist in a textual form stems from a number of assumptions about the nature of language, including that language has fixed and objective meanings. These ideas are deeply rooted in the philosophy of positivism (see Definition), the idea that the social world can be studied scientifically, in other words that social phenomena can be quantified and measured, that general laws and principles can be established, and that objective knowledge is produced as a result.

DEFINITION Positivism

While Comte, a nineteenth-century French philosopher, founded what is now called positivism, Durkheim was arguably the first to translate these ideas into the realm of sociology. Durkheim was concerned to make sociology into a science, and advocated the use of a positivistic philosophy. This philosophy assumes that cause and effect can be established between social phenomena through the use of observation and testing, and that general laws and principles can be established. These general laws and principles constitute objective knowledge.

The third key element of the objectivist epistemology is that it privileges explicit knowledge over tacit knowledge (Marabelli and Newell 2014). This relates to and flows from the previous assumption, about the possibility to produce objective, codified knowledge. Primarily, explicit or codified knowledge is regarded as equivalent to objective knowledge. Tacit knowledge on the other hand, knowledge which is difficult to articulate in an explicit form, is regarded as more informal, more personal and individualized, less rigorous, and highly subjective, being embedded within the cultural values and assumptions of those who possess and use it. Nonaka et al. (2000), for example, make this explicit by suggesting that

> explicit knowledge can be expressed in formal and systematic language and shared in the form of data, scientific formulae . . . In contrast, tacit knowledge is highly personal . . . Subjective insights, intuitions and hunches fall into this category of knowledge.

However, a key element of Nonaka's perspective on epistemology, as will be seen in Chapter 7, is that he challenges the privileging and prioritization of explicit knowledge, which he regards as being characteristic of the way knowledge is conceptualized in 'Western' societies, and suggests that greater attention should be paid to the role of tacit knowledge.

The final major assumption is that knowledge is regarded as a cognitive, intellectual entity. As Cook and Brown (1999: 384) suggest, knowledge 'is something that is held in the head'. From this perspective, the development and production of knowledge comes from a process of intellectual reflection (individual or collective), and is primarily a cognitive process. Newell (2015: 8) explains this aspect of the objectivist perspective by arguing that knowledge is a cognitive entity that people possess, with the mind being conceptualized as a personal repository or 'carrier of knowledge'.

The knowledge-based theory of the firm

The knowledge-based theory of the firm represents the dominant theory which adopts the objectivist perspective on knowledge. For example, Nonaka and Peltokorpi's (2006) analysis of the twenty most cited knowledge management articles found that articles using or developing the knowledge- (and/or resource-) based theory of the firm were prominent in this list. Hence it is worth spending time examining it in a little detail.

The knowledge-based theory of the firm, which represents a specific development from the resource-based view of the firm, was initially articulated and developed by a number of writers including Spender (1996), Kogut and Zander (1996), and Grant (1996). Over time the theory has been developed and refined partly through theoretical development, and partly through empirical testing (Nahapiet and Ghoshal 1998; Berman et al. 2002; Bogner and Bansal 2007; Haas and Hansen 2007; Wang et al. 2009; Cuervo-Cazurra and Un 2010; Sullivan and Marvel 2011; Judge et al. 2015; Agarwal et al. 2016). Finally, it is a perspective that underpins much knowledge management literature (Voelpel et al. 2005; King and Marks Jr 2008; Donate and Guadamilas 2010; Stock et al. 2010; Williams 2011; Harzing et al. 2016). There are two central tenets to the knowledge-based theory of the firm. First, it assumes that knowledge which is difficult to replicate and copy can be a significant source of competitive advantage for firms. Knowledge that is assumed to be difficult to replicate is firm-specific knowledge, which builds from and links to existing knowledge within an organization, and which is related to firm-specific products, services, or processes (Wang et al. 2009). Second, it assumes that organizations provide a more effective mechanism than markets do for the sharing and integration of knowledge between people. Thus, two of the key focuses of research which utilizes the knowledge-based theory of the firm are on the development of firm-specific knowledge (see, for example, Nag and Gioia 2012), and the relationship between the development and use of such knowledge and firm performance (see, for example, Bognor and Bansall 2007).

The compatibility of the knowledge-based view of the firm with Schultze and Stabell's (2004) neo-functionalist discourse (see Chapter 1) is visible in the fundamental, unquestioned assumptions made by those adopting this perspective that organizational knowledge is an increasingly important source of competitive advantage for firms; and, further, that the interests of workers and organizational managers and owners in attempting to protect this are compatible and not contradictory.

The compatibility of the knowledge-based view of the firm with the characteristics of the objectivist perspective on knowledge just outlined is also typically quite apparent. For example, such work typically adopts an entitative view of knowledge (see, for example, Szulanski 1996), with Glazer (1998: 176) explicitly talking about 'knowledge as a commodity'. Second, this perspective is also founded on the idea that there are separate and distinctive types of knowledge, such as tacit and explicit, and group and individual knowledge (see, for example, Berman et al. 2002; Haas and Hansen 2007; Williams 2011). Finally, assumptions in this perspective regarding the objective character of knowledge are apparent in the view that the quality and character of organizational knowledge can be quantified and measured. For example, one of the key objectives of Glazer's (1998: 176) article is to facilitate efforts to 'develop reliable and valid measures of knowledge'. Further, Haas and Hansen (2007), in examining how the acquisition of tacit and explicit knowledge can improve task performance, assume unproblematically that it is possible to measure the quality of both types of knowledge (defined as 'rigour, soundness and insight' (p. 1137)) through asking relevant questions in a survey.

Finally, the compatibility of those utilizing and developing the knowledge-based theory of the firm with the objectivist perspective on knowledge is evident in the use of positivistic methods to investigate and analyse organizational knowledge and knowledge management processes (see, for example, Harzing et al. 2016). This is apparent in the assumptions that the variables under investigation can be objectively measured (typically via quantitative methods involving the collection of large bodies of statistical data), and that objective causal relationships between these variables can be revealed via the development and testing (via statistical analysis) of specific hypotheses. Such characteristics are visible in the various illustrated examples provided in this chapter.

Typologies of knowledge

As has been outlined, one of the primary features of the objectivist perspective on knowledge is the privileging of explicit/objective knowledge over tacit/subjective knowledge. This distinction between tacit and explicit knowledge, which are regarded as quite separate and distinct types of knowledge, flows from an either/or logic of binary oppositions which is a fundamental character of this perspective (discussed later). Thus, one feature of the writing of those adopting an objectivist perspective on knowledge is to make and develop typologies that identify and distinguish between fundamentally different types of knowledge. Two of the most common distinctions made which are examined here are between tacit and explicit knowledge, and individual and collective or group knowledge.

Tacit and explicit knowledge

The tacit–explicit dichotomy is largely ubiquitous in analyses into the characteristics of organizational knowledge. One feature of those utilizing an objectivist epistemology is that tacit and explicit knowledge are regarded as separate and distinct types of knowledge. Explicit knowledge, from an objectivist perspective, is synonymous with objective knowledge, therefore it is unnecessary to restate in detail its characteristics (see Table 2.2). Suffice to say first that explicit knowledge is regarded as objective, standing above and separate from both individual and social value systems; and, second, that it can be codified into a tangible form.

Tacit knowledge on the other hand represents knowledge that people possess, and which may importantly shape how they think and act, but which cannot be fully made explicit. It incorporates both physical/cognitive skills (such as the ability to juggle, to do mental arithmetic, to weld, or to create a successful advertising slogan) and cognitive frameworks (such as the value systems that people possess). The main characteristics of tacit knowledge are therefore that it is personal, and is difficult, if not impossible, to disembody and codify. This is because tacit knowledge may not only be difficult to articulate, it may even be subconscious (see Table 2.2). Two of the most commonly referred to examples of tacit knowledge are the ability to ride a bike or to swim, with the knowledge possessed by people of how to carry out these activities being difficult to communicate, articulate, and share. Examples of work-related tacit knowledge include the ability to write good computer software, the ability of a skilled craftsperson to produce high quality goods, the ability to be an effective leader, and the ability to solve complex problems (see Illustration 2.1).

This distinction between tacit and explicit knowledge is by no means unique to the objectivist epistemology of knowledge, but the specific way that the distinction is theorized within this perspective is quite particular. Importantly, as will be seen later in the chapter, some major implications flow from this depiction of the dichotomy in terms of the way knowledge sharing processes are conceptualized. Within the objectivist epistemological framework an either/or logic predominates, resulting in tacit and explicit knowledge being regarded as separate and distinctive types of knowledge. This characterization of the dichotomy is explicit in the following quotation: '[t]here are two types of knowledge: explicit knowledge and tacit knowledge' (Nonaka et al. 2000). Thus from this perspective tacit and explicit knowledge do

Table 2.2 The Characteristics of Tacit and Explicit Knowledge

Tacit Knowledge	Explicit Knowledge
Inexpressible in a codifiable form	Codifiable
Subjective	Objective
Personal	Impersonal
Context-specific	Context-independent
Difficult to share	Easy to share

not represent the extremes of a spectrum, but instead represent two pure and separate forms of knowledge.

Typically, this polarized dichotomy is argued to be based on the work of Michael Polanyi (1958, 1983). Nonaka for example makes this reference explicit. However, as will be shown in Chapter 3, there is another, distinctly different interpretation of Polanyi's work, which questions this conceptualization of the tacit–explicit dichotomy. More details on Nonaka's conceptualization of knowledge are presented in Chapter 7.

 Illustration 2.1 The role played by the acquisition of tacit and explicit knowledge in improving task productivity

Haas and Hansen (2007) examined the impact that the acquisition by work groups of tacit and explicit knowledge from beyond their group/team had on what they called task productivity. This was done within the empirical context of sales teams in a large management consultancy firm in the USA. The management consultancy firm examined provided tax and audit advice to clients in a wide range of industries including energy, communications, healthcare, automotive, and financial services. The study focused narrowly on the acquisition and use of knowledge in the work done by sales teams in pitching for business with prospective clients. One of the key elements involved in preparing such bids, which was the knowledge sharing/acquisition process examined by Hass and Hansen, was to draw on and utilize knowledge or experience from previous bids that was felt to be relevant. The data on the knowledge and work processes they examined was acquired from surveys that were distributed to the team leaders of a random selection of sales bids carried out during the time of the research. Three dimensions of task productivity were examined including time saved, task quality, and the extent to which the bid team were considered to be competent by external stakeholders such as clients. In terms of knowledge sharing, two mechanisms were examined, with one being related to each type of knowledge that was examined. Fundamentally it was assumed that explicit knowledge was shared through the acquisition and use of documentation, whereas tacit knowledge was acquired through person-to-person interaction.

The most fundamental and general finding of their study was that the acquisition of both tacit and explicit knowledge from outside the bid teams did positively impact on task productivity, but in quite different ways. For example, the acquisition of explicit knowledge had positive time saving benefits, but the acquisition of tacit knowledge did not. Further, the higher the quality of the explicit/codified knowledge that was used, the greater the time saving. By contrast, the sharing of tacit knowledge improved both task quality and client's perception of competence, with both being positively related to the quality of the tacit knowledge that was shared. This study doesn't privilege tacit over explicit knowledge and shows that both tacit and explicit knowledge have their own distinctive benefits for task productivity.

Question

Does this empirical evidence undermine assumptions regarding the superiority of explicit over tacit knowledge?

Individual-group knowledge

While some argue that knowledge can only ever exist at the level of the individual, this idea is disputed by a range of writers. These writers argue that while much knowledge does reside within individuals, there is a sense in which knowledge can reside in social groups in the

Table 2.3 Generic Knowledge Types

	Individual	Social
Explicit	Conscious	Objectified
Tacit	Automatic	Collective

Source: Adapted from Spender (1996).

form of shared work practices and routines, and shared assumptions or perspectives (Collins 2007; Ebbers and Wijnberg 2009; Hecker 2012; Razmerita et al. 2014). This insight is used as the basis for a further dichotomy of knowledge types: into individual and group/social level knowledge. One of the most well-known advocates of such a perspective is Spender (1996), who combined the tacit–explicit dichotomy with the individual–group dichotomy to produce a two by two matrix with four generic types of knowledge (Table 2.3).

Objectified knowledge represents explicit group knowledge, for example a documented system of rules, operating procedures, or formalized organizational routines. *Collective* knowledge on the other hand represents tacit group knowledge, knowledge possessed by a group that is not codified. Examples of this include informal organizational routines and ways of working, stories, and shared systems of understanding. For example, the value systems that people possess have a collective element, as they are related to values and ideas that circulate in the particular social milieu that people work within. The massive expansion of the culture management industry that has occurred since the mid-1980s, which attempts to inculcate specific value systems within organizations, suggests that there is an optimism among organizational management that such shared systems of values can be developed.

However, collective knowledge can exist within different types of community, of different sizes and characteristics. For example, at a relatively small-scale level, collective knowledge can exist within teams or communities. One specific example of this small-scale level of community knowledge that is increasingly being referred to is that possessed and held within communities of practice (see Chapter 12). However, other types of group or community within which collective knowledge can be developed include departments, sites, organizations, or business units within multinational corporations (MNCs). At a more macro level, Lam (1997) also found that the national cultural context could play an important role in shaping the nature of organizational knowledge.

One of the most detailed analyses of collective knowledge was produced by Hecker (2012). Constraints of space make it impossible to fully articulate the model of collective knowledge developed by Hecker. However, it is worth highlighting the distinction Hecker makes between three types of collective knowledge (see Table 2.4). The first type of collective knowledge identified by Hecker is shared knowledge. This represents knowledge that is possessed by a range of different members within a community. For example, within a sales team, this may be shared knowledge regarding how to manage customer interactions. The second type of complementary knowledge identified by Hecker is complementary knowledge. This is where there is a knowledge-based division of labour within a community, where people possess different bodies of (overlapping) but specialized knowledge. The shared, complementary knowledge in this context is the knowledge and understanding people have about the distribution of expertise within the community, where community members' knowledge of each

Table 2.4 Hecker's (2012) Three Types of Collective Knowledge

Type of Collective Knowledge	Definition	Locus	Relationship to Individual Knowledge	Origin	Example
Shared knowledge	Knowledge held by individuals in a group	Individuals	Overlapping, common knowledge	Shared experiences	A set of rules and norms shared within a community, and which govern behaviour in social interactions, for example, shared organizational culture.
Complementary knowledge	Knowledge regarding the division of expertise within a group	Interdependencies between individual knowledge		Specialized division of knowledge within group	An organizational IT team, where separate individuals possess knowledge of different IT systems, and where team members understand the distribution of expertise among people, and can use this understanding to co-ordinate expertise to solve problems.
Artifactual knowledge	Knowledge embedded in collective, group artifacts	Artifact	Combinations of individual knowledge in an articulated form	Codification and articulation of knowledge	A computer database of sales information collectively produced and used by a team of sales people.

Source: Hecker (2012).

other's expertise helps them to effectively coordinate their work activities such that their collective efforts are greater than the sum of their individual knowledge and efforts (see Illustration 2.2). The third and final type of collective knowledge identified by Hecker is knowledge embedded in artifacts which are developed and used collectively by community members. Examples of such artifacts are documentation (such as a shared presentation or database), or technological artifacts such as collectively developed products. Razmerita et al. (2014) argue that knowledge management systems which consist of a repository of codified knowledge accessible to all organizational members allow the development of collective knowledge. In Hecker's terms, knowledge management repositories are an example of artifactual collective knowledge, which facilitates the development of shared collective knowledge through people's use of the knowledge management repository.

Illustration 2.2 Sharing collective knowledge: the role of the 'collective bridge'

Zhao and Anand (2013: 1513) define collective knowledge as 'knowledge embedded among individuals regarding how to coordinate, share, distribute, and recombine individual knowledge'. This is compatible with what Hecker (2012) defined as 'complementary knowledge' (see Table 2.4). Such knowledge is qualitatively different from individual knowledge possessed by a specific person, as it is mutually shared among a group of people. Zhao and Anand suggest that collective knowledge is important for organizations as it can be a source of competitive advantage, and its complexity makes it difficult to replicate. Collective knowledge includes not only routines, and shared language/syntax, but also how an individual's actions will impact on the work and knowledge of interdependent others. Zhao and Anand illustrate the benefits of collective knowledge in the context of an engineering, design, and manufacturing company, where the existence of collective knowledge between a design engineer and a manufacturing engineer would allow the design engineer to design a product that was straightforward to manufacture.

However, the complexity of collective knowledge also creates challenges for organizational attempts to share it internally, between different parts of an organization. The complexity of collective knowledge is related to the extent of the interdependencies that exist between different areas of specialist knowledge, with highly complex collective knowledge involving a significant degree of interdependency between different areas of expertise. The challenge of sharing highly complex, interdependent collective knowledge is that this process involves the transferral of not simply isolated, individual expertise between people, but also the interdependencies that exist between different bodies of specialist knowledge.

Zhao and Anand argue that the sharing of complex, interdependent collective knowledge involves the use of what they define as a 'collective bridge'. This is a direct set of inter-personal ties between a group of people in the two units that collective knowledge is to be shared between. Developing a collective bridge to facilitate such a knowledge transfer thus involves developing inter-personal relations between a range of people in the two units involved. A successful example of the development of such a bridge was achieved within Volkswagen, between the German and Chinese units of its research and development (R&D) department. This was achieved when a group of Chinese engineers underwent an extensive training programme in Germany. The participation of the Chinese engineers in this programme meant that when they returned to China they had developed an understanding of the collective knowledge of the German R&D unit, and were also able to effectively communicate with them when they needed any ongoing technical support.

Question

Can you identify other means, apart from training programmes, where a 'collective bridge' of social relationships can be developed between two separate groups of workers?

An objectivist perspective on the sharing and management of knowledge

Having examined both the fundamental character of knowledge, and the way knowledge can be categorized into different types, the final section of the chapter examines the implications of these ideas for the sharing and management of knowledge. This section begins by making explicit the general model of knowledge sharing which flows from objectivist

24

assumptions regarding knowledge, before concluding by outlining the way knowledge man-agement processes are characterized.

Conduit model of knowledge sharing

Building from previous assumptions, the sharing of knowledge from an objectivist per-spective represents what has been referred to as the conduit or transmitter/receiver model (see Figure 2.1). This model suggests that knowledge is shared by being transferred from an independent sender, to a separate receiver, via a specific transmission channel/mecha-nism. Thus, the key components in this model of knowledge transfer/sharing are: a sender, a receiver, a transmission channel/mechanism, the knowledge being transferred, and a context in which the transfer occurs. Further, the success of such transfers are assumed to be based on a number of conditions including that the sender is knowledgeable and willing to transfer knowledge, that an appropriate transmission channel is used (which is related to the character of the knowledge being transferred—discussed later), and that the receiver has the capacity to absorb and utilize the knowledge being transferred (Hartmann and Dorée 2015).

Such assumptions are often made explicit. For example, Szulanski (1996: 28) suggests that knowledge sharing involves 'the exchange of organizational knowledge between a source and a recipient'. Khan et al.'s (2015: 659) analysis of knowledge transfer processes with local suppliers in international joint ventures also reveals such assumptions, using terms such as 'knowledge sender', 'transfer mechanism', and 'recipient'. Finally, Williams (2011: 338), who utilizes the knowledge-based view of the firm to analyse the sharing of knowledge between some clients and offshore engineers they work with, says that 'knowledge transfer involves both [the] transmission of knowledge from sender to recipient, as well as its integration and application by the recipient'.

While the basic principles and components of this knowledge transfer model are relatively simple, research in this area has resulted in the development of complex models and analy-ses, which examine the interactions between the model's different components, as well as conceptualizing the components of the model in complex ways (Szulanski et al. 2016), with the end of chapter Case study being a good example of such an analysis.

For example, a key element in the success of such knowledge transfer processes is the abil-ity of the receiver to absorb and utilize the knowledge being sent. This capability to absorb external knowledge, integrate it with existing knowledge, and effectively apply and utilize it is defined as a receiver's absorptive capacity. This concept was initially developed by Cohen and Levinthal (1990), but has subsequently expanded to be a significant area of research, with complex analyses being developed regarding the factors influencing it, and its impact on organizational performance and innovation (Marabelli and Newell 2014). (This concept will be returned to in Chapter 7 on innovation, where it will be discussed more fully.)

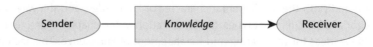

Figure 2.1 **The Conduit Model of Knowledge Sharing**

As outlined earlier, a key component of the objectivist perspective on knowledge is that tacit and explicit knowledge represent separate and distinct types of knowledge. This assumption is reflected in analyses regarding the character of knowledge transfer processes, with it being assumed that the effective transferral of tacit and explicit knowledge requires different transfer mechanisms. In broad terms, those utilizing this perspective on knowledge assume that the transferral of explicit knowledge is more straightforward than the transferral of tacit knowledge. With respect to codified knowledge, which is typically shared via information and communication technologies (ICTs) and documentation, it is assumed that the sender, in isolation from the receiver, can produce some fully codified knowledge and then transfer it remotely to the receiver. The receiver then takes this knowledge and is able to understand it and use it without any other form of interaction with the sender. Further, it is assumed that no important aspects of this explicit knowledge are lost in the transfer process, and that both sender and receiver derive the same meaning from the knowledge. With respect to the sharing of tacit knowledge, it is typically assumed that this involves more inter-personal interaction and communication (such as via meetings and one-to-one dialogue). However it is still assumed that such tacit knowledge is an entity which can be directly transferred from one person to another.

Knowledge management processes

Building from these assumptions regarding the sharing of knowledge, we can now examine the nature of knowledge management processes from an objectivist perspective (Table 2.5).

Based on the strict dichotomy on which the objectivist perspective is founded, where tacit and explicit knowledge are regarded as distinctive and separate types of knowledge with quite specific characteristics, the sharing of tacit and explicit knowledge are also regarded as being fundamentally different (the case study by Haas and Hansen is a good illustration of this, as is the study by Williams 2011). From this perspective, while the sharing of tacit knowledge is acknowledged to be difficult, complex, and time-consuming, the sharing of explicit knowledge, by contrast, is regarded as much more straightforward. In fact, from the objectivist perspective, the easy transferability of explicit knowledge represents one of its defining characteristics. For example, Grant (1996: 111) suggests that 'explicit knowledge is revealed by its communication. This ease of communication is its fundamental property.'

The typical starting point in objectivist conceptualizations of knowledge management is the processes of codifying relevant knowledge, converting tacit to explicit knowledge (a process which Nonaka and his collaborators refer to as 'externalization'—see Chapter 7). From this

Table 2.5 An Objectivist Perspective on Knowledge Management

Knowledge Management: Objectivist Perspective
Convert tacit to explicit knowledge (codification)
Collect knowledge in centralized repository
Structure/systematize knowledge (into discrete categories)
ICT plays a key role

perspective there is an acknowledgement that much organizational knowledge may be tacit. But this is accompanied by an optimism that it is possible to convert much of this knowledge to an explicit form. For example, while all the assembly instructions for putting together a car, or all the stages in a telesales customer interaction, may not be totally explicit, with effort and work it is assumed to be possible to make all this knowledge explicit, and codify it into a complete set of instructions/body of knowledge. This can be achieved by getting relevant workers to articulate all their knowledge about such processes, making explicit all the assumptions, behaviours, and actions they utilize in accomplishing the task being examined.

Thus, the first stage in any knowledge management initiative, from this perspective, is to identify what knowledge is important and then make it explicit. The typical optimism that exists with regard to the extent to which tacit knowledge can be made at least partially explicit means that the difficulties involved in sharing tacit knowledge and the nature of such processes are not typically central to objectivist models of knowledge management (see Time to reflect).

 Time to reflect   'Externalizing' tacit knowledge

Think about an example of tacit knowledge that you possess. To what extent could this knowledge be converted into an explicit form? Could it be codified such that someone else could utilize it? Further, how easy and how time-consuming is this process likely to be?

The next stage in the knowledge management process involves collecting all the codified knowledge together into a central repository, and then structuring it in a systematic way to make it easily accessible to others (Durcikova and Gray 2009; Taskin and Van Bunnen 2015). Thus for example, the knowledge may be collected in a central database, where it is not only stored, but also categorized, indexed, and cross-referenced. The importance of doing this effectively is related to the next part of the knowledge management process: making this knowledge accessible to all people who may want to use it. One of the primary rationales for organizations managing their knowledge is to allow knowledge to be more widely and effectively shared within organizations (Fadel and Durcikova 2014; Taskin and Van Bunnen 2015). This makes organizing knowledge, and making it accessible, as important as the codification process. The knowledge management system examined by King and Marks Jr (2008) fits with these objectives, being described as a 'repository' whose purpose is to facilitate the dissemination of best-practice knowledge among the case study organization's globally dispersed workforce.

Finally, ICTs typically play a key role in knowledge management processes utilizing the objectivist perspective. For example, ICTs can play an important role in almost every element of the knowledge management process (Gilbert et al. 2010). First, they can provide a repository (for example, databases) in which codified knowledge can be stored (Cha et al. 2008). Second, they can play a role in the organizing of knowledge (for example, with electronic cross-referencing systems). Finally, they can provide conduits and mechanisms through which knowledge can be transferred into, or extracted from, a central repository (for example, through an intranet system or search engine). It is thus no surprise that many studies into the role of ICTs in knowledge management initiatives utilize an objectivist perspective on knowledge (see, for example, Voelpel et al. 2005; King and Marks Jr 2008). The role of ICTs in knowledge management processes, from an objectivist perspective, is examined more fully in Chapter 9.

Conclusion

This chapter has outlined the defining characteristics of the objectivist perspective on knowledge, which represents the mainstream perspective in the knowledge management literature on how to conceptualize knowledge. The most fundamental assumptions of this perspective on knowledge are that knowledge can take the form of a discrete entity, separate from people who may understand or use it; and that knowledge can take different forms, distinguishing most importantly between tacit and explicit knowledge. Within this perspective there is also typically an assumption and optimism that much of the organizational knowledge possessed by workers can be codified into an explicit form. Some subsidiary features of this perspective on knowledge are that tacit and explicit knowledge are regarded as quite separate and distinctive types of knowledge, with explicit knowledge typically being privileged and prioritized over tacit knowledge. This is largely because explicit or codified knowledge is typically characterized as being objective, while tacit knowledge is, in contrast, assumed to be more personal, subjective, and context-specific.

These assumptions about the nature of knowledge have significant implications for how the management and sharing of knowledge is conceptualized. The privileging of explicit knowledge within this perspective means that there is a bias towards and focus upon the management and sharing of explicit, codified knowledge. The emphasis on codified knowledge is also due to assumptions that it is much easier to manage and share codified knowledge than it is to manage and share tacit knowledge. The optimism regarding the codifiability of knowledge means that those adopting an objectivist perspective on knowledge typically emphasize processes of codification. Thus, from this perspective, an initial step in the management and sharing of knowledge is to codify as much knowledge as possible. The sharing of such knowledge between people has the characteristics of a 'transmitter–receiver' model, where it is assumed codified, explicit knowledge can be passed from one person to another unmodified. This perspective on knowledge typically also suggests that computer and communication technologies can play a key role in knowledge management processes through providing one important medium, or conduit, via which codified knowledge can be shared.

 Case study Factors shaping the successful transfer of knowledge within an MNC: an objectivist analysis

A potential advantage that MNCs have over other types of organization is the ability to improve business practices through the sharing of knowledge between different divisions/subsidiaries. Thus, less knowledgeable subsidiaries can benefit from the knowledge and experience of more knowledgeable ones. Such processes can result in the development of technological capabilities in less knowledgeable subsidiaries, with potential competitiveness benefits for both the subsidiary and the MNC owner. However, the successful transfer of knowledge between subsidiaries within MNCs is by no means simple, and success in such activities is never guaranteed.

Jasimuddin et al. (2015)'s analysis of the acquisition of knowledge by Chinese subsidiaries from the Japanese MNCs which own them provides insights into some of the factors which influence the success of such activities. This empirical focus is particularly interesting and important due to the significance of the role such knowledge transfers have played in recent decades in the massive economic development and growth of China. In their analysis, the specific focus is on the role played by the Chinese subsidiary in the acquisition of knowledge. More specifically, Jasimuddin et al. (2015) examine how some key characteristics of these subsidiaries affects the acquisition of knowledge, as well as how the type of transfer mechanisms used mediate the relationship between these characteristics and the success of the focal knowledge acquisition processes.

The fact that Jasimuddin et al.'s (2015: 465) analysis utilizes an objectivist perspective on knowledge is visible in two primary ways. First, it explicitly utilizes the sender/receiver model of knowledge sharing/transfer, talking about how knowledge transfer processes involve a 'source' and 'recipient'. Second, in considering the different mechanisms via which knowledge can be transferred it talks of tacit and codified knowledge as distinct and separate types of knowledge, with different transfer mechanisms being appropriate for the transfer of each.

In examining how the characteristics of the Chinese subsidiary (the receiver) affects the acquisition of knowledge from the Japanese MNCs which own them (the source of knowledge), Jasimuddin et al. (2015) distinguish between two variables: the motivation to acquire knowledge, and the ability to acquire knowledge. The ability to acquire knowledge is conceptualized as the absorptive capacity. This refers to 'an organizations ability to understand, absorb, and use new knowledge' (p. 466). (This represents one of the key concepts underpinning processes of innovation and knowledge creation, and is discussed again in Chapter 7 on innovation). Jasimuddin et al. (2015) hypothesize that both the motivation and the ability of a subsidiary to acquire knowledge will be related to the success of knowledge acquisition processes.

Jasimuddin et al. (2015) also examine the role played by the type of transfer mechanism in mediating the success of knowledge acquisition processes. In doing so they distinguish between tacit and codified knowledge, and suggest that different transfer mechanisms are likely to be effective for the acquisition of both types. For the acquisition of codified knowledge, they hypothesize that the use of ICTs will be the most effective acquisition mechanism (codification-based strategies), while in contrast they hypothesize that the acquisition of tacit knowledge will require the use of more inter-personal communication, via face-to-face interactions (personalization-based strategies).

Jasimuddin et al. (2015) tested the validity of their hypotheses via the statistical analysis of a survey that was distributed among Chinese subsidiaries of Japanese MNCs in the Dalian region of China. Their analysis found that all hypotheses tested were supported. Thus, the successful acquisition of knowledge by Chinese subsidiaries was related not only to their motivation to engage in such activities, but also to their ability to absorb and utilize external knowledge. Second, they also found that the success of these knowledge acquisition processes was mediated by the extent to which both codification and personalization-based knowledge acquisition strategies were utilized.

These findings have a number of practical implications for those interested in facilitating the successful transfer of knowledge in such contexts. The first, and arguably the most important, practical implication is that the successful acquisition of knowledge by subsidiaries is not solely dependent on them being motivated and willing to acquire external knowledge, but also, crucially, by their ability to absorb such knowledge. Thus, organizations interested in the success of such activities should not only be willing to absorb eternal knowledge, but be committed to devoting effort in developing their ability to do so (absorptive capacity). Second, to ensure the success of knowledge acquisition processes organizations should also utilize a mixture of codification-based and personalization-based strategies.

Source: Jasimuddin, S., Li, J., and Perdikis, N. (2015). 'Knowledge Recipients, Acquisition Mechanisms, and Knowledge Transfer at Japanese Subsidiaries: An Empirical Study in China', *Thunderbird International Business Review*, 57/6: 463–79.

Questions

1. If the ability to absorb external knowledge (absorptive capacity) is so crucial to knowledge transfer processes, what can be done to develop it?

2. If the sharing of tacit knowledge requires face-to-face interaction between people, how are such processes shaped by the extent to which people are culturally different?

Review and Discussion Questions

1. The objectivist perspective assumes that 'pure' explicit knowledge exists, where tasks, activities, or jobs can be fully codified. Can you think of any jobs or activities where knowledge is highly (or totally) codified?

2. Think about your experience of social/group knowledge. Is it largely tacit or explicit? Did it exist in the form of systems of rules, routines, stories, etc.?

3. National culture and communities of practice have been discussed as two types of social context/ setting where collective knowledge can be seen to exist. In what other social contexts have you witnessed collective knowledge to exist—organization, family, geographic region, peer group, friendship network, profession?

4. Based on any work experiences you have, is it common that explicit/codified knowledge tends to be privileged and regarded as more objective than tacit knowledge?

 ## Suggestions for Further Reading

R. Grant (1996). 'Towards a Knowledge Based Theory of the Firm', *Strategic Management Journal*, 17, Winter Special Issue: 109–22.
One of the earliest papers explicitly concerning itself with articulating and theoretically developing the knowledge-based view of the firm.

A-W. Harzing, M. Pudelko, and S. Reiche (2016). 'The Bridging Role of Expatriates and Inpatriates in Knowledge Transfer in Multinational Corporations', *Human Resource Management*, 55: 679–95.
Makes an empirical and conceptual contribution to the development of the knowledge-based view of the firm by examining the role of expatriates and inpatriates in knowledge transfer processes within MNCs.

K.J. Fadel and A. Durcikova (2014). 'If It's Fair, I'll Share: The Effect of Perceived Knowledge Validation Justice on Contributions to an Organizational Knowledge Repository', *Information and Management*, 51: 511–19.
An examination of the factors influencing workers' willingness to contribute knowledge to a knowledge management repository.

A. Hecker (2012). 'Knowledge Beyond the Individual? Making Sense of a Notion of Collective Knowledge in Organization Theory', *Organization Studies*, 33/3: 423–45.
A conceptual paper which considers the different ways in which collective knowledge is conceptualized.

 To further your understanding of knowledge management in organizations explore the book's accompanying online resources at **www.oup.com/uk/hislop4e/**

3 | The Practice-Based Perspective on Knowledge

Introduction

Chapter 2 provided one specific answer to the question 'what is knowledge?' However, the objectivist perspective has been widely challenged, and for a number of different reasons. Arguably the most fundamental challenge and critique of it is that it is based on flawed epistemological assumptions. Chapter 3 therefore presents an alternative answer to the question 'what is knowledge?' This chapter is based on fundamentally different epistemological assumptions and, as will be seen, characterizes knowledge and knowledge management practices quite differently from the objectivist perspective.

The practice-based perspective conceptualizes knowledge not as a codifiable object/entity, but instead emphasizes the extent to which it is embedded within and inseparable from work activities or practices (see Definition). Cook and Brown (1999) labelled this perspective an 'epistemology of practice' due to the centrality of human activity to its conception of knowledge. Ripamonti and Scaratti adopted a similar perspective, talking about knowledge being 'action-oriented and implicit . . . [and] acquired by experience in a specific context' (2011: 185). Thus, the embeddedness of knowledge in human activity (practice) represents one of the central characteristics of this epistemological perspective. Finally, Tooman et al. (2016: 19) go a little further, arguing that knowledge is not only embodied in people, and inseparable from the activities they undertake, but also embedded in the contexts in which activity takes place, arguing, 'what is known, the one who knows it, and the context of action are bound together'.

The practice-based view on knowledge is indicative of a wider acknowledgement of the importance of practices in work, in management and organization studies, and in the social sciences more broadly (Marshall 2014; Zeynep et al. 2014), In the domain of knowledge management, interest in practice-based perspectives on knowledge is visible in the number of books (such as Gherardi and Strati 2012; Nicolini 2013; Orr et al. 2016), and research publications (see the remains of this chapter), which have utilized it.

> **DEFINITION Practice**
>
> Practice refers to purposeful human activity. It is based on the assumption that activity includes both physical and cognitive elements, and that these elements are inseparable. Knowledge use and development is therefore regarded as a fundamental aspect of activity.

While the objectivist perspective was closely aligned with a positivistic philosophy, the practice-based one is compatible with a number of different theorists and philosophical perspectives (Nicolini 2011). For example, the work of Heidegger, Wittgenstein, and the American pragmatists, Pierce and Dewey, underpins much contemporary writing, and more contemporary theorists such as Bourdieu and Garfinkel are also utilized (Bain and Mueller 2016; Rivera and Cox 2016). In the domain of knowledge management, the work of Nicolini, Gherardi, and Strati is the most prominent (Strati 2007; Gherardi 2009; Nicolini 2011, 2013; Gherardi and Rodeschini 2016), with Lave and Wenger's work on communities of practice also utilizing a practice-based perspective (see Chapter 12). However, constraints of space make it impossible to describe and compare these diverse perspectives here.

The chapter follows a similar structure to Chapter 2 and begins by outlining the way knowledge is characterized within the practice-based perspective. The chapter then examines how knowledge management processes are conceptualized. As the chapter proceeds, the vast differences that exist between the practice-based and the objectivist perspectives on knowledge will become more apparent.

Features of a practice-based perspective on knowledge

The practice-based epistemology can be understood in terms of five specific, but interrelated, factors each of which are now examined in turn (Table 3.1).

The embeddedness of knowledge in practice

Perhaps the most important difference between the objectivist and practice-based epistemologies of knowledge is that the practice-based perspective challenges the entitative conception of knowledge. From this perspective, knowledge is not regarded as a discrete entity/object that can be codified and separated from people. Instead, knowledge, or as some of the writers from this perspective prefer, knowing, is inseparable from human activity (Orlikowski 2002; Gherardi 2006; Corradi et al. 2010). Nicolini (2011: 604) summed this up as follows: 'knowledge is inherently tied to the pursuit of an activity and is constituted

Table 3.1 Practice-Based Characteristics of Knowledge

Characteristics of Knowledge from Practice-Based Epistemology
1. Knowledge is embedded in practice
2. Knowledge is multidimensional and non-dichotomous
3. Knowledge is embodied in people
4. Knowledge is socially constructed
5. Knowledge is culturally embedded
6. Knowledge is contestable

and renovated as actors engage with the organizational world in practice'. Thus all activity is, to some extent, knowledgeable, involving the use and/or development of knowledge (see Illustration 3.1.).

As well as challenging the knowing–doing dichotomy, this perspective also challenges the mind–body dichotomy that is inherent in the objectivist perspective (see more detail in the later 'Knowledge is embodied' section). As outlined, the objectivist perspective, drawing on the classical images of science, conceptualizes knowledge as being primarily derived from cognitive processes, something involving the brain but not the body. The practice-based perspective instead views knowing and the development of knowledge as occurring on an on-going basis through the routine activities that people undertake. Knowing thus can be seen as less of a purely cognitive process and more of a holistic one involving the whole body (Hindmarsh and Pilnick 2007; Strati 2007). From this perspective, thinking and doing are fused in knowledgeable activity, the development and use of embodied knowledge in undertaking specific activities/tasks.

Strati (2007) conceptualized the role of the body in practices of knowing via the development of the term 'sensible knowledge'. Central to Strati's conceptualization of knowledge is the idea that knowing is not an activity conducted purely within the brain, with knowing involving the whole body. For Strati (2007: 67), work practices and processes of knowing in organizations are 'not only mental and logical-analytical but also corporeal and multi-sensorial'. The concept of sensible knowledge relates to knowing that involves workers using the human senses of touch, sight, taste, hearing, and smell, with a number of empirical examples being given to illustrate the arguments being made. One of these examples concerned sawmill workers from the north-east of Italy (Strati 2007: 67–9). In this example, the workers in the mill (who did not wear gloves) were able to identify the thickness of the planks they were moving without formally measuring them, simply through the process of lifting and feeling them. Their sense of touch was such that they were able to differentiate between planks whose thicknesses varied by half a centimetre. For Strati this represented an example of sensible knowing, where the sawmill workers' hands, through their sense of touch, were intimately involved in knowing how thick the planks they handled were.

 Illustration **3.1** A practice-based perspective on telemedicine

Nicolini (2011) utilizes a practice-based epistemology to analyse the work of nurses looking after patients with heart problems who required continuous monitoring in between regular hospital visits, with the monitoring process being carried out via regular calls to the patients to check up on them. Nicolini's focus was the various interrelated practices the nurses undertook, and the knowing that was embedded within them. The focus here is narrowly on one practice, the nurses' phone calls to patients. These phone calls represented the primary way that patient care was managed in between formal visits. These phone calls involved checking on the general health of the patients, identifying any problems they were experiencing, and checking whether they were taking their medication as prescribed and whether this medication was causing any problems. With these phone calls knowing was embedded within and emerged through what the nurses and patients said to each other, and how the nurse made sense of and responded to what the patients told them. Thus, nurses (attempted to) manage the conversation in order to gain particular types of information from the patient, which typically involved trying to organize the conversation according to a particular sequence. However, they had to be active in managing this, as due to patients developing an understanding of what was being sought, they may not give information in the order that it is sought, or they may not be willing to reveal easily some information to the nurses. Thus, the nurses' knowledge was deeply embedded in these conversations, and the evolving and unpredictable interactions they had with patients, and was not knowledge that could be codified.

Question

Can you identify other tasks/practices which general nursing staff undertake where knowledge is embodied and not codified?

Knowledge as multidimensional and non-dichotomous

One key difference between the objectivist and practice-based perspectives on knowledge, as highlighted by Schultze and Stabell (2004) is their attitudes towards binary oppositions. Within the objectivist perspective an either/or logic dominates, which results, as outlined in Chapter 2, in the development of taxonomies of distinctive categories of knowledge. From this perspective, knowledge can be either tacit *or* explicit, and knowledge can be individual *or* collective in character. However, such a logic is rejected by those advocating and utilizing a practice-based perspective on knowledge, who suggest that, while such an approach may have analytical benefits, it underestimates the complexity of organizational knowledge. Tsoukas (1996), for example, suggests that dichotomies such as tacit–explicit and individual–group are unhelpful as they disguise the extent to which these elements are inseparable and mutually defined. Blackler (1995: 1032) makes a similar point by suggesting that 'knowledge is multi-faceted and complex, being both situated and abstract, implicit and explicit, distributed and individual, physical and mental, developing and static, verbal and encoded.'

Thus the practice-based perspective rejects the taxonomy-based approach to categorizing knowledge into distinctive types which are independent of each other. Instead of the objectivist perspective's either/or logic, a both/and logic predominates. This perspective is most obvious in how those utilizing a practice-based perspective conceptualize the relationship between tacit and explicit knowledge. The practice-based perspective suggests that rather than tacit and explicit knowledge representing separate and distinctive types of knowledge, they represent two aspects of knowledge and in fact are inseparable, and are mutually constituted (Werr and Stjernberg 2003). One consequence of this is that there is no such thing as fully explicit knowledge, as all knowledge will have tacit dimensions. For example, text, which is often referred to as a form of codified knowledge, has tacit components without which no reader could make sense of it (see Illustration 3.2). Examples of these tacit elements include an understanding of the language in which they are written, or the grammar and syntax used to structure them. Polanyi (1969: 195) suggests that 'The idea of a strictly explicit knowledge is indeed self-contradictory; deprived of their tacit co-efficients, all spoken words, all formulae, all maps and graphs, are strictly meaningless.'

Illustration 3.2   This book as partially explicit knowledge

This book represents a piece of partially explicit knowledge for two reasons. First, as authors, we have not been able to make fully explicit all the ideas, assumptions, theoretical frameworks, and values which underpin what we have written. From the point of view of the reader it can also be considered partially explicit, as to read it you have to have a good grasp of the English language, and some knowledge of other relevant academic topics.

While, as outlined in Chapter 2, Polanyi's work is often used to justify the idea that tacit and explicit knowledge are two separate and distinctive types of knowledge, a number of writers suggest that this misunderstands his analysis (Brown and Duguid 2001; Tsoukas 2003). These writers suggest that his analysis is grounded more in the practice-based perspective which builds from the assumption that there are tacit and explicit dimensions to all knowledge, and that they are inseparable. Thus, from this perspective, there is no such thing as pure tacit or pure explicit knowledge, as all knowledge contains elements of both.

The both/and logic of the practice-based perspective not only shapes how tacit and explicit knowledge are interrelated, it also extends to understanding how other aspects of knowledge are conceptualized. Three dichotomies, which are challenged by those adopting the practice-based epistemology, are outlined in Table 3.2. For example, those adopting a practice-based perspective (such as Strati and his example of sawmill workers) reject the Cartesian distinction between mind and body, which assumes that knowing is primarily an intellectual and cognitive process related to the brain and instead takes knowing and doing to be inseparable, with all knowing involving some element of doing or action and vice versa (see later section on the embodied nature of knowledge for further elaboration). Finally, those adopting a practice-based epistemology challenge the dichotomy between individual and collective knowledge, suggesting that all knowledge has both individual and collective aspects (Tooman et al. 2016; see Illustration 3.3). For example in relation to communities of practice (see Chapter 12), which are typically examined from a practice-based perspective, the knowledge developed and utilized by people who are part of such communities simultaneously has individual and collective elements. Bouty and Gomez (2010) adopt a similar perspective in their analysis of knowledge developed and utilized by chefs and kitchen staff within an haute cuisine restaurant kitchen. Finally, Hsiao et al. (2012) use the concept of 'collaborative knowing' to highlight the shared, collective, and collaborative nature of knowledge in organizations (see Time to reflect).

Table 3.2 Challenging Objectivist Dichotomies

Practice-Based Perspective	Objectivist Perspective
Knowledge as tacit and explicit	Knowledge as either tacit or explicit
Knowledgeable activity (knowing and doing)	Knowledge as purely cognitive, separate from the activities in which it is applied/used
Knowledge as both individual and collective	Knowledge as either individual or collective

Time to reflect   The multidimensionality of knowledge

Think of some specific organizational knowledge that you possess. To what extent is it simultaneously tacit and explicit, as well as being both individual (possessed by you) and collective (learned in a community, partially shared by others, and based on shared values/assumptions) in character?

 Illustration 3.3   The individual and collective character of knowledge and practice in the advertising industry

Grahle and Hibbert (2016) utilize a practice-based perspective on knowledge to examine the interconnectedness of knowledge and practices in advertising. A key feature of such knowledge/practice is its collaborative and collective character, being developed, used, and applied by teams of people in advertising firms, in collaboration with the clients they work for. They refer to the collective nature of such work as involving 'the collaborative enactment of practice' (p. 103). In analysing knowledge and work inside advertising firms they identify five key practices in the development process, which include kicking off the creative process, developing strategies, generating ideas, realizing concepts, and evaluating the effects of ideas. The focus here is narrowly on the first practice, kicking off the creative process. This process varied from project to project, as every project was unique, and all clients had different needs and different ways of working. Thus, knowledge in each project was developed through collaborative interactions between the advertising team and their client. Further, all relevant knowledge is not held individually by any specific individual, but is shared collectively among staff working on each project.

The key aims of the kicking off process were twofold, being first to make sense of the problem that the client was wanting addressed; and, second, beginning to outline a potential solution to it. Addressing these aims involved the team from the advertising agency working closely with the client as well as examining diverse sources of information. Initial consultations with clients involve the analysis of their 'briefing documents'. However, clients are often somewhat unclear regarding their precise needs, thus client briefs are often developed collaboratively, via the advertising team probing client staff on their needs and any ambiguities in 'briefing documents'. Thus, the information that was utilized to develop initial solution to client needs was coproduced by the dynamic interaction and communication that occurred between people from the advertising team and client staff, which was collectively developed and shaped by the particular behaviours of the specific people involved in each project.

Question

While this suggests a collective aspect to the knowledge possessed by staff in advertising agencies, can you identify any knowledge which is more personal/individual in character?

Knowledge is embodied

The objectivist perspective on knowledge assumes that knowledge can exist in a fully explicit and codified form and can exist independently of human beings. This position is fundamentally challenged by the practice-based perspective on knowledge, which sees all knowledge or knowing as personal. The practice-based perspective therefore assumes that it is impossible to totally disembody knowledge from people in a fully explicit form. This assumption is therefore closely related to and flows from the previous two issues examined, that all knowledge has tacit dimensions and that knowledge is embedded in and insepara-ble from practice. Thus, knowledge that is embedded in work practices is simultaneously embodied by the workers who carry out these practices (Strati 2007; Yakhlef 2010; Gherardi and Rodeschini 2016).

The practice-based nature of knowing/knowledge assumes that knowledge develops through practice: people's knowledge develops as they conduct activities and gain experi-ence. Further, the inseparable and mutually constituted nature of tacit and explicit knowledge means that it is not possible to make such knowledge fully explicit. While it may be possible to partially convert tacit knowledge into an explicit form, in contradiction to the objectivist perspective, the practice-based perspective assumes that such processes can never be com-plete. Thus, even after efforts to codify knowledge, there will always be an element whereby knowledge resides in the head/body of those who developed and possess it.

For example, in terms of a situation most readers are likely to be familiar with from one context or another, consider the nature of knowledge sharing in a mentoring-type relation-ship, where someone experienced attempts to share their knowledge with a more inexperi-enced colleague. The practice-based perspective assumes that the practice-based nature of the knowledge and expertise the 'mentor' possesses means that this knowledge will be to some extent embodied, and cannot be fully articulated and made explicit. Further, the prac-tice-based perspective assumes that for the mentee to learn the knowledge of the mentor requires that they communicate, interact, and work together, typically over an extended pe-riod of time. Hindmarsh and Pilnick's (2007) study of pre-operative anaesthetics illustrates the embodied nature of knowledge through processes of knowledge sharing that involved little verbal communication. In their study they found that anaesthetics staff collaborated ef-fectively to physically manipulate the body of patients in certain ways, as well as coordinate these movements with those of other anaesthetics staff, with these activities having to be done quickly, with little verbal communication.

A further sense in which knowledge is embodied (and simultaneously embedded in practice) relates to what Tsoukas (1996) referred to as the 'indeterminacy of practice', where the essential distinctiveness of all situations that people act in requires them to continually make personal judgements. No matter how explicit and well-defined the rules are that may guide action, there will always be some element of ambiguity or uncertainty that creates a need for actors to make inferences and judgements. Thus, knowledge/knowing involves the active agency of people mak-ing decisions in light of the specific circumstances in which they find themselves. A good example of such decision-making was found by Ripamonti and Scaratti (2011) in a study of dock workers in an Italian port (see Illustration 3.4).

 Illustration 3.4 The indeterminacy of practice and ad hoc decision-making in an Italian dock

One of the catalysts for Ripamonti and Scaratti's (2011) study of Italian dock workers was that management were unable to effectively explain the highly variable productivity levels of their dock workers. Management found that the number of containers that could be processed per day varied enormously but were unable to effectively explain this variability. Ripamonti and Scaratti conducted an observation- and interview-based study in order to explain this variability. They felt that to fully understand the nature of the work in question, they had to gain a detailed qualitative understanding of exactly what the dock workers did. They concluded that the key reason for the variability in productivity levels was that the nature of the work they had to do was highly variable, with some jobs being straightforward and others being complex. This variability meant that they couldn't use standardized working practices as what they did was shaped by the specific nature of each ship and cargo. Further, in deciding how to load or unload each cargo, they had to continuously have discussions with each other and make decisions about how to proceed. Thus they argued that the dock workers experienced 'continuous learning to cope with ever-changing circumstances' (2011: 193). The reason why management were unable to explain the variable productivity levels was because they assumed that the work of the dockers was routine and low-skilled, and didn't appreciate the extent to which it involved ongoing decision-making.

Questions

To what extent can standardized routines and rules be used in any job? Can you think of other apparently routine jobs which involve a degree of discretion to cope with uncertainties and differing, unpredictable circumstances?

The socially constructed and culturally embedded nature of knowledge

Two factors that are closely interwoven are that knowledge is socially constructed and culturally embedded. It is therefore necessary to examine them simultaneously. In stark contrast to the 'knowledge is truth' assumption of the objectivist perspective on knowledge, where it is suggested that codified knowledge can exist in an objective form independent of social and cultural values, the epistemology of practice perspective argues that all knowledge is socially constructed in nature, which makes it somewhat subjective and open to interpretation. Thus, knowledge is never totally neutral and unbiased and is, to some extent, inseparable from the values of those who produce it.

As with the objectivist perspective, this viewpoint is based on a particular understanding about the nature of language. In relation to the practice-based perspective it is assumed that the meaning of language is inherently ambiguous. This subjectivity or interpretive flexibility in language thus undermines any claims about the objective status of any knowledge, whether it is highly tacit and personal, or whether it is partially explicit and codified.

The socially constructed nature of knowledge applies to both its production and its interpretation. Polanyi (1969) referred to these two processes as sense giving and sense reading, while Boland and Tenkasi (1995) used the terms 'perspective making' and 'perspective taking'. Thus both the production of knowledge and the reading/interpretation required to develop an understanding of it involve an active process of meaning construction/inference. For example, a written report is a piece of partially explicit knowledge, whose meaning is constructed by its author(s). However, different readers may infer a different meaning and analysis. This aspect of the practice-based perspective therefore has profound implications for the way knowledge is shared and managed, as the attractive simplicity of the transmitter–receiver model is questioned (see Time to reflect).

Further, this process of meaning construction/inference is typically culturally embedded. As Weir and Hutchins argue (2005: 89), 'knowledge cannot be understood outside of the cultural parameters that condition its emergence and modes of reproduction'. For example, the meanings people attach to language/events are shaped by the values and assumptions of the social and cultural context in which they live and work. Rivera and Cox (2016) provide an example of the impact of cultural values on knowledge management. Their investigation into the reasons for the failure of an IT-based knowledge management system within the human resources department of a Mexican university found that the values of human resources practitioners were a key factor. Ultimately, human resources practitioners' very limited utilization of the knowledge management system that was implemented was due to the fact that it was not perceived as reflecting the existing values of the human resources practitioner community. Thus, a recurring comment from interviewees was that the knowledge management system 'does not fit how things are done here' (2016: 22). The system that was implemented required people to codify their knowledge into a repository and then search/use the repository when undertaking their work. This was perceived as being an ineffective and impersonal way to share knowledge which didn't reflect the existing values of the human resources community, which were focused around a strong emotional engagement with work, and sharing of knowledge inter-personally, within trusted, close networks.

 Time to reflect   Perspective making and taking

Can you think of an example from any organizational experience you may have where a range of people inferred different meanings from a report? Could these differences partly be explained by the fluidity of meaning in language?

The socially constructed and culturally embedded nature of knowledge becomes visible when examining collaborations which span communities or groups with different and distinctive values and knowledge (see e.g. Hong et al. 2010), with the characteristics of such collaborations being the focus of Chapter 13.

The socially constructed and culturally embedded nature of organizational knowledge can also be illustrated through considering how national cultural factors impact on both the nature of organizational knowledge and the character of knowledge management processes. For example, Secundo et al. (2015) examined the knowledge retrieval practices of comparable engineers in Japan and Italy who had similar characteristics and were undertaking similar types of work, and found some significant differences, which were argued to be due to differences in the way work was organized in the two countries. One of the most significant differences in the information retrieval practices of the engineers related to the importance of routine knowledge. The retrieval of this information was argued to be more important for the Italian engineers than for the Japanese engineers, as the Italian engineers were argued to be less likely to possess this knowledge themselves than the Japanese engineers. The Japanese engineers were more likely to possess such knowledge due to the typically longer tenure levels they had with their employers than the Italian engineers, which allowed them to develop, absorb, and remember such routine organizational knowledge. Thus, they were less likely to need to retrieve such knowledge externally from others, as they possessed it themselves, developing it experientially over time. The impact of national cultural values on knowledge management activities is also considered in Chapter 11 when examining how national culture affected people's attitudes towards knowledge sharing activities. Finally, the impact of national cultural values on knowledge management activities is also visible in the analysis of the Nonaka and Takeuchi's (1995) SECI (socialization, externalization, combination, and internalization) model of knowledge creation, which some writers suggest is not universally applicable as it is based upon social and organizational characteristics that are specific to Japan (Glisby and Holden 2003; Weir and Hutchins 2005). This is an issue that is returned to in Chapter 7, when the work of Nonaka and Takeuchi is considered in detail (See Time to reflect.).

 Time to reflect   The complexity of cross-cultural knowledge sharing

These ideas suggest that the sharing of knowledge between people from different cultures is likely to be difficult. Such situations are likely to be common in multinational corporations. From a management point of view, what, if anything, can management in multinationals do to address such problems?

The contestable nature of knowledge

The final key aspect of the practice-based perspective is the acknowledgement that the subjective, socially constructed, and culturally embedded nature of knowledge means that what constitutes knowledge is open to dispute (see e.g. Marshall and Rollinson 2004; Yanow 2004; Kamoche and Maguire 2011; Ferguson and Taminiau 2014). This therefore challenges and undermines the idea central to the objectivist perspective that it is possible to produce truly objective knowledge. Thus, competing conceptions of what constitutes 'legitimate' knowledge can occur where different groups/individuals develop incompatible and contradictory analyses of the same events, which may lead to conflict due to attempts by these groups to have their knowledge legitimated (see e.g. Mørk et al. 2010; Heizmann 2011; and the relevant sections in Chapter 14 on conflict regarding the legitimacy of knowledge claims).

One of the main consequences flowing from this, therefore, is that issues of power, politics, and conflict become more important than is acknowledged by the objectivist perspective. Most fundamentally, Foucault's (1980) conception of power/knowledge suggests that these concepts are inseparable (Marshall and Rollinson 2004; Heizmann 2010; Mueller et al. 2016). Finally, Nicolini (2007, 2011), who utilizes a practice-based epistemology, argues that the analysis of knowledge and work practices requires issues of power and conflict to be accounted for, as the collaborative nature of work practices and the application of knowledge tend to 'produce and reproduce a landscape of inequalities' (2011: 616). The importance of acknowledging and taking account of the contested and political nature of knowledge is magnified by the fact that this aspect of knowledge and knowledge management initiatives (e.g. see Illustration 3.5) is typically either neglected or ignored by the majority of the knowledge management literature. These issues are examined more fully in Chapter 14.

Illustration 3.5 Conflict resolution in diverse groups through ongoing negotiation

Ferguson and Taminiau (2014) use a practice-based perspective to analyse conflict, learning, and the negotiation of knowledge claims in online communities. Their empirical focus was on online cross-organizational networks/forums concerned with international development. The two networks examined varied in terms of the level of diversity of members, with one group being relatively homogeneous, and the other group being more diverse. This diversity related to geographic location, professional affiliation of participants, the occupational role of participants, and the aim of the network. In the homogeneous network participants were from the same region of the USA, were all funded by the same agency, and all carried out similar roles in similar types of organization (research institutes and non-governmental organizations). In the diverse network, participants were spread across a number of countries and undertook a range of roles in quite diverse organizations (including African non-government organizations, local and national political groups, and non-government organizations from the USA and Europe).

Utilizing a practice-based perspective, based on the assumption that people's knowledge and understanding is socially constructed and shaped by people's cultural context, it was assumed that in the diverse social networks there would be more evidence of conflict, related to competing and diverse knowledge claims, and that these conflicting knowledge claims would inhibit learning. In contrast to expectations, mutual learning among participants within the diverse network was found to be greater than in the more homogeneous network. Mutual learning in the diverse network occurred through a 'subtle evolving process of negotiations' (Ferguson and Taminiau 2014: 888). This process is best illustrated via a specific example.

In the diverse network, its focus was on the role of technology as a facilitator of international development, however, there was much diversity within the community regarding the particular ways that technology could be used to facilitate development. One online discussion, which ultimately produced mutual learning, initially highlighted the differences of opinion within the community and provoked some heated arguments. This discussion related to using technology to discuss the issue of family planning, with community members being quite divided on this topic. However, as the debate/argument over this topic evolved in the community, participants were able to reflect upon and remember the core values which united the online community, which was to provide an open forum for debate that African development activists were in control of. When participants (re)learned these common community values, the dispute over the issue of family planning was resolved, and the sense of community among participants became strengthened.

Questions

How typical is this example? When differences of interest and/or identity exist between people, is conflict and dispute over knowledge claims likely to occur?

A practice-based perspective on the management and sharing of knowledge

Having considered in detail how the practice-based epistemology conceptualizes knowledge, it is now time to examine the implications of these ideas for understanding the character of organizational knowledge sharing and knowledge management processes (see Table 3.3). Fundamentally, the assumptions in this epistemology that knowledge cannot be codified into

Table 3.3 A Practice-Based Perspective on Knowledge Management

Knowledge Management from a Practice-Based Epistemology
1. Knowledge sharing/acquisition requires 'perspective making' and 'perspective taking'—developing an understanding of tacit assumptions
2. Knowledge sharing/acquisition through: • 'rich' social interaction • immersion in practice—watching and/or doing
3. Management role to facilitate social interaction

a discrete entity as it is deeply embodied in people and simultaneously embedded in and inseparable from people's work practices, means that knowledge isn't regarded as something which can be directly managed. Instead, those adopting this perspective conceptualize the role of management in the management of knowledge as facilitating inter-personal communication and collaboration between people.

One of the central components of the practice-based perspective on knowledge management is that it eschews the idea that it is possible for organizations to create a disembodied library or repository of codified knowledge (Goodall and Roberts 2003). Tsoukas (1996: 15), quoting Hayek, suggests that a belief in the ability to achieve such a state represents the 'synoptic delusion ... that knowledge can be surveyed by a single mind'. Thus managerial understanding of organizational knowledge will always be fragmented and incomplete, and attempts to collect knowledge in a central location likely to be limited. The following quotation from Tsoukas (1996: 22) sums this up, and points towards the practice-based perspective's conceptualization of knowledge sharing processes:

> the key to achieving coordinated action does not so much depend on those 'higher up' collecting more and more knowledge, as on those 'lower down' finding more and more ways to get connected and interrelating the knowledge each one has.

The practice-based perspective further suggests that the transmitter–receiver model of knowledge sharing is questionable because the sharing of knowledge does not involve the simple transferral of a fixed entity between two people. Instead, the sharing of knowledge involves two people actively inferring and constructing meaning. The adoption of a practice-based epistemology implies that to be effective the sharing of knowledge requires individuals to develop an appreciation of (some of) the tacit assumptions and values on which the knowledge of others is based—the processes of 'perspective making' and 'perspective taking' (see Definition) outlined earlier (Boland and Tenkasi 1995). This challenges the assumption embedded in the transmitter–receiver model that the knowledge exchanged in such processes is unchanged. Bolisani and Scarso (2000) suggest the practice-based perspective on knowledge sharing represents a 'language game', due to the importance of dialogue and language to such processes. Boland and Tenkasi (1995: 358) argue that effective knowledge sharing involves 'a process of mutual perspective taking where distinctive individual knowledge is exchanged, evaluated and integrated with that of others in the organization'.

> **DEFINITION Perspective making and taking**
>
> Perspective making is the process through which an individual develops, strengthens, and sustains their knowledge, beliefs, and values. Perspective taking is the process through which people develop an understanding of the knowledge, values, and 'worldview' of others.

These perspective making and perspective taking processes typically require an extensive amount of social interaction to be effective. The acquisition and sharing of knowledge typically occurs through two distinct, but closely interrelated, processes (see Table 3.3): immersion in practice (either from doing a task or from closely observing someone else) and 'rich' social interactions between people. These processes are interrelated because learning by doing is likely to simultaneously involve an element of social interaction and vice versa.

Immersion in practice is the process whereby people develop, share, and communicate knowledge through either undertaking a particular task or closely observing (and communicating with) someone else who is carrying out a particular task. An example of such a process is presented by Bouty and Gomez (2010) which describes the way in which knowledge in restaurant kitchens is communicated and shared between the chefs and other kitchen staff, which occurs via actually preparing food for customers. Another example of knowledge sharing/development via a process of 'immersion in practice' is the collective problem-solving of the dock workers highlighted by Ripamonti and Scaratti (2011). Here knowledge was developed through the dock workers having to find ways to deal with the highly variable types of cargo they had to process. Rich social interactions can take an almost infinite range of forms, but to be 'rich' they need to allow people to be able to effectively communicate their knowledge, values, and assumptions with each other. Listed later is a range of ways in which this could be done.

From a practice-based perspective, the managerial role in facilitating the management and sharing of knowledge is therefore to encourage and facilitate the type of communication and social interaction processes that will allow effective perspective making and taking to occur. This can be done through an enormously diverse range of ways including (to highlight just a few examples):

- developing a knowledge sharing culture (through rewarding people for sharing);
- facilitating the development of organizational communities of practice;
- providing forums (electronic or face-to-face) which create opportunities for social interaction between people;
- implementing a formalized 'mentoring' system to pair experienced and inexperienced workers;
- designing job roles to facilitate and encourage inter-personal communication and collective problem-solving.

Many of these issues are examined in more detail in subsequent chapters. Chapters 12 considers the knowledge sharing dynamics within communities of practice, which applies practice-based principles to the context of homogeneous groups. Chapter 13 examines the characteristics of knowledge processes within diverse groups, which emphasizes issues examined here such as the culturally embedded nature of knowledge. Finally, Chapter 14, on power, politics, and conflict, links to and builds from the contestable nature of knowledge and the scope for conflict that can exist when attempting to manage knowledge.

 ## Conclusion

Chapters 2 and 3 have outlined two distinctive epistemological perspectives, which characterize knowledge in extremely different ways. These perspectives also conceptualized knowledge sharing and knowledge management processes differently. They therefore have very different managerial implications with regard to how knowledge management efforts should be organized and structured:

- *Objectivist perspective*: focus on the codification and collection of knowledge; create mechanisms to allow this knowledge base to be searched and accessed such as setting up a searchable database and encouraging staff to codify their knowledge and store it there.

- *Practice-based perspective*: facilitate inter-personal knowledge sharing and processes of perspective making and taking through diverse forms of interaction and communication.

 Case study The collective knowledgeability of care: a case study of an Italian care home

Gherardi and Rodeschini (2016) use the findings from an ethnographic study of a single Italian care home for the elderly to examine the nature of the knowledge involved in the provision of care. They adopt what is here labelled a practice-based perspective on knowledge, particularly emphasizing the collective nature of the knowing involved in the provision of care.

Their focus is the practices involved in the provision of care by nursing and medical staff. In the home examined, the provision of care was defined as 'fostering well-being among the cared-for persons' (2016: 273). The collective provision of care was achieved not via workers using codified knowledge to make decisions, but was instead an 'emergent process' (p. 268) whereby knowledgeable staff worked together, to provide care based on their evaluation of the specific circumstances which they encountered when dealing with each patient. Two key aspects of this knowing was first its close connection to the body and the human senses, with it being described as 'body work' involving touching, moving, cleaning, etc., the bodies of patients. This is conceptualized as an 'embodied competence' that is learnt with the body, while 'working with other bodies' (p. 270). Second, the knowledgeability of care is argued to be 'hidden' within the practices, being 'corporeal, preverbal, and non-rational' (p. 270). Fundamentally, the knowing of care embodied by the staff examined was highly tacit, was something that staff were only partly conscious of, and was something they would find difficult articulating.

A key feature in the collective provision of care is the 'common orientation' possessed, developed, and utilized by all medical staff. An important aspect of this 'common orientation' was the shared definition of caring that existed in the home (see definition earlier). This ethos was embedded in all care practices, and was sustained via the way people collectively coordinated with each other to carry out the work. This is illustrated in the following quote provided by a care assistant: 'here proper value is given to our mission, which is getting them [the residents] to feel well. I mean, we're here for them, and we do everything possible for their well-being' (p. 273). The sense of collective practices is illustrated via the use of the pronoun 'we'.

The day-to-day work in the home was focused around three generic types of practice. First, there were practices related to the bodies of the residents such as washing, dressing, examining, and massaging them; administering medication; moving them between rooms (such as from bedrooms to toilets, etc.); and entertaining residents. A second group of practices related to care for the premises such as tidying rooms, cleaning, etc. Finally, a third group of practices involved administrative, bureaucratic, and managerial work such as attending meetings, filling in paperwork documenting patients' health and the care provided to them.

The collective, practice-based, and emergent nature of the practice of caring can be usefully illustrated via the description of a single, detailed episode. This is based on the researchers' fieldnotes, which say:

> the patient says that she has copious catarrh. The doctor ausculates her and finds nothing seriously wrong. He prescribed flumocil, and then in a low voice asks the nurse co-ordinator Carla if they have the aerosol. After she answers in the affirmative, he adds some aerosol to the therapy, and again in a low voice tells the nurse: this way we'll put on a bit of a show and make her feel better. (p. 273)

This episode illustrates how the provision of care emerges from the coordinated talk, activities, and ad hoc decision-making of the nurse and doctor, who combine together to ensure the well-being of the patient. From this perspective, care emerges from the ongoing negotiations and decision-making which is in response to emergent contingencies related to how patients look, act, and talk, which evolves on a daily basis.

Source: Gherardi, S., and Rodeschini, G. (2016). 'Caring as Collective Knowledgeable Doing: About Concern and Being Concerned', *Management Learning*, 47/3: 266–84.

Questions

1. Building from this perspective on knowing, to what extent can the knowledgeability of care be codified?

2. What would be the potential benefits of attempting to (partially) codify this knowledge, and what are the likely challenges from attempting to do so?

3. Does this account of a practice-based perspective on care underestimate the role of codified knowledge on medical procedures, health and safety guidelines, etc., in the provision of care?

 ## Review and Discussion Questions

1. Think about an example of partially explicit knowledge you are familiar with, for example a set of instructions for how to conduct a certain task. What tacit knowledge is necessary for you to make sense of them? What does this say about the inseparability of tacit and explicit knowledge?

2. Think about interactions you have had with people of different nationalities. Have there been examples from these interactions where people's contrasting understandings of the same phenomenon have revealed the socially constructed and culturally embedded nature of knowledge?

3. Compare the two perspectives on knowledge outlined in Chapters 2 and 3. Which one more closely models the nature of knowledge in the organizations that you have worked in?

Suggestions for Further Reading

E. Zeynap, A. Schneider, and G. von Krogh (2014). 'The Multi-Faceted Nature of Social Practices: A Review of the Perspectives on Practice-Based Theory Building about Organizations', *European Management Journal*, 32: 712–22.
Presents a good review of the diverse literature utilizing a practice-based perspective, which includes the literature on knowledge/knowing.

N. Marshall (2014). 'Thinking, Saying and Doing in Collaborative Projects: What Can we Learn from Theories of Practice?', *The Engineering Project Organization Journal*, 4/2–3: 107–22.
An interesting case study which utilizes and develops the practice-based perspective in the analysis of a two-year ethnographic study of project-based working in the UK water industry.

K. Orr, S. Nutley, S. Russell, R. Bain, B. Hacking, and C. Moran (2016). *Knowledge and Practice in Business and Organizations*. Routledge: London.
A useful edited book which contains a diverse range of theoretical and empirical chapters all utilizing a practice-based perspective.

D. Nicolini (2011). 'Practice as the Site of Knowing: Insights from the Field of Telemedicine', *Organization Science*, 22/3: 602–20.
A detailed and insightful paper which contributes empirically and conceptually to the development of the practice-based view on knowledge.

 To further your understanding of knowledge management in organizations explore the book's accompanying online resources at www.oup.com/uk/hislop4e/

PART 2

An Introduction to Key Concepts

Part 2 contains two chapters both of which examine concepts that are fundamental to the topic of knowledge management. As has been outlined in previous chapters, the knowledge management literature contains a wide range of perspectives on the question of the nature of knowledge, and this diversity extends to all of the concepts examined here. Thus a separate chapter is required to fully explore and elaborate the diversity of perspectives and debates that surround each topic.

Chapter 4 begins this section by examining the topic of knowledge management itself. Fundamentally the chapter shows that there is no single, simple, agreed definition of what knowledge management is and that there are an enormous diversity of ways in which organizations can attempt to manage their knowledge. The chapter explores the diversity of perspectives on this topic by suggesting that in exploring the topic of knowledge management what 'management' constitutes requires as much attention as the nature of organizational knowledge. The chapter also discusses the various processes involve in the management of knowledge (creation, storage, application . . .), and distinguishes between an organization's knowledge and knowledge management strategies. The chapter then examines the diversity of factors, including the type of strategy adopted by organizations, which shape the type of approach to knowledge management that organizations should adopt, as well as examining some of the most well-known typologies developed to characterize the diversity of knowledge management strategies that exist.

As Chapter 1 outlined, the knowledge society rhetoric suggests that much work has become increasingly knowledge intensive. However, there is still a debate within the knowledge management literature over what constitutes knowledge work and which organizations can be defined as knowledge intensive. Chapter 5 engages with and examines the different perspectives that exist on these debates.

4 What is Knowledge Management?

Introduction

Now it is time to consider what is meant by the term 'knowledge management'. A whole chapter is needed to explore this topic to take account of the heterogeneous ways in which knowledge management is defined and in which organizational knowledge can be managed. Almost every book or article published on the topic of managing knowledge in organizations has a different definition of knowledge management. Many authors therefore emphasize the lack of consensus regarding how knowledge management is defined and conceptualized (Lloria 2008; Mehrizi and Bontis 2009). One general distinction that can be made in terms of how to manage knowledge is between technology- and people-centred approaches. Thus, while some suggest that knowledge management can be equated with the implementation and use of particular types of information and communication technologies (ICTs) (see Part 4 for more detail on the role of ICTs in knowledge management), others focus on more indirect methods of managing knowledge, via managing the people who possess and utilize knowledge (see Part 6 for further details on this approach to knowledge management). Holsapple (2005) claims that the two approaches can be not be separated and that modern knowledge management is inseparable from technology, meaning that the actual implementation of knowledge management in organizations is always a combination of the two.

However, before exploring these issues, the question of what is knowledge management is considered. After this the chapter explores the diverse range of factors that influence the approach to knowledge management that firms adopt. By studying these approaches, distinct patterns can be referred to as knowledge management strategies. The chapter concludes with examining several frameworks and taxonomies that have been developed to categorize how the management of organizational knowledge can be achieved.

What is knowledge management?

In the introductory chapter of this book it was already indicated that knowledge plays an important role in the post-industrial society which is characterized by an increased share of services in the economy, by knowledge and information intensity of economic/social life, and by the growing importance of theoretical knowledge in work. Knowledge became an important production factor, in other words essential for creating value, and an important resource for competitive advantage (Newell 2015). This is also reflected by the ideas of the knowledge-based theory of the firm presented in the third section of Chapter 2. Consequently, knowledge needs to be nurtured and developed within the organization and protected from leaking outside the organization boundaries to prevent losing the competitive edge of the organization (Von Krogh 2012). It is therefore no surprise that organizations started to think about managing this important production factor just like they did with other production factors in the industrial area (e.g. workforce management, financial management, production management). These concerns led to a popularization of the term 'knowledge management' (Scarbrough and Swan 2001).

Knowledge management is a broad concept which refers to leveraging knowledge assets to the benefit of the organization (Alavi and Leidner 2001; Hislop 2010). These benefits include more efficient processes, from preventing the reinvention of the wheel at different places in the organization to an increase in innovativeness and hence strategic advantage for the organization (Von Krogh 1998). Knowledge management is therefore more than just managing knowledge, which implies it is mainly a technological challenge that can be solved by applying knowledge management systems. Although this approach was common in the early days of knowledge management, it was soon realized that knowledge management also includes organizational factors such as culture, structure, human resource management (HRM), and leadership (Heisig 2009). Therefore, knowledge management is considered as the managing of knowledge processes and knowledge work rather than just the management of knowledge itself (Newell 2015). The number of knowledge processes that are considered varies considerably in the literature. Heisig (2009) studied 117 knowledge management frameworks and found that the number of knowledge processes (also referred to as 'KM activities') ranges from a minimum of two processes to a maximum of nine; the average number of knowledge processes he found in his research was five. Studying the co-occurrence of knowledge processes in the frameworks finally led to the identification of four core knowledge processes: create, store, share, and apply. Together they form the knowledge management life cycle. This indicates it is a circular process where knowledge is first created. Next it is stored in some way so that it can be shared with others. Once it has been shared it can be applied so that value is created for the organization. The application of knowledge results in feedback and might lead to another cycle of create, store, share, and apply (see Time to reflect).

 Time to reflect   Knowledge management life cycle

The knowledge management life cycle (create, store, share, apply) is central to many knowledge management definitions. Yet, if you look at the business process descriptions of organizations, there is never a mention of any of these knowledge processes. What do you think can explain this omission of knowledge processes in process descriptions? Hint: Should knowledge processes be considered as separate processes or are they embedded in the primary business processes (e.g. sales, marketing, production) of the organization?

Definitions of knowledge management therefore typically contain references to the knowledge processes to be managed and the organizational factors that are involved. One of the earliest definitions of knowledge management can be found in the seminal book *Working Knowledge* by Davenport and Prusak (1998):

> Knowledge management is concerned with the exploitation and development of the knowledge assets of an organisation with a view to furthering the organisation's objectives. The knowledge to be managed includes both explicit, documented knowledge, and tacit, subjective knowledge. Management entails all of those processes associated with the identification, sharing and creation of knowledge. This requires systems for the creation and maintenance of knowledge repositories, and to cultivate and facilitate the sharing of knowledge and organisational learning. Organisations that succeed in knowledge management are likely to view knowledge as an asset and to develop organisational norms and values, which support the creation and sharing of knowledge.

A later definition of knowledge management states (Dalkir 2005):

> Knowledge management is the deliberate and systematic coordination of an organization's people, technology, processes, and organizational structure in order to add value through reuse and innovation. This coordination is achieved through creating, sharing and applying knowledge as well as through feeding the valuable lessons learned and best practices into corporate memory in order to foster continuous organizational learning.

But the broad definition of knowledge management still leaves room for different interpretations of knowledge management depending on the perspective that is chosen. In this book we use the two most commonly used perspectives towards knowledge management: the objectivist perspective and the practice-based perspective (which are similar to the 'knowledge as an object' and 'knowledge as a process' perspective from Alavi and Leidner 2001). The objectivist perspective considers knowledge as a separate entity that can be collected and stored in repositories which allows employees to access and search this knowledge. Hence, it is a very technical approach and focuses on the selection and deployment of the right knowledge management technologies. The practice-based perspective considers knowledge as embodied in human beings and therefore focuses on facilitating interpersonal knowledge sharing and processes. This requires an organizational approach and involves establishing a culture in which knowledge is shared and where managers evaluate their employees on their contribution to knowledge management and not only on financial productivity.

The broadness of the knowledge management concept is also demonstrated by the number of theories in which it is rooted. This is nicely demonstrated in an overview article by Baskerville and Dulipovici (2006) who provide an overview of the different theories underlying the knowledge management field (see also Table 4.1). They divide the theories into three high level categories. The first category provides the rationale for knowledge management and includes information, economics and strategic management theories. The second category concerns the management of knowledge processes and includes organizational culture, organizational structure, organizational behaviour, and knowledge-based systems theories. The third and last category concerns evaluation or measuring of knowledge management and includes quality management and organizational performance management theories. All those theories have influenced thinking about knowledge management and resulted in many different perspectives on knowledge management (see Time to reflect).

Table 4.1 Theoretical Foundations of Knowledge Management Theories

Applied Purpose in Knowledge Management	Theoretical Foundation	Key Theories Drawn from this Foundation	Developed Key Knowledge Management Theories	Examples of Theories as Applied in Knowledge Management
Rationale	Information economics	Intellectual capital, intellectual property	Knowledge economy, knowledge networks and clusters, knowledge assets, knowledge spill overs, continuity management	Tordoir (1995), Inkpen and Tsang (2005), Teece (2000), Foray (2004), Beazley et al. (2002)
	Strategic management	Core competencies, dynamic capabilities	Dumbsizing, knowledge alliances, knowledge strategy, knowledge marketplace, knowledge capability	Conner and Prahalad (1996), Eisenberg (1997), Inkpen and Dinur (1998), Conner and Prahalad (1996), Kafentzis et al. (2004), Baskerville and Pries-Heje (1999)
Process definition	Organizational culture	Cultural values, power, control, and trust	Knowledge culture	Graham and Pizzo (1996), De Long and Fahey (2000)
	Organizational structure	Goal-seeking organizations	Knowledge organizations	Starbuck (1997), Dyer and Nobeoka (2000)
	Organizational behaviour	Organizational creativity, innovation, organizational learning, organizational memory	Knowledge creation, knowledge codification, knowledge transfer/reuse	Nonaka and Takeuchi (1995), Nonaka and Toyama (2003), Wiig (1997), Hansen et al. (1999), Markus (2001)
	Artificial intelligence	Knowledge-based systems, data mining	Knowledge infrastructure, knowledge architecture, knowledge discovery	Davenport et al. (1998), O'Leary (1998), Zhuge (2002), Fayyad et al. (1996), Shaw et al. (2001)
Evaluation	Quality management	Risk management, benchmarking	Knowledge equity, qualitative frameworks	Glazer (1998), Jordan and Jones (1997), King and Zeithaml (2003)
	Organizational performance measurement	Financial performance measures	Performance indices	Ahn and Chang (2004), Chang Lee et al. (2005)

Source: Baskerville and Dulipovici (2006).

Time to reflect Knowledge management or not?

Considering the following two practices that can be found in an international engineering organization, discuss if you would label these practices as knowledge management and explain why.

Practice 1: Maintain a handbook of commonly applied engineering standards and make it available online to all engineers in the organization.

Practice 2: Send engineers to international conferences on construction technologies.

Factors influencing organizational approaches to knowledge management

In the previous section it was suggested that the way in which management personnel in an organization attempt to manage knowledge is likely to be shaped by the particular approach to management that is adopted. This section builds on this insight to look at the diverse range of factors that influence both the wide range of distinctive knowledge-based issues/challenges different types of organization face, as well as the approaches to managing knowledge that they adopt. The first issue explored here is the link between an organization's general business strategy and its approach to knowledge management. After this, a range of factors related to both the nature of the business environment and the characteristics of organizations are considered. What this section attempts to illustrate is that the enormous diversity in the strategies that firms utilize, in the character of their business environment, and in basic organizational features, means that there is likely to be a vast range of ways in which organizations attempt to manage knowledge. This diversity is reflected here in the heterogeneous range of illustrations, examining knowledge management in small firms, multinational corporations, and a public sector organization.

A number of writers and analysts suggest that it is essential to link knowledge management initiatives to concrete business strategies (Hansen et al. 1999; Pan and Scarbrough 1999; McDermott and O'Dell 2001; Hunter et al. 2002). The logic of such perspectives is that an organization's knowledge management strategy should link to and flow from its business strategy. This is done via developing an understanding of the role of knowledge resources and processes in an organization's business strategy, and developing a knowledge management strategy to sustain and enhance these knowledge resources/processes. For example, contrast the situations of two different companies in the same industry pursuing different strategies, such as the car manufacturers Nissan and Jaguar. While both companies design, manufacture, and sell cars, the nature of their products and the strategies pursued by the companies are vastly different, with Nissan primarily focusing on high-volume family cars, while Jaguar is more focused on the luxury car market. Fundamentally, the type of knowledge-based challenges they face, the type of knowledge processes they have to manage (creation, codification, sharing . . .), and thus the approaches to managing knowledge that they adopt are consequently likely to be different. Hence, besides aligning the knowledge management strategy with the business strategy, the actual knowledge management processes should also be aligned with the knowledge management strategy in order to reap the benefits from knowledge management initiatives (Bosua and Venkitachalam 2013).

Table 4.2 Massingham's (2004) Model of Knowledge-Based Strategy-Making Processes

Stage Number	Stage Title	Actions
1	Clarify strategy.	Decide on the generic strategy to be used and get 'buy in' to it from senior management.
2	Identify strategic themes.	Determine the activities that are key to achieving this strategy.
3	Identify knowledge resources.	Identify the role of knowledge resource in the activities which are key to the agreed strategy.
4	Evaluate knowledge resources.	Evaluate whether the firm's existing knowledge resources are adequate to allow the effective execution of the firm's strategic activities.
5	Knowledge decision.	Decide what actions are necessary to develop and/or sustain the firm's knowledge resources.

Source: Massingham (2004).

Writers examining the link between business strategy and knowledge management activities typically propose neat sequential stage models for linking knowledge-related issues into strategy-making processes. For example, Massingham's (2004) model of knowledge-based strategy-making is outlined in Table 4.2. Zack (1999), Earl (2001), and Van der Spek and Hofer-Alfeis (2002) develop similar models to conceptualize the relationship between business and knowledge management strategies. However, such a conceptualization of the knowledge management–strategy relationship has idealistic and rationalistic overtones. Thus, there are assumptions that business strategies are developed on the basis of thorough and objective analyses of the business/market environment, and that the implications of these business strategies are then used in a logical and structured fashion to determine organizational practices (such as HRM policies, information technology (IT) strategy).

In Mintzberg et al.'s (1998) terms, such a conceptualization of strategy-making follows the Design School or Planning School models, which neglects the extent to which strategy is ad hoc, emergent, based on limited searches and hunches, and the possibility that business strategies are as much the result of political battles as careful market analyses. Arguably, this is because the issue of strategy has been given inadequate attention in the knowledge management literature, and as a consequence strategy models are relatively basic and unsophisticated. Empirical support for the ad hoc and emergent model of strategy-making is provided by Meroño-Cerdan et al. (2007). They report on a study looking into the knowledge management strategies adopted by a selection of Spanish and Austrian small and medium-sized enterprises (SMEs). One of the main conclusions from their study was that few of the SMEs examined had clear, deliberate, and consistent approaches to the management of knowledge. This finding is also confirmed by Bolisani et al. (2015) who suggest that deliberate strategies are more likely to be found in large organizations, while emergent strategies seem to be a better fit for small organizations.

Illustration 4.1 (Informal) knowledge management in SMEs

Hutchinson and Quintas (2008) report on the findings of a study into knowledge management initiatives within some UK SMEs. They conducted an interview-based study of a diverse range of SMEs, with these including farms, IT consultancies, and a roofing contractor. Of the thirteen SMEs they examined, ten didn't recognize the term 'knowledge management', and didn't engage in any formal knowledge management activities. However, in all thirteen firms examined, they did find extensive evidence of what they refer to as informal knowledge management. Informal knowledge management is defined as knowledge processes/activities that are specifically concerned with the management of knowledge but which are not 'systematized within policies, roles, programmes or budgets that are governed by the terminology or concepts of KM' (2008: 141). Thus knowledge management activities were identified but they were relatively ad hoc and personalized. Further, informal examples of knowledge creation, knowledge sharing, knowledge searching, and knowledge synthesis were identified as being undertaken by a range of people in the companies examined. For example, one of the farmers engaging in what was labelled informal knowledge creation said, 'I discuss how things could be improved with the butcher that I supply. We make discoveries accidentally. You could say we have a partnership' (p. 141). An example of informal knowledge sharing in one SME simply involved different people chatting and sharing ideas within an open-plan office. Finally, informal knowledge searching within one manufacturing company involved a range of activities including attending industry conferences, developing contacts with two professors at a local university, and chatting with suppliers.

Question

Think about the potential advantages and disadvantages to SMEs of trying to formalize these informal knowledge activities. Do you think the benefits of formalization outweigh the disadvantages?

As outlined earlier, the type of knowledge-related challenges and approaches to managing knowledge that are appropriate for different firms will be affected not only by the type of strategies that organizations pursue, but also by the characteristics of an organization, and also by the nature of the environment that businesses operate in. Both these issues are briefly examined now, starting with how an organization's characteristics will affect its approach to knowledge management. As Illustration 4.1 suggests, organizational size, in terms of the number of employees it has, may be an important variable, with the type of knowledge-based challenges faced by small companies likely to be quite different to those faced by a global multinational employing thousands of workers. However, in considering organizational size, it is also necessary to simultaneously take account of other organizational characteristics that are likely to be linked to the number of employees, including the extent to which an organization's workforce is geographically dispersed and the extent to which an organization's workforce is culturally diverse. Thus, while global multinationals may employ a culturally diverse workforce which is dispersed across sites and locations which are thousands of miles apart, a small firm may be located on only one site and employ a culturally homogeneous workforce. Further, the knowledge-related challenges faced by these two types of company are likely to be significantly different, and they are thus likely to manage knowledge in quite different ways. Such a contrast is visible if Illustration 4.1, representing informal knowledge management in

SMEs, is contrasted with Illustration 4.2, representing IT-based knowledge management adopted by some multinationals. For example, multinationals are likely to face the challenge of sharing knowledge between workers of different cultures (see Chapters 11 and 13), and may need to make extensive use of IT to facilitate communication and knowledge sharing between workers who are geographically dispersed (see Chapter 10). Overall therefore, factors such as the structure, size, and cultural diversity of an organization are likely to have a significant impact on the ways in which it attempts to manage knowledge.

 Illustration **4.2** The challenges of knowledge sharing across sites within multinationals

Kasper et al.'s (2010) paper is concerned with how six multinational firms address a problem that all multinationals face, that of sharing knowledge across sites. Sharing knowledge between sites can be particularly challenging if the knowledge to be shared is highly tacit, and contextually rich. The generic solution to this challenge adopted by all the multinationals they examined was to give up attempts to share contextually rich knowledge between sites, and to instead focus on the sharing of what they referred to as 'thinned' knowledge. One writer who talked about thick and thin knowledge was Geertz (1973), who contrasted the 'thick', rich, detailed descriptions that ethnographic anthropologists could produce with the thin, briefer, more summarized knowledge of other anthropologists. Another illustration of thin knowledge is two-dimensional technical drawings, which provide a thin (two-dimensional) description of three-dimensional objects. Thin knowledge is thus brief, summarized knowledge that is stripped of its contextual richness. The benefit of thin knowledge in addressing the problem of cross-site knowledge sharing is that such knowledge is relatively easy to transmit.

While Kasper et al. (2010) argue that all six multinationals shared thin knowledge between sites, they identified three different thinning strategies, with the strategies they adopted being related to the nature of the work done within them and the type of knowledge that needed to be shared. Two of the multinationals examined were consultancies. In both these companies what was labelled a *topographical approach* to thinning was adopted. This involved developing electronic expertise maps, which codified details of who possessed what expertise and knowledge and where in the organization they were located, but not the details of the knowledge. These electronic maps could be accessed and searched by anyone within the company who was interested in locating people with specific expertise. This was typically people-centred knowledge. This type of knowledge was important in these organizations as it allowed both consultants to advertise their knowledge and experience to others in the organization, and project leaders to identify relevant people for their projects.

An alternative *statistical approach* to thinning knowledge was adopted by the two industrial materials companies that were examined. In these companies, the type of knowledge that needed to be shared between sites was site-specific knowledge, related to a site's performance, which allowed people to benchmark and compare performance across sites. With the statistical approach to thinning, the thinned knowledge was statistical information (on topics such as product quality levels, productivity levels, error levels, etc.), with collections of such statistical information presenting thin knowledge on site performance. The third and final approach to knowledge thinning adopted by the two high-technology companies was referred to as a *diagrammatic approach* to thinning. In both these organizations product design responsibilities were highly centralized with dispersed sites being responsible for the standardized production of products that were designed at the corporate centre. In this context, the knowledge to be shared between the corporate centre and production sites was product design specifications, which were shared in the form of diagrams and technical drawings.

The multi-nationals described in this illustration decided to abandon the sharing of contextually rich knowledge (i.e. tacit knowledge) given that this case study is from 2010 (and probably a bit earlier since the case study was conducted well before its publication date) and the fact that information technology has developed considerably since that time (e.g. the first iPad was introduced in 2010).

Question

Would you reconsider this decision of sharing thinned knowledge if you would be responsible for knowledge management at one of these multi-nationals at the present day?

The final range of factors examined here that affect an organization's approach to knowledge management relates to the character of the environment that organizations operate in. First, due to the embodied and tacit nature of much knowledge, the nature of the labour markets that organizations recruit from can have significant implications for their knowledge management strategies. For example, research on knowledge-intensive work suggests that labour market shortages in particular sectors can make it easy for knowledge workers to move between firms, making the retention of such workers difficult (see Chapter 14). In such circumstances, methods developed to retain such workers can be conceived of as an important element of an organization's knowledge management strategy.

Second, the nature of an organization's markets and the character of competition in them are also likely to be important factors. Thus, whether markets are highly competitive or not and whether competition is on the basis of cost, product quality, or product/service innovation are likely to affect the strategic role of knowledge processes within firms. For example, in business sectors such as pharmaceuticals, IT/software, mobile technologies, and consumer goods such as televisions, levels of technological change are high, thus for companies involved in the development of products in these sectors processes of knowledge creation are likely to be important. By contrast, in business sectors such as furniture manufacture and sales or food production, where levels of technological innovation are lower, organizations are likely to place less emphasis on knowledge creation processes.

Finally, whether an organization is a private business, which has to make profit, etc., or whether it is a public sector organization or a charity, is fundamental to the type of knowledge processes that are likely to be important. While the vast majority of research on knowledge management is focused on private business, some studies have been done on knowledge management activities in other types of organizations, such as public sector organizations (Dawes et al. 2009; Waring and Currie 2009; Kothari et al. 2011; Seba et al. 2012) and not-for-profit organizations (Hume and Hume 2008; Matzkin 2008; Cruz et al. 2009).

Summarizing, the previous arguments suggest that there is no universal knowledge management that holds in all environments or situations. This leads to the idea of a contingency model towards knowledge management, suggesting different knowledge management strategies for different environments or situations (Kim et al. 2014).

Conceptualizing the diversity of knowledge management approaches

While the focus thus far in the chapter has been on the general and strategic factors which can shape the type of knowledge management approaches organizations adopt, the focus shifts here to provide some specific details of four of the most influential frameworks and typologies that have been developed to characterize some of the key features of different approaches to the management of organizational knowledge. These approaches are also referred to as knowledge management strategies. Denford and Chan (2011) identified that there are three different meanings of 'knowledge management strategy' used in the literature. Each of the meanings of knowledge management strategy addresses a different organizational level, in other words strategic, tactical, and operational.

On the strategic level they talk about a 'knowledge strategy' which means that organizations follow a strategy that focuses on knowledge-based competitive advantage. To describe the knowledge strategy of an organization Denford and Chan (2011) distinguish six knowledge strategy dimensions: knowledge source, knowledge process, knowledge focus, radicalness of learning, speed of learning, and scope of knowledge. On the tactical level a knowledge management strategy refers to the 'approach towards knowledge management'. It considers the knowledge to be managed (e.g. explicit or tactit) and the focus for knowledge management (e.g. technology, process, people) (Saito et al. 2007). Hence, the approach defines the basic assumptions and guidelines for managing the knowledge processes. The last meaning refers to knowledge management strategy on an operational level and considers it as the 'implementation of specific knowledge management initiatives'. This includes the knowledge management practices and technologies that are implemented. In practice, an organization will deal with all these three different meaning of knowledge management strategy by starting with a knowledge strategy that will be translated to a knowledge management approach on the tactical level and a knowledge management implementation on the operational level.

The frameworks discussed in this section address the first two levels: strategic and tactical. They are referred to as knowledge strategy framework and knowledge management strategy frameworks, respectively.

Knowledge strategy frameworks

This section discusses two well-known knowledge strategy frameworks of Von Krogh et al. (2001) and Kim et al. (2014). A knowledge strategy framework defines different strategies for how an organization can achieve competitive advantage by leveraging knowledge assets.

Von Krogh et al. (2001): leveraging, expanding, appropriating, and probing

The first typology is a typical management model, in other words a 2 × 2 matrix, it is based on two dimensions resulting in four different strategies. It was developed on basis of the insights of an in-depth case study of the knowledge initiative in the culinary category (i.e. meal sauces, cold sauces, and cooking ingredients) of Unilever in the late 1990s. The first dimension of the strategy typology focuses on developing existing or new knowledge domains of a company where domains are defined as 'vibrant domains where experts create and share knowledge on

		Knowledge process	
		Transfer	Creation
Knowledge domain	Existing	Leveraging strategy	Expanding strategy
	New	Appropriating strategy	Probing strategy

Figure 4.1 Von Krogh's Knowledge Management Typology

Source: Von Krogh et al. (2001).

a continuous basis' (Von Krogh et al. 2001). An example of a knowledge domain in the context of the case study is sauce manufacturing. In terms of the knowledge-based theory of the firm, knowledge domains are the company's knowledge assets that result in a competitive advantage. The second dimension of the typology concerns the knowledge processes of knowledge creation and knowledge transfer, which can be applied to knowledge domains (either existing or new). Knowledge transfer concerns diffusion of existing knowledge within and among knowledge domains while knowledge creation concerns the creation of new knowledge with a focus on innovation. Choices along the dimensions are among other things influenced by the nature of the industry. In stable and mature industries a company is more likely to choose knowledge transfer in existing knowledge domains, while in highly volatile environments a company is more likely to choose knowledge creation to develop new knowledge domains.

Combining both dimensions leads to four strategies as shown in the 2 × 2 matrix in Figure 4.1.

- Leveraging—Ensures the internal transfer of existing knowledge within and among existing knowledge domains in the company. It aims for achieving efficiency in operations as well as reducing risks in operations.

- Expanding—There is limited knowledge creation based on bringing existing expertise in the company together as well as outside expertise related to the existing knowledge domains. It aims for incremental innovation such as variants of existing products or the launch of an existing product in a new market.

- Appropriating—Characterized by an external focuses and bringing together external knowledge sources to build up a new knowledge domain for the company. It is achieved by building links and partnerships with other companies and institutions, which also avoids the risk of overtaxing resources and the deterioration of the value of knowledge.

- Probing—To increase the chance of future growth and relevance of the company, it requires radical innovation. This is realized by developing a new knowledge domain, requiring the creation of knowledge, relying on internal resources that also need to form a new community around this new domain. It is the most risky approach since it requires the creation of knowledge in a new knowledge domain.

The knowledge strategy should be aligned with the business strategy and therefore depends on the strategic goals of a company. In the research, these strategic goals are efficiency, innovation, and risk management. If the strategic goals are increasing efficiency and low risk, then the leveraging strategy is the best fit with the business strategy. At the other side of the spectrum, the strategic goals are innovation and high risk. In this case the probing strategy best fits with the business strategy.

Kim et al. (2014): internal and external codification, internal and external personalization

The second model is also a typical management model. It is inspired by the technology-organization-environment (TOE) framework and consists of two key contextual factors. The first is *environmental knowledge intensity* and addresses the level of innovation in the environment required to stay competitive. The environment knowledge intensity is low if incremental innovation is sufficient (e.g. food and beverages) and is high when radical innovation is required (e.g. electronics and pharmaceuticals). The other factor is *organizational information systems maturity* and refers to 'the internal development of information resources, the proper integration of computer-based systems, and the ability of users to utilize organizational systems'. A higher level of organizational information systems maturity enables employees to reuse knowledge but also enables employees to identify valuable information that can be used to create new knowledge. Based on the two factors they identify four different knowledge management strategies: external codification, internal codification, external personalization, and internal personalization. The codification and personalization strategies are direct reference to the codification and personalization strategies of Hansen et al. (1999), which will be discussed later in this section. The empirical study of Kim et al. (2014), conducted among 141 Korean companies, provides the proof that each of the strategies only influences the performance of the organization in a certain situation (e.g. low environmental knowledge intensity and high organization information systems maturity) and has no significant effect on performance in other situations, although this could not be proven for the internal personalization strategy. Finally, an important limitation of the study is it regional bias since it was only conducted in Korea. Generalization to other regions and industries is therefore limited.

Knowledge management strategy frameworks

This section discusses two well-known knowledge management strategy frameworks of Hansen et al. (1999) and Alvesson and Kärreman (2001). A knowledge management strategy framework defines different strategies for managing the knowledge processes in an organization.

Hansen et al.'s (1999) codification versus personalization framework

One of the earliest, but arguably most influential, typologies of knowledge management approaches was developed by Hansen et al. (1999). The extent of its influence is visible in the fact that according to Google Scholar it had been cited more than 5,700 times by January 2017. Examples of recent studies which have linked to their framework include Kim et al. (2014), Kumar and Ganesh (2011—see Illustration 4.3), Lin (2011), and Jasimuddin et al. (2012). Of the two knowledge management typologies examined here, Hansen et al.'s is the simplest, as it only differentiates between two broad knowledge strategies: codification and personalization (see Table 4.3). The codification strategy is argued to be most relevant for companies whose competitive advantage is derived from the reuse of codified knowledge and is centrally concerned with creating searchable repositories for the storage and retrieval of codified knowledge. The personalization strategy, by contrast, is most relevant for companies whose competitive advantage is derived from processes of knowledge creation and the provision of innovative, customized products/services. The personalization knowledge strategy assumes that much of the key knowledge of its workers is tacit and cannot be codified, and thus focuses on ways to improve the face-to-face sharing of this tacit knowledge between workers.

To determine what strategy best fits the organization, it should ask itself three fundamental questions. The first question is whether the organization offers standardized or customized products to its customers. In case of a standardized product, processes are repetitive and typically well-documented. So the organization would benefit from a codification approach. When the organization offers customized products, it needs to adapt the product to the wishes or situation of the customer. Since these needs vary for each customer, the organization relies more on the use of tacit knowledge. Therefore, a personalization strategy is more appropriate. The second question is whether the organization has a mature or innovative product. When producing mature products, an organization can rely on reuse economics and a codification strategy is a logical choice. But a strategy based on innovative products requires knowledge creation in which personal knowledge transfer plays an important role. Hence this situation would call for a personalization strategy. The third and last question is whether an organization mainly relies on explicit or tacit knowledge to resolve problems. Explicit knowledge is knowledge that can be codified and therefore the codification approach should be chosen. Tacit knowledge is knowledge that cannot be codified and is embodied in people. Tapping into this knowledge therefore requires a personalization strategy towards knowledge management (see Time to reflect).

Answering the three questions will hint what knowledge management strategy would best fit the organization. However, the authors warn that two other issues may complicate the choice for a strategy: existence of multiple business units and commoditization of knowledge over time. Organizations that consist of multiple business units should apply the three questions to each individual business unit. Each business unit might have different strategic goals and therefore might also require a different knowledge management strategy. Commoditization of knowledge might require a shift in knowledge management strategy over time. An organization that offers innovative and knowledge-intensive products might find that their product becomes a commodity over time. Take for example IT service providers offering implementation services in the early days of customer relations management (CRM). In those

Table 4.3 Codification and Personalization Knowledge Strategies

knowledge Strategy	Codification	Personalization
Business–Knowledge Link	Competitive advantage through knowledge reuse	Competitive advantage through knowledge creation
Relevant Knowledge Process	Transferring knowledge from people to documents	Improving social processes to facilitate sharing of tacit knowledge between people
HRM Implications	Motivate people to codify their knowledge. Training should emphasize the development of IT skills. Reward people for codifying their knowledge	Motivate people to share their knowledge with others. Training should emphasize the development of interpersonal skills. Reward people for sharing knowledge with others

Source: Hansen *et al.* 1999.

Time to reflect   Refinement of Hansen, Nohria, and Tierney's model of personalization and codification

An important piece of advice from Hansen et al. is that organizations should not straddle but should choose one strategy as their predominant knowledge management strategy. The other strategy should then only be used to support the dominant strategy and they think of it as an 80/20 rule. So 80 per cent of their knowledge management strategy should be based on the dominant strategy and 20 per cent should be based on the supportive strategy. Organizations that do not make a clear choice for one strategy or the other will find themselves in the middle (50/50). The authors warn that this is a dangerous situation because both strategies require different IT technologies and different types of people for example. Therefore both strategies cannot be successfully integrated and they even provide an example where this situation led to a bankruptcy. However, they do not provide more rigorous evidence for the 80/20 rule. This evidence is provided by Scheepers et al. (2004) although their insights also led to a refinement of Hansen et al.'s model (see also Denford and Chan 2011). Scheeper et al. studied the knowledge strategy emphasis in four case organizations. They found that organizations initially benefited from a clear choice for either the personalization or codification strategy (i.e. supporting 80/20 rule). However, they also found that the strategy mix changes over time and evolves to a 50/50 mix of personalization and codification (i.e. not supporting the 80/20 rule). Therefore, they arrive at the conclusion that the 80/20 rule is good advice when there is no knowledge strategy yet. In that situation, a clear focus benefits organizations in developing knowledge management within the organization. But due to the intertwined nature of knowledge processes, organizations might find it necessary to adapt their strategy mix over time.

 Illustration **4.3**   The use of codification and personalization strategies within Indian manufacturing companies

Kumar and Ganesh (2011) undertook a survey-based study of the knowledge management strategies utilized within the product development facilities of some Indian manufacturing companies. They examined both the extent to which codification and personalization strategies to manage knowledge were adopted, and the extent to which product development performance was linked to the use of either approach to knowledge management. They found that, in virtually every product development unit they examined, both approaches to knowledge management were utilized simultaneously. However, in general terms significantly greater use was made of the personalization-based approach to knowledge management. Second, in terms of the link between the use of these knowledge management strategies and product development performance, which was measured in terms of the extent to which product development activities were carried out according to planned cost and time schedules, they found a positive link between both approaches and product development performance. Thus, both approaches to knowledge management appeared to facilitate product development performance.

Kumar and Ganesh also analysed the differences between firms in terms of the extent to which they utilized each knowledge management approach. In terms of the use of a codification-based approach they found little variation between firms, with this being argued to be due to the increasing standardization of IT facilities that were being used by Indian manufacturing firms. However, they did find some variation between firms in terms of the extent to which the personalization-based approach to knowledge management was used. It was suggested that this variation may be related to differences between firms, both in terms of the types of knowledge they utilized, and the types of business strategies they adopted. Fundamentally, the more orientated a firm is to the creation of new knowledge, the more important a personalization-based approach to knowledge management is likely to be.

Question

Imagine that you are the newly appointment knowledge manager of a large law firm. You have been recruited specifically to improve this firm's knowledge management processes. As a start, you plan to introduce a suitable knowledge strategy in this firm. Based on the Hansen et al. model, what knowledge management strategy would you suggest and why?

early days it concerned an innovative product requiring customization. But as time passed by it slowly turned into a commodity offered by many IT service providers. So initially a personalization approach would be appropriate for the provision of CRM implementation services, but when it turned into a commodity the IT service provider should switch to a codification strategy (or offer new products/services that fit with their personalization strategy).

Alvesson and Kärreman's (2001) four knowledge management approaches

Finally, it is useful to examine Alvesson and Kärreman's (2001) typology of knowledge management strategies. They used a framework of four management philosophies as the basis for developing four specific approaches to knowledge management (see Figure 4.2). Alvesson and Kärreman make clear that the distinctions they make between the four different approaches to knowledge management are analytical rather than empirical. Thus they suggest that organizations are unlikely to exclusively use one approach to knowledge management and that management in any particular organization are likely to simultaneously use a combination of their four approaches. The four approaches to knowledge management they identify are structured around two dimensions: the mode of managerial intervention and the medium of interaction (see Figure 4.2). The mode of managerial intervention dimension relates to the strength of managerial control dimension outlined earlier, with the 'coordination' mode relating to a relative weak philosophy of management, and the 'control' mode referring to a stronger form of management control. The medium of interaction dimension relates to the distinction, outlined earlier, between management systems focused on controlling behaviour and those focused on workers' attitudes, with the 'social' dimension relating to attitudinal control, and the 'technostructural' dimension relating to behavioural controls. We will now describe the four approaches that result from the combination of these dimensions.

Starting at the bottom left of Figure 4.2 is the *extended library* approach to knowledge management, which combines technostructural focused controls with a relatively weak form of coordinated management. This approach to knowledge management is relatively bureaucratic, centrally controlled, and top–down in character. IT systems play an important role in this approach, with senior management creating central databases and archives where employees are encouraged to codify their knowledge and experiences. Such databases are searchable and can be accessed by staff looking for sources of particular types of knowledge.

The *community* approach to knowledge management combines the coordinated form of weak and limited managerial interventions with socially focused managerial controls. This approach to knowledge management gives a very limited role to IT systems, due to the acknowledgement that much organizational knowledge is highly tacit, with it being focused around encouraging the direct sharing of knowledge between people. Management efforts

MODE OF MANAGERIAL INTERVENTION

	Coordination: 'weak' management	Control: 'strong' management
Social: attitude centred	COMMUNITY: Sharing of ideas	NORMATIVE CONTROL: Prescribed interpretations
Technostructural: behaviour focused	EXTENDED LIBRARY: Information exchange	ENACTED BLUEPRINTS: Templates for action

MODE OF INTERACTION

Figure 4.2 Alvesson and Kärreman's Knowledge Management Approaches

Source: Adapted from Alvesson and Kärreman (2001).

in this approach are focused on creating a positive environment, context, or culture which is likely to encourage staff to share knowledge with each other, for example through facilitating the development of communities of practice.

The *normative control* approach to knowledge management combines the same focus on socially focused control as the community approach, but allies it with a stronger form of managerial intervention. This is knowledge management via culture management, whereby management invest significant efforts in creating a culture which encourages, values, and rewards employee participation in organizational knowledge processes, and encourages employees to 'buy into' the culture.

Alvesson and Kärreman's final approach to knowledge management is the *enacted blueprints* method which combines a strong form of managerial intervention with technostructural type managerial controls. As with the normative control approach to knowledge management, the enacted blueprints model involves significant managerial efforts. These efforts are focused on creating codified databases of knowledge on particular roles and tasks that provide employees with templates to guide their action. This means of knowledge management is intended to facilitate the codification and dissemination of 'best practice' ways of work. However, the way in which this method limits the scope of workers to use their autonomy leads Alvesson and Kärreman to label it a form of Taylorism.

 ## Conclusion

Following on from Chapters 2 and 3, where two different perspectives on the character of knowledge in the knowledge management literature were examined, this chapter moved on to grapple with the question of what knowledge management is. The general conclusion of the chapter, which was illustrated through examining two knowledge strategy typologies (Von Krogh et al. and Kim et al.) and two separate knowledge management typologies (those of Nohria et al. and Alvesson and Kärreman), was that there is a large diversity of ways in which to manage knowledge in organizations. Each of the typologies is inspired by the knowledge-based theory of the firm but is built up from different dimensions. This shows that there is still no consensus on what are the predominant dimensions for choosing a knowledge strategy or knowledge management strategy.

The chapter also considered the factors that influence the approach to knowledge management that organizations adopt. In this respect it was found that a large diversity of heterogeneous factors came into play, including the types of business strategies that organizations pursue, management approach adopted by the organization, the characteristics of organizations such as number of employees, level of geographic dispersal, etc., and the nature of the environment that organizations operate in. It demonstrates that there is no universal model for knowledge management which is applicable in all possible situations. This demands a contingency view on knowledge (management) strategies as advocated by Kim et al. (2014). Hence, organizations should select a knowledge management strategy with care and include local circumstances and situational factors in their final choice. The resulting knowledge management strategy is only the starting point for knowledge management and not the end. It provides a general direction for knowledge management initiatives that will shape knowledge management at an operational level within the organization.

 Case study Centralizing knowledge management: McKinsey's Knowledge Network

McKinsey is one of the most well-known management consultancy companies worldwide. They employ more than 14,000 employees and they serve clients in every continent (except for Antarctica). Management of the company is based on a partnership model, meaning that each of the 1,400 partners owns and is responsible for part of the company. The global managing partner is elected by the other partners and also the board consists of partners that have been elected. McKinsey is specialized in management consultancy and many of the Fortune 500 companies are among their clients. They are hired for their state-of-the-art knowledge of industries and technological trends as well their problem solving capacity. This enables their consultants to assist their clients with complex and challenging business problems. Employees that are hired by McKinsey are therefore experienced business people or graduates from the top business schools. Once employees start at McKinsey they are expected to continuously increase their knowledge and expertise and to climb the ranks in the company. If they fail in doing so, they are expected to leave the company ('up or out' principle).

McKinsey is a truly knowledge-based company because knowledge is the main asset of the company that provides them a competitive advantage. One of the key knowledge management challenges that McKinsey faces is to keep the knowledge of their consultants up-to-date and to make sure that they can tap into the knowledge that is required for client projects whenever they need it. Consequently, the company invests heavily in maintaining and updating their knowledge assets. According their own data (www.mckinsey.com) they invest $600 million yearly in their knowledge assets. The focus on knowledge is also reflected in the composition of the workforce, which consists of 12,000 consultants and 2,000 research and information professionals supporting the consultants in their projects with clients. These research and information professionals are part of McKinsey's global Knowledge Network, which is responsible for the development and dissemination of knowledge inside the organization and to the clients of the company.

The knowledge of the network covers twenty-two industries and eight core business disciplines and is centralized in several competence centres. Supply Chain Management is one of the competence centres, which has expertise on analysing supply chains and big data analysis for example. Furthermore, they develop their own supply chain tools, build a supply chain case library and have a Supply Chain Academy. These knowledge products are the result of their own research and of collaboration with external parties. Dissemination of knowledge products to client service teams is one of the main priorities of the practice managers and knowledge professionals in the competence centres. One of the channels for dissemination is the global Knowledge Portal and the competence centres are responsible for keeping this portal up-to-date. However, the research and information professionals are also directly involved in client service teams to bring their knowledge to the team, especially when it involves tacit knowledge that is not easily shared in documented form through the Knowledge Portal (which contains over 50,000 documents). Good informal networks and a directory of resources are therefore also key to the success of knowledge management in the company.

The start of the knowledge management initiatives dates back to the late 1970s. At that time, though, the company experienced competition from other consulting companies. It was concluded that McKinsey focused too much on geographic expansion and relied too much on a generalist approach towards the consulting business. Rather than have specialist expertise on certain topics, it relied on a consulting approach and more general problem solving skills. At that time an important strategic decision was made to establish competence centres and practice areas that would focus on developing specialist expertise. It was recognized that specialist expertise was becoming an important part of the consultancy business and that a generalist approach would now longer suffice. In the late 1980s they also started to develop the IT system that developed into their current global Knowledge Portal. As described earlier, this system relied on a combination of a codification and a personalization approach. Over time the company further developed their knowledge management practices: in 1999 they launched their first knowledge centre in India and in 2013 launched the Digital Labs initiative. The Knowledge Center is a concentration of expertise from the knowledge network in a particular geographic region. It supports the region by conducting geographic information research and benchmark studies. Digital Labs brings together expertise from different knowledge areas ranging from experience design to product engineering and agile transformation. Experts from Digital Labs work together with consultants to support clients in building solutions to enable their digital business.

The McKinsey case shows that the company chose a knowledge strategy many years ago and that it is still in place today. According the typology of Von Krogh et al. (2001) this knowledge strategy can be best described as a probing strategy. The firm actively looks for new areas of expertise to gain competitive advantage and actively develops communities around it in the form of competence centres. What has changed over the years is their knowledge management strategy, which is illustrated by the many different new initiatives that have been launched to support knowledge management at the firm. Their knowledge management strategy is a combination of codification and personalization in terms of Hansen et al.'s framework. The knowledge portal is used for storing and disseminating codified knowledge while at the same time personal links between employees and direct involvement of experts in consulting projects is also key to the success of the firm. It is likely that the knowledge strategy is here to stay but that the knowledge management strategy will further evolve over time.

Sources: McKinsey, the McKinsey Knowledge Network, http://www.mckinsey.com/knowledge-network/ (accessed 26 September 2017).
McKinsey, Research Analyst job description, available at: https://mckinsey.secure.force.com/EP/job_details?jid=a0xA0000008IupMIAQ (accessed 26 September 2017).
McKinsey, 'About Us', available at: http://www.mckinsey.com/about-us/who-we-are (accessed 26 September 2017).

Questions

1. McKinsey chose a centralization strategy when it came to knowledge management. It has specialized knowledge management professionals for creating and sharing knowledge that is used by others in the organization (i.e. the consultants). What are the advantages of this strategy?

2. Can it successfully integrate the experience that consultants get from their clients' engagements?

Review and Discussion Questions

1. Knowledge management concerns organizing the knowledge processes: create, store, share, and apply in an organization. But knowledge processes can also be identified in your personal life. Can you think of any knowledge creation and/or knowledge sharing processes in which you are involved? Are these processes formalized in some way or would you consider them as informal knowledge management?

2. This section argues that organizations should develop a knowledge strategy. But as with any other strategy there is an expiry date for such strategies. What interval would you propose for revising the knowledge strategy? What are your arguments for suggesting this interval and does it take into account Mintzberg's idea of emergent strategies?

3. Von Krogh et al. and Kim et al. propose two different knowledge strategy frameworks. Investigate the dimensions of both models and determine to which extent both models overlap (or not). Based on your analysis of the dimensions of the two frameworks, would you recommend an organization to use both knowledge strategy frameworks when defining a knowledge strategy or should they stick to one of the two frameworks?

 Suggestions for Further Reading

M. Mehrizi and N. Bontis (2009). 'A Cluster Analysis of the KM Field', *Management Decision*, 47/5: 792–805.
A relatively up to date article which gives an overview of the literature on knowledge management.

R. Baskerville and A. Dulipovici (2006). 'The Theoretical Foundations of Knowledge Management', *Knowledge Management Research & Practice*, 4/2: 83–105.
Provides a good overview of the main theories that underpin the field of knowledge management.

H. Kasper, M. Lehrer, J. Mühlbacher, and B. Müller (2010). 'Thinning Knowledge: An Interpretive Field Study of Knowledge Sharing Practices of Firms in Three Multinational Contexts', *Journal of Management Inquiry*, 19/4: 367–81.
Examines cross-site knowledge sharing, one of the key challenges faced by knowledge-related multinationals, as well as highlighting a diversity of responses to it which are shaped by different organizational factors.

V. Hutchinson and P. Quintas (2008). 'Do SMEs do Knowledge Management? Or Simply Manage What they Know?', *International Small Business Journal*, 26/2: 131–54.
Highlights the significance of informal knowledge management practices within small companies.

 To further your understanding of knowledge management in organizations explore the book's accompanying online resources at **www.oup.com/uk/hislop4e/**

5 Knowledge-Intensive Firms and Knowledge Workers

Introduction

As discussed in Chapter 1, many commentators and writers characterize contemporary society as being a knowledge society, with the importance of knowledge to work and economic activity having grown enormously in the last quarter of the twentieth century. The growing importance of knowledge to the world of work is also argued to have transformed both the character of the work activities people undertake, as well as the nature of organizations. Key to these transformations has been the growing importance of knowledge workers and knowledge-intensive firms and their contribution to innovation. In fact, if contemporary society is a knowledge society, then almost by definition knowledge-intensive firms and knowledge workers represent constituent elements of it.

This chapter has two primary purposes. First, it provides a detailed definition of the terms 'knowledge-intensive firms' and 'knowledge workers' and second, it examines the character of work and the dynamics of the knowledge processes within knowledge-intensive firms. However, as the chapter progresses it will be shown that a number of debates exist on these topics, most fundamentally with the definition of knowledge workers, knowledge worker productivity, and the extent to which knowledge workers are distinctive from other types of workers being topics on which there is much disagreement (Hislop 2008; Bosch-Sijtsema et al. 2010).

The chapter begins by looking at how writing on knowledge workers and knowledge-intensive firms is typically embedded in the knowledge society rhetoric. The second section then considers how knowledge-intensive firms are defined and the overlap that exists between knowledge-intensive firms and professional service firms. Following this, the next two sections present different perspectives on the definition of knowledge work, starting with the mainstream 'professional knowledge work' perspective, knowledge worker productivity, and then moving on to the alternative 'all work is knowledge work' perspective. The fifth section then begins to consider the nature of the work carried out within knowledge-intensive firms, examining the extent to which ambiguity represents a distinguishing feature of, and inherent element in, knowledge work. The sixth section then considers the character of knowledge processes within knowledge-intensive firms, which links to the topics of intellectual capital, social capital, and innovation. The chapter concludes by examining the debate regarding the extent to which knowledge workers represent the ideal employee, being always willing to participate in relevant knowledge processes, and working long hours for their employers. Topics not examined here that are dealt with in later chapters include what organizations can do to retain (Chapter 8) and manage (Chapters 15 and 16) knowledge workers.

The knowledge economy and the growing importance of knowledge-intensive firms and knowledge workers

Since approximately the mid-1970s, as discussed in Chapter 1, the character of work has changed significantly. These changes are argued to have produced an enormous expansion in the number of knowledge workers and knowledge-intensive firms (Joo 2010; Matson and Prusak 2010; Huang 2011). More specifically, such analyses typically utilize the knowledge society rhetoric and argue that not only have the number of knowledge workers increased, and the knowledge intensity of work gone up, but the effective use of knowledge is now a significant source of competitive advantage for many companies (Bosch-Sijtsema et al. 2010; Carleton 2011; Dul et al. 2011), and that abstract and theoretical knowledge has taken on a heightened level of importance (Giauque et al. 2010; Joo 2010; Huang 2011).

One writer who was among the first to popularize such analyses was Robert Reich (Blackler 1995; Rifkin 2000). Reich's analysis was focused largely on the USA, but his argument was relevant to all of the most industrialized economies (Reich 1991). He argued that the shift towards high value-added, knowledge-intensive products and services in these economies gave rise to a category of workers he labelled 'symbolic analysts'. These are workers who first 'solve, identify and broker problems by manipulating symbols' (p. 178); and second need to make frequent use of established bodies of codified knowledge (p. 182). Thus, typical of symbolic analytical occupations are research and product design (problem solving), marketing and consultancy (problem identification), and finance/banking (problem brokering). According to Reich's analysis, by the late 1980s this category of work had grown to account for 20 per cent of employment in the USA, and was one of the USA's three key occupational categories. Statistical analysis from the UK suggests that the proportion of professional/knowledge-intensive workers in Britain was also 20 per cent in the early 1990s (Elias and Gregory 1994). As outlined immediately above, few people provide contemporary statistical data in support of knowledge workers. However, contemporary writing on knowledge workers and knowledge-intensive firms restates these claims with the likelihood that about a quarter to half of workers in advanced twenty-first century economies would be knowledge workers with their primary tasks the manipulation of information and knowledge (Davenport 2005; see Time to reflect).

 Time to reflect   *How important are knowledge workers?*

If knowledge workers constitute approximately 20 per cent of the workers in the most industrialized nations, does this suggest their importance to these economies has been exaggerated, or is their contribution to knowledge creation and wealth generation disproportional to their numbers?

Chapter 1 presented a critique of the knowledge society rhetoric on which much of the literature on knowledge work and knowledge-intensive firms is founded and there is no need to revisit it here. The main purpose of linking back to the concept of the knowledge economy here was to highlight the way in which the concepts of knowledge work and knowledge-intensive firms are so closely tied to it. The chapter now shifts focus to consider the challenges involved in providing a precise definition of what a knowledge-intensive firm is.

Defining and characterizing knowledge-intensive firms

Considering the characteristics of knowledge-intensive firms and how to define them it is necessary to acknowledge that there is no consensus on how to define a knowledge-intensive firm. Thus some types of organizations labelled as knowledge-intensive include IT service companies (Grimshaw and Miozzo 2009), law firms (Malhotra et al. 2010), biotechnology companies (Bunker Whittington et al. 2009; Luo and Deng 2009), and business consultancies and engineering services (He and Wong 2009). In labelling law firms as knowledge-intensive firms it needs to be acknowledged that there is an overlap and interrelationship between knowledge-intensive firms and professional service firms.

In terms of the diversity of definitions, they vary from those which are relatively broad, such as Alvesson (2000: 1101) who defines knowledge-intensive firms as: 'companies where most work can be said to be of an intellectual nature and where well qualified employees form the major part of the workforce', to Swart et al. (2003) who define them in terms of a wide range of features which distinguish them from more traditional, hierarchical organizations including the way they are structured, the character of their workforce, the nature of work processes within them, and the character of their products and services. Despite this breadth in definitions, knowledge is considered to be a knowledge-intensive firm's primary asset and deemed more important than other kinds of firm inputs and resources with regards to achieving competitive advantage (Teece 2000; see Illustration 5.1 and Time to Reflect).

 Illustration 5.1 IT service firms as knowledge-intensive

Grimshaw and Miozzo (2009) examine the human resource management (HRM) practices within two global information technology (IT) service firms which they define as knowledge intensive. These organizations are labelled knowledge-intensive firms as the work/service they provide (IT services) involves supplying and maintaining complex high level technological systems for clients, which requires a significant proportion of their workforce to possess both specialized skills and professional knowledge. The need for this type of service has grown significantly in recent years as many large organizations have shifted to 'outsource' and contract such work to external firms rather than provide such services themselves. This work often involves transferring employees to client firms, and requires detailed knowledge of IT systems and services, and the specific and distinctive requirements and needs of individual clients, which typically vary greatly.

Questions

If you think of the specialized skills and professional knowledge in an IT service firm—how is this firm's knowledge different from the knowledge of a law firm? Are there any differences and if so what are they?

Time to reflect   Would you consider a startup company knowledge intensive?

Give reasons why you argue for or against this.

In discussing the character of knowledge-intensive firms the taxonomy of knowledge-intensive firms developed by von Nordenflycht (2010) is utilized. Not only is it sensitive to the diversity of firms that can be labelled knowledge intensive, it also links to the concept of professional service firms. While some writers link professional service firms and knowledge-intensive firms together by arguing that professional service firms are simply a specialized sub-set of a wider population of knowledge-intensive firms (see Malhotra et al. 2010), von Nordenflycht develops a taxonomy with three dimensions.

The three dimensions in von Nordenflycht's taxonomy are the knowledge intensity of work carried out within them, their level of capital intensity, and the extent to which their workforce is professionalized (see Table 5.1). The knowledge intensity of a firm is defined in terms of the extent to which the development and use of complex knowledge is involved in the creation of its outputs (products/services). In terms of capital intensity, von Nordenflycht argues that knowledge-intensive firms have a low capital intensity, which means that its output is not dependent upon significant amounts of non-human assets such as factories, equipment, patents, copyrights, etc. The third dimension in von Nordenflycht's taxonomy is the extent to which a firm employs a professionalized workforce, with a professionalized workforce being defined by the possession of specialized knowledge, where this knowledge is institutionally regulated (such as by a professional body/association), and where a code of ethics governing behaviour operates. In applying this taxonomy (see Table 5.1) von Nordenflycht argues that knowledge-intensive firms vary in their degree of professional service intensity, with law firms having a high level and biotechnology firms having a low level of professional service intensity.

Table 5.1 Von Nordenflycht's (2010) Taxonomy of Knowledge-Intensive Firms

Category	Knowledge Intensity	Low Capital Intensity	Professionalized Workforce	Exemplars
Technology developers	X			Biotechnology firms and R&D laboratories
Neo-professional service firms	X	X		Consultants and advertising agencies
Professional campuses	X		X	Hospitals
Classic professional service firms	X	X	X	Accountants and architects

Source: von Nordenflycht (2010).

Defining knowledge workers: the professional knowledge work perspective

As with the concept of knowledge-intensive firms, providing a precise definition of knowledge workers is not straightforward, as there is a lack of general consensus on the topic (Bosch-Sijtsema et al. 2010). To reflect this debate two different definitions are presented in the chapter, with this section presenting the mainstream definition of knowledge work/ers (see Definition), before introducing this perspective's critique in the following section, which leads to another definition of knowledge work/ers.

Precise definitions vary between authors, with some being relatively broad and others being more specific. For example, Dul et al. (2011) provide one of the broadest (and vaguest) definitions of knowledge work by defining knowledge workers as people 'who perform "brain work"' (p. 722). In contrast, Bosch-Sijtsema et al. (2010) define a knowledge worker as: 'anyone who creates, develops, manipulates, disseminates or uses knowledge to provide a competitive advantage or some other benefit contributing towards the goal of the organization' (p. 183). Such definitions typically suggest that knowledge workers possess high level, formal academic qualifications (see Giauque et al. 2010; Joo 2010; Huang 2011). Despite enormous variation in wording with regards to how knowledge workers are defined there are a number of features that are typically common to all of what are here labelled the mainstream perspective on knowledge work. Common elements are that knowledge workers constitute an elite and quite distinctive element of the contemporary workforce, that they possess high level formal qualifications, that their output typically contributes significantly to their employers' performance, and that their work is highly creative and involves a significant amount of problem solving and the creation and use of knowledge. Finally, this definition of knowledge work fits with Reich's definition of symbolic analysts.

> **DEFINITION   Knowledge worker ('professional knowledge work' perspective)**
>
> Someone whose work is primarily intellectual, creative, and non-routine in nature, and which involves both the utilization and creation of abstract/theoretical knowledge.

Based on such definitions, an enormous range of occupations can be classified as knowledge work. Typical occupations characterized as such are: IT and software engineers/designers (Swart and Kinnie 2003; Bosch-Sijtsema et al. 2010), lawyers (Hunter et al. 2002; Malhotra et al. 2010), consultants (Robertson and Swan 2003; Swart and Kinnie 2010; Dul et al. 2011), advertising executives (Alvesson 1995; Beaumont and Hunter 2002; Swart and Kinnie 2010), accountants (Morris and Empson 1998), scientists and engineers (Beaumont and Hunter 2002; Huang 2011), and architects (Frenkel et al. 1995). Knowledge worker definitions therefore overlap with and include classical professions (such as lawyers, architects, etc.), but also extend beyond them to include a wide variety of other occupations (such as consultants, advertising executives, IT developers, etc.).

One problem with the definitions of knowledge workers is that they are a little vague. However, Frenkel et al.'s (1995) somewhat neglected framework develops a more detailed definition, and conceptualizes knowledge work in relation to three dimensions (see Table 5.2). The first dimension, creativity, is defined as a process of 'original problem solving', from which an original output is produced (p. 779), with the level of creativity in work varying on a sliding scale from low to high. Thus, work with a high level of creativity would include software design, where programmers design and produce new software to meet the specific requirements of their clients. The second dimension is the predominant form of knowledge used in work, with knowledge being characterized as either theoretical or contextual. Theoretical knowledge represents codified concepts and principles, which have general relevance, whereas contextual knowledge is largely tacit and non-generalizable, being related to specific contexts of application. The third dimension is skill, with skills involved in work being divided into three categories: intellective, social, and action-based skills. Action-based skills relate to physical dexterity, social skills to the ability to motivate and manage others, while intellective skills are the ability to undertake abstract reasoning and synthesize different ideas.

Using these dimensions, Frenkel et al. (1995) define a knowledge worker as anyone who first has a high level of creativity in their work; second, is required to make extensive use of intellective skills; and finally, also uses theoretical rather than contextual knowledge. This framework fits within the professional knowledge work perspective as the label 'knowledge worker' is restricted to those whose work has the three characteristics listed in Table 5.2.

Also common within the mainstream perspective on knowledge workers and knowledge-intensive firms is the use of the term 'knowledge-intensive work', which provides the same function as Frenkel et al.'s framework in maintaining the idea that knowledge workers represent an elite and exclusive element in the contemporary workforce. Thus, what distinguishes knowledge workers from other types of workers is the intensity of their knowledge use. However, as Alvesson (2000) clarifies, knowledge intensiveness is a somewhat vague concept and suggests in a later paper that 'any evaluation of "intensiveness" is likely to be contestable' (Alvesson 2001: 864). Arguably, there will always be room for debate on which occupations can be defined as knowledge-intensive work.

Peter Drucker (1999) wrote extensively on the philosophical and practical foundations of modern business corporations and asserts that the most valuable asset of twenty-first century institutions will be its knowledge workers and their productivity. Steady advances in productivity

Table 5.2 Frenkel et al.'s Three Dimensional Conceptualization of Work

Dimensions	Characteristics
Creativity	Measured on a sliding scale from low to high
Predominant form of knowledge used	Characterizes work as involving the use of two predominant forms of knowledge: 1. Contextual knowledge 2. Theoretical knowledge
Type of skills involved	Characterizes work as involving three main categories of skill: 1. Intellective skills 2. Social skills 3. Action-based skills

Source: Frenkel et al. (1995).

have been made over the past fifty years through a deeper understanding, analysis and management of the constituting tasks of a 'job'. Examples include management techniques and technological innovations originating from industrial engineering and scientific management to make manual workers' tasks more productive. However, automation is changing the way we work, and the emphasis is now on making *knowledge workers more productive*. Drucker highlights six factors that determine knowledge worker productivity: understanding how to perform a specific task, individuals carrying responsibility for their productivity, continuous innovation as part of work and tasks, engaging in continuous learning and teaching, focusing on quality outputs, and firms seeing and treating knowledge workers as an organizational 'asset' as opposed to a 'cost'. The chapter now examines an alternative definition of knowledge work that can be found in some knowledge management literature.

Defining knowledge workers: the 'all work is knowledge work' perspective

Explicitly embedded in Frenkel et al.'s conceptualization of knowledge work is the privileging of theoretical knowledge over contextual knowledge (Hislop 2008). Thus, occupations that involve using high levels of contextual knowledge and low levels of theoretical knowledge, such as care workers, examined by Nishikawa (2011), or highly skilled flute makers, examined by Cook and Yanow (1993), are not classified as knowledge work by Frenkel et al. This privileging of abstract/theoretical knowledge is typical, either explicitly or implicitly, in the mainstream conceptualization of knowledge work, and provides the basis of one of the main critiques of such definitions.

Such a privileging of theoretical knowledge, and the use of the term 'knowledge worker' to refer to an exclusive group of workers, is a subjective and somewhat arbitrary definition. The main problem with such definitions is that the privileging of abstract and theoretical knowledge in them typically leads to the significance, role, and even legitimacy of (often tacit) contextual knowledge in work being downplayed. The 'all work is knowledge work' perspective (see Definition) suggests that when such knowledge is taken account of, virtually all types of work can be considered to be knowledge work (Alvesson 2000; Grant 2000; Thompson et al. 2001). Knights et al. (1993) argue by drawing on Giddens' (1979) argument that all behaviour involves a process of self-reflexive monitoring and is thus knowledgeable. Such arguments lead to an awareness that most types of work involve the development and use of tacit knowledge. Davenport (2005) confirms this point by stating that knowledge workers 'think' for a living and are essential to spark innovation and growth in organizations (see the sixth section of this chapter). Further, Beaumont and Hunter (2002) report the findings of a study which concluded that knowledge generation/creation was not simply the domain of a small, elite group of workers, and that knowledge was created at all levels within organizations (Cutcher-Gershenfeld et al. 1998).

Nishikawa's (2011) argument that care workers can be labelled as knowledge workers is compatible with the 'all work is knowledge work' perspective. The lack of formalized, codified knowledge in care work means that it is not classified as knowledge work using the professional knowledge work perspective outlined above. However, Nishikawa argues that tacit and collectively developed knowledge of the specific context in which care is provided is fundamentally important to the quality of care, and that if account is taken of this contextual knowledge, care workers could be defined as knowledge workers.

Key to this perspective on knowledge work is that account is taken of tacit and contextual knowledge, as well as abstract and codified forms of scientific knowledge. Those adopting a practice-based perspective on knowledge typically adopt this perspective, and have examined the role of knowledge in a wide range of workers from flute makers (Cook and Yanow 1993), construction workers (Styhre et al. 2006), copier engineers (Orr 1996), open-source software developers (Hemetsberger and Reinhardt 2006) to manual workers in a sawmill (Strati 2007).

Further, Hislop (2008) developed an analysis which suggested that Frenkel et al.'s (1995) framework, outlined earlier (due to the fact it takes into account both contextual and theoretical knowledge and the range of skills involved in work), could be adapted to be compatible with the 'all work is knowledge work' perspective by stripping it of exclusivist 'professional knowledge work' assumptions. Thus, from this perspective, any job involving the use of a reasonable amount of theoretical and/or contextual knowledge can be classified as a form of knowledge work (see Illustration 5.2).

> **DEFINITION Knowledge worker ('all work is knowledge work' perspective)**
>
> Anyone whose work involves the use of a reasonable amount of tacit and contextual and/or abstract/conceptual knowledge.

 Illustration 5.2 Office equipment service engineers as knowledge workers

Hislop (2008) illustrated how Frenkel et al.'s framework could be made compatible with the 'all work is knowledge work' perspective using the modified framework to describe and understand the work of some management consultants and office equipment service engineers as knowledge workers. Data on the engineers was collected in three small office equipment servicing companies based in the same city in the English Midlands. Using Frenkel's modified framework, these workers were classified as knowledge workers, with the skills, knowledge, and level of creativity involved in their work summarized in Table 5.3. First, the level of creativity required by the engineers was relatively low because the majority of jobs done by the engineers were common, simple, and required little diagnostic analysis by the engineers. In terms of skills involved in their work, there was an identifiable need to make a reasonable use of all three skill types. First, action-based skills were needed as most jobs involved some amount of physically disassembling and reassembling equipment. Social skills were also necessary to allow effective communication not only with clients, but also with colleagues (typically via mobile phones).

The repetitiveness and apparent simplicity of most jobs undertaken by the engineers disguised the extent to which intellective skills were used. This was because these skills were relatively tacit, and were developed on the job, over time, through experience. What such 'experience' provided was summed up by one engineer:

> when you have first done a machine because you have not got experience on it you spend a lot of time fault finding, figuring out what the faults are. But once you get to know the machine you walk in and straight away a customer says it is doing this and you know what it is and you will go in there and you will fit the part.

Finally, in terms of knowledge, while the engineers made little if any use of theoretical knowledge, they developed and utilized contextual knowledge. This knowledge consisted of an understanding, developed over time, of not only what the business needs and uses of their client's office equipment were, but how this impacted on the type of problems that could develop. One engineer described this as

Table 5.3 The Knowledge, Skills, and Creativity Involved in Office Equipment Service Engineering

Skills	Action-based	Medium
	Social	Medium—social interaction with customers and colleagues is important
	Intellective	Medium—regular need to draw on experience to solve non-standard problems
Knowledge	Contextual	Medium—important
	Theoretical	Low
Degree of creativity		Low—medium

Source: Adapted from Hislop (2008).

follows: 'you get to know what they expect from the machine, which might be quite different from what someone else's identical machine expects.'

Thus, the way clients used office equipment affected the type of faults that their equipment developed, and having an understanding of this constituted contextual knowledge that the engineers drew on in their efforts to diagnose and repair these faults. As with the engineer's conceptual skills, such knowledge was relatively tacit in nature.

Question

If the contextual knowledge and conceptual skills of the engineers were developed through experience, 'on the job', rather than through formal educational processes and training, what can the employers of such workers do to facilitate the development of their skills and knowledge?

Knowledge work and ambiguity

Thus far this chapter has shown the ambiguity that exists in defining knowledge workers and knowledge-intensive firms. Alvesson (2001, 2011), in an interesting critique of the mainstream perspective on knowledge workers/knowledge-intensive firms, argues that such ambiguity actually represents one of the defining characteristics of the work done in knowledge-intensive firms. The arguments regarding the ambiguity in knowledge-intensive firms were initially developed in the 2001 article, but are revisited in the 2011 article, which reflects on the ideas developed in the original article. The argument developed by Alvesson suggests that these mainstream conceptions are too closely wedded to objectivist perspectives on knowledge, and that greater account needs to be taken of the way knowledge is conceptualized from a practice-based perspective. Fundamentally, Alvesson suggests that doing so reveals three key areas of ambiguity that are irresolvable and represent an intrinsic element of the work carried out by knowledge workers (see Table 5.4). Thus, for Alvesson there are ambiguities not only in the nature of the knowledge workers possessed in knowledge-intensive firms, but there are also ambiguities regarding both the extent to which their work involves the use of knowledge and regarding the measurability of the impact of their work (see Illustration 5.3).

Table 5.4 The Ambiguities Inherent to Knowledge Work

Topic	Mainstream Perspective	Area of Ambiguity
Knowledge: what it is and what it is like.	Knowledge is codified, objective, scientific.	Knowledge is subjective, socially constructed, context specific, equivocal.
The significance of knowledge as an element of knowledge work.	Using institutionalized knowledge systematically and creating knowledge are the core activities of knowledge workers.	The systematic utilization of formal bodies of knowledge, the need for high level cognitive capabilities are not necessarily the most significant elements in knowledge work.
The results of knowledge work.	The contribution of the knowledge and intellectual effort of knowledge workers in the provision of client solutions, and in underpinning the economic performance of knowledge-intensive firms, is regarded as transparent.	The complexity of the work undertaken by knowledge workers makes the quality of their advice/solutions/products difficult to establish, and makes the unambiguous establishment of the contribution of the efforts of knowledge workers to such products/services problematic.

Source: Alvesson (2001).

Swart et al. (2003) provide one example of the ambiguity inherent in the work of knowledge workers. They suggest that a key source of ambiguity in knowledge-intensive firms that knowledge workers have to deal with, relates to the nature of their client's needs and requirements. Fundamentally they suggest that, particularly in the early stages of a project's development, clients may have quite broad, vague, and unclear requirements, with one of the tasks of knowledge workers being to try and reduce such ambiguity through communicating with clients in order to develop a more detailed understanding of their needs and requirements. Both Matson and Prusak (2010) and Carleton (2011) reinforce this point, arguing that there are significant ambiguities in the nature of their work and the type of problem solving activities they commonly have to undertake.

 Illustration 5.3 The ambiguous impact and output of some management consultants

Alvesson's 2011 article is largely conceptual, presenting a sceptical perspective regarding the mainstream claims that exist on knowledge-intensive firms. However, the article has a short anecdote that usefully illustrates his arguments regarding the ambiguity involved in knowledge-intensive work. The anecdote relates to the impact of some consulting work done by a firm of global management consultants for a large life science firm.

Alvesson suggests that on the basis of the research done, three types of ambiguity existed regarding the consultants' work. First, there were ambiguities regarding what work they actually did, with different interviewees giving significantly different stories regarding the consultants' intervention. Another ambiguity in the case related to benefits the client firm derived from the consultants' work. The senior consultant, perhaps unsurprisingly, argued that their work had provided significant and positive benefits to the company, and any limitations in the impact of their work related to problems in the client firm. This perspective was challenged to some extent by some junior consultants who argued that the benefits derived by the client were somewhat limited, with this being the fault of the client firm, who failed to effectively implement the majority of the consultants' proposals. A third perspective was presented by the client managers who dealt with the consultants, who argued that the benefits derived from the consultants' work were limited, as the proposals made typically took too little account of the cost to implement them.

A third area of ambiguity related to the impact of the consultants' presentations. Client managers typically emphasized the extent to which the consultants utilized presentations to outline their proposals and recommendations. While some client managers regarding these presentations as simply self-publicity exercises that contained little in the way of effective advice, other client managers felt that these presentations were effective and helped sustain the idea that the consultants' work had been successful.

Question

The ambiguities outlined in this case flow from the variation in perspectives possessed by different people in both the consultancy and the client firms. Would it be possible to reduce these ambiguities through a detailed investigation of the various claims made, or are these ambiguities and differences unavoidable?

Knowledge and knowledge processes in knowledge-intensive firms

As the definitions section has made clear, the utilization of knowledge represents one of the defining aspects of the work undertaken in knowledge-intensive firms. Thus, to understand the character of knowledge-intensive firms and the knowledge management challenges which exist within them, it is necessary to develop a fuller understanding of the type of knowledge processes undertaken by knowledge workers. The key knowledge processes within knowledge-intensive firms which are overlapping and closely interrelated, are knowledge creation and knowledge integration/application, as described later on.

Knowledge workers, intellectual capital, and innovation

As mentioned earlier in this chapter, knowledge workers contribute substantially to innovation and growth in organizations. These aspects are confirmed by the resource-based theory of competitive advantage proposed by Robert Grant (1996, 2000). This theory emphasizes the importance of knowledge as a *valuable, rare, inimitable, and non-substitutable organizational asset*. The collection of a firm's resources and capabilities in the form of financial, human, physical, and organizational assets are used to develop its products, processes, and services to its customers. The human resources (HR) of a firm include all its employees' knowledge, experience, wisdom, judgement, and propensity to take risks. Knowledge, in particular tacit knowledge embodied in a firm's knowledge workers, is therefore the distinguishing factor that contributes to a firm's competitive advantage. Competitive advantage arises when an organization outperforms its rivals by offering clients new products, processes, and services of better and greater value. The ideal is that a firm continuously develops its unique capabilities to sustain competitive advantage in a business arena characterized by continuous change.

Tushman and Nadler emphasized in 1986 that 'organizations can gain competitive advantage only by managing effectively for today while simultaneously creating innovation for tomorrow'. Hence, in today's fast-changing business arena the notion of competition forces an organization to be innovative—a capability that is closely tied to its intellectual capital.

A number of sources describe an organization's intellectual capital as the sum of all knowledge that firms utilize for competitive advantage (Nahapiet and Ghoshal 1998; Youndt et al. 2004). Intellectual capital comprises three elements: human, organizational, and social capital. *Human capital* is defined as the skills, abilities, and knowledge that reside in and are used by individuals, while *organizational capital* comprises the collective institutional knowledge and codified expertise that reside in organizational databases, systems, structures, and processes (Youndt et al. 2004). *Social capital* relates to the knowledge embedded in and available through the personal relationships that people possess, and the resources people draw on and utilize as a result of the networking within and between individuals in these networks (Nahapiet and Ghoshal 1998).

While innovative ideas draw on knowledge and skills that reside in individuals, innovation as a process of inventing and implementing new ideas is a collective achievement that draws on interactions in groups and networks. The ability to combine knowledge management processes with intellectual capital is therefore the essence of innovation. While the three aspects of intellectual capital are conceptually separate, each of these aspects distributes and accumulates knowledge differently either through individuals, organizational structures, processes, and systems, or through relationships and networks. Innovation in knowledge-intensive firms therefore depends on innovation through processes of knowledge creation and integration/application, as outlined in the next two sections.

Knowledge creation

A key aspect of the work in knowledge-intensive firms is that it is typically not routine, repetitive work. Instead, knowledge-intensive firms provide customized, specifically designed products/services, rather than off-the-shelf ones. For example, Robertson and Swan (2003: 833) suggest one of the key characteristics of knowledge-intensive firms is 'their capacity to solve complex problems through the development of creative and innovative solutions'. The production/creation of such client-specific, customized solutions requires and involves both the application of existing bodies of knowledge and the creation of new knowledge (Alavi and Leidner 2001; Morris 2001; Dul et al. 2011). Thus, the ongoing creation and development of knowledge represents an important and intrinsic feature of a knowledge worker's work and innovation. This helps explain why there is a significant body of research into the topics of knowledge creation and innovation within knowledge-intensive firms (see Amara et al. 2009; Bunker-Whittington et al. 2009; Luo and Deng 2009; Dul et al. 2011).

Knowledge integration/application

Developing client-specific, customized solutions involves more than knowledge creation, it also involves the acquisition, integration, and application of different bodies of knowledge, both between workers in knowledge-intensive firms, and between the workers in knowledge-intensive firms and staff from client organizations (Fosstenløkken et al. 2003; Amara et al. 2009). Due to this need to acquire and share knowledge, and the limits to codification that exist, most typically this is done through inter-personal interaction. For example, two specific mechanisms that can be utilized to achieve this process of knowledge integration/application are through extensive interactions between workers from knowledge-intensive firms and their clients (see He and Wong 2009), or through outsourcing processes, which involves having staff from knowledge-intensive firms work on extended secondments with client firms (see Grimshaw and Miozzo 2009). The dynamics of social interactions/networking and knowledge processes give access to and utilize the social capital that exists in intra- and interorganizational networks (Yli-Renko et al. 2001; Swart and Kinnie 2003; Kärreman 2010; see Illustration 5.4).

 Illustration 5.4   Pfizer's approach to managing its knowledge workers

Pharmaceuticals are considered knowledge intensive since knowledge management is critical to improving their research and development (R&D) productivity and reduce product cycle times. With drug pipelines (the process of bringing a drug to market from idea conception to final approval) of between ten and fifteen years, drug development is a knowledge-intensive process requiring many years of dedicated teamwork to develop a successful and superior product. Moreover, drug development brings together a variety of skills and expertise through multidisciplinary, dispersed project teams. In addition, knowledge sharing is important in pharmaceuticals since R&D professionals need to share findings and conclusions within and between dispersed teams that are involved in the drug pipeline.

Pfizer, a leading American pharmaceutical corporation, has its general headquarters in New York City and its research headquarters in Connecticut. As one of the largest pharmaceuticals in the world, Pfizer aims to attract only the best talent, in other words knowledge workers that will, in the Pfizer environment, get opportunities that allow them to be the best they can be. Pfizer's talent management involves training processes and procedures that enable new knowledge workers to quickly integrate into the company.

Prior to 2007, Pfizer invested in knowledge workers by planning for the kind of talent they believed would be needed during the next ten years and then developed talent from within. However, since 2007 the company changed its approach to talent management by investing in employees who can easily move from one position to the next. While earlier recruitment processes focused on hiring candidates according to job description, new recruitment practices evaluate the *competencies* candidates demonstrate. Hence, Pfizer's new focus is on developing employees based on their unique competencies. Examples include appointing a worker with project management skills and moving him/her from manufacturing to research over time, and moving an employee working on heart disease products to another project that helps people quit smoking.

This change in culture towards investment in and education of knowledge workers manifested in a new learning culture, the so-called 'OWNIT! Culture' that seeks to empower all workers to explore new things, invest in open, candid conversations, and build collaborative networks and relationships that deliver on commitments. This programme aims to continue Pfizer's cultural transformation in order to equip colleagues with the necessary skills to thrive in a changing environment while taking introspective risks allowing for innovation. This ownership-focused culture represents a major change allowing workers to become increasingly resilient and to learn through experiences. Pfizer's approach to support knowledge workers, by enhancing their capacity to manage and stimulate change, has allowed Pfizer to improve its competitive position from the second highest in the world in 2014 to the first in 2016.

Sources: *Eyeforpharma* (2002) 'Knowledge Management at Pfizer: Starting from the Inside Out. Exclusive Interview Claire Hogikyan, Worldwide Head of Information', 26 February, http://social.eyeforpharma.com/uncategorised/knowledge-management-pfizer-starting-inside-out-exclusive-interview-claire-hogikyan (accessed 22 September 2017).

Pfizer (2014) Annual Report, http://www.pfizer.com/files/investors/financial_reports/annual_reports/2014/business_colleagues.htm (accessed 22 September 2017).

Workforce (2007) 'Pfizer Overhauls Talent Strategy', 23 February, http://www.workforce.com/2007/02/23/pfizer-overhauls-talent-strategy/ (accessed 22/09/17).

Questions

This case highlights the importance of talent management in knowledge-intensive firms such as Pfizer. Who do you think carries the major responsibility for talent management? The Pfizer case illustrates the company's commitment to develop its workers allowing them to learn through experience. What do you think are other key processes that would be part of a talent management programme in an organization such as Pfizer?

Social capital, knowledge workers, and knowledge-intensive firms

The close and inseparable relationship that exists between the networks of relations that people possess, and the resources they have access to through them, means that there is a lack of consensus within the social capital literature about the precise definition of social capital. For some, social capital refers purely to the networks of relations people possess, while for others it encompasses not only these networks, but also includes the resources people have access to through them (Nahapiet and Ghoshal 1998). Here it is used in the narrow sense, to refer purely to the networks of social relationships that people have. Further, Nahapiet and Ghoshal (1998) suggest that social capital has three key dimensions or facets: the structural, the relational, and the cognitive (see Table 5.5).

In the context of knowledge-intensive firms, the importance of social capital to knowledge workers is that it is only through social capital (i.e. bonds, bridges, linkages, shared norms, values, and understanding) that individuals are able to gain access to and utilize the knowledge

Table 5.5 The Three Dimensions of Social Capital

Dimension	Character
Structural	The overall pattern of social relations a person possesses. For example, number of contacts and type of people in the network.
Relational	The strength of relationship between people, varying from weak to strong relationships involving high levels of trust. This social capital dimension is typically built up over time, through repeated interactions.
Cognitive	The extent to which people have shared cognitive resources such as shared knowledge, common assumptions, interpretations, and beliefs.

Source: Nahapiet and Ghoshal (1998).

of others they require to do their work effectively (Swart and Kinnie 2003). This is because for people to be willing to share knowledge with others, some degree of inter-personal trust is required (a topic that is discussed more extensively in Chapters 11 and 13), and the existence of social capital implies that an element of trust exists between people (the relational dimension of social capital).

The types of knowledge that knowledge workers use in their work require their networks of social capital to include both staff from their own organization (who may be working on different projects) and staff in client firms (Yli-Renko et al. 2001; Swart et al. 2003; Grimshaw and Miozzo 2009; He and Wong 2009). As outlined, the typical project-based nature of work in knowledge-intensive firms means that the knowledge base within knowledge-intensive firms is typically fragmented, with different workers possessing different bodies of expertise linked to different client firms and projects. Having a network of social relations (social capital) that spans such project boundaries thus provides knowledge workers with a way of accessing potentially relevant knowledge possessed by colleagues working on other projects (Swart and Kinnie 2003). The importance for knowledge workers of possessing social capital with representatives of client firms, is that such networks can provide access to relevant client knowledge which is necessary for their work. However, as outlined, knowledge workers' need to continually interact with representatives of their client firms over the course of a project typically means that the development of social capital and good relations with specific client staff is often not difficult to develop (Alvesson 2000; Fosstenlokken et al. 2003).

The willingness of knowledge workers to participate in knowledge processes: contrasting perspectives

One of the key themes developed and examined in Part 4 of this book, is that the willingness of any worker to participate in organizational knowledge management processes should *not* be taken for granted. In any type of work setting, be it individual or in a team, the motivation and participation of knowledge workers in knowledge processes essentially starts at the individual level. In fact, dealing with motivational issues and creating a socio-cultural environment in which workers are prepared to participate in knowledge management initiatives, represents one key challenges and difficulty of knowledge management. However, another area of divergence in the literature on knowledge workers and knowledge-intensive firms, relates to the extent to which knowledge workers are always willing to participate in knowledge management processes and initiatives, with two contrasting perspectives existing, both of which are outlined below.

Knowledge workers: the ideal employee?

A reasonable amount of (largely case study) evidence exists to suggest that in many ways knowledge workers represent the ideal employees. Primarily, this evidence suggests that such workers are prepared to invest significant amounts of time and effort into their work, and that motivating them to do so is not difficult (Alvesson 1995; Deetz 1998; Robertson and Swan 2003). As these workers are prepared to make such efforts with minimal levels of supervision, and without regarding such effort as being problematic, Alvesson suggests such workers represent the ideal subordinates (2000: 1104). Alvesson (2000) suggests four reasons why knowledge workers are prepared to make such efforts:

1. They find their work intrinsically interesting and fulfilling.
2. Such working patterns represent the norms within the communities they are a part of.
3. There is a sense of reciprocity, whereby they provide the organization with their efforts in return for good pay and working conditions.
4. Such behaviour reinforces and confirms their sense of identity as knowledge workers, where hard work is regarded as a fundamental component.

Robertson and Swan (2003) provide a further explanation: the structure of the employment relationship is less clear than for other workers, and the potential for conflict on the basis of this relationship thus becomes dissipated. They suggest that the employer/employee, manager/managed relationship is not as clear cut in knowledge-intensive firms as in other, more hierarchically based, organizations. In knowledge-intensive firms such boundaries are fuzzy, and evolve over time, and therefore the interests of employers and employees are more likely to be shared.

Factors inhibiting knowledge workers' work efforts and knowledge management activities

As will be discussed in more detail in Chapters 11 and 13, two general factors which may inhibit workers from participating in organizational knowledge management efforts, are the unavoidable potential for conflict between workers and their employers that is embedded in the employment relationship, and the potential for intra-organizational conflict (between people and groups/teams) that arguably exists in all organizations. In contrast to the perspective adopted by writers discussed in the previous section, some analysts suggest that these two potential sources of conflict are as likely in knowledge-intensive firms as in any other type of organization, and that the willingness of knowledge workers to participate in knowledge management initiatives should not be taken for granted. Thus, Starbuck (1993) described the knowledge-intensive company he examined as being 'internally inconsistent, in conflict with itself . . . An intricate house of cards.' Further, Empson (2001b) presented an example of a knowledge-intensive firm in a post-merger situation, where workers from the two pre-merger companies were unwilling to share their knowledge with each other. Kärreman (2010), in reviewing the contribution of Starbuck's (1993) article, also emphasized the importance of the attention it paid to issues of power and conflict.

A number of writers highlight the issue of the conflicting senses of identities that knowledge workers may experience, and how this may shape and inhibit their willingness to participate in organizational knowledge management processes (Alvesson 2000). Due to the amount of time many knowledge workers may spend working with individual client organizations and particular staff within them (see previous section), one source of identity-based conflict that knowledge workers can experience is feeling a sense of belonging to both their employer's and their client's firm (Swart et al. 2003). Ravishankar and Pan (2008) present a case where such client-based identity by the knowledge workers they studied (an Indian IT outsourcing vendor), resulted in some staff being unwilling to participate in their employer's knowledge management initiatives. Grimshaw and Miozzo's (2009) study of outsourcing with IT-based business services reached similar conclusions, mentioning 'the tensions of the competing claims on the identity of knowledge workers in a context of inter-organizational networks' (p. 1544).

Other evidence which suggests that knowledge workers may have divergent interests from their employers, relates to the problem many knowledge-intensive firms experience in trying to retain their employees for extended periods. Fundamentally many knowledge-intensive firms have quite high turnover rates, which suggests that knowledge workers have only a limited amount of loyalty to their employing organization. This is partly due to labour market conditions, where the skills and knowledge of knowledge workers are typically relatively scarce, creating conditions for knowledge workers which are favourable to labour market mobility (Flood et al. 2001; Malhotra et al. 2010; Van Nordenflycht 2010; Huang 2011).

Having a high turnover rate is a potentially significant problem for knowledge-intensive firms (Alvesson 2000; Flood et al. 2000; Beaumont and Hunter 2002). For example, client knowledge or social capital, the knowledge of and relationships with key individuals within their client organizations, can be a key source of knowledge for knowledge-intensive firms. Individual knowledge workers develop such knowledge and social capital through working closely with clients. Such knowledge is typically tacit and highly personal, and therefore, when knowledge workers leave their jobs, they take such knowledge with them. Not only that, but through the social capital they possess with individuals in client firms, there is also a risk for their employers that when a knowledge worker leaves they may take some clients with them (see also Chapter 8). The question of how to develop the loyalty and commitment of such workers is one of the key issues addressed in Chapter 15.

 Conclusion

The importance of knowledge workers and knowledge-intensive firms is closely tied to the rhetoric regarding the contemporary rise and emergence of the knowledge society. The debate over defining knowledge workers identified two perspectives. The mainstream perspective suggests that knowledge workers are a distinctive and elite element in the contemporary workforce, while the other argues that this neglects to account for the extent to which all work is knowledge work, and thus how all workers can be defined as knowledge workers. With regard to knowledge-intensive firms, multiple definitions were found to exist.

In relation to the work in knowledge-intensive firms, it was shown that the possession and use of client-related knowledge was as important as the possession of formalized technical knowledge. Further the acquisition of such knowledge requires knowledge workers to possess and utilize any networks of social capital they have, and such knowledge is acquired from both colleagues (who may work on different projects) and staff from the clients they work with.

Finally, some case study evidence suggests that knowledge workers arguably represent the ideal employee due to their willingness to work autonomously. Others suggest that for a number of reasons, such as tensions that may exist between a knowledge worker and their employer over how their knowledge is utilized, it cannot always be assumed that knowledge workers will be willing to participate in the knowledge management processes their employers may desire.

Case study The linkages between learning orientation, knowledge assets, and HR practices in professional service firms

Swart and Kinnie (2010) report findings of a study conducted on a diverse range of sixteen professional service firms from the UK and US that included law firms, management consultants, software development companies, and advertising agencies. Conceptually their paper focuses on the links between a firms' learning orientation, the types of knowledge assets needed to sustain it, and the type of HR practices which help facilitate the links. In the paper they define organizational learning as involving both the refinement and the renewal of organizational knowledge.

In doing this they develop a conceptual framework which distinguishes between four separate learning orientations. The learning orientation framework they develop is based on two key dimensions, the mode of learning undertaken by an organization and the temporal frame in which learning and knowledge creation required, occurs. With respect to the mode of learning they differentiate between exploration-based learning and exploitation-based learning (see Chapter 6). While exploitation-based learning concerns incremental innovation related to the development of an organization's existing knowledge, services, and products, exploration-based learning concerns development of new knowledge, products, and services. With respect to the temporal frame they differentiate between accelerated timescales, where learning has to be undertaken quickly in short timescales, and planned timescales, which are more long-term. When these two dimensions are linked, four different learning orientations are created.

For each learning orientation Swart and Kinnie examine the type of knowledge assets necessary to sustain them and the type of HR practices that facilitate them. Constraints of space mean that it is impossible to examine all the links between these variables for all four learning orientations. Thus, only two are examined here.

First, the *creative combination* learning orientation combines an accelerated timescale with exploration-based learning. This type of learning thus involves and underpins the creation of new products or services in short timescales. A specific example of the need for this learning orientation was created within one advertising agency where a client gave the company a week to develop a brief to highlight the music-playing potential of a mobile phone. In terms of knowledge assets, Swart and Kinnie found this learning orientation required a combination of creativity, experimentation, and quick adaptability of ideas. Further, they found that these knowledge assets were facilitated by a range of different HR practices. First, to facilitate creativity and experimentation, recruitment and selection processes need to emphasize these skills. Second, to facilitate quick adaptability they argued that people need to work with a range of different clients who have their own unique specific demands, which can be facilitated by regularly rotating people between different projects, or getting people to work on different projects simultaneously. Finally, to facilitate and support people's efforts to be creative and experimental, organizations need to have cultures which encourage risk-taking and which don't automatically punish failure.

Second, another learning orientation examined by Swart and Kinnie is labelled *expert solutions*. In contrast to creative combination, this learning orientation links exploitation-based learning with planned timescales. This type of learning is quite different from creative combination, and concerns the incremental development of existing products and services for established clients over long-term timescales. An example of this mode of learning was found in law firms where well-established procedures were utilized for personal injury or employment law cases. For this learning orientation Swart and Kinnie found that people needed good client capital (knowledge of and relationships with clients and their needs), procedure-based organizational capital, where people had a good knowledge of established procedures, and project-based knowledge, where people have experience working on long-term projects. Swart and Kinnie found a range of HR practices that facilitated these knowledge assets. For example, one way of developing good client capital was through the recruitment of staff from clients, which not only gave firms good knowledge of their clients' needs and expectations, but also gave them people with good social capital within client firms. Second, procedure-based knowledge was found to be facilitated by a combination of on-the-job training and one-to-one coaching.

While Swart and Kinnie identified four specific learning orientations they do not argue that companies typically only utilize one. Instead they argue that all companies examined were required to utilize a range of learning orientations, and had to be flexible and adaptable in utilizing the appropriate learning orientation at the appropriate time.

Question

1. Given that each learning orientation is linked to a particular timescale and that different modes of learning require the use of different knowledge assets, which are facilitated by different HR practices, how challenging is it likely to be for any organization to utilize more than one learning orientation, and to flexibly switch between them when appropriate?

Review and Discussion Questions

1. What do you think of the 'all work is knowledge work' perspective? Can all forms of work be defined as knowledge work even if they don't require the use of abstract/conceptual knowledge? Think about a range of jobs and the types of knowledge, skills and level of creativity involved in them. Can you identify any that you don't feel should be labelled 'knowledge work'?

2. Do you agree with Alvesson's perspective regarding the ambiguity of knowledge work? Is it possible to reduce/eliminate the types of ambiguity identified by Alvesson or are they unavoidable?

3. One factor that was found to be a potential source of conflict and tension for knowledge workers, and that could affect their attitude to participating in organizational knowledge management initiatives, was their identification with both their employer and the client firms they work for. Given the nature of the work undertaken by knowledge workers and the typical need that exists to work extensively with their clients, is it likely to be inevitable that knowledge workers will typically always have some level of identification with and loyalty to client firms?

4. Imagine that you are the knowledge manager of a large knowledge-intensive multinational organization and you aim to facilitate the sharing of knowledge within the organization. What mechanisms would you potentially introduce to facilitate knowledge acquisition and sharing in this type of organization?

Suggestions for Further Reading

M. Alvesson (2011). 'De-essentializing the Knowledge Intensive Firm: Reflections on Sceptical Research Going Against the Mainstream', *Journal of Management Studies*, 48/7: 1640–61.
A useful review article that highlights Alvesson's sceptical perspective on the claims of the mainstream work on knowledge-intensive firms.

A. von Nordenflycht (2010). 'What is a Professional Service Firm? Towards a Theory and a Taxonomy of Knowledge-Intensive Firms', *Academy of Management Review*, 35/1: 155–74.
Reviews the debate on how to define professional service firms and knowledge-intensive firms and develops a taxonomy that differentiates between distinctive types of knowledge-intensive firm.

D. Hislop (2008). 'Conceptualizing Knowledge Work Utilizing Skill and Knowledge-Based Concepts: The Case of Some Consultants and Service Engineers', *Management Learning*, 39/5: 579–97.

Elaborates the debate on how knowledge work is defined and illustrates the argument via use of two contrasting examples.

J. Swart and N. Kinnie (2010). 'Organizational Learning, Knowledge Assets and HR Practices in Professional Service Firms', *Human Resource Management Journal*, 20/1: 64–79.

Interesting empirical analysis of learning and HR practices in a range of professional service firms.

P. F. Drucker (1999). 'Knowledge-Worker Productivity: The Biggest Challenge', *California Management Review*, 41/2: 79–92.

An interesting paper that elaborates on the 'productivity journey', since the earliest form of work, through the era of Taylorism up to the nineteenth century.

W. Reinhardt, B. Schmidt, P. Sloep, and H. Drachsler (2011). 'Knowledge Worker Roles and Actions—Results of Two Empirical Studies', *Knowledge and Process Management*, 18/3: 150–74.

The authors draw on empirical data to propose a new way of classifying knowledge worker roles and the knowledge actions they perform during their daily work.

 To further your understanding of knowledge management in organizations explore the book's accompanying online resources at www.oup.com/uk/hislop4e/

PART 3

Innovation, Knowledge Creation, and Unlearning

While most chapters in this book take a general approach to knowledge management and don't focus specifically on particular types of knowledge processes, the three chapters in this part of the book are different. Thus, Chapter 6 examines the topic of learning, Chapter 7 is concerned narrowly with processes of knowledge creation, while Chapter 8 has an exclusive focus on processes of unlearning and forgetting. These processes deserve particular attention for a number of reasons. First, the turbulent and dynamics business environments that many companies compete in means that the ability to innovate and change is a crucial organizational competence. For different reasons, the ability of organizations to innovate is affected by their ability to learn and/or create new knowledge, and also to give up or abandon knowledge whose contemporary value has become questionable. Chapter 6 examines the linkages between the related topics of knowledge management and learning in organizations, which will involve engaging with the debate on the question of the character of the 'learning organization' concept, as well as examining Crossan's influential model on the learning organization which links processes of learning at individual and organizational levels. Chapter 7 on knowledge creation takes a deliberately narrow focus, examining Nonaka's theory of knowledge creation. There are two fundamental reasons for this focus. First, within a single book chapter it isn't possible to effectively examine the various perspectives on innovation and knowledge creation that exist. Second, the reason for choosing Nonaka's work to focus on is fundamentally due to its widespread popularity. Chapter 8 focuses on unlearning. This topic is generally because it is neglected and under-examined in the learning and knowledge management literatures. Thus, part of the reason for examining organizational unlearning is to suggest that it is a topic which requires greater levels of attention by those interested in the topics of innovation and knowledge management.

6 Learning and Knowledge Management

Introduction

For a number of reasons the topic of learning in organizations encompasses a vast literature. First, its origins date back more than forty years, and can be traced to the work of Cyert, March, and Simon (Cyert and March 1963; March and Simon 1993). Second, it is a subject that is truly multidisciplinary, being written about and conceptualized (quite differently) in a range of academic disciplines from economics, management science, psychology, and sociology to anthropology (Styhre et al. 2006; Easterby-Smith and Lyles 2015). Third, since the early 1990s there has been a mushrooming of interest in the topic, with this interest predating the growth of interest in knowledge management by a few years (Scarbrough and Swan 2001). Contu et al. (2003) suggest this blossoming of interest in organizational learning connects with a wider interest in and discourse on the value and importance of learning in contemporary globalized, knowledge-based economies/societies. Due to the enormity and diversity of this literature it is characterized by heterogeneity, debate, and a lack of theoretical consensus on a wide range of topics, from whether learning should be conceived primarily in behavioural or cognitive terms, to the relationship between individual and organizational learning, to whether organizations learn at all (Crossan et al. 1999; Berthoin Antal et al. 2001; Antonocopoulou 2006).

Thus, to attempt to outline and review all the features, characteristics, and debates in this literature it would be necessary to write a book on the topic (examples of books which provide an overview on the topic include Starkey et al. 2003 and Easterby-Smith and Lyles 2015). Further, the interrelated and overlapping nature of the relationship between learning and knowledge management (Thomas et al. 2003; Chiva and Allegre 2005) means that another book could be written on how the topic of learning relates to and connects with knowledge management. In the space of a single chapter, it is not possible to do either of these tasks. Instead, a deliberately narrow, partial, and specific focus is taken in examining learning in organizations.

This chapter has three primary objectives. First, it aims to, very briefly, give a sense of the diversity of the ways that learning is conceptualized. Second, it examines the issue of organizational learning and the complex and dynamic relationship between individual, group, and organizational-level learning. In doing this, the primary focus is on the influential 4I learning framework developed by Crossan et al. (1999, 2011). Finally, it presents two perspectives on the debate surrounding the concept of the learning organization. In presenting the critique of the learning organization, the chapter connects both to some themes that will be shown in later chapters to resonate with the knowledge management literature, and the objective of the book to adopt a critical perspective to mainstream literature and concepts.

The chapter begins by very briefly examining the difficulties involved in defining what learning is, and considering the diversity of topologies or ways in which learning occurs. After this, the next major section examines the dynamics of organizational learning, and the relationship between individual, group, and organizational-level learning processes. The largest section in the chapter then examines the debate on the learning organization concept, which provides a useful way of discussing some of the key issues which link the learning and knowledge management literatures. As will be seen, issues raised by the critics of the learning organization rhetoric, such as the need to account for power, as well as the broad context of the employment relationship, link closely with some of the key issues developed in Part 5 of the book, and in Chapters 11 and 14 in particular.

The heterogeneity of learning

It would seem sensible to begin the chapter by defining learning and considering the various learning types, processes, and mechanisms via which learning in organizations can occur. However, such a task is by no means easy due to the diversity of ways in which learning is defined, and the heterogeneity of methods via which learning can occur. This section therefore provides a very brief overview of both learning topologies and learning mechanisms and processes.

Characterizing learning in organizations

The heterogeneity and lack of theoretical consensus in the learning literature means that providing a single, simple definition of learning is impossible. Instead of providing a single definition of learning, Table 6.1 gives an overview of some of the most important ways that learning in organizations has been characterized (for a more detailed examination of the different taxonomies of learning which exist, see Pawlovsky 2001). These typologies are not examined in detail because not only do constraints of space make it impossible to do justice to the depth of debate, but the debate on these typologies became somewhat dormant during the mid-1990s (Easterby-Smith et al. 2000). Thus, most of the contemporary learning literature makes only passing reference to these frameworks. Presenting such a summarized overview illustrates the complexity of the topic and the diversity of ways in which learning has been conceptualized.

Learning mechanisms and processes

Due to the diversity of ways that learning is conceptualized and characterized, it is no surprise that the learning literature suggests that learning can occur via a wide range of different mechanisms and processes. These can be characterized into three distinctive types: learning via formal training and education, learning via the use of interventions in work processes,

Table 6.1 Typologies of Learning

Learning Topologies	Concepts/Levels	Description
Learning modes	Cognitive	Learning as a change in intellectual concepts and frameworks (at individual or group level).
	Cultural	Change in inter-subjective, group-based values, concepts, or frameworks.
	Behavioural/ action-based	Learning occurs primarily through action followed by a process of critical reflection.
Learning processes	Single-loop	Incremental changes within a coherent framework of theory.
	Double-loop	Learning where existing theories/assumptions are questioned and reflected on.
	Deutero	The highest level of learning which involves the process of learning and reflection itself being questioned.
Learning levels	Individual	Changes in the behaviour or theories and concepts of an individual.
	Group	Changes in group-level, shared understandings or practices.
	Organizational	Institutionalization at organizational level of changes in behaviour/theory.
	Inter-organizational	Learning at a supra-organizational level—for example within a network or sector.

and learning that is embedded in and emerges from day-to-day work activities (and people's reflections on them).

Before learning became a fashionable idea it was a relatively neglected backwater of a subject and was regarded as being most closely linked to the topics of training and education. Thus, from this perspective, learning occurred and was facilitated via workers attending and participating in formal processes of training and education. The growing interest in the topic of learning led to an acknowledgement that learning could also occur in and be facilitated by a range of practices, values, and activities embedded in work processes of which some activities can be enabled and supported by information and communications technologies (see Chapters 9 and 10). From this perspective learning can be facilitated via the creation of 'learning cultures', where learning, reflection, debate, and discussion are encouraged (López et al. 2004; Raz and Fadlon 2006), the embedding of learning opportunities in organizational decision-making processes (Carroll et al. 2006), and where project-based work is common via processes such as post-project reviews (von Zedtwitz 2002; Ron et al. 2006). Finally, writers who adopt a practice-based perspective on knowledge see learning as occurring via and embedded in day-to-day work practices (see for example Styhre et al. 2006; Hong and Snell 2008).

In conclusion, there is significant diversity and disagreement in the literature on learning on both the topics of what learning is and how it occurs in organizations. More so, learning (including teaching) is an inherent, dynamic, and ongoing process that is integral to the work that knowledge workers do. This chapter now changes focus to consider the dynamic inter-relationship between individual, group, and organizational levels of learning.

The dynamics of organizational learning

While the central concern of the chapter is on learning within organizations, this does not mean that there is an exclusive focus on organizational-level learning. As will be seen, learning in organizations is a continuous process and can be characterized as involving a dynamic reciprocity between learning processes at the individual, group, and organizational level (Antonocopoulou 2006; Berends and Lammers 2011; Crossan et al. 2011). In fact, many organizations learn through their individual knowledge workers. These individuals may form groups, departments, or even communities of practice as described later on in Chapter 12. Even though individuals learn on behalf of organizations, an organization 'remembers' and builds its own *organizational memory* over time. This memory, also referred to as an institutional or corporate memory, can be viewed as a large repository of all of a firm's archived experiences, decisions, actions, routines, processes as well as the knowledge embedded in human minds (Walsh and Ungson 1991). Organizational memory can be seen as both an individual- and an organizational-level construct that plays an instrumental role in both individual and organizational learning.

Before presenting a conceptual model that outlines the interrelationship between learning processes at the individual, group, and organizational level, it is useful to define and discuss the term organizational learning in more depth (see Definition). Organizations can be understood to learn, not because they 'think' and 'behave' independently of the people who work within them (they cannot), but through the embedding of individual and group learning in organizational processes, routines, structures, databases, systems of rules, etc. (Shipton 2006). For example, organizational learning would be where insights developed by an individual or group result in a systematic transformation of the organization's work practices/values.

However, it is wrong to equate organizational learning with being simply the sum of individual and group learning processes (Vince 2001). Organizational learning only occurs when learning at the individual or group - level impacts organizational-level processes and structures. But, such a transition is by no means automatic (for a good illustration of this see the end-of-chapter case study of Berends and Lammers 2010, which examined how discontinuities disrupt the flow of learning between levels). The literature on project-based working also shows how project-based learning is often not transferred to an organizational level (Scarbrough, Bresnan, et al. 2004; and Scarbrough, Swan, et al. 2004).

> **DEFINITION Organizational learning**
>
> The embedding of individual- and group-level learning in organizational structures and processes, achieved through reflecting on and modifying the norms and values embodied in established organizational processes and structures.

This complex interrelationship between learning at different levels is taken into account in the Crossan/Zietsma framework of organizational learning. This framework was initially devised by Crossan et al. (1999), but was usefully modified by Zietsma et al. (2002), with the addition of two action-based learning processes (attending and experimenting) to supplement the more cognitively focused processes of Crossan et al. The relationship between the six learning processes and three levels of learning in the Crossan/Zietsma framework are illustrated in Figure 6.1. The

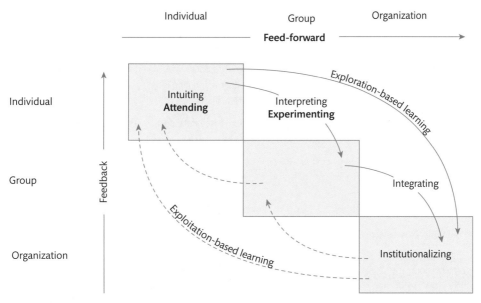

Figure 6.1 The Modified Crossan et al. Model

Source: Zietsma et al. (2002).

significance and influence of Crossan et al.'s organizational learning framework is that the article in which it was initially articulated (Crossan et al. 1999) was the most cited article in the *Academy of Management Review* in the 2000s (Crossan et al. 2011).

Descriptions of the learning processes, and the levels at which they exist, are outlined in Table 6.2. In the framework, the six learning processes link the three levels of learning through two opposing dynamics: feed-forward and feedback loops. The feed-forward loop, alternatively referred to as an *exploration*-based learning process, involves the development and assimilation of new knowledge. Exploration thus starts with individual-level learning, through intuition or attending, and then builds to both group- and organization-level learning through interpretation, experimentation, integration, and institutionalization processes. The feedback loop, by contrast, referred to as an *exploitation*-based learning process, involves the utilization of existing knowledge, whereby institutionalized learning guides and affects how groups and individuals act and think. However, while feed-forward and feedback learning loops involve moving between learning processes at different levels, such movement cannot be assumed to happen automatically or unproblematically. Thus, for example, it can be difficult for someone to take an individual-and level insight and articulate it to a group, and then further develop this into a shared, agreed-upon, collective insight.

One of the core themes in the Crossan/Zietsma framework is the tension that exists between *exploration* (the development and acquisition of new knowledge) and *exploitation* (the utilization of existing knowledge). This tension exists because processes of exploration may bring into question, challenge, undermine, and even replace institutionalized norms (knowledge and practice) embedded in exploitation processes. This is a potentially serious tension because, as Crossan et al. argue (1999: 534), 'learning that has become institutionalized at the

Table 6.2 Characteristics of Learning Processes in the Crossan/Zietsma Model

Learning Process Name	Level	Process Description
1. Intuition	Individual	Cognitive process involving the preconscious recognition of patterns. Intuition is highly subjective and rooted in individual experience.
2. Attending	Individual	Action-based individual process of actively searching for and absorbing new ideas.
3. Interpretation	Individual-group	Explaining personal insights through words or actions. It can be an individual process, where an individual actively interprets his/her own insights, or a group process where individual insights are shared and discussed collectively.
4. Experimenting	Individual-group	Attempting to implement and utilize new learning through actual practices of change.
5. Integration	Group-organization	Developing shared understandings and practices, which can occur through both dialogue and coordinated action.
6. Institutionalization	Organization	The process of ensuring that routinized action occurs through embedding insights in organizational systems and processes.

Source: Crossan et al. (1999); Zietsma et al. (2002).

organizational level is often difficult to change.' Thus the institutionalization of learning has the potential risk that such a process can introduce rigidities and an inability to adapt and change through a blinkering process that leaves institutionalized norms unquestioned. Thus, when institutionalized norms become powerful and dominant, for example through being successful, they can turn into what has been defined as 'competency traps' where organizations become locked in to prior successful routines through not noticing or effectively accounting for changed circumstances (Levinthal and March 1993; Bettis and Prahalad 1995). See Chapter 8 for further discussion of competency traps in relation to the topic of unlearning.

Despite the tensions between processes of exploitation and exploration, and the difficulties that organizations face when attempting to do both simultaneously, an increasing number of writers suggest that it can be highly beneficial to an organization's dynamic innovative capability to be able to do both simultaneously (Gibson and Birkinshaw 2004; He and Wong 2004). The ability to do so is referred to as ambidextrous learning (Kang and Snell 2009; Turner and Lee-Kelley 2012; see also special issue of *Organization Science* 2009, 20(4), for example Raisch et al. 2009).

The learning organization: emancipation or exploitation?

The past two sections cover the heterogeneity and dynamics of learning, in other words the interplay between learning at the individual, group, and organizational level. As outlined in the Introduction, the literature on organizational learning is characterized by a diversity of theoretical perspectives. One specific topic that has produced an enormous amount of debate and heated argument is the learning organization. It is worthwhile examining the contours of this debate, as doing so sheds light on some key issues.

Crudely, those engaged in this debate can be classified into two broad camps: the *advocates* (who are the visionaries or utopian propagandists), and the *sceptics* or gloomy pessimists (Friedman et al. 2001). The visionary/propagandists camp, whose most well-known and prolific writers include Peter Senge (1990) and Mike Pedler (in Pedler et al. 1997), is largely dominated by consultants and industrial practitioners (Driver 2002) and is very prescriptive in nature (Shipton 2006). This camp portrays the learning organization as an achievable ideal with significant benefits for both organizations and their workers. On the contrary, the sceptic/pessimistic camp, which is largely populated by academics, challenges this perspective and pours scorn on the claims of the learning organization propagandists (Weick and Westley 1996; Levitt and March 1988). Primarily these writers, with Coopey (1995, 1998) being one of the most incisive, argue that despite the emancipatory rhetoric of the learning organization discourse, in reality it is likely to provide a way to buttress the power of management and is thus likely to lead to increased exploitation of and control over workers, rather than to their emancipation and self-development (Hong and Snell 2008).

This section more closely examines these two dominant perspectives in this debate, uncovering and examining issues such as power, the nature of the employment relationship, and trust, as will be shown later in Chapters 11 and 14, connect the topics of learning and knowledge management as they are factors which can also play a crucial role in shaping organizational knowledge management processes.

The learning organization: the advocates' vision

Constraints of space make it impossible to elaborate all the different learning organization frameworks developed by its different advocates (Pedler, Senge, Garvin, among others—see Shipton 2006). This section focuses centrally on the way Pedler et al. and Senge conceptualize it, where the illustrated example (universities as learning organizations) links to Senge's learning organization model (see Definition). However, there is much commonality to these frameworks, therefore there is a general resonance between the broad characteristics of these different models. Pedler et al. (1997: 3) define the learning organization as an 'organization which facilitates the learning of all its members and consciously transforms itself and its context'. Their learning organization framework is also elaborated into eleven specific characteristics (see Table 6.3). A key element of this definition is that there is a mutual, positive synergy between the organizational context and the learning of its members. Thus in a learning organization, the organizational context should facilitate the learning of organizational staff, with this learning in turn sustaining and contributing to the ongoing transformation of the organizational context. Therefore, organizational memory described earlier in this chapter forms an integral part of the organizational context that contributes to both the learning organization and learning in the organization.

One of the articulated organizational advantages of the learning organization framework is that it is appropriate to the contemporary business environment, which is typically characterized as being highly competitive and turbulent (Harrison and Leitch 2000; Salaman 2001; Bontis et al. 2002). Thus, in such circumstances organizations require to continually adapt and change, with the adoption of the learning organization framework being argued to

Table 6.3 The Learning Company Framework of Pedler et al. (1997)

Learning Organization Focus	Core Characteristics	Description
Strategy	1. Learning approach to strategy	Strategy making-implementation-evaluation structured as learning processes—for example, with experiments and feedback loops.
	2. Participative policy making	Allow all organizational members opportunity to contribute to making of major policy decisions.
Looking in	3. Informating	Use of information technology (IT) to empower staff through widespread information dissemination and having tolerance to how it is interpreted and used.
	4. Formative accounting and control.	Use of accounting practices which contribute to learning combined with a sense of self-responsibility, where individuals/groups are encouraged to regard themselves as responsible for cost management.
	5. Internal exchange	Constant, open dialogue between individuals and groups within an organization, and encouraging collaboration not competition.
	6. Reward flexibility	New ways of rewarding people for learning contribution which may not be solely financial, and where principles of reward systems are explicit.
Structures	7. Enabling structures	Use of loose and adaptable structures which provide opportunities for organizational and individual development.
Looking out	8. Boundary workers as environmental scanners	Bringing into an organization ideas and working practices that have been developed and used externally— cultivating an openness and receptivity to learning from others.
	9. Inter-company learning	Use of mutually advantageous learning activities with customers, suppliers, etc.
Learning opportunities	10. Learning climate	Facilitate the willingness of staff to take risks and experiment, which can be encouraged by senior management taking the lead. People not punished for criticizing orthodox views.
	11. Self-development opportunities for all	Have opportunities for all staff to be able to develop themselves as they see appropriate.

Source: Pedler et al. (1997).

make this possible. One of the defining characteristics of a learning organization is therefore that it is flexible, and that this provides organizations with the ability to achieve and retain a position of competitive advantage. A number of papers (including Bui and Baruch 2011—see Illustration 6.1) examine the extent to which organizations have the characteristics of learning organizations (such as Elkin et al. 2011), or examine the relationship between learning organizations and organizational performance (see, for example, Shieh 2011). Implicitly (and sometimes explicitly) the learning organization is regarded as the antithesis of traditional bureaucracies, which are regarded as having highly centralized and hierarchical systems of management and control (Contu et al. 2003). Instead, the learning organization is typically conceptualized as having a relatively flat structure, open collaboration and communication systems, limited top-down control, and autonomous working conditions (Driver 2002).

> **DEFINITION Learning organization (propagandists)**
>
> An organization which supports the learning of its workers and allows them to express and utilize this learning to the advantage of the organization, through having an organizational environment which encourages experimentation, risk taking, and open dialogue.

However, the advocates such as Pedler are clear that the benefits of utilizing the learning organization framework are by no means confined to improving organizational performance. Instead, an inherent element of these frameworks is that management and workers alike will benefit from their adoption. In fact, one of the articulated consequences of utilizing these frameworks is that the divisions between management and workers are likely to become blurred. As is clear from all eleven characteristics of the learning organization framework (see Table 6.3), workers benefit through the creation of a working environment where levels of participation in major decisions are high, where opinions of all are valued, and where there are opportunities for workers to be creative and develop themselves. These features of learning organizations present them in a very positive light, as a 'visionary ideal' (Shipton 2006: 240), and as a 'utopia of democracy' (Contu et al. 2003: 939). Illustration 6.1 applies these principles through a study of two universities from different cultural parts of the world.

 Illustration 6.1 Universities as learning organizations

Bui and Baruch (2011) test for Senge's model of the learning organization in two universities, one of which was in the UK, and one of which was in Vietnam. They define a learning organization as an organization which 'works to create values, practices and procedures, in which learning and working are synonymous', and which 'align people's learning and development continuously to corporate vision, mission and strategy' (p. 2). They conducted a survey-based study in both universities, and examined not only whether they had the characteristics of a learning organization, but also the extent to which the components of a learning organization they examined, were linked to particular antecedents and outcomes. There are five disciplines or elements in Senge's model of a learning organization: systems thinking; personal mastery; mental models; team learning; and a shared vision. Systems thinking is the capacity to identify underlying causes in events, personal mastery refers to a person's commitment to learn and develop, mental models refer to the assumptions people have which shape how they see the world, team learning is the commitment of people to work collaboratively, while shared vision is the extent to which people have shared values and ideas. Senge argues that the existence of these disciplines in an organization will result in positive benefits in terms of both organizational performance and employee satisfaction and commitment.

Bui and Baruch identify particular antecedents linked to each of Senge's five disciplines, with for example, the antecedents of team learning being suggested as being team commitment, leadership, goal setting, development and training, organizational culture, and individual learning. They also examined a range of individual and organizational outcomes including work performance (in terms of teaching, research, and administration), self-efficacy, work-life balance, and knowledge sharing. In terms of outcomes, they examined the extent to which the existence of the five disciplines of a learning organization were positively linked to these outcomes, and also mediated the relationship between the antecedents and outcomes they examined.

Limitations of space mean that it's only possible to give a broad overview of their research findings. First, they did identify the characteristics of learning organizations in both organizations, and provided support for Senge's learning organization model. All the hypotheses tested were either partially or fully supported, and the existence of the five disciplines of a learning organization was positively linked to the outcomes investigated. One interesting conclusion was that the Vietnamese university scored higher than the UK one on all disciplines of the learning organization model. It was suggested that this might be due to the fact that Vietnam has a more collectivist culture than the UK.

Question

Do you think that this final conclusion can be generalized such that the stronger the sense of collectivism in a country, the easier it will be to create learning organizations?

One element which is argued to be necessary and central to the creation of such a working environment, is a particular type of *leadership style* (Sadler 2001; Snell 2001; Biu and Baruch 2011; Crossan et al. 2011). For example, leaders in learning organizations are required to be learners as much as teachers, and they should also have roles as coaches or mentors. Such a leadership style is necessary not only to actively stimulate the curiosity and learning of workers, but to also make leaders sensitive and responsive to the opinions of workers. However, the contradictions of the learning organization advocates regarding the role and style that organizational management should have, is discussed later when looking at the critique of this perspective.

The learning organization: the pessimists' or sceptics' perspective

The arguments of the learning organization advocates have produced an enormous amount of debate (Easterby-Smith 1997; Tsang 1997). This section examines the critique put forward by those who have been labelled the pessimists or sceptics. The critique is structured into three broad but interrelated areas: the nature of the employment relationship, the need to account for power, and how individual factors such as emotion, shape people's willingness to learn. The sub-sections that follow explore these three interrelated areas using the following factors as themes: learning and the employment relationship; power, politics, and learning; and emotions and attitudes to learning. The last two themes (power, politics, and learning, and emotions and attitudes to learning) are both illustrated using different empirical studies.

Learning and the employment relationship

Central to Coopey's (1995, 1998) critique of the learning organization rhetoric, is that there is a fundamental contradiction that is not addressed regarding the power and authority of management. On the one hand, as outlined previously, Pedler's vision of the learning organization—characterized by the support and encouragement given to open discussion and risk free critical debate, as well as the importance of democratic decision-making processes—requires organizational managers to share power much more than in traditional organizations. However, on the other hand, Pedler takes for granted the legitimacy of both shareholder rights, enshrined in company law, as well as management's authority and right to manage in their shareholders' interests (Coopey 1995: 195; see Time to reflect). Thus, while the learning organization rhetoric suggests that more democratic decision-making is necessary, it doesn't explain how this can be effectively achieved. Given that empirical evidence suggests that organizational management are often unwilling to share power, it is arguably unlikely that such a process will occur voluntarily (Dovey 1997). Illustration 6.2 describes employee learning at adidas.

 Illustration 6.2 The adidas group learning campus

In 2011, the adidas CEO Herbert Hainer announced a new initiative—the building of a corporate university for all employees to learn and develop. Founded in 1949, adidas is a leading worldwide sports brand, which designs and develops footwear and streetwear apparel and accessories. Hainer stated that since 'Innovation is our most discerning competitive advantage', adidas had to reposition and rewire 'learning' in the twenty-first century. To retain its position as a market leader the adidas Group invests heavily in elements that drive its design, production, and retail processes as well as its systems and branding. New ideas require a stimulating environment focused on continuous development and learning of new things. Hainer realized that new ways of learning are required in order for the company to become a leader in learning, attract the best talent, and develop and retain the right people.

Prior to establishing the Group Learning Campus, 95 per cent of adidas's learning initiatives were one-time and formal, taking employees out of workflows following a top-down training approach. The company's new learning concept entitled 'the new way of learning' is based on the 70:20:10 model of Charles Jennings whereby 70 per cent of the learning is on the job; 20 per cent of the learning is through interactions with other people; and 10 per cent of the learning is through coursework. This new learning approach shifts formal learning to informal learning, bringing learning back into the workplace as a fun activity delivered by colleagues, friends, peers, in teams, online, and in real life. The new way of learning is a life-long learning experience with employees deciding when and where they learn, choosing how and what they learn.

adidas's new way of learning is based on five core principles:

1. Working is learning and learning is working—learning is an integral part of work and needs to be embedded in an employee's daily work practices.

2. Learning occurs in an open, collaborative, connected social learning environment—employees learn from and among peers and contribute to the learning of others.

3. Leadership means sharing, learning, and teaching—every employee share his/her knowledge, being a teacher and student at the same time.

4. Innovation is part of everyone's daily work—innovation is unrestricted to specific roles or functions and occurs in every area of the business and is attainable by everybody.

5. A self-driven life-long learning culture—the learning campus provides an environment in which everybody can learn and share everything, enabling everyone to be a student as well as a teacher.

The new adidas Group Learning Campus was launched in July 2014 in Herzogenaurach in Germany and consists of three pillars: physical learning spaces, the virtual learning campus, and the future workplace. At this campus called the 'Shed', all activities in this open, physical, flexible space relate to learning, training, knowledge sharing, collaboration, and innovation. Virtual learning occurs through an open, collaborative, digital intranet platform comprising content in the form of videos, podcasts, texts, and presentations. The learning portal draws all these together allowing for learning through classrooms, forums, and e-learning courses or learning events. The future workplace integrates the new way of learning with the future workplace that houses its employees.

Source: Adapted from Hüttner and Brem (2017).

Question

What do you think are key challenges of adidas's new way of learning?

 Time to reflect   Authority, law, and democracy

If management's authority to manage is enshrined in company law, does this limit the extent to which organizational decision-making can be made democratic?

Coopey's argument, a perspective also taken by Contu and Willmott (2003), is that within the socio-economic context of capitalism, power is structurally embedded in the employment relationship, and that this typically places workers in a subordinate position to management. This is an issue that is returned to in both Chapters 11 and 14. Such institutional arrangements are argued to produce a 'democratic deficit' where the values, ideas, and interest of workers are largely downplayed, and where the authority and knowledge of management is privileged and taken for granted (Coopey 1998). In such situations it is arguable that the vision of the learning organization articulated by its propagandists is unlikely to be achieved. The relevance of these arguments for the topic of learning is that these features of the employment relationship are likely to significantly shape the nature of organizational learning processes.

Power, politics, and learning

Neglecting to adequately take account of power, politics, and conflict is another criticism made of the learning organization propagandists. However, such a neglect is typical of the majority of the learning literature (Hong and Snell 2008; Bunderson and Reagans 2011). Further, the propagandists not only downplay such issues, but are typically unwilling to even acknowledge that they are relevant to the analysis of learning processes (Driver 2002). However, since the mid-1990s, issues of power and politics have been given a greater level of attention (LaPolombara 2001; Vince et al. 2002). The need to account for power and politics in learning processes flows from three closely interrelated factors (see Figure 6.2). Each of these factors impact on organizational learning processes.

First, as will be discussed more fully in Chapter 14, power and knowledge are either intimately interrelated or totally inseparable (the precise way the power-knowledge relationship is understood depends on how power is conceptualized). Thus, if learning is about the development and use of knowledge, then account needs to be taken of issues of power (Vince 2001). Coopey (1998), for example, drawing on Foucault (1980), suggests that managerial authority

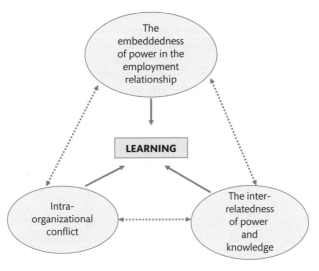

Figure 6.2 Linking Power and Politics to Learning

relates to the inseparability of power and knowledge, where management's power is reflected in the privileging of their knowledge, and vice versa. Second, as discussed in the previous section, the need to account for power in learning processes relates to the embeddedness of power in the employment relationship. Third and last, some argue that power and politics need to be accounted for due to the typical lack of value consensus which exists in most organizations, and the potential for conflict and disagreement this creates (Salaman 2001; Huzzard and Ostergren 2002). This is another issue that was discussed more fully in Chapters 11 and 14. Illustration 6.3 demonstrates the impact of power and culture on learning processes.

 Illustration 6.3 Power inequalities and cultural differences in learning within Japanese subsidiaries in China

Hong and Snell (2008) conducted a detailed qualitative study into the dynamics of learning within five Japanese subsidiary companies in China. The subsidiary companies they examined were all based in the same region, and were of a reasonable size, employing between 500 and 2,500 staff. The study found that all five of the Japanese parent companies made significant efforts to impose their corporate culture within the subsidiaries, despite the existence of some identified culture differences. One of the culture differences identified between the working style of the Chinese workers and Japanese managers was in relation to teamworking. For the Japanese managers, effective teamworking involved all team members making significant efforts to contribute to group tasks and problem solving activities. The Japanese managers didn't feel that the Chinese workers were prepared to participate in such activities effectively. Thus, one manager said, 'within the traditional culture of Canon, we encourage close cross-departmental cooperation and total employee participation . . . the workers here perceive their work differently. They tend to have a clear demarcation of duties, titles and power' (p. 262). Another manager said, 'In general, the Chinese are not aggressive enough to engage in the problem solving process' (p. 263). Hong and Snell argued that these differences were not due to any laziness of the Chinese workers, but were instead due to cultural differences.

However, despite these culture differences, no attempts were made to take account of them and make some cultural adjustments. The Japanese managers were totally convinced about the superiority and value of the corporate culture their company had developed, and made great efforts to impose it within the Chinese subsidiary plants. This was achieved through the inflexible imposition of particular types of work practice, combined with an intensive programme of culture management. Hong and Snell found evidence of cultural adjustment over time among some of the Chinese workers where 'some of the local Chinese had gradually developed the kinds of work-related attitudes and behaviours that were valued by the Japanese headquarters' (p. 267). Hong and Snell conclude that the power inequalities that existed between the Japanese managers and Chinese workers in the subsidiary factories were such that they were able to impose their preferred style of culture and work practices on the Chinese staff.

Question

In all types of subsidiary organizations, do corporate management have the same level of power to be able to impose their preferred work styles on people, or do workers in such situations have any power to challenge and resist such efforts?

The critics of the learning organization rhetoric argue that taking adequate account of these factors means the vision of the advocates is unrealistic, and that there are likely to be some stark contradictions between their rhetoric, and the way the adoption of learning organization practices impact on organizational relations (see Definition). Thus, rather than workers having a greater potential for creativity and self-development, the use of learning organization practices may mean they are subject to greater levels of control. Further, rather than empowering workers, learning organization practices have the potential to bolster and reinforce the power of management (Driver 2002; Hong and Snell 2008—see Illustration 6.3).

The adoption of the rhetoric and practice of the learning organization can be perceived as increasing the potential to control workers, because, as with the use of culture-based management practices generally (Kunda 1992), it involves a form of socially based control, where goal alignment between worker and organization is achieved through persuading workers to internalize the organizational value system (Driver 2002). Such control systems are more subtle, less visible, and have the potential to be more effective than traditional bureaucratic methods (Alvesson and Willmott 2001).

DEFINITION **Learning organization (sceptics)**

An organization where socially based control systems are used to create value alignment around the benefits to all of learning, which has the potential to reinforce management power, and contradict the logic of emancipation embodied in the learning organization rhetoric.

Some writers, however, conclude that conflict is not necessarily detrimental to learning processes, and that if conflict and differences of opinion are managed and negotiated through a certain type of dialogue, they can actually facilitate learning (Coopey and Burgoyne 2000; Huzzard and Ostergren 2002). For example, conflict can facilitate learning if it is dealt with in a communication process which does not privilege any particular point of view, where people are able to communicate without fear, where the communication is a two-way process, and where ultimately the objective of the process is not to achieve a consensus, but for people to develop a greater understanding of the viewpoint of others. Such processes therefore have much in common with the processes of perspective making and taking outlined in Chapter 3, which are an important element of the practice-based perspective on knowledge. Further, while Bunderson and Reagans (2011) highlight how power inequalities within organizations can negatively affect the dynamics of learning processes, they argue that a 'socialized' style of leadership, which is sensitive to such issues, can stimulate and facilitate learning in groups where such power inequalities exist.

Emotion and attitudes to learning

The final factor that the learning organization advocates inadequately account for is the role that people's emotions play in shaping attitudes and behaviours towards learning processes. However, a growing number of writers now acknowledge how emotion importantly affects the dynamics of learning processes (Vince 2001; Crossan et al. 2011; Shepherd et al. 2011; Zhao 2011). At the individual level, learning can be regarded as potentially positive and exciting—discovering new knowledge, improving levels of understanding, developing more effective ways of working, etc. But there is also a potential negative side—giving up the familiar, embracing some level of uncertainty—which may be anxiety inducing for people (Kofman and Senge 1993; Shipton and Sillince 2012). Learning is therefore likely to bring up conflicting emotions for people. Learning and changing can also be understood to affect an individual's sense of self-identity (Child 2001), which may be regarded positively or negatively. Arguably, the attractiveness of defensive routines (Argyris 1990) is that they provide people with a sense of security and self-identity (Giddens 1991). Thus, a potentially frightening side of learning is that it can be felt to involve giving up that which makes people feel competent and secure. Illustration 6.4 describes the impact of emotional experiences and motivation on undergraduate students' learning.

 Illustration 6.4 The impact of emotion, context, and personality on people's ability to learn from errors

Zhao (2011) presents the findings of a laboratory experiment that involved undergraduate students which was centrally concerned with examining the relationship between experiences of negative emotions and people's ability to learn from errors. This study hypothesized that negative emotional experiences would be negatively related to people's ability to learn from errors by reducing their motivation to learn. The paper starts from the assumption that while errors can provide potentially valuable learning opportunities, they often create negative emotions in people that can inhibit them from learning from these experiences. Errors are defined as: 'individuals' decisions and behaviours that (a) result in an undesirable gap between an expected and real state; and (b) may lead to actual or potential negative consequences for organizational functioning that could have been avoided' (p. 436). In terms of the relationship between experiences of negative emotionality and learning from errors, three specific hypotheses are tested. First, they hypothesize that experiences of negative emotionality will be negatively related to people's motivation to learn. Second, they hypothesize that people's motivation to learn will be positively related to the ability to learn from errors. Finally, they hypothesize that motivation to learn will mediate the relationship between the experience of negative emotionality and the ability to learn from errors.

In this study, Zhao also examined two antecedents of negative emotionality, with these being people's emotional stability and their perception regarding managerial intolerance of errors. They hypothesize that emotional stability is negatively related to experiences of negative emotion, in other words the more emotionally stable people are the less likely they are to experience negative emotions. Second, they hypothesize that people's perceptions of managerial intolerance of errors will be positively related to experiences of negative emotion. In the tests that were conducted, both of these hypotheses were supported.

In terms of the relationships between negative emotion and learning from errors, while it was found that motivation to learn was positively linked to the ability to learn from errors, their hypothesis that motivation to learn would be negatively related to people's emotional experiences was not supported. In fact, in contradiction to what was expected, experiences of negative emotions were found to be positively linked to people's motivation to learn. Two suggestions were put forward to explain this. First, the level of negative emotions people experienced were relatively low, which may have been due to the fact that the research data was collected in a student simulation test, where participants didn't have to experience and deal with the consequences of real errors. Second, it was suggested that the level of negative emotion experienced may actually be an important variable. Thus experiencing low levels of negative emotions may motivate people to learn as this does not create a lot of fear, anxiety, etc., in people, whereas when high levels of negative emotions are experienced, this may act to inhibit people's motivation to learn in line with the level of fear experienced.

Finally, in terms of managerial implications, the study suggests that management behaviour can influence the extent to which people experience negative emotions related to errors. To avoid or minimize this, it is suggested that managers should behave in a way that indicates a tolerance for making errors and that people should feel safe admitting to and discussing the reasons for any errors they make.

Question

To what extent do you agree with the suggestion that the relationship between experiencing negative emotions and people's motivation to learn is affected by the level of negative emotion that people experience?

Finally, as Illustration 6.4 highlights, learning from errors and mistakes is a situation where emotion can strongly influence the dynamics of learning processes (see also Shepherd et al. 2011). This topic is revisited in Chapter 8 when the topic of unlearning is examined.

 ## Conclusion

The chapter has shown that the enormous literature on organizational learning that has been produced since the mid-1990s is of great relevance to those wishing to understand the dynamics of organizational knowledge processes. This should be relatively unsurprising given the relatedness of learning to knowledge management. Through utilizing the Crossan/Zietsma framework the complexity and multilevel nature of organizational learning was explored, showing how organizational learning cannot simply be regarded as the sum of the learning of an organization's workers.

The chapter also showed how the concept of the learning organization has been the subject of significant debate, with its advocates arguing that it provides both organizations and workers with

Table 6.4 Factors Affecting Learning in Organizations

Factors Affecting Learning	Level
The emotional character of learning.	Individual
Competency traps and the difficulty of giving up established values and practices.	Individual-group-organization
The politics and power involved in implementing learning and challenging established norms.	Individual-group-organization
The interrelatedness of learning, knowledge, and power.	Supra-organizational
The embeddedness of power in the employment relationship.	Supra-organizational

many benefits, while the critics argue that the emancipatory rhetoric of the learning organization disguises and denies the way in which the practices of the learning organization may impact negatively on workers, for example leading to increased levels of exploitation and control. This debate was not resolved, but it did provide a useful way of revealing the diversity of factors which make learning within the context of work organizations difficult and complex (see Table 6.4).

This chapter concludes with a case study that uses Crossan's 4I learning framework to analyse organizational learning within in a large Dutch bank.

 Case study The role of time and discontinuities in shaping the complex dynamics of organizational learning

Berends and Lammers (2010) use Crossan et al.'s multilevel model of organizational learning to analyse the dynamics of a knowledge management initiative that was undertaken within a large Dutch bank. They not only apply Crossan et al.'s model, but also contribute to its development through their use of the concept of discontinuities and how they affected the dynamics of learning within the project and wider organization. Discontinuities are defined as occurring when 'one of the four learning processes is interrupted or where learning does not flow from level to level' (p. 1048). Their analysis also highlighted how factors of time, the social context of the organization, and politics played crucial roles in shaping the dynamics of learning. Their analysis was based on a detailed, qualitative study of the knowledge management project that involved both interviewing people at various times and observing key project meetings. While the knowledge management project was ultimately unsuccessful, their analysis of it provides detailed insights into the dynamics of organizational learning. To give some insights into their analysis, this brief overview gives some examples of the four learning processes within the project as well as some of the discontinuities that interrupted learning. The way in which factors such as time and the social context impacted on learning in the project are also highlighted.

As outlined earlier, central to Crossan et al.'s model of organizational learning are the four processes of intuiting, interpreting, integrating, and institutionalizing, which move learning between individual, group, and organizational levels through feed-forward and feed-back processes. An example of individual-level intuition in the project occurred at an early phase, when interest in knowledge management was in its infancy and was relatively limited. At this stage interest in the topic and understanding of the relevance of knowledge management to the bank occurred through the intuition of various individuals. The growth of interest in knowledge management, which grew out of these intuitions, resulted in knowledge management becoming a topic that the bank considered investing in via a research project. One outcome of this growth of interest was the organization of various workshops and meetings that brought relevant people together, and where a group-level process of interpretation began. However, the emergence of various discontinuities, which interrupted the evolution of the project, meant that these initial interpretations of knowledge management were not sustained throughout the project. An example of one such discontinuity occurred immediately after the project was awarded funding, when it was decided to replace the initial project team with a new and highly successful project manager. However, this decision both delayed the project, as the new project manager wasn't available to start immediately, and also resulted in the focus of the project changing, as the new project manager developed his own ideas about how to implement knowledge management. This meant that the initial focus and priorities of the project became changed.

An example of knowledge integration occurred later in the project during the conduct of some small pilot projects within particular departments. Here a process of knowledge integration occurred as the insights developed within the knowledge management project were integrated with local department-specific knowledge to help address particular local challenges and problems. A partial process of integration also flowed out of this as some of the findings from the pilot projects (though not all) were institutionalized into formalized departmental procedures. A final example of discontinuity occurred towards the end of the project, at a time when there was growing concern among senior management regarding the organizational benefits that were being derived from the project. In analysing the knowledge derived from the pilot projects and the ways in which this understanding could be institutionalized into organizational procedures, senior managers decided not to continue funding the project, and decided to merge the knowledge management project and subsume it within a new intranet project.

The role of time crucially shaped the project in various ways, fundamentally through various features of the organization's temporal structures. For example, the timing of various management committees crucially shaped funding for and evaluation of the project's progress. Further, factors such as when key people were available to participate, as well as the timing of holidays, also impacted the project's progress. The social structure of the organization also shaped the progress of the knowledge management project and the learning that occurred. The project spanned various departments (such as IT and HRM), and involved people from a wide range of hierarchical levels. This shaped the project in various ways. First, it contributed to the conflict that existed regarding the general character of the knowledge management project, such as the extent to which it should be IT focused. Fundamentally, there was a wide range of different views regarding what the knowledge management project should focus on. Second, the social structure of the project and the wider organizational context also influenced the politics that developed within the project, whereby various actors used different strategies in order to have their vision of knowledge management privileged over others. An example of this occurred early in the project, where an IT focused view predominated, which led to the downplaying of HRM issues and the exclusion from the project team of HRM staff.

Berends and Lammers' conclusion regarding the general character of organizational learning was that due to the various discontinuities that occurred, learning was 'fragmented', and that overall learning within and from the project was 'non linear' and 'more complex than process models suggest' (p.1060), where learning 'resembled a changing delta of meandering flows, some of which get blocked, while new flows emerge and others get reinforced' (p. 1059).

Question

1. While this case is based on a single project, do you think that it is atypical or typical of how learning occurs during the life of large cross-departmental projects?

Review and Discussion Questions

1. The advocates of the learning organization suggest that critical self-reflection and open debate on norms and values are fundamental to learning organizations. However, Coopey and Burgoyne (2000) suggest few organizations provide the 'psychic space' where such reflection can occur. Do you agree with this analysis? If so, what factors are key in stifling such processes?

2. Compare the two definitions of the learning organization outlined in the chapter. Which do you most agree with and why?

3. The research of Hong and Snell (2008) suggested that national culture shaped the learning styles of Japanese and Chinese workers. How important is national culture in shaping the way people learn?

4. If experiencing strong negative emotions can negatively influence people's ability to learn, to what extent does experiencing strong positive emotions affect people's willingness to learn?

 ## Suggestions for Further Reading

M. Crossan, C. Maurer, and R. White (2011). 'Reflections on the 2009 AMR Decade Award: Do We Have a Theory of Organizational Learning?', *Academy of Management Review*, 36/3: 446–60.
This article reviews developments in theory of organizational learning which link to and build from the Crossan et al. framework.

J. Bundeson and R. Reagans (2011). 'Power, Status, and Learning in Organizations', *Organization Science*, 22/5: 1182–94.
A conceptual paper which draws on a range of literature to examine the way in which power and status differences within teams and organizations affect learning processes.

H. Bui and Y. Baruch (2012). 'Learning Organizations in Higher Education: An Empirical Evaluation within an International Context', *Management Learning*, 43/5: 515–44.
An empirical paper which examines the existence of Senge's learning organization framework within two universities.

D. Shepherd, H. Patzelt, and M. Wolfe (2011). 'Moving Forward from Project Failure: Negative Emotions, Affective Commitment and Learning from the Experience', *Academy of Management Journal*, 54/6: 1229–59.
An empirical study which considers the role that negative emotions (and a number of other variables) have on the extent to which people can learn from experiencing project failure.

D. Vera, M. Crossan, and M. Apaydin (2011). ' Chapter 8: A Framework for Integrating Organizational Learning, Knowledge, Capabilities, and Absorptive Capacity', *Handbook of Organizational Learning and Knowledge Management*, 2: 153–82.
This contemporary paper proposes an integrative model that identifies conceptual boundaries of and relationships between a number of concepts (organizational learning, knowledge management, dynamic capabilities, and absorptive capacity) and firm performance.

 To further your understanding of knowledge management in organizations explore the book's accompanying online resources at www.oup.com/uk/hislop4e/

Innovation and Knowledge Processes

Introduction

While the focus of this chapter, on the role of various knowledge processes (creation, absorption, integration utilization) in organizational innovation processes, can be stated relatively succinctly, this topic encompasses a vast literature and a diverse range of perspectives. Thus, within the space of a single book chapter, it is only possible to provide a brief overview and examine a limited range of topics. Some of the reasons for the scale of interest include the elasticity of the term innovation, the fact that innovation can occur at diverse levels (individual, team, organization, sector, country . . .), and also that innovation can be thought of as a process and an outcome. These ideas are encapsulated in Crossan and Apaydin's (2010) definition of innovation, which is intended to be all encompassing. Thus, their definition of innovation is:

> production or adaptation, assimilation, and exploitation of a value-added novelty in economic and social spheres; renewal and enlargement of products, services, and markets; development of new methods of production; and establishment of new management systems. It is both a process and an outcome. (2010: 1155)

In this chapter, the focus is on organizational level innovation only and the examination of innovation as a process. The consideration given to how knowledge processes shape innovation processes is due to the growing recognition that knowledge processes are a fundamentally important element shaping innovation dynamics (Richtnér et al. 2014), which is acknowledged by the prominence of learning and knowledge management theories in the analysis of innovation processes (Crossan and Apaydin 2010). Further, two separate perspectives are examined here. First, Nonaka's knowledge creation theory is examined; and, second, relevant parts of Crossan and Apaydin's (2010) multidimensional framework on innovation are considered. The reason why these perspectives are focused on is outlined later. However, only selective elements of both perspectives are examined.

In examining the role of knowledge processes in shaping innovation dynamics it is virtually impossible to ignore Nonaka's knowledge creation theory as it represents arguably the single most influential and widely referenced theory in the knowledge management domain (Nonaka et al. 2006; Güldenberg and Helting 2007). The influence of this work is visible in citation data. The two most cited publications which articulate knowledge creation theory are Nonaka's (1994) article in *Organization Science*, and Nonaka and Takeuchi's (1995) book *The Knowledge-Creating Company*, which by July 2017 had been cited over 21,000 and 33,000 times, respectively, according to Google Scholar.

Crossan and Apaydin's (2010) framework is the other perspective examined, as it is a comprehensive, multidimensional framework, which was developed through synthesizing almost thirty years of academic work on the topic. It is also a widely cited framework. While an overview is given of the whole model, the focus here, due to the central concern of this book with knowledge processes and knowledge management, is narrowly on the role of knowledge and learning processes, which are a core element of the model. This model suggests that linking to and utilizing external sources of knowledge represents a fundamentally important way to facilitate innovation. In examining these processes the highly relevant concept of absorptive capacity is elaborated and examined.

The structure of the chapter is relatively simple. Some of the key components of knowledge creation theory are presented, including the distinctive epistemology it is founded on, how knowledge creation is achieved through the conversion of knowledge from one form to another, and the role of space (*ba*) in knowledge. The chapter then examines some of the main critiques that have been made of knowledge creation theory which relate to its epistemology and its level of cultural generalizability. The chapter then elaborates relevant parts of Crossan and Apaydin's (2010) model and closes with an extended illustration on the role of absorptive capacity in innovation processes.

The scope and evolution of Nonaka's knowledge creation theory

Nonaka's theory is extremely wide-ranging, and Nonaka and his various collaborators have published extensively on various aspects of it. In terms of its scope, not only is it a theory of knowledge and knowledge creation, it also engages with topics such as *ba*, leadership and management, organizational structure/form, and business strategy. In terms of publications, the body of work in which this theory has been developed is substantial, spanning a timescale of more than thirty years, and includes (in terms of English-language publications only) a number of books (Nonaka and Takeuchi 1995; von Krogh et al. 2000; Ichijo and Nonaka 2006; Nonaka et al. 2008) and more than twenty refereed journal articles (including Nonaka 1991, 1994; Nonaka and Konno 1998; Nonaka et al. 2006; Nonaka and von Krogh 2009; von Krogh et al. 2012; Nonaka and Hirose 2015). Thus, all that can be done is give an overview of some of its key features, most fundamentally the SECI knowledge creation spiral, which arguably represents the core of the model.

Another key feature of this theory is that it has evolved and developed over time, partly due to the refinement and elaboration of the theory (such as von Krogh et al. 2012, on the topic of leadership; and Nonaka and Toyama 2015, on knowledge creation theory and dialectics), as well as responses to some of the critiques that have been made of it (such as Nonaka and von Krogh 2009, on the topics of tacit knowledge and knowledge conversion). Thus, knowledge creation theory should be understood as dynamic rather than being a static body of ideas which have remained unchanged over time.

The epistemology of knowledge creation theory

There are three fundamental elements to the way knowledge is conceptualized in knowledge creation theory. First, there is the basic definition of knowledge as 'justified true belief'. Second, knowledge gives people the ability to define and understand situations, and act accordingly. Finally, there is the distinction between tacit and explicit knowledge, which implies that they represent distinctive and different forms of knowledge. Further, one of the themes in knowledge creation theory is the distinction between Japanese and Western epistemology, and that the high level of importance attributed to tacit knowledge in knowledge creation theory distinguishes it from the dominant Western epistemology in academia which is argued to be more centrally focused on explicit knowledge.

For Nonaka, defining knowledge as 'justified true belief' refers to the knowledge that individuals develop based on their particular experiences and work practices. While distinctions are made in knowledge creation theory between individual, group, and organizational knowledge, and it is argued that through the process of knowledge conversion knowledge can 'move' between these levels (see following section), within knowledge creation theory knowledge is fundamentally individual, being possessed by and embodied within people. In this respect it has resonances with the practice-based perspective on knowledge articulated in Chapter 3. Further, it is a highly subjective and relative definition of knowledge, as knowledge constitutes what an individual believes to be true. Thus, Nonaka et al. (2006: 1182) say that 'knowledge is never free from human values and ideas'. Ultimately, knowledge conceptualized in this way refers to what an individual can justify as being true, based on their experience of and interaction with the world. However, an important element of people's experiences are their interactions with others, whose understanding of the same events may be different. People's knowledge or justified true beliefs emerge from a process of dialogue with others, where people become exposed to others with different perspectives, with people's knowledge being 'born of the multiple perspectives of human interaction' (Nonaka et al. 2008: 12). In this process of dialogue, conflict may exist between competing perspectives, with knowledge resulting from the process via which people (attempt to) justify their personal beliefs.

The second feature of knowledge is that it provides people with the ability to define and understand situations and then act in accordance with these insights. Thus knowledge is closely linked to and inseparable from how people act and behave. This implies, as discussed earlier, that knowledge is highly practice-based and also that the relationship between knowledge and action is two-way. Thus, not only does people's knowledge (justified true beliefs) shape how they act and behave, but the relationship also operates in the opposite direction, with consequences of people's actions shaping their knowledge.

The third key dimension of Nonaka's epistemology is the distinction between tacit and explicit knowledge as being fundamentally different. Thus, 'knowledge that can be uttered, formulated in sentences, captured in drawings and writing, is explicit', while 'knowledge tied to the senses, movement skills, physical experiences, intuition, or implicit rules of thumb, is tacit' (Nonaka et al. 2006: 1182). In this respect, Nonaka's epistemology is closer to the objectivist perspective articulated in Chapter 2. Thus, Nonaka's theory of knowledge creation cannot easily be characterized as embedded in either the objectivist or practice-based perspectives on knowledge, as it embodies elements of both (see Time to reflect).

Time to reflect

Compare the earlier summary of Nonaka's conceptualization of knowledge with how the objectivist and practice-based perspectives are defined in Chapters 2 and 3. Which perspective do you think it is closest to?

This distinction between tacit and explicit knowledge as two distinct and separate types of knowledge is something that has been generally consistent and unchanged in knowledge creation theory (see e.g. Nonaka 1994; Nonaka and Takeuchi 1995; Nonaka et al. 2006). However, the conceptualization of the distinction between tacit and explicit knowledge has been refined in later work (Nonaka and von Krogh 2009) in response to various comments and critiques. This refinement of epistemology will be examined later, following the critique that is presented towards the end of the chapter.

SECI and knowledge creation/conversion

The distinction Nonaka makes between tacit and explicit knowledge is fundamental to his model of knowledge creation, as it is via the conversion of knowledge between forms (tacit and explicit) that knowledge is created. In Nonaka's knowledge creation spiral (Figure 7.1) there are four modes of knowledge conversion and the SECI mnemonic with which it is labelled utilizes the first letter of the four knowledge conversion processes (socialization, externalization, combination, and internalization). First, socialization involves the conversion of tacit knowledge into new forms of tacit knowledge. Second is externalization, which involves the conversion of tacit knowledge into explicit knowledge. The third conversion process, labelled combination, involves the integration of different forms of explicit knowledge to create new forms of

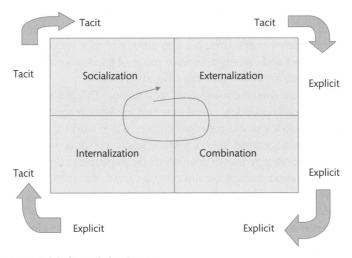

Figure 7.1 The SECI Model of Knowledge Creation

Source: Nonaka and Takeuchi (1995). By permission of Oxford University Press.

Table 7.1 Nonaka's Four Modes of Knowledge Conversion

	Socialization	Externalization	Combination	Internalization
Knowledge Conversion Type	Tacit to tacit	Tacit to explicit	Explicit to explicit	Explicit to tacit
Change in Level of Knowledge	Individual to individual (between people)	Individual to group	Group to organization	Organization to individual
Illustrative Example	Where a new member of a work group acquires the tacit knowledge possessed by other group members through dialogue, observation, or cooperative working.	Where an individual is able to make their tacit knowledge explicit, e.g. through a process of communication and dialogue with others.	The linking together of discrete bodies of knowledge, to create a more complex body of knowledge.	Where an individual converts explicit knowledge into tacit knowledge, through applying it to their work tasks.

explicit knowledge. Finally, internalization involves the conversion of explicit knowledge into tacit knowledge. For Nonaka, socialization is typically the starting point of knowledge creation processes, as it is the impulse of individuals to collaborate and communicate or share explicit knowledge which provides the initial catalyst for knowledge creation.

It is important to note that knowledge creation evolves through a spiral rather than circular motion. This is because the SECI knowledge conversion/creation processes involve a double, simultaneous conversion. Thus, with each mode of knowledge creation, not only is knowledge created via changing forms, but simultaneously knowledge moves between individual, group, and organizational levels (see Table 7.1). The movement of knowledge 'up' from the individual level, through to group level, and finally to organizational level is referred to as a process of amplification (Nonaka et al. 2008: 25). Thus at an organizational level knowledge creation contributes to the expansion of an organization's knowledge system. Such systems include not only a store of explicit knowledge codified into information technology (IT) systems, formalized rules, or operating procedures, but also a body of tacit knowledge existing within an organization's culture and value system. Each mode of knowledge creation/conversion is examined in a little more detail later (see also Illustration 7.1).

The first process of knowledge conversion is socialization. This process involves the interpersonal sharing of tacit knowledge, where new tacit knowledge for one person is created through gaining access to the tacit knowledge of others as they work together on a day-to-day basis. This type of knowledge creation occurs when people work together collaboratively and usually occurs over extended periods of time, which allows people to develop not only shared working practices, but also common systems of values and understanding. Thus socialization involves the movement of knowledge from one individual to another.

The second process of knowledge creation, where knowledge is transformed from a tacit to an explicit form, is externalization. This knowledge creation process involves the movement of knowledge from the level of the individual to a group. This is a process via which individuals articulate, communicate, and justify their individual knowledge to a group of peers. It involves transforming knowledge from a tacit to an explicit form via people using language, images, models, and concepts, etc., to begin the process of codifying tacit knowledge. Dialogue is important to this process, as the articulation of knowledge by one person will involve them being questioned (or possibly challenged) by peers to clarify and develop their knowledge and ideas.

The third process of knowledge creation is combination. This involves creating new forms of explicit knowledge from existing forms of explicit knowledge, and involves the movement of knowledge from the level of the group to the level of the organization. This process involves combining different bodies of somewhat disparate explicit knowledge to create more complex and interrelated systems of knowledge. Further it involves the institutionalization of group-level knowledge into formalized, organizational-level knowledge, such as an organization-wide system of rules or working practices.

 Illustration 7.1 Knowledge creation theory and customer relationship management systems

Khodakarami and Chan (2014) argue that customer relationship management (CRM) systems can provide organizations with an effective and important means for acquiring, managing, and utilizing customer-related knowledge. They utilize Nonaka's knowledge creation theory to understand the ways in which different types of CRM systems support customer-related knowledge processes. In their analysis they distinguish between three different types of CRM system. First, there are operational systems, used to automate and make customer processes more efficient. Second, there are analytical systems, which utilize important knowledge about customers. Finally, there are collaborative systems, which are concerned with managing the knowledge shared with a customer.

Their analysis, based on examining seven diverse organizations that utilized CRM systems, found the following. First, in terms of knowledge creation via socialization, operational and collaborative systems provide a reasonable level of support. This is because the use of both types of system involves real-time interaction with customers, which allows organizational workers to acquire some tacit knowledge about their customers. In terms of knowledge creation via externalization, collaborative systems provided the greatest level of support, as the knowledge acquired via real-time interactions (see previously) can be codified into an explicit form. In terms of knowledge creation via combination, analytical systems provided the highest level of support, creating systems capable of combining different sources and types of knowledge. Finally, for knowledge creation via internalizations collaborative systems provided the highest level of support. This is because collaborative systems provide workers with access to codified customer knowledge which can be absorbed tacitly.

Question

If the aim of management is to use CRM systems which support the greatest number of knowledge creation modes, what are the managerial implications of this analysis?

The fourth and final process of knowledge creation is internalization. This is where knowledge is converted from an explicit form to a tacit form, and where knowledge moves from the level of the organization to the level of the individual. This is therefore a process of absorption or embodiment, where people's use of explicit knowledge (such as systems of rules, operating manuals, etc.) becomes absorbed into their work practices so that they eventually do not have to utilize the explicit knowledge which has shaped their (tacit) practices. Finally, the process of knowledge creation/conversion is potentially infinite, as the internalization of explicit knowledge by people does not mean that knowledge at this point becomes static and unchanging, as internalization has the potential to lead to and initiate a new process of socialization, whereby new tacit knowledge is created out of the existing tacit knowledge people possess and utilize.

Ba

Ba is a Japanese concept which translates into English as 'shared space or context'. While it was a concept that was not referred to in the earliest formulations of knowledge creation theory (Nonaka 1994; Nonaka and Takeuchi 1995), it was fully articulated by Nonaka (in Nonaka and Konno 1998) and has evolved to constitute an important element of knowledge creation theory. *Ba* represents an important element of the organizational context which facilitates knowledge creation processes or, in Nonaka's terms, provides the 'enabling conditions' for knowledge creation. *Ba* enables knowledge creation by facilitating inter-personal interactions between people. Such interactions facilitate knowledge creation as they provide an 'existential place where participants share contexts and create new meanings' (Nonaka et al. 1994: 34) and which provides a person an opportunity to 'get involved and transcend one's own limited perspective' (p. 36).

While Nonaka's conceptualization of *ba* includes shared physical space, *ba* refers to more than simply a shared physical context where people create knowledge through face-to-face collaboration. *Ba* also includes shared virtual space, where people can communicate, interact, and collaborate via IT systems such as e-mail. Further, *ba* also refers to shared mental space in terms of common assumptions, values, practices, and knowledge that people can develop and share. For example, Nonaka et al. (2006: 1185) suggest that an example of this type of *ba* in the context of product development activities refers to common interpretations regarding technical data, test results, product features in terms of quality, etc.

Nonaka also suggests that the type of *ba* that facilitates and supports each type of knowledge conversion is likely to be different.

Nonaka argues that the key reason why an appropriate *ba* is necessary to support different knowledge creation processes is that knowledge creation is a typically fragile social process in which people articulate and justify their knowledge to others in a group-based context. If the organizational context within which this type of activity occurs is inappropriate it is likely to inhibit people's efforts to communicate and interact. However, the concept of *ba*, and the relationship between different type of *ba* and particular modes of knowledge conversion, has been largely empirically untested and remains somewhat abstract. For example, in their 2006 review article Nonaka et al. (2006) refer to only a couple of studies on the topic.

The critique of Nonaka's knowledge creation theory

While Nonaka's theory is widely cited and highly influential, it has also been the subject of a number of criticisms. Three considered here are that the empirical evidence supporting the theory is unconvincing, that the model has conceptual problems, and that its universal applicability is limited as it is only relevant to companies utilizing Japanese business practices. One of the most extensive critiques of Nonaka's knowledge creation theory has been developed by Gourlay (2006) and his work is here utilized in the development of the first two critiques of Nonaka's theory.

Gourlay (2006) argues that one of the main criticisms of Nonaka's theory is that, despite the fact that his work is typically replete with illustrative examples, the evidence supporting it is brief, anecdotal, and unconvincing. In substantiating his argument, Gourlay reviews the evidence and examples presented by Nonaka which are argued to provide illustrative and supporting evidence for each of the four modes of knowledge creation. Here, for illustrative purposes, only the evidence supporting socialization is considered.

In *The Knowledge-Creating Company* (Nonaka and Takeuchi 1995) the key exemplar provided to illustrate the process of socialization (converting tacit knowledge into new forms of tacit knowledge) is how the process of bread making was learnt in the development of a domestic bread-making machine. To overcome some initial problems in the bread-making process (the inability to produce 'tasty bread') it was decided that a member of the product development team would watch a master chef making bread. Through doing this it was realized by the developer that the chef was both twisting and stretching the dough. These insights were then integrated into the design of the bread machine and it was argued that the tasty bread problem had been solved. This process of learning by watching undertaken by the developer is argued to be an example of socialization. While Gourlay acknowledges that this may represent an example of socialization he argues that the anecdotal nature of the example and the lack of detailed evidence makes it far from convincing that what has been revealed is an example of socialization.

Even if Nonaka's many illustrative examples are regarded as convincing, there are other limitations regarding the extent to which the theory has been tested and evaluated by others. Teece goes further, questioning whether at present knowledge creation theory is a 'testable theory' (2008: xiv), as it is not articulated in the form of testable propositions. However, Teece was generally positive that hypothesis formulation and testing of the theory was possible.

A second critique developed by Gourlay is that there are a number of conceptual problems not only in the SECI model, but in what he argues is a radically subjective definition of knowledge, and the epistemological assumption that it is possible to completely convert tacit knowledge into explicit knowledge. Again, for illustrative purposes, the focus here is narrowly on the extent to which tacit knowledge can be made explicit. While Nonaka draws on Polanyi in making the distinction between tacit and explicit knowledge, and arguing that tacit knowledge can be converted wholly into an explicit form, Gourlay argues that Polanyi's position on these questions is more ambiguous. Further, Gourlay takes the perspective, shared by a number of theorists (Ribeiro and Collins 2007; Collins 2007), that there is an irreducibly tacit element to any and all explicit knowledge, and that it is never possible to make fully explicit any tacit knowledge.

This critique of Nonaka's epistemology was explicitly acknowledged and responded to by Nonaka and von Krogh (2009). The focus here is the response to the critique regarding the nature of tacit and explicit knowledge and the relationship between them. Nonaka and von Krogh's (2009) paper develops a subtle but significantly different way of articulating their relationship. While Nonaka's earlier work, as outlined in the previous section, suggested that tacit and explicit knowledge were separate types of knowledge, in the response to the critique that tacit knowledge cannot be made fully explicit, they argue in their 2009 article that tacit and explicit knowledge exist 'on a continuum' and that 'tacit and explicit knowledge are not two separate types but inherently inseparable' (p. 637). The idea of tacit and explicit knowledge being part of a continuum is reinforced later when they talk about how knowledge loses some of its 'tacitness' and 'increasingly explicit knowledge' (both p. 642). Thus while continuing to highlight the important distinction between tacit and explicit knowledge, and with knowledge conversion between forms remaining the centre of knowledge creation theory, Nonaka and von Krogh's (2009) paper represents a retreat from the idea that tacit and explicit represent two separate and distinct forms of knowledge.

The third and final critique of Nonaka's knowledge creation theory questions its tacit universalistic assumptions, arguing that it is based on values very much embedded in Japanese work practices and culture. This is an argument that Nonaka has thus far not responded to. Glisby and Holden (2003), as well as Weir and Hutchins (2005), argue that all knowledge is culturally embedded, and that the universality of Nonaka's knowledge creation model is limited by the fact that it is embedded within and reflects the values and culture of Japanese business. Thus its relevance to business cultures which do not share these values is argued to be limited. Glisby and Holden illustrate their argument by considering the way that Nonaka's conceptualization of each of the four modes of knowledge conversion reflects business practices that are common in Japan, but much less frequently utilized elsewhere.

In examining processes of socialization, Glisby and Holden distinguish between the internal sharing of tacit knowledge by employees within an organization, and the external sharing of knowledge by people across organizational boundaries. Glisby and Holden argue that the external sharing of knowledge referred to by Nonaka reflects the close and interlocking inter-organizational relations that are typical in Japan. In countries where the management of inter-firm relations is typically more arms' length, the sharing of tacit knowledge across organizational boundaries is argued to occur much less frequently. Equally, Glisby and Holden argue that the frequent sharing of tacit knowledge between employees discussed by Nonaka is likely to be shaped by the typically high commitment levels Japanese workers have for the organizations they work for, and that in countries where levels of organizational commitment and loyalty are lower, the sharing of tacit knowledge between employees is also likely to be lower. Glisby and Holden make a similar argument with respect to processes of internalization, the conversion of explicit knowledge into tacit knowledge. For Nonaka, this is closely linked to processes of learning by doing which emerge when job rotation occurs. However the type of job rotation referred to by Nonaka, while being common within Japanese companies, is much less common in other countries. The embeddedness of knowledge creation theory in Japanese values and practices is reinforced by the fact that, almost without exception, the illustrative examples utilized by Nonaka are taken from Japanese companies.

Hong (2012) adds a further contribution to this critique by arguing that the behaviours and assumptions underpinning each of Nonaka's knowledge conversion modes are embedded in particular Japanese cultural values. This argument is developed utilizing Hofstede's perspective on national culture (see Table 7.2). For example, in relation to socialization, the assumption underpinning it is that people have a willingness to identify and work closely with others. Hong argues that this willingness will be facilitated by national cultural values that have a high level of collectivism (as Japan does). Second, Hong argues that externalization can be

Table 7.2 Assumptions and Cultural Values Underpinning Knowledge Conversion Modes

Mode of Knowledge Conversion	Underlying Assumptions	Embedded Japanese Cultural Values (from Hofstede)
Socialization	A desire to identify and interact with others.	• High collectivism • Large power distance
Externalization	A strong motivation to reduce ambiguity.	• High uncertainty avoidance • Masculinity
Combination	Importance of producing things via collaboration with others.	• High collectivism • Large power distance
Internalization	Willingness to be open to new ideas, reflect on own ideas/practices, and continuously improve.	• High uncertainty avoidance • Masculinity.

Source: Hong (2012).

understood as an attempt by people to reduce ambiguities, with people's desire to engage in this type of activity being facilitated by national cultural values concerned with uncertainty avoidance (as is the case with Japan). This line of argument thus implies that in countries where cultural values are different to those in Japan, people may be less likely and willing to engage in SECI knowledge conversion processes, as the behaviours and assumptions they involve are not embedded in their cultural values.

 Illustration 7.2 The (partial) applicability of knowledge creation theory in Russia

Andreeva and Ikhilchik (2011) reflect on the extent to which each of the four modes of knowledge creation in Nonaka's SECI model are applicable in Russia. The arguments they present are based on their own direct knowledge of business practices and cultural values in Russia rather than on the collection of any specific research data. To analyse the applicability of the SECI processes to Russia they argue that there are certain societal/organizational conditions, as well as managerial tools/practices, which facilitate each mode of knowledge creation. They then reflect on the extent to which these conditions exist in Russia. Only part of their analysis is presented here, with the focus being on socialization alone.

In relation to socialization they argue that it is facilitated by factors including employees with high levels of loyalty, a willingness among employees to cooperate with each other, organizations which are embedded in collaborative partnerships with other organizations, jobs which allow people to collaborate and share ideas, and good mentoring systems.

In terms of employee commitment and loyalty, Andreeva and Ikhilchik argue that levels of loyalty and commitment are either low or medium rather than high, due to the levels of job insecurity and economic instability most Russian employees have experienced in the recent past. Second, in relation to Russian employees' general willingness to cooperate with colleagues, they also argue that such values are typically limited, with it being more usual for employees to have a competitive attitude towards each other that limits their willingness to collaborate extensively with colleagues. In terms of the extent to which Russian companies are linked into collaborative networks, Andreeva and Ikhilchik argue that this varies significantly between industries, but is typically something that Russian companies are not good at. Finally, in terms of having jobs that encourage collaboration and communication, and the existence of extensive mentoring schemes, Andreeva and Ikhilchik argue that these are both types of work practices that are used to a limited extent. For example, mentoring is typically limited to new or probationary employees and experienced managers may be unwilling to share their knowledge and experience with others due to a fear of being replaced by younger employees.

In conclusion, they argue that knowledge creation theory has partial applicability in Russia as not all the cultural conditions or business practices necessary to support and facilitate SECI processes exist there.

Question

To what extent are the business practices, history, and cultural values that exist within a country likely to affect the extent to which employees are willing to participate in Nonaka's SECI knowledge creation processes?

Innovation, knowledge processes, and absorptive capacity

As outlined, Crossan and Apaydin (2010) developed a multidimensional framework to provide a comprehensive means of understanding the character of innovation processes and the factors which shape them. The framework was deliberately designed to be multidisciplinary, bringing together all the diverse perspectives on innovation into a single framework. What is provided here is a brief overview of the whole framework and then a more detailed focus specifically on the role of learning and knowledge management in the framework.

Figure 7.2 provides a visual summary of the determinants of innovation identified by Crossan and Apaydin. These are divided into three distinct categories of factors. First, there are determinants related to the role of senior management in facilitating innovation processes, which are divided into the roles played by an organization's chief executive officer, its top management team, and its board. There is extensive research which highlights the role of all three elements of leadership in facilitating innovation. The second category of factors relate to the role of business processes in facilitating organizational innovation. These include the process of initiation and decision-making at the start of innovation processes, the process of development and implementation, portfolio management, project management, and commercialization. All these processes are internal organizational processes concerned with the management of innovation, and research suggests that the effective management of such processes can improve the effectiveness with which organizational innovations are developed.

The third category of factors are labelled 'managerial levers', which are concerned with factors distinct from the stages of innovation examined previously, and are concerned with a range of processes and factors that management have control over, which can be utilized

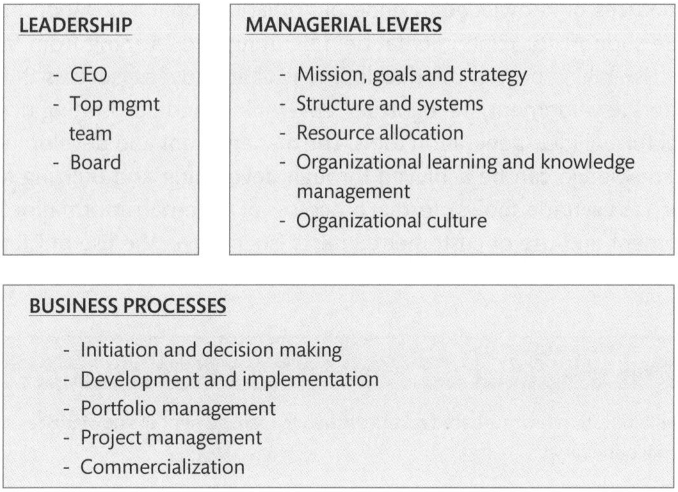

```
┌─────────────────────┐  ┌──────────────────────────────────────────┐
│ LEADERSHIP          │  │ MANAGERIAL LEVERS                        │
│                     │  │                                          │
│   - CEO             │  │   - Mission, goals and strategy          │
│   - Top mgmt        │  │   - Structure and systems                │
│     team            │  │   - Resource allocation                  │
│   - Board           │  │   - Organizational learning and knowledge│
│                     │  │     management                           │
│                     │  │   - Organizational culture               │
└─────────────────────┘  └──────────────────────────────────────────┘

┌─────────────────────────────────────────────────────────────────────┐
│ BUSINESS PROCESSES                                                  │
│                                                                     │
│   - Initiation and decision making                                 │
│   - Development and implementation                                 │
│   - Portfolio management                                           │
│   - Project management                                             │
│   - Commercialization                                              │
└─────────────────────────────────────────────────────────────────────┘
```

Figure 7.2 Crossan and Apaydin's Determinants of Organizational Innovation

Source: adapted from Crossan and Apaydin (2010).

to facilitate innovation processes. Knowledge management and learning processes represent one of these key 'managerial levers'. Before considering them in detail, the other managerial levers are briefly outlined. Crossan and Apaydin (2010) identify five managerial levers which have been found to be important determinants of organizational innovation. These are the development of organizational goals, mission, and strategy, the way in which innovation processes are structured and organized within the broader organizational structure (such as the degree of centralization of innovation), the way in which innovation resources are allocated, the culture of the organization, and organizational learning and knowledge management processes.

While Crossan and Apaydin's (2010) model is very comprehensive, it is somewhat tentative, as the interrelationship between its various elements is somewhat sketchy and unclear. For example, how the various managerial levers link together is not articulated, and the link between the three types of factor is also relatively unspecified, with a relatively simplistic causal change being proposed which leads from leadership factors, to managerial levers to business processes. What Crossan and Apaydin propose is a framework which requires to be empirically evaluated. However, the aim here is to examine the role of learning and knowledge management processes in this model, rather than to critique their framework, and the remainder of this section thus has this focus.

In examining organizational learning and knowledge management processes, Crossan and Apaydin identify a number of mechanisms to facilitate the management and development of internal sources of knowledge (from existing employees), and also from external sources of knowledge from outside the organization. It is assumed that effective innovation involves the integration of both types of knowledge. While they don't explicitly use the term, this characterization of innovation processes has been conceptualized as 'open innovation' (West and Bogers 2014; Lakemond et al. 2016; see Definition). The effective management of internal sources of knowledge to underpin organizational innovation involves providing adequate support for experimentation; tolerating and learning from failed ideas; the adoption of risk-taking norms; the development of employees (such as through investing in training and development); recognizing, developing, and celebrating diversity; and the utilization of formal idea-generation tools. The management and development of external sources of knowledge can be achieved through developing and utilizing formal external linkages (such as via trade shows), formal processes of (external) information gathering, and the development and use of customer contacts (such as via the use of CRM systems—see Illustration 7.2).

> **DEFINITION Open innovation**
>
> A distributed innovation process based on the deliberate management of knowledge across organizational boundaries.

In considering innovation as involving the utilization of both internal (organizational) knowledge and external sources of knowledge highlights the important role played by knowledge integration in innovation processes. With the type of open innovation considered by Crossan and Apaydin, innovation does not occur via either using internal knowledge or external knowledge, but through the effective synthesis and combination of internal and external sources of knowledge. In considering this issue, the concept of absorptive capacity is highly relevant (see Definition). An organization's absorptive capacity refers to its ability to identify, integrate, and utilize external sources of knowledge. This was a concept and topic that was already touched on towards the end of Chapter 2.

> **DEFINITION Absorptive capacity**
>
> An organization's ability to understand, absorb, and use external knowledge.

An organization's absorptive capacity refers to its ability to effectively utilize external sources of knowledge. An enormous amount has been written about the concept since it was developed by Cohen and Levinthal (1990). Research has examined the antecedents of absorptive capacity, the extent to which absorptive capacity affects knowledge acquisition and innovation, as well as the development and refinement of the concept (Zahra and George 2002). In refining the concept it has been broken down into a number of discrete knowledge processes including acquisition, assimilation, transformation, and exploitation (Miller et al. 2016). However, constraints of space prevent the full examination of these topics, which are instead illustrated by a couple of empirical examples (discussed later in the chapter; see Illustration 7.3). A key issue to highlight, in the context of this chapter, is that empirical research has identified the positive role that absorptive capacity can play in processes of organizational innovation (Su et al. 2013; Costa and Montiero 2016; Lakemond et al. 2016; Miller et al. 2016).

Illustration **7.3** University knowledge transfer processes: open innovation and absorptive capacity

Miller et al. (2016) characterized the transfer and commercialization of university knowledge as a process of open innovation. This is because it involves a diverse range of different stakeholders including universities, government, and industry. They use the concept of absorptive capacity, differentiated into discrete processes of acquisition, assimilation, transformation, and exploitation, to understand the factors which influence the success of such cross-organizational knowledge transfer processes. Their research found that five key factors influenced the effectiveness of these knowledge transfer processes. First, there were human-centric factors, such as people's attitude towards engaging in such activity as well as the extent to which they are embedded in relevant networks. Second, there were organizational factors, such as processes used to organize knowledge transfer (equivalent to the business processes in Crossan and Apaydin's model—see Figure 7.2). Third, there were issues of power and conflict, with the interests of participants not always totally overlapping. Fourth, there were issues related to the character and quality of the social relationships in the knowledge transfer network (such as trust levels). Finally, the characteristics of the knowledge being transferred were also relevant, such as the extent to which it was tacit or explicit.

Questions

What are the managerial implications of these findings? Which of the five factors identified are most amenable to managerial control and influence?

The discussion of innovation here, which examined the concepts of absorptive capacity and open innovation, and which emphasized that organizational innovation processes increasingly involve collaboration with external organizations, links to issues discussed in Chapter 13. That chapter is on boundary-spanning knowledge processes, where people who collaborate may have a different sense of identity and work for different organizations. Thus the issues discussed there, such as the importance and challenges of developing trust in this context, and the facilitative role that can be played by people acting as boundary-spanners, are all relevant to understanding the character of the open innovation processes examined here. Thus in considering the type of open innovation processes emphasized by Crossan and Apaydin's model, it is useful to read Chapter 13 in parallel.

Conclusion

While examining innovation and knowledge creation processes, the focus in this chapter has been deliberately narrow, examining only two specific frameworks: Nonaka's SECI model of knowledge creation, and Crossan and Apaydin's multidimensional innovation model. Nonaka's framework was examined as it is highly influential and extensively referenced.

The majority of the chapter has thus been devoted to briefly articulating some of the key elements of Nonaka's knowledge creation theory. At the centre of this theory is the distinction between tacit and explicit knowledge, with knowledge being created through the conversion of knowledge from one form to another. However, Nonaka's theory also incorporated ideas regarding the type of organizational context and environment likely to facilitate knowledge creation processes. In doing this Nonaka developed the concept of *ba*, or shared space, to highlight how each type of knowledge creation is facilitated by a different type of interaction between people, with these interactions being shaped by the character of the space they occur in. While Nonaka's theory is very influential and extensively referenced, there are still a number of limitations to it, not least that many aspects of it remain to be fully empirically evaluated. Further critiques relate to the way tacit knowledge and knowledge conversion processes are conceptualized and the extent to which it is a theory which is relevant beyond the Japanese business and cultural context that it was developed in.

However, there are a wide range of perspectives with which to analyse processes of innovation and knowledge creation, and thus it is important to consider more than Nonaka's work. Crossan and Apaydin's framework on innovation was examined as it represents one of the broadest and most comprehensive frameworks on innovation. A key feature of this framework is the importance attached to utilization of both internal sources of knowledge. In understanding how organizations utilize external sources of knowledge it was argued that the concept of absorptive capacity was useful.

 Case study Knowledge creation, absorptive capacity, and product innovativeness

Su et al. report on the findings of a study into the factors influencing the effectiveness of new product development (NPD) processes within Chinese manufacturing firms. NPD is defined as a form of product innovation, where products are adapted and developed. A firm's product innovativeness refers to its ability to develop and combine new knowledge to solve product-related problems. This is acknowledged to involve both the development and use of new knowledge within a firm (defined as knowledge creation capability), and also with the identification, integration, and use of external sources of knowledge (defined as absorptive capacity).

Su et al. develop a research model to test the relationship between these variables and an organization's level of product innovativeness. They hypothesize that both a firm's knowledge creation capability and absorptive capacity will be positively related to its level of product innovativeness. Further, they argue that product innovativeness is not just related to the use of these two separate sources of new knowledge, but also to how they are combined and integrated. Thus they also hypothesize that a positive synergy between knowledge creation capability and absorptive capacity will be positively related to an organization's product innovativeness.

They also investigate how technological turbulence, defined as the amount of technological change in an industry, affects these relationships. Increasing levels of technological turbulence are argued to positively moderate the relationship between knowledge creation capability and product innovativeness. This is because, when levels of turbulence are high, organizations need to continually develop new knowledge to remain innovative. In contrast, the researchers suggest that increasing levels of technological turbulence will negatively moderate the relationship between absorptive capacity and product innovativeness. This is because when levels of turbulence are high, there is a likelihood that external knowledge that is absorbed may quickly become out of date and thus of limited use.

Su et al. tested their research model via conducting a survey-based study of a diverse range of Chinese manufacturing firms from a number of different regions. Surveys were completed in 2009 and 2010 by over 240 organizations.

When the statistical analysis of the survey data was completed, all hypotheses were supported. Thus, a firm's product innovativeness was positively related to not only its ability to create new forms of internal knowledge, or acquire and utilize external sources of knowledge, but the extent to which it is able to combine both forms of knowledge together. Further, the greater the level of technological turbulence, the more important knowledge creation capabilities are, and the less important absorptive capacity is.

In terms of managerial implications, to optimize its level of product innovativeness firms should simultaneously develop both their knowledge creation capabilities and absorptive capacity, and also make efforts to combine the knowledge produced by these efforts.

Source: Su, Z., Ahlstrom, D., Li, J., and Cheng, D (2013) 'Knowledge Creation, Absorptive Capacity, and Product Innovativeness', *R&D Management*, 43/5: 473-85.

Question

1. From a managerial perspective, to what extent are there likely to be difficulties and challenges involved in simultaneously developing an organization's ability to create new knowledge and utilize external sources of knowledge?

 ## Review and Discussion Questions

1. To what extent, if at all, can tacit knowledge be articulated and made explicit?

2. Think of a country whose culture and business practices you are relatively familiar with, and reflect on the extent to which business organizations there would be able to effectively utilize Nonaka's knowledge creation theory.

3. To what extent do you agree with the critique of Nonaka's knowledge creation framework that the evidence presented by Nonaka in support of it is anecdotal and unconvincing?

4. Of the two perspectives on innovation presented, which do you find the most convincing and why?

 ## Suggestions for Further Reading

I. Nonaka and G. von Krogh (2009). 'Tacit Knowledge and Knowledge Conversion: Controversy and Advancement in Organizational Knowledge Creation Theory', *Organization Science*, 20/3: 635–52.
A response to the epistemological critique of knowledge creation theory made by Gourlay and others.

T. Andreeva and I. Ikhilchik (2011). 'Applicability of the SECI Model of Knowledge Creation in Russian Cultural Context: Theoretical Analysis', *Knowledge and Process Management*, 18/1: 56–66.
Considers the relevance of SECI knowledge creation process to the context of Russia.

M. Crossan and M. Apaydin (2010). 'A Multidimensional Framework of Organizational Innovation', *Journal of Management Studies*, 47/6: 1154–91.
A comprehensive review of the academic literature on innovation which develops a multidimensional model of its key determinants, one of which is learning and knowledge management.

J. West and M. Bogers (2014). 'Leveraging External Sources of Innovation: A Review of Research on Open Innovation', *Journal of Product Innovation Management*, 31/4: 814–31.
A review of the literature on open innovation which examines the importance of utilizing external knowledge sources.

 To further your understanding of knowledge management in organizations explore the book's accompanying online resources at **www.oup.com/uk/hislop4e/**

8 Unlearning, Knowledge Loss, and the Protection of Knowledge

Introduction

While processes of unlearning and forgetting or losing knowledge (accidentally or deliberately abandoning, giving up, or losing knowledge) and knowledge protection are neglected and rarely addressed in the knowledge management literature and textbooks, they are arguably crucial elements in organizational knowledge management change processes more generally. Primarily, this is because forgetting and unlearning are closely related to learning and the creation and acquisition of new knowledge (Lee 2011; Zahra et al. 2011). Unlearning as a special from of 'knowledge loss' necessitates replacement of obsolete knowledge that occurs as a result of knowledge loss or attrition. In addition, protection or guarding valuable knowledge against loss is also important for knowledge creation and sharing. Organizations need to protect their competitive knowledge from rivals and competitors in early stages of new product or service development. Knowledge protection is often overlooked in organizations as knowledge managers are more focused on encouraging flows and the sharing rather than protecting of knowledge.

Fundamentally, the *in*ability to unlearn or forget can produce rigidity in thinking and acting, and create a blinkering of outlook, which prevents change being implemented when necessary (Akgün, Byrne, et al. 2006; Tsang 2008). This can occur when existing views are never questioned or challenged. Further, the inability to reflect upon and question what may have been successful organizational norms, values, practices, and knowledge can create what have been referred to as 'competency traps' (see Chapter 6 and Shipton 2006), where useful competencies become outdated through never being challenged, revised, or abandoned.

Thus, the ability to unlearn and give up existing knowledge (routines, assumptions, values, behaviours, etc.) can be a catalyst to change, and can allow organizations to be adaptable (Becker 2010; see Illustration 8.1). Most fundamentally, the ability to acquire, develop, or create new knowledge is directly related to an organization's or person's ability to begin unlearning, through recognizing and acknowledging the limitations of existing knowledge (Tsang and Zahra 2008). In dynamic business environments where high levels of turbulence and change occur, the capacity to do so effectively is arguably crucial to organizational performance. This therefore helps explain why unlearning has been examined within the context of change, innovation, or learning processes. For example, studies have examined the role of unlearning in the context of knowledge transfer processes (Tsang 2008; Yildiz and Fey 2010), the implementation of tech-nological change (Becker 2008), processes of exploration and exploitation based learning in organizations (Cegarra-Navarro et al. 2011), in new product development teams (Akgün et al. 2007b; Lee and Sukoco 2011), and in processes of internationalization (Casillas et al. 2010).

Another reason for examining processes of unlearning is that research suggests that organi-zations and people find the process of giving up old ways of thinking and doing challenging and difficult. For example, research suggests that even the experience of failure in organiza-tions *rarely* results in the adequacy of existing knowledge/values/ideas/practices being reflected upon and that consequently few organizations are systematically able to un/learn from failure (Baumard and Starbuck 2005; Cannon and Edmondson 2005). This therefore raises questions regarding why people and organizations find such processes so difficult, which is one of the key topics addressed in this chapter.

This chapter's focus will cover three themes: first, unlearning as a means of deliberate for-getting or accidental loss of knowledge, learning, and change (see Illustration 8.1); second, knowledge leakage; and, third, knowledge protection. The chapter starts by differentiating between unlearning and forgetting (see Definition), and then examines the close and insepa-rable interrelationship between unlearning, learning, and change. Thereafter, different in-dividual and organizational-level factors that can act as barriers to forgetting are examined. Knowledge leakage is then introduced to distinguish between 'leakage' and 'loss', with a final section that describes how knowledge could be protected in organizations.

DEFINITION Unlearning versus forgetting

Unlearning refers to the ability to deliberately dispose of or discard obsolete, outdated, or unwanted knowledge. Forgetting refers to the loss of knowledge that is not necessarily intended or planned.

 Illustration 8.1 The role of unlearning in joint ventures

Tsang (2008) uses the concept of unlearning to understand what inhibited the transfer of knowledge during some international joint ventures involving Chinese companies. Further, in relation to unlearning, Tsang's focus was on the unlearning of organizational routines, with routines, following Feldman and Pentland, being defined as: 'repetitive patterns of interdependent actions carried out by multiple organizational members involved in performing organizational tasks' (Tsang 2008: 7). For Tsang unlearning represents a deliberate process, whereby old routines are discarded in favour of newer ones.

In the context of the type of acquisition-based joint ventures Tsang examined, the process of unlearning organizational routines represented an important stage crucial to their success. This is because with such joint ventures, the adaptation of an existing site and the retraining of an existing workforce, which are intrinsic elements in such initiatives, require the workers involved to give up and unlearn organizational routines as well as to learn new ones. For Tsang, this process of unlearning is thus both unavoidable and crucially important, as without it, workers are unlikely to learn new routines, and in such circumstances joint ventures have a high chance of failure.

Tsang conceptualized the transfer of knowledge during joint ventures as involving four separate but overlapping and interrelated processes. First, there is the initiation stage, which consists of processes leading up to the decision to undertake the joint venture. Second is the implementation stage during which knowledge is transferred from one party in the joint venture to the other. Third is the ramp-up stage where the recipients of the acquired knowledge begin to make use of it in carrying out their work. Fourth and last is the integration stage, whereby the newly acquired knowledge and routines become established and institutionalized. While Tsang's analysis examined what inhibited unlearning during each of these stages, the focus here is purely on the ramp-up and integration stages.

At the ramp-up stage a key indicator of unlearning was that despite this being a phase when workers were meant to be utilizing the new routines, they often continued to utilize the old work routines that they were more familiar with. This was most likely to occur when the joint venture partner only sent a few managers to the site of the joint venture to help with the utilization of the new routines. It was also likely to occur where the old, established routines concerned were highly socially embedded. Finally, at the integration, as with the ramp-up phase, a key indicator of unlearning was that a number of workers still continued to use existing routines rather than utilize the new ones. However, over time, as people's memories faded and the new routines became more familiar, such processes became less pronounced. Time thus facilitated the abandonment of old routines, partly through the fact that staff who had been familiar with the old routines left the organization.

Question

Suppose you are one of the managers who oversees the uptake of a new routine in a particular new joint venture site. You notice that the uptake of this routine is not as fast as expected. What would you do to expedite the uptake of this routine?

Unlearning and forgetting in organizational contexts

While the topics of unlearning and forgetting are neglected in the knowledge management literature, and are generally underresearched topics (Tsang and Zahra 2008), there is a growing body of conceptual and empirical work on topics such as the nature of forgetting, unlearning, and their relationship to change and learning (Akgün et al. 2007a; Tsang and Zahra 2008; Easterby-Smith and Lyles 2011), what the antecedents of unlearning are (Lee 2011; Cegarra-Navarro et al. 2012, 2013), and what the consequences of unlearning are (Tsang 2008; Casillas et al. 2010; Wong et al. 2012).

The ability to deliberately forget and give up existing knowledge is a necessary and important precursor to the creation and development of new knowledge. This means that deliberately forgetting/giving up knowledge and knowledge creation are closely related topics. For example, the creation of new knowledge may require the discarding of old routines (unlearning) to make way for new routines (learning). Notably, unlearning and forgetting can occur at the individual, team, or group levels in organizations and relate to both the objectivist and practice-based perspectives on knowledge (see Part 1). For example, unlearning or forgetting impacts human activity and might result from unlearning or forgetting of tacit and/or explicit knowledge, and vice-versa.

Unlearning as a type of deliberate forgetting

Although the terms unlearning and forgetting overlap, they are different. Unlearning encourages the replacement of knowledge while forgetting refers to the actual 'shedding' or 'getting rid' of knowledge. While it has been suggested thus far in the chapter that, in general terms, the ability to unlearn, forget, and give up knowledge can be a useful organizational capability, it is important to make clear that not all forms of abandoning or giving up knowledge are functional for organizations, and they can have potentially dysfunctional consequences (Easterby-Smith and Lyles 2011). Intentional forgetting is required when firms need to expand and build their knowledge base since old practices and procedures may not necessarily be applicable any more when new routines require the development and adoption of new capabilities and procedures. Institutionalized knowledge may be difficult to unlearn or 'erase' from an organization's memory, while forgetting can be detrimental to an organization. For example the loss of a key source of knowledge, which can occur when specialist staff leave an organization, may have quite negative organizational implications (Massingham 2008—see also Chapters 5 and 15).

Distinguishing between what constitutes useful and dysfunctional knowledge loss requires defining and differentiating between the specific and distinctive forms that it can take. One of the most fundamental distinctions that can be made is between the *accidental* and *deliberate* loss of knowledge. Accidental knowledge loss is where knowledge and capabilities are lost inadvertently, while deliberate knowledge loss involves a conscious process of giving up and abandoning knowledge, values, and/or practices, which are deemed to have become outdated. In general terms, unintentional or accidental processes of loss are typically understood as having generally negative and dysfunctional consequences, while deliberate processes of loss are regarded as having positive consequences for the organizations which undertake them (De Holan and Phillips 2004; Akgün, Byrne, et al. 2006; Zahra et al. 2011). Thus, organizations need to get the balance right between retaining, protecting, and developing knowledge that is useful and important, while simultaneously being able to discard, forget, unlearn, or give up knowledge which has become outdated and of limited contemporary use. Achieving such a balance is by no means easy.

A useful typology that helps differentiate between different types of knowledge loss is De Holan and Phillips's (2004) typology of organizational forgetting (see Figure 8.1). This typology combines the distinction between accidental and deliberate forgetting, with a distinction between newly acquired/developed knowledge and established knowledge, which constitutes an accepted and existing part of an organization's knowledge base.

The first form of forgetting is the accidental forgetting of existing or established knowledge, which de Holan and Phillips (2004) define as memory loss. This form of forgetting is typical when knowledge is used infrequently. In such situations, organizations may forget knowledge through the loss to the organization of the people who possess it, or where an organization loses the ability to carry out long unused, informal, and uncodified work routines because the capability to carry them out has been forgotten through lack of use (see Time to reflect). The second form of forgetting is the accidental forgetting of new knowledge, which is defined as a failure to capture new knowledge. This occurs when new knowledge is acquired and developed by one individual or a small group of workers, which, through not becoming institutionalized, becomes forgotten or lost by the wider organization. A common example of this form of forgetting occurs with project-based working in which, when project teams break up, often most of the learning they have acquired/developed is then lost to the wider organization through not having been effectively shared or codified (Scarbrough, Bresnan, et al. 2004).

MODE OF FORGETTING

	Accidental	Intentional
From existing stock	MEMORY LOSS	UNLEARNING
SOURCE OF KNOWLEDGE		
Newly innovated	FAILURE TO CAPTURE	AVOID BAD HABITS

Figure 8.1 Typology of Organizational Forgetting

Source: de Holan and Phillips (2004).

While Figure 8.1 focuses on organizational forgetting, there are also other examples of knowledge loss that significantly impact organizations. Examples are attrition of knowledge through retirement with an ageing workforce, the retrenchment of workers as a result of mergers and acquisitions, downsizing, and redeployment in organizations (Martins and Martins 2011). Another example of knowledge loss is when senior or highly experienced employees resign and move across to competitor organizations to take up new or higher positions. These employees take multiple years of experience with them which can advantage the new organization. So, while the loss of an expert to one organization is the gain to another organization, this is an interesting problem from a human resources perspective, which can be addressed in many different ways for example with an embargo, which prohibits an employee from working for a rival organization for a certain amount of time after leaving the organization.

 Time to reflect   Technology and unintentional forgetting

To what extent does the development of technology, such as computer and communications technologies and industrial robotics, lead to particular technical skills and capabilities being forgotten by organizations? Can you think of examples of specific skills (spelling, letter writing) that have been forgotten in this way due to the development of computers and mobile phones? Is the loss of such capabilities likely to ever be a problem for business organizations? Can you think of specific situations where the loss of such technical skills/competencies might cause problems for organizations?

The other two forms of forgetting are quite different, involving the deliberate and conscious process of forgetting organizational knowledge. First is the intentional forgetting of newly acquired knowledge, referred to as avoiding bad habits. This form of forgetting starts from the assumption that not all learning is necessarily positive, and that as a consequence, whenever new knowledge, values, ideas, routines, practices, etc., are learned, a conscious process of reflection should occur to decide whether they are useful to retain or not. An example of when such a process may be useful is during and after joint ventures, where efforts could be made to ensure any potentially dysfunctional habits learned do not become institutionalized. Finally, the fourth form of forgetting is the intentional forgetting, loss, or abandonment of established organizational knowledge, referred to by de Holan and Phillips (2004) as unlearning. This definition of unlearning as deliberately abandoning or giving up knowledge is the most common way in which unlearning is defined in relevant literature (Tsang and Zahra 2008). Organizations and their staff generally find this to be a challenging and difficult process. Part of the reason why unlearning is difficult is that it involves reflecting on and being prepared to give up knowledge and practices which may be taken for granted, and which are deeply embedded in organizational routines and cultures.

Unlearning, learning, and change

The challenges involved in unlearning of established knowledge and behaviours link to the themes raised in Chapter 11 and beyond regarding the problems and challenges of motivating workers to participate in knowledge management processes such as unlearning.

As outlined earlier, the ability to unlearn is particularly useful during processes of change, as change arguably involves both the ability to unlearn and to learn. Thus Hayes (2002: 7) characterizes change as requiring people to both 'unlearn old ways and develop new competencies'. This therefore raises questions regarding the relationship between unlearning, learning, and change, which is the topic that is briefly examined here.

In terms of the relationship between learning and unlearning, Tsang and Zahra (2008) consider that various relationships are possible, and that unlearning may precede, occur simultaneously with, or be independent of learning. The dominant perspective in the unlearning literature is that unlearning is a distinctive process and is a prerequisite to, and a precursor of, learning (Becker et al. 2006; Akgün et al. 2007a; Cegarra-Navarro et al. 2010). However, there is also another way to conceptualize the relationship between learning and unlearning and that is to consider unlearning as a specific and particular type of learning (Antonacopoulou 2009). This is the perspective that is also utilized by Argyris and Schön (1996: 3–4), who argued that

> we may also speak of the particular kind of learning that consists of 'unlearning': acquiring information that leads to subtracting something (an obsolete strategy, for example) from an organization's existing store of knowledge.

Overall therefore, while it is acknowledged that learning and unlearning are closely interrelated, there isn't a consensus in the unlearning literature regarding the nature of their relationship.

Illustration 8.2 Facilitating unlearning during change

Becker (2010) reports the findings of a survey-based study into the factors which facilitated and inhibited unlearning during a process of change in a single Australian company. The company concerned was a large government-owned corporation in the energy sector that had approximately 5,000 employees. The change process examined was the implementation of an organization-wide enterprise information system, and the survey was given to over 200 people who had a direct role in the change programme. The analysis identified seven factors which had significantly influenced people's attitude to unlearning, with five of these being individual-level factors related to employees, and two of which were organization-level factors. The five individual factors were: the extent to which people had a positive outlook, the extent to which people had negative feelings regarding the change, the extent to which people experience good levels of informal peer support, the extent to which people understood the need for change, and finally, the extent to which people perceived the new ways of working to be an improvement on the old ones.

Here, only two of these factors are considered in detail. First, in terms of feelings and emotions the survey found that the more negative and apprehensive people felt about the change that was being implemented, the more likely they would be to resist the change, and the greater the barriers there would be to unlearning old and established ways of working. Second, in terms of the final individual factor, it was found that the more people perceived the change to be positive and beneficial, the more likely they would be to unlearn and abandon old ways of working.

The two organizational-level factors that affected people's attitude to unlearning were: people's previous experiences of change in the same organization, and the extent to which people were given formal support and training. In relation to previous experiences, it was found that the more people had had negative previous experiences of change, the more likely they would be to resist any further change, and the less likely they would be to unlearn. Finally, unsurprisingly, the more formal support and training people were provided, the more positive their attitudes to unlearning were likely to be.

Question

Based on this analysis, what recommendations and advice would you give to a company wanting to create a positive attitude to unlearning with respect to a forthcoming change initiative?

While the vast majority of the unlearning literature suggests that unlearning is a precursor for or facilitator of change (see for example Becker 2010, discussed in Illustration 8.2), only a few papers consider the relationship between unlearning and change in any depth. One such paper is Akgün et al.'s (2007a) conceptual paper. Akgün et al. (2007b) explicitly link to Lewin's (much criticized) three-stage model of change. This relatively simplistic model of change suggests that change happens via the sequential processes of unfreezing, change, and refreezing (Hayes 2002: 52; Akgün et al. 2007b). Akgün et al. assume that unlearning and learning together constitute the second stage in Lewin's model. Tsang and Zahra (2008) also examine the relationship between learning, unlearning, and organizational change. They distinguish between two distinct types of change (continuous and episodic) and suggest that each type of change will involve a different form of unlearning. They define continuous change as change that is incremental and gradual in character. By contrast, episodic change is typically discontinuous, infrequent, and greater in scope than continuous change.

Table 8.1 Types of Unlearning

Type of Unlearning	Wiping	Deep Unlearning
Catalyst	Change programme	Unexpected individual experience
Level/type of impact	Typically focused on behaviours	Unlearning of behaviours and knowledge/values/beliefs
Speed of unlearning	Variable	Typically sudden
Emotional impact	Variable	Typically significant

Source: Rushmer and Davies (2004).

Tsang and Zahra (2008) thus raise the idea that there may be different types of unlearning—an idea also examined by some other writers on the topic (see for example Akgün et al. 2007a). One of the most useful unlearning typologies, which is focused on individual rather than organizational unlearning, is developed by Rushmer and Davies (2004). While they distinguish three types of unlearning, which they label fading, wiping, and deep unlearning, fading, which involves the accidental and gradual loss of knowledge over time, is more akin to what is here defined as forgetting. Rushmer and Davies argue that each type of unlearning differs significantly (see Table 8.1).

For Rushmer and Davies, the typical catalyst for the type of unlearning they define as wiping is a change initiative external to the person (see, for example, Becker 2010). Wiping is thus a process of unlearning that results from a deliberate process of change that has been externally imposed on people. Wiping is deliberate and conscious and is typically focused on a relatively narrow practice or activity where a person consciously gives up a particular way of behaving. The other type of unlearning referred to by Rushmer and Davies is deep unlearning. This radical form of unlearning is argued to occur rapidly as a result of an external event whose characteristics and/or outcomes are unexpected, and which suddenly brings into question some basic assumptions that people have. It is argued to have a significant impact on the individuals who experience it, leading them to question their values and beliefs. Deep unlearning may result in people experiencing strong emotions such as anxiety, fear, and confusion. However, the vast majority of the unlearning literature talks about unlearning in generic terms, and does not distinguish between different types of unlearning. Thus in the remains of the chapter, no further reference will be made to different types of unlearning.

Antecedents of unlearning

As outlined previously, research into unlearning suggests that there are many factors that influence the willingness of people and organizations to unlearn. The focus of this section is on examining these factors, the antecedents of unlearning, where it will be shown that a heterogeneous range of factors have been found to inhibit and facilitate people's wiliness to unlearn. This section separates these factors into two distinct types. First to be examined are individual-level factors, those related to the character, personality, and attitude of people. The second type of factor to be considered is more related to the organizational context.

Individual-level antecedents of unlearning

The first potential individual-level barrier to unlearning is the negative emotions that un-learning and giving up knowledge can generate. As was highlighted in Chapter 6, learning of any type, while being potentially positive and enjoyable, can also stir up negative emotions in people. The feelings of fear and anxiety that unlearning can generate relate to admitting the limitations to, and giving up knowledge and practices which may have provided a person with a sense of competence, self-identity, and self-esteem. For example, the studies of Becker (2010) and Lee and Sukoco (2011) both found that people's emotional state, and the extent to which people experience negative feelings of anxiety, was negatively related to their willing-ness to unlearn.

Research also suggests that unlearning which is related to admitting to and learning from failure can be an even more difficult process for people to undertake (Baumard and Starbuck 2005; Shepherd et al. 2011; Zhao 2011). One of the general conclusions of research in this area was that people don't like admitting to failure. This was partly due to the stigma that can be attached to being involved in or responsible for failure. Thus, Wilkinson and Mellahi (2005) suggest this typically means that failure is a brush to be tarred with rather than something to be admitted and learned from. Cannon and Edmondson's (2005) research suggests that deep psychological factors, related to the importance people attach to, sustaining feelings of self-competence and, how people's esteem and competence is judged by others, help explain why people are unwilling to admit to and learn from failure. Thus they suggest that 'being held in high regard by other people, especially those with whom one interacts in an ongoing manner, is a strong fundamental human desire, and most people tacitly believe that revealing failure will jeopardize this esteem', and that as a consequence 'most people have a natural aversion to disclosing or even publicly acknowledging failure' (Cannon and Edmond-son 2005: 302). (See Time to reflect).

 Time to reflect   Admitting to and learning from failure

In your own experience, is admitting to failure and using it as a positive learning experience uncommon? Can you think of examples where failure has been regarded in this way and where people have been willing to admit responsibility for failure?

Another general factor, which can act as an individual-level barrier to unlearning, re-lates to how people may perceive undertaking a process of unlearning as threatening and undermining their self-interest through the way it may impact not only their status and esteem, but also the power they possess and the interests they are trying to pursue. Fundamentally, if people perceive that unlearning threatens to reduce the power they possess, this may inhibit them from doing so. This links to a point made in Chapter 13, in relation to cross-community knowledge processes that was made by Carlile (2002, 2004). Carlile, adopting a practice-based perspective on knowledge, suggested that the way in which people's knowledge is 'invested in practice' means that they may be reluctant to participate in processes they perceive will threaten their interests through requiring them to adapt and change their knowledge and practices.

In such situations, people may actively try and resist unlearning through carrying out what have been called defensive routines. Tranfield et al. (2000), based on an empirical study whose analysis built on Argyris's (1990) work on defensive routines, found that different groups of workers utilized particular defensive routines which acted as barriers to unlearning. Tranfield et al. (2000) define routines as 'habits', repetitive patterns of behaviour, which are often un-conscious and which have cognitive, behavioural, and structural elements to them. Argyris (1990) defined a defensive routine as: 'any policies or actions that prevent organizational players from experiencing embarrassment or threat while preventing the organization from uncovering the causes of the embarrassment or threat in order to reduce or get rid of them.' Defensive routines are thus repeated behaviours that allow people to avoid admitting to and dealing with any limitations that exist in their thinking and/or actions. Thus, if people are unwilling to unlearn, they might do more than passively resist engaging in such processes: they may proactively behave in ways that undermine attempts to unlearn through reinforcing existing knowledge, behaviours, and practices.

Cognitive-level factors can also act as a potential barrier to unlearning, through blinkering people's thinking and creating a sense of cognitive myopia and inertia. Nystrom and Starbuck (2003) suggest that unlearning can be conceptualized as a process of cognitive reorientation, in which people need to give up traditional and accepted ways of understanding and em-brace the need to develop and utilize new ones. However, people's cognitive structures shape how they see, interpret, and understand events. If particular views, values, ideas, and practices have been successful in the past, people can become (unconsciously) quite attached to them and be unwilling to give them up, and may become unaware how they blinker and constrain how they understand and interpret events. In the vocabulary of the learning literature, this can result in what may have previously been core competencies evolving into 'competency traps' (Shipton 2006), which trap people in past-focused ways of understanding the world.

Finally, when unlearning is linked to a change initiative, the attitude of people to the change process has been found to affect the extent to which people are prepared to engage in unlearn-ing. For example Becker's (2010—see Illustration 8.2) study of unlearning during a process of change in an Australian organization found that people's attitude to unlearning was affected both by the extent to which people felt change was necessary, and by the extent to which they felt that the changes being implemented were a positive improvement. Thus, if people do not believe that change is necessary, or if they believe that the type of changes being implemented are not beneficial, this is likely to negatively affect their willingness to unlearn.

Organizational-level antecedents of unlearning

Research on unlearning also suggests that a number of factors related to the organizational con-text can also play a significant role in influencing whether people are willing to unlearn (Cegarra-Navarro et al. 2011, 2012), and it is such organizational-level factors that are considered here.

Nystrom and Starbuck (2003) suggest that the embedding and institutionalization of knowl-edge, values, and practices in standard operating procedures and specific work practices can create an inertia that makes them difficult to change. Typically, the longer that work practices have been institutionalized, the more they become taken for granted and unquestioned, and the more difficult they become to change as people become unused to questioning the as-sumptions on which they work, and new staff members become socialized into particular ways of working. This links to the findings of Tsang's (2008–Illustration 8.1) study, where the extent to which routines were socially embedded in an organization affected the extent to which people were prepared to unlearn existing ways of working, and embrace new ones.

One of the findings from Baumard and Starbuck's (2005) study of fourteen failures in a single European telecommunications company was the following: the strong unwillingness among people to admit to involvement in or responsibility for failure produced a number of distortions in organizational communication systems which acted as a barrier to unlearning. Cegarra-Navarro et al. (2011) reinforce this and found that the nature of communication processes was an important element of the organizational context which affected people's attitude to unlearning. Some specific examples of the distorted forms of communication that Baumard and Starbuck (2005) found included:

- Failures were not reported (often in the hope/expectation that any problems would disappear over time).
- Findings/events which contradicted institutionalized beliefs/norms were often dismissed and ignored.
- The nature of any failures that were admitted were explained as having limited significance through being regarded as transitory 'blips' that would not be repeated.
- Small-scale successes were exaggerated.
- There was a general tendency to challenge/resist/subvert/hide analyses which implicated people as being in some way responsible for failure.

Another organizational-level factor which has been found to affect people's attitude to unlearning is the nature of their jobs. Lee (2011) examined the role that challenge and hindrance stressors had on people's attitude to unlearning. Both these factors relate to the nature of people's jobs. Challenge stressors relate to the complexity of people's jobs and the opportunities that jobs provide people to be creative and solve problems. Lee found that such stressors were positively linked to people's attitudes to unlearning. Hindrance stressors are more negative factors related to people's jobs such as the extent to which administrative factors inhibit the completion of work tasks or the degree of ambiguity that exists in people's roles. Lee (2011) found that such stressors were negatively related to people's attitude to unlearning. Thus, from a managerial point of view, the implications of Lee's (2011) study are that to facilitate unlearning, people should have clear unambiguous jobs, and also have jobs that require people to routinely be creative and solve problems.

One means to actively facilitate unlearning involves deliberately introducing new, external ideas, knowledge, practices, and values into an organization with the objective of encouraging or forcing people to reflect on and question their existing values and assumptions. A number of specific ways that this can be done have been suggested. One of Nystrom and Starbuck's (2003) suggestions on how to do this, fitting with their argument that senior management have a major responsibility for discouraging unlearning, is to sack senior management and replace them with a new senior management team. This radical way of facilitating unlearning is argued to work through bringing new, enthusiastic people into the organization, allowing senior management to carry the major responsibility for any problems and failures, and through encouraging existing staff to engage in a process of cognitive reorientation by engaging with the ideas brought into the organization by the new senior management team.

Two other less radical ways of introducing new ideas into an organization were identified by Tranfield et al. (2000), who found two specific enabling routines that facilitated unlearning by this means. First, the enabling routine entitled 'envisioning what we might become' involved bringing external consultants into an organization who, through how they organized meetings and discussions, forced people to justify and reflect on their taken-for-granted assumptions and values. This is comparable with Akgün, Lynn, et al.'s (2006) suggestion to challenge and undermine existing ideas through forcing work teams to deal with outsiders who played the role of a 'devil's advocate', deliberately questioning people's beliefs. The second enabling routine entitled 'benchmark others' achievements' by Tranfield et al. (2000) introduce new ideas to staff by organizing exchange visits with comparable firms who carry out their work differently, and organizing secondments allowing people to move between business units within the same organization to learn different business practices.

A number of suggestions have also been made regarding the way in which management can facilitate a process of unlearning and learning from failure. For example, Cannon and Edmondson (2005) and Provera et al. (2010) suggest that middle managers can do this via carrying out blameless discussions, and generally creating 'a safe environment where errors can be openly discussed' (Zhao 2011: 458).

Another general means of enhancing an organization's capacity to unlearn is through the retraining of existing staff. First, Akgün, Lynn, et al. (2006) suggest that training staff in lateral thinking has the potential to endow workers with the capability to contemplate ideas that challenge their existing norms and values. Second, Becker (2010) found that providing access to training represented a way to facilitate attitudes to unlearning during change initiatives.

A couple of team-level factors have also been found to affect people's attitude to unlearning. Thus, one of the seven factors identified by Becker (2010) that positively affected the attitude of people to unlearning was the amount of informal support from peers they received. Second, Lee and Sukoco (2011—see this chapter's case study) found that levels of reflexivity in teams, which refers to the ability of a team to question and reflect on the ongoing utility of existing knowledge and practices, was also positively related to a team member's attitude to unlearning.

Knowledge leakage

While the deliberate forgetting and loss of knowledge in organizations is useful and in some instances necessary, there is also another form of knowledge loss, which is referred to as *leakage*(see Definition). Leakage is different to knowledge loss in the sense that loss leaves a significant gap that requires change to occur in the form of learning. Leakage relates to vital/ competitive organizational knowledge that leaves a safe environment, moving into or being released into another environment where this knowledge can be used or applied in either the same way or in new competitive ways (Ahmad et al. 2014). Leakage can either be deliberate or accidental and can occur at the individual, group, or organizational level. A typical example is the leakage of sensitive knowledge that is essential for the firm to retain its position in the business market. Imagine the erosion of competitive advantage that may follow this leak in the event of this knowledge being intercepted and exploited by rivals, and the potential damage to the reputation of the organization from which this leak occurred. An example of deliberate leakage is a disgruntled employee who may feel that s/he is unfairly treated or underpaid. This employee may *deliberately share confidential knowledge* with rival organizations, which can eventually turn out to be harmful to the organization being exposed. Or an employee may unintentionally share confidential insights or knowledge about a product in an informal conversation which may be overheard by a rival. Although these may seem to be knowledge loss, it can rather be classified as knowledge leakage. What is true is that the leakage of confidential knowledge may result in the loss of competitive organizational knowledge (Ahmad et al. 2014). (See Time to reflect.)

DEFINITION   **Knowledge leakage**

The accidental or deliberate disclosure of confidential organizational knowledge which, when intercepted, may significantly erode or impact the competitive advantage of the firm from which the knowledge leaked.

 Time to reflect   Leakage and technology

Information leakage through technology is more prominent in the news nowadays—do you think that knowledge can 'leak' through technology use?

Another example of accidental knowledge leakage occurs in strategic alliances, in other words an agreement between two or more parties to share resources while undertaking a mutually agreed project while the organizations remain independent. In this scenario this type of relationship exposes both firms' knowledge, which opens up opportunities for expropriation hazards (Jiang et al. 2013). Another example of accidental leakage could occur when organizations collaborate, for example offshoring or outsourcing of some of a firm's operations could incur the loss of an organization's core competences (Ritala et al. 2015). The organization being outsourced to could glean new insights of the other organization which implies accidental leakage. To overcome challenges associated with leakage in these types of collaborations, non-disclosure agreements (NDAs) or other legal agreements are required to protect sensitive organizational organizational knowledge.

Leakage from tacit and explicit knowledge perspectives

It can be useful to view leakage from two perspectives—a tacit and explicit knowledge perspective, or an objectivist or practice-based knowledge perspective (refer to Part 1), as a discussion about knowledge protection would be different when considering either of these. Since tacit knowledge is highly personal and based on experience and subjective insights, one can argue that tacit knowledge as 'individual insights that exist in one's mind' is more difficult to leak as tacit knowledge is self-protecting. This is because tacit knowledge is difficult to operationalize or imitate (Wu and Lin 2013) and is by nature sticky and closely bounded to those that possess it. These attributes make it difficult to translate or convert tacit knowledge into explicit knowledge (Polanyi 1983). However, explicit knowledge is subject to deliberate or accidental leakage as explicit knowledge is usually stored or embedded in manual or electronic files, folders, and repositories. Therefore, highly competitive tacit knowledge that can be converted into a formal or informal explicit form is vulnerable and susceptible to leakage.

Informal forms of explicit knowledge include handwritten notes, diagrams, or figures, while examples of formal explicit knowledge (also referred to as codified knowledge) are artefacts that embed knowledge, for example: policies, standard operating procedures, lessons learnt, methodologies, or procedural guidelines. Notably, the risk of accidental or deliberate leakage of an organization's competitive knowledge (in either tacit or explicit form) could be catastrophic if a rival organization has the *capability to absorb leaked knowledge* to its own advantage (Ahmad et al. 2014). Note that even though leakage is of high concern to the organizations that are the source of the leak(s), not all individuals or organizations at the receiving end of the leak may have the capability (or know-how) to exploit leaked knowledge in a way that will seriously damage the reputation or erode the competitive advantage of the original organization. Besides, the organization from which the leak has occurred might have the capability to rapidly recover from a leak through reconfiguration of existing knowledge assets (Ritala et al. 2015).

The objectivist perspective of knowledge confirms that knowledge as an object can be made explicit, can exist independently of a human's mind, and therefore can leak more easily than tacit knowledge (see Chapter 2). Objective knowledge can leak from individuals or groups since collective group knowledge can be embedded in group-developed artefacts over time. Accidental or deliberate sharing of artefacts created by individuals or groups can easily fall into the wrong hands, particularly when using modern information and collaboration technologies to network and interact with other individuals and teams internal and external to the organization (see Chapters 9 and 10).

Also, the practice-based knowledge perspective views knowledge as being embedded in and inseparable from work activities and practices (see Chapter 3). Knowledge is therefore not only an object but is action-oriented and strongly tied to a specific context, which means that know-what and know-how is intertwined. Leakage of practice-based knowledge or know-how can occur when individual or group actions are observed (see Illustration 8.3). Take for example the highly specialized process of making flutes, which depends on highly skilled craftsmanship (Cook and Brown 1999). This process requires high quality standards and throughout this process parts of each flute need to be assessed according to specific standards that have been derived from many years of experience in the craft. If a part does not 'feel right', it is returned for further work and improvement. Hence, it is rather difficult to exploit and capitalize on 'observed' leaks, since replication or imitation of observed practices of an individual or group requires high levels of skill and know-how to already be in place. Imagine how difficult it would be to imitate the fine craftsmanship of flute making that has developed over many years of action-based know-how and the passing down of traditional skills from one flute makers to another.

 Illustration 8.3 Guarding against knowledge leakage—Coca-Cola

Coca-Cola (also referred to as Coke) is one of the largest American beverage companies in the world. Established 130 years ago, Coca-Cola operates from its headquarters in Atlanta and is renowned for its variety of carbonated soft drinks. It was founded by Confederate Colonel John Pemberton, and Pemberton's original formula—the Coca-Cola formula—is Coca-Cola's secret recipe for Coca-Cola syrup, which is combined with carbonated water to create the company's flagship cola soft drink. Since its inception, this company has grown from strength to strength into a word-wide giant that sells a variety of products that we all like and consume.

Knowledge protection

From a knowledge protection viewpoint, the exact formula of Coca-Cola's natural flavourings is a *trade secret that has never leaked* since Coca-Cola's inception. Even though its ingredients are listed on the side of each bottle and can, the original formula was held for eighty-six years in Sun Trust Bank's main vault in Atlanta. This was moved from the vault to a new vault containing the formula in December 2011. The only information that we have about this unique formula up to this point in time is that Coca-Cola's two key ingredients were cocaine and caffeine, with cocaine derived from the coca leaf and caffeine from the kola nut, leading to the name Coca-Cola (with the 'K' in Kola replaced with a 'C' for marketing purposes).

Company founder Asa Candler initiated the surrounding veil of secrecy of the formula in 1891 as a *publicity, marketing, and intellectual property protection strategy*. While several recipes have been published over a number of years, each claiming to be the authentic formula, the company maintains that the actual formula remains a secret, known to only a limited number of anonymous employees. To protect its trade secret, Coca-Cola has a rule that restricts access to its special formula to only *two executives*. Each knows the entire formula as well as other formulas along with the formulation process. This is an excellent example of secure knowledge management whereby both the know-what and know-how have been and still are being protected through the physical lock-down of the formula with only two top executives having the ability to 'know' more about the unique formula.

Questions

1. What is your view on the protective mechanisms applied by Coca-Cola to prevent against leakage of its recipe? What do you think makes this arrangement successful?

2. Do you think the physical locking away of a recipe in a vault is a safe protective measure?

Knowledge protection

In terms of protection against leakage there are many different aspects that need to be considered. Ahmad et al. (2014) synthesized knowledge protection literature and identified four key important knowledge protection areas: first, strategic management initiatives; second, operational-level knowledge protection processes; third, a supportive technology infrastructure; and, fourth, legal knowledge protection structures. Notably many organizations use NDAs, patents, and contracts to protect their sensitive knowledge assets, for example innovation processes for new products and services (Olander et al. 2009; Olander and Hurmellina 2010). However, literature reports that humans are considered the weakest link in the world of information security (Nohlberg 2009; Bulgurcu et al. 2010). Mechanisms are therefore required to educate humans in this regard, so the importance of security training, education, and awareness in this regard cannot be underestimated (see Time to reflect).

The increased use of social media platforms, tools, and technologies poses unique challenges to the protection of sensitive competitive knowledge. Even though online social networks greatly facilitate the sharing of and access to knowledge and expertise, the risk of knowledge leakage is exacerbated through the use of these different tools and technologies (see Chapters 9 and 10). Work patterns are also rapidly changing, requiring mobile workers to move around using mobile devices and smart phones. New forms of communication between mobile workers (e.g. open wireless communication networks) further challenge leakage, as these forms of networking are susceptible to hacking operations.

The storage of and access to sensitive explicit knowledge, and securing this knowledge, is an important knowledge management challenge which knowledge managers often defer to their organization's security function. The protection of explicit knowledge embedded in organizational artefacts can be accomplished through a supportive technology infrastructure, the use of a variety of tools and techniques that authenticate and control role-based access to sensitive codified knowledge, while the locking of content areas is also common (Ahmad et al. 2014; see Illustration 8.4). Audit trail logs can be used to identify and track who accessed and used sensitive content stored in repositories or knowledge bases over time. In addition, monitoring of social networking traffic could also reveal the unauthorized sharing of sensitive content in teams and networks within and between organizations. Based on the former discussion of tacit and explicit perspectives of knowledge leakage, Table 8.2 provides a short summary of knowledge process activities, protective activities, and examples of useful mechanisms that can be put in place to monitor and prevent tacit and explicit knowledge leakage.

 Time to reflect   Where does responsibility lie?

Who do you think needs to carry major responsibility to prevent or guard against leakage of sensitive competitive knowledge in an organization?

 Illustration 8.4   Knowledge protection at William Bethwey and Associates, Australia

William Bethwey and Associates (WB&A) is a small independent management consulting firm that specializes in knowledge management, business process improvement, enterprise content management, and change management. Founded in 2002, WB&A conducts consulting work in Australia, New Zealand, and Southeast Asia and prides itself on the calibre of organizations that are part of its regular client list.

One of WB&A's core competitive assets is its unique methodology used in its consulting services. This methodology is the result of WB&A's distinctive consulting experience developed over a period of ten-plus years in the form of a set of best practices that can be customized to deliver specialized consulting services in any of the four areas that WB&A specializes in. Conscious of this competitive asset (a unique consulting methodology) and that WB&A also works with sensitive client information and knowledge as an outcome of their consulting process, WB&A uses two methods to prevent leakage.

Firstly it prevents leakage of this knowledge and any accompanying expertise by deliberately keeping tacit any methodology-related tacit knowledge. Consequently none of the consultants are allowed to codify any aspects of this methodology. This approach makes the tacit knowledge self-protecting, meaning no other consulting organization can imitate WB&A's unique methodology.

The second method relates to client-specific information or explicit knowledge that derives from decisions made as part of the client consulting process. In cases whereby sensitive client-related knowledge needs to be stored and handled, WB&A uses a taxonomy to classify sensitive explicit knowledge which then assists in identifying policies and procedures to control the flow of sensitive client-related information. So the taxonomy helps to identify the sensitivity levels of all the different pieces of client-specific information (or explicit knowledge). Governance is then applied to this information/explicit knowledge to identify who information can be shared with, who cannot be involved in the sharing processes, who can 'see' specific information/explicit knowledge, who is not authorized to 'see' this information, who are authors of specific information/explicit knowledge, and how much protection is required for each of the specific client-related information/explicit knowledge.

Questions

1. What are your views on the notion of 'keeping tacit knowledge tacit'? Is this a good method to fully guard against knowledge leakage?

2. WB&A is a small organization—in your opinion, would this method to protect its consulting methodology work in a large organization?

3. Do you think WB&A's method to protect its know-how and know-what may impact knowledge sharing in this organization?

Table 8.2 Tacit and Explicit Knowledge Protection Activities and Example Mechanisms

Tacit and Explicit Knowledge Process Activities	Protective Activity Focus	Examples of Useful Mechanisms
Tacit knowledge		
Knowledge creation for new product or process design (innovation)	Keeping tacit knowledge tacit (particularly in early stages of innovation processes)	• NDAs, patents, and intellectual property (IP) agreements • Confidentiality agreements for sharing sensitive, competitive knowledge
Individual and/or group sharing of tacit knowledge in face-to-face or electronic networks	• Restricting the sharing of sensitive, confidential knowledge when collaborating/communicating through networking activities • Educating employees on the type of knowledge that may or may not be shared and with whom	Rules and regulations related to: • sharing specific sensitive competitive tacit knowledge, • who tacit knowledge can be shared with in both intra- and inter-organizational networks
Explicit knowledge		
Creation of, access to, and reuse of explicit knowledge stored in knowledge bases, repositories, and file structures	• Restrictions on creating storing, accessing, and reuse of sensitive, competitive knowledge embedded in artefacts • Protective activities to guard against unauthorized access to and reuse of sensitive explicit knowledge	• Restrictions on what may be codified. • Role-based access restrictions to knowledge artefacts/containers of knowledge artefacts • Compartmentalizing sensitive competitive knowledge • Audit trails that log access to sensitive content areas
Exchange and integration of knowledge artefacts (explicit knowledge) through intra- and inter-organizational collaboration	• Restricting access to confidential knowledge containers/repositories/knowledge bases • Protective activities to observe unauthorized behaviour, access to and reuse of sensitive explicit knowledge	• Monitoring the exchange and use of content in internal and external networking activities • Monitoring unauthorized use of knowledge artefacts in collaborative and networking activities

Conclusion

One of the key conclusions of this chapter is that despite forgetting, unlearning, loss, leakage, and protection being neglected topics in the knowledge management literature, they are crucially important to an organization's ability to adapt, change, and survive, as well as to access, develop, and utilize new knowledge. This is particularly the case with unlearning, the deliberate abandonment of existing knowledge and/or practices. Without being able to acknowledge the limitations of existing knowledge, values, norms, and practices, and without being prepared and able to give up established knowledge which may have become outdated, organizations are unlikely to be able to change and acquire or develop new knowledge. Thus, arguably, unlearning is as important an element of knowledge management as knowledge creation, codification, or knowledge sharing processes are.

While the ability to unlearn is a capability that is extremely useful for organizations to possess, there are a number of reasons which can make people unwilling to do so which can limit an organization's ability to unlearn. These range from the threat to a person's self-esteem that can be associated with having to give up established forms of knowledge, the amount of stress and anxiety people experience, and the nature of people's job roles. Despite these challenges, there are a range of methods that organizations can use to improve their ability to unlearn, as highlighted in the last section of the chapter.

Finally, the leakage of know-what and know-how imposes further challenges as organizations invest strategically in new forms of global collaboration and cooperation. While the increased use of modern technologies facilitates the movement of information and knowledge across multiple boundaries, organizations need to rethink ways in which the movement of knowledge is enabled but also monitored and tracked to identify leakage vulnerabilities. In addition, knowledge-intensive firms need to be cognizant of leakage, and derive mechanisms to recover from leakage incidents in today's challenging and connected business world.

 Case study The impact of team reflexivity and stress on unlearning and innovation in new product development teams

Lee and Sukoco (2011) examined the impact of team reflexivity and perceptions of stress on both levels of unlearning and product innovation within new product development teams in Taiwan. In their paper they define unlearning as: 'actively reviewing and breaking down the organization's long-held routines, assumptions and beliefs' (p. 412). The fundamental assumption they start with is that due to the rapidly changing technological environment that high technology companies have to deal with, the ability of new product development teams to reflect on and give up existing knowledge and beliefs (unlearning) is important to their innovativeness. Thus, one of the hypotheses that they test is that team unlearning is positively related to team innovation.

They also examine the impact of two other variables on both unlearning and innovation. The first of these factors is team reflexivity. Team reflexivity, the ability to critically reflect on taken-for-granted ideas and knowledge, is defined as: 'a team's collective efforts to review and raise awareness toward task-related issues during the development of new products' (p. 411). They argue that the more teams are able to be reflexive, the more they are likely to be willing to unlearn and abandon existing knowledge or behaviours, thus they hypothesize that team-level reflexivity will be positively related to both unlearning and product innovation. The second factor they examined was team stress, which is defined as the extent to which teams have a sense of crisis or anxiety. They argue that teams which experience high levels of stress are likely to fear receiving negative feedback, selectively focus on what is regarded as threatening information, and tend to interpret unclear information in a negative way. They hypothesize that team stress will be positively linked to unlearning, but negatively linked to product innovation.

To test their hypotheses they conducted a survey-based study of new product development teams that were located in three science parks in Taiwan. Survey responses were received from 298 people who were members of seventy-seven different new product development teams, with the majority of these teams working in high technology industries. All but one of their hypotheses were supported. Thus, as hypothesized, they found that unlearning was positively related to levels of product innovation. The ability to unlearn was found to be positively related to the performance of new product development teams. Further, as hypothesized, they found that team reflexivity was positively related to both unlearning and product innovation. In terms of the stress hypotheses, they found that stress levels were negatively related to levels of product innovation, but that, in contrast to what they hypothesized, team stress was also found to be negatively related to levels of unlearning. It appears that feelings of stress result in teams acting defensively, where they tend to rely upon what they perceive to have been traditionally successful beliefs and behaviours, which makes them less willing to embrace change. Thus, they found that unlearning was facilitated by the team's ability to be reflexive, but inhibited by the extent to which teams experienced feelings of stress.

Question

1. From an organizational point of view, can you think of ways that the levels of stress experienced by people in new product development teams can be reduced, and levels of reflexivity be developed and enhanced?

 ## Review and Discussion Questions

1. If the distortion of communication is a barrier to unlearning, what, if anything, can organizations do to address this issue? Is this an inevitable and unavoidable feature in business organizations?

2. One of the organizational-level barriers to learning from failure is that being involved in or responsible for failure is often punished, for example via career opportunities being inhibited. Are you aware of or can you find any instances when the opposite occurred, for example where failure was not punished, or where active experimentation and learning from failure was encouraged?

3. The consequences of the accidental forgetting of of knowledge, such as through the loss of knowledgeable staff members, are usually regarded as negative. Can you think of any potentially positive consequences that might result from an organizational accidentally forgetting or losing some knowledge?

4. While opportunities to be creative and solve problems in people's jobs have been found to facilitate unlearning, feelings of stress and anxiety were found to inhibit unlearning. Is it possible that these factors could become interrelated if a person's work requires such high levels of creativity that this could be a source of stress?

5. Do you think leakage will increase in a more digitized and technology-enabled society? What recommendations would you give startup firms to guard their sensitive, competitive knowledge assets?

6. Are there any people-specific aspects to consider in order to protect competitive organizational knowledge, and if so what are they?

7. Do you think that the HR department has a responsibility in terms of secure knowledge management, and if so what would it be?

Suggestions for Further Reading

E. Tsang and S. Zahra (2008). 'Organizational Unlearning', *Human Relations*, 61/10: 1435–62.
Conceptual paper which provides a comprehensive review of the literature on organizational unlearning, and which links unlearning explicitly to the topic of change.

K. Becker (2010). 'Facilitating Unlearning During Implementation of New Technology', *Journal of Organizational Change Management*, 23/3: 251–68.
Empirical case study of a single Australian company which examines the factors which facilitate and inhibit unlearning of individuals during a change process.

L. Lee and B. Sukoco (2011). 'Reflexivity, Stress, and Unlearning in the New Product Development Team: The Moderating Effect of Procedural Justice', *R&D Management*, 41/4: 410–43.
An empirical study of the factors influencing unlearning and product innovation in Taiwanese new product development teams.

E. Tsang (2008). 'Transferring Knowledge to Acquisition Joint Ventures: An Organizational Unlearning Perspective', *Management Learning*, 39/1: 5–20.
Examines the role of unlearning and knowledge transfer in joint ventures using empirical data on joint ventures involving Chinese companies.

 To further your understanding of knowledge management in organizations explore the book's accompanying online resources at www.oup.com/uk/hislop4e/

PART 4

Introduction to ICTs and Knowledge Management

Information and communication technologies (ICTs) have always played a prominent role in knowledge management processes and research. However, the reason for this interest and the type of technologies used has evolved over time. The very first knowledge management systems emerged from the field of artificial intelligence (AI), especially in the oil exploration industry, where there was a lot of interest. In this industry, AI was used to elicit geologists' knowledge about the composition of the Earth's layers. The knowledge from geologists was stored in rule-based systems that were used to predict prospective oil drilling locations (cf. Duda et al. 1979; Cannon et al. 1989). Rule-based systems made oil companies less dependent on expert geologists who were a scarce resource. Furthermore, the technology made it possible to find new oil drilling locations much quicker.

In the late 1990s interest in knowledge management started to develop further and new ICTs were introduced in knowledge management initiatives. Reporting on a 1997 survey, Ruggles (1998) found that the four most popular types of knowledge management projects at that time involved the implementation of intranets, data warehouses, decision support tools, and groupware. Scarbrough and Swan (2001) found that this emphasis was also reflected in academic research on knowledge management, with the vast majority of published research focusing on IT-related issues. There was also a general optimism among many organizations that simply implementing a relevant ICT system would lead to the successful management of knowledge. Over time, both these assumptions have been questioned and challenged.

However, ICTs have still retained a high profile role in knowledge management activities and research. This continued interest is arguably due to two related factors. First, developments in ICTs have facilitated collaboration between people and teams which are geographically dispersed, with a variety of labels being used for this type of working, including virtual working and (globally) dispersed working. One significant strand of research into this type of collaboration has been concerned with understanding the character and dynamics of knowledge processes in such contexts. Since the mid-2000s there has been a significant amount of research on this broad topic (Kotlarsky et al. 2007; Robert et al. 2009; Wang and Haggerty 2009; Chiravuri et al. 2011; Faraj et al. 2011; Mueller et al. 2011; Paasivaara and Lassenius 2014). Second, and relatedly, it has increasingly been acknowledged that ICTs can facilitate knowledge management activities, not just via the codification of knowledge, but through facilitating rich and interactive forms of communication enabling knowledge sharing and creation. This is most visible in research into the role that social media technologies can play in facilitating knowledge management activities (Helms et al. 2017). Most recently, big data and data analytics technologies have been added to the spectrum of knowledge management technologies. Big data and data analytics support knowledge discovery in vast amounts of data and hence support knowledge creation processes in organizations. This also brings us back to the roots of knowledge management since the analysis of (big) data is done through technologies from the field of AI, most notably machine learning.

Inseparability of knowledge management and computer-based technology

In his 2005 article in the *Journal of Knowledge Management*, Clyde Holsapple observed that there seemed to be two camps when it came to knowledge management and ICTs. One camp he called the *identification* camp, which considered ICT and knowledge management to be synonymous. But he argued that this camp simplified knowledge management by ignoring social and organizational aspects of knowledge management. The other camp was called the *exclusive* camp who stated that ICTs are not part of knowledge management. If technology is included they consider this data or information management, rather than knowledge management. In his article, Holsapple introduced a new perspective called the *inclusive* perspective. In this perspective, the boundary between ICT and knowledge management was considered to be highly permeable and ICTs were considered to be essential for getting value from knowledge management initiatives. He stated that eliminating ICTs from the equation was an illusion since our work is highly digitized. At the same time it should be realized that there are also other issues involved socio-cultural factors such as trust. In this book we also apply the inclusive view towards ICTs in knowledge management, hence accepting that ICT and knowledge management are inseparable.

The different technologies that can support knowledge management processes in organizations are examined in detail in this part of the book. This introductory chapter begins by providing an overview of the diversity of ways that ICTs can be used to facilitate knowledge management initiatives, which is done via linking back to the typologies of knowledge management examined in Chapter 4. One of the key conclusions of this section is that the role assigned to ICTs in knowledge management initiatives is significantly shaped by the assumptions about knowledge that are made.

Linking knowledge management and ICTs

As was discussed explicitly in Chapter 4, and as should be apparent implicitly throughout this book, there are a vast range of ways in which organizations can attempt to manage their knowledge. A specific issue that was touched on in Chapter 4, and that is examined more fully here, is how the role that ICTs can play in such activities will vary significantly depending upon the particular approach to knowledge management that an organization adopts. The objective of this section is to return to the knowledge management typologies outlined in Chapter 4 to consider the particular roles that ICTs play in them.

Table I illustrates the extent of the role that ICTs can play in knowledge management processes, as articulated in the different knowledge management strategies examined in Chapter 4. It is suggested here that the roles allocated to ICTs by these different styles of knowledge management can be classified into six generic types, three of which relate to each epistemological perspective. From the table it is clear that different approaches towards knowledge management require different technologies to support them. The different approaches might suggest that an organization has to choose one of them, but in practice an organization can use a mix of these approaches, depending on which organizational goals are being pursued.

Table I Divergent Approaches to ICT-Enabled Knowledge Management

ICT-Enabled Knowledge Management from Objectivist Perspective		
Purpose	KM Strategies Linked with	Empirical Examples
Repository-based approach to IT-based knowledge management.	Alvesson and Kärreman's extended library Earl's systems-based school Hansen et al.'s codification-based approach.	Scarso and Bolisani (2016): Adoption and use of Wikis in small and medium size enterprises Taskin and Van Bunnen (2015): Impact of introducing knowledge repositories into the workplace Dixon et al. (2009): The use of knowledge codification to capture and store knowledge within a US public healthcare organization Gray and Durcikova (2005–6): Knowledge repository used by technical support staff in a call centre environment.
Process and domain knowledge model approach to IT-based knowledge management.	Alvesson and Kärreman's enacted blueprints Earl's engineering school Hansen et al.'s codification-based approach.	Joram et al. (2017): Describes a knowledge-based system prototype to support the process of life insurance underwriting Huang (2009): Describes a knowledge-based system to support the strategic planning process based on the Balance Score Card Arnold et al. (2004): Explains the importance of the ability of knowledge-based systems to explain how they arrived at an outcome or decision.
Sensor-based approach to IT-based knowledge management (Internet of Things, big data).	Newell's Sensor-based approach Earl's Systems-based school.	Uden and He (2017): Use of Internet of Things to support knowledge management by including real-time data Khan and Vorley (2017): Big data text analytics as a means to enhance the effectiveness of knowledge management.
ICT-Enabled Knowledge Management from Practice-based Perspective		
Network-based approach to IT-based knowledge management.	Earl's cartographic approach Alvesson and Kärreman's community Hansen et al.'s personalization-based approach.	Choi et al. (2010): The role of IT systems to create transactive memory and facilitate the sharing of knowledge within two South Korean companies Hacker (2017): Linking social media capabilities to tacit knowledge sharing requirements Hwang et al. (2015): Knowledge sharing in online communities crossing hierarchical and geographic boundaries.

Table I (*Continued*)

Purpose	KM Strategies Linked with	Empirical Examples
Collaboration tools to facilitate ICT-based communication and knowledge sharing.	Earl's organizational school Earl's spatial school Hansen et al.'s personalization-based approach.	Mäntymäki and Riemer (2016): The use and value of Enterprise Social Networking tools from a knowledge management perspective Leonardi (2017): Considers social media as leaky pipes of communication that contribute to knowledge sharing and learning in the organization Ellison et al. (2015): The use of Enterprise Social Networks in multinational organizations using the theory of affordances.
Crowd-based approach to IT-based knowledge management.	Newell's crowd-based approach Earl's strategic school Hansen et al.'s personalization-based approach.	Ghezzi et al. (2017): Review of the crowd sourcing literature and suggestions for future research Ebner et al. (2009): Case study of how SAP applied ideas competitions to tap into knowledge of their partners O'Leary (2013): Facilitating knowledge management and innovation with crowd sourcing Majchrzak et al. (2009): Case study of how IBM is using social networking to get in touch with the wisdom of the crowd.

Table II shows an alternative way for classifying ICTs for knowledge management, as used by several authors (cf. Alavi and Leidner 2001; Alavi and Tiwana 2003; Becerra-Fernandez and Sabherwal 2014), and uses knowledge management processes as a basis for classification. It shows the many different technologies that can be labelled as knowledge management systems or technologies. Furthermore, it shows that the different systems and technologies support specific knowledge processes. In practice, the technological infrastructure for knowledge management in an organization will consist of a blend of different technologies and there is no one size fits all type of solution.

Chapters 9 and 10, which make up this part of the book, build from the distinctions outlined in Table I and examine in more detail the different ways that ICTs can be used in organizational knowledge management processes when the objectivist and practice-based perspectives are utilized. Chapter 9 focuses on the objectivist perspective, while Chapter 10 focuses on the practice-based perspective, with each chapter examining the three generic roles identified in Table I that ICTs can have in knowledge management processes.

Table II ICT Support for Knowledge Management Processes

Creation	Storage and Retrieval	Transfer	Application
e-Learning systems	Knowledge repositories	Knowledge directory	Expert systems
Collaboration support systems	Data warehouse and business intelligence	Online communities	Decision support systems
Knowledge discovery and analytics	Document and content management	Communication support	AI and intelligent agents
	Wikis	Blogs	Workflow management systems
	Sensors and Internet of Things	Social networking	
		Enterprise information portals	
		Media sharing	

9 Objectivist Perspectives on ICTs and Knowledge Management

Introduction

This chapter links to and builds from the Introduction to Part 4 outlined previously. The specific focus in this chapter is on examining the diverse ways in which information and communication technologies (ICTs) can be used to facilitate knowledge management processes which are compatible with the objectivist perspective on knowledge (see Chapter 2). Table I in the introduction to Part 4 identified three separate ways to utilize ICTs to facilitate knowledge management activities. Each of these is examined in more depth here. The chapter begins by revisiting the key features of the objectivist perspective on knowledge, focusing on their implications regarding the role that ICTs can play in knowledge processes. After this, the chapter then examines each of the different approaches to knowledge management compatible with the objectivist perspective that were identified in Table I. Following this, Chapter 10 will discuss knowledge management processes which are compatible with the practice-based perspective.

Objectivist perspective on ICT-enabled knowledge management

The popularity of the objectivist perspective on knowledge management, and the idea that through codification ICTs can play a crucial role in knowledge management processes, is visible in the number of ICT-enabled knowledge management initiatives in which codification activities are central. Examples include Siemens' ShareNet initiative (Voelpel et al. 2005), the US public health organization examined by Dixon et al. (2009), the globally dispersed military procurement organization examined by King and Marks (2008), the semiconductor equipment company examined by Hsiao et al. (2006), and the World Bank, where the objective of its knowledge management strategy in the late 1990s was to make itself a 'technology broker, transferring knowledge from one place where it is available to the place where it is needed' (van der Velden 2002: 30).

Epistemological assumptions and ICTs

Chapter 2 outlined in detail both how the objectivist perspective on knowledge conceptualizes knowledge and how it characterizes knowledge sharing processes. However, it is worth briefly restating some of the key assumptions of this perspective, as they help explain the roles that this perspective assumes ICTs can play in knowledge management processes. First, this perspective conceptualizes knowledge in entitative terms, with knowledge being regarded as a discrete object that can exist separately from the people who possess and use it. Second, there is an optimism embedded in this perspective that much knowledge either exists in an explicit form or that it can be made explicit through a process of codification (Steinmueller 2000). Third, this perspective conceptualizes knowledge sharing as being based on a transmitter–receiver or conduit model (see Figure 2.1), and assumes that it is relatively straightforward to share codified knowledge. Building from these assumptions those utilizing an objectivist perspective believe that ICTs can play a direct role in knowledge management processes, with ICTs simply representing one key channel/medium through which explicit knowledge can be shared.

Three ICT-enabled knowledge management approaches based on the objectivist perspective

The meta-analysis of the role of ICT systems in the knowledge management typologies examined in Chapter 4 is articulated in Table I. This suggests that despite the diversity of approaches to knowledge management embedded in these typologies, when objectivist assumptions about the nature of knowledge are utilized, there are three specific ways in which ICTs can facilitate knowledge management processes. All of these roles for ICT-enabled knowledge management build on the twin assumptions outlined earlier: that knowledge can be codified and that once codified it can be transferred and shared between people via ICTs. In the remainder of this section, each of the three approaches is discussed in more detail.

Repository-based approach to ICT-based knowledge management

The first role for ICTs is in creating searchable repositories or libraries of knowledge (see Definition; see also Illustration 9.1). As outlined in Table I this relates to three specific knowledge management strategies, including Hansen et al.'s codification approach, Earl's systems approach, and Alvesson and Kärreman's extended library approach. All three strategies assume that knowledge can be codified in some form. Examples of codified knowledge in an organizational context include documented tips and tricks, best practices, checklists, and process descriptions. Once knowledge is codified, it can be stored in a repository, or library, and made accessible for others in the organization. If people in the organization are looking for knowledge on a particular issue or issues then they can search the repository for it. The use of knowledge repositories has several benefits for the organization and is illustrated using the following example.

> **DEFINITION Knowledge repository**
>
> A computer-based system for storing and organizing codified organizational knowledge, in all sorts of different formats, with the aim to make this knowledge easily accessible for other people.

A common application area for knowledge repositories are technical support environments (Gray and Durcikova 2005; Hsiao et al. 2006; Scarso and Bolisani 2016); examples include the helpdesk of an Internet service provider or the support department of a manufacturer of aeroplane engines. In the repository, support engineers can store their knowledge on how to solve particular technical problems. When other support engineers encounter a particular problem during a call with a customer or in a maintenance job, they can search the repository to see if others have encountered a similar problem before and what is the best way to solve it.

Hence a repository can be used to increase the efficiency of the support engineers because they need less time to solve the problem and it prevents them from 're-inventing the wheel'. At the same time the quality of their work might increase because they use a proven solution from the repository. Additionally, less qualified (and hence cheaper) staff are able to do the job because they can consult the knowledge repository which is filled with knowledge from experts. Furthermore, this is also useful when the number of experts is limited but the company has to support customers worldwide. Experts can only be in one location at the time but a repository makes it possible to bring expert knowledge to many locations at the same time.

As well as of improving efficiency, a repository can also be used to enhance learning of support engineers (Gray and Durcikova 2005). In this case the repository should provide a rich description of the problem and the solution. The rich description results in an increased understanding of the problem rather than providing a 'recipe' for solving the problem. The increase of learning will help the support engineers in new situations that they encounter and that are not stored in the repository yet. In these situations their increased understanding might help them to solve this new problem.

For knowledge repositories to be successful a number of factors are necessary. First, people must be willing to codify their knowledge (see Time to reflect). Second, a system of categorizing and structuring knowledge must be found which allows people looking for knowledge to find it. Finally, people must be willing to search such systems, in other words trust the knowledge in the system when they require assistance (Gray and Durcikova 2005–6; Bock et al. 2006; Paroutis and Al Saleh 2009). Gray and Durcikova (2005) showed that time pressure and credibility are two important factors influencing the use of a repository. First of all, when support engineers feel that they are under time pressure, it is less likely that they will consult the repository. In a situation of time pressure they might turn to alternative sources for knowledge, such as a colleague (Helms et al. 2011; Trusson et al. 2014). Good accessibility of knowledge in the repository is therefore an important design criterion. Second, it is important that the users of the repository trust the knowledge that is stored in the repository. Therefore it is important to consider who can add to the knowledge repository (i.e. what is their reputation?), to screen the knowledge that is added (i.e. to check if the solution works and to avoid duplicates), and to maintain the repository (i.e. remove outdated knowledge).

Time to reflect   Willingness to share knowledge

Knowledge repositories are implemented because from an organizational perspective there are many benefits to be gained from sharing knowledge, such as re-using knowledge. However, this requires that employees are willing to share their knowledge with others. Can you think of reasons why employees would not be willing to share their knowledge in codified form? Are these reasons different from sharing knowledge in tacit form? Are there any personal gains from sharing knowledge in codified form?

A case study at Infosys illustrates the negative effect of poor repository management (Garud and Kumaraswamy 2005). Infosys introduced a knowledge repository and encouraged their employees to share their on-the-job experiences using the knowledge repository. When introducing a knowledge repository there is always a 'chicken and egg' problem. Employees will not be motivated to contribute knowledge to the repository because no one is using it. And no one is using it because there is no knowledge in the repository. Therefore, InfoSys used financial rewards to stimulate submissions to their knowledge repository. The effect was overwhelming since it resulted in an avalanche of contributions to the repository. In fact, there were so many contributions that the organization decided to publish them in the repository without a proper screening. Hence, besides the valuable contributions to the repository, there were also many low quality and erroneous contributions that made it to the repository. Consequently, employees lost their trust in the repository and abandoned it. This example shows that screening of content is an important part of good repository management. When designing such a screening process it also important to realize that the screening process should be fair. If contributors consider the screening process to be unfair they will be less likely to contribute to the repository (Fadel and Durcikov 2014).

 Illustration 9.1   Design of a repository

A knowledge repository consists of several components. At its core is a multimedia database to store knowledge fragments such as a solution to a particular technical problem. Knowledge fragments can be web pages, documents, or multimedia files such as an instruction video. On this database there should be version management to support updates and maintenance of the knowledge fragments in the database. Users have access to the repository through the user interface, which should both support contributors to the knowledge base as well as users that retrieve fragments from the knowledge base. The contributors should be supported by functionality to upload or enter new knowledge to the repository. Besides the knowledge fragment itself, a contributor should also provide meta-data to support findability of the knowledge fragment. Users that search for knowledge in the repository need to be supported by functionality to retrieve knowledge fragments. Two basic approaches here are the structured and the unstructured search. An example of an unstructured search is using a search engine than can search full text, for example Google desktop search. An example of a structured search is using a folder structure similar to Windows Explorer, which is also known as taxonomy-based search. But also a timeline can be considered as structured search. (A nice demonstration of different retrieval mechanisms can be found on the following website: http://www.eternalegypt.org/.)

Wiki's are an example of a technology that can be used for knowledge repositories (Scarso and Bolisani 2016). Knowledge fragments are mainly stored as web pages and access is provided by full text search and hyperlinked pages. The hyperlinks make it possible to discover related knowledge not included in the search terms.

Questions

Two methods for retrieving knowledge from a knowledge repository are full text search and taxonomy-based search (e.g. browsing a hierarchical folder structure). What are the advantages and disadvantages of both methods? Would it be possible to combine both methods to get the best of both worlds?

Process and domain knowledge model approach to ICT-based knowledge management

The second role for ICTs is in embedding process and domain knowledge in task execution. As outlined in Table I this relates to the enacted blueprint approach of Alvesson and Kärreman, Earl's engineering school of knowledge management, and Hansen et al.'s codification approach. With this approach the information technology (IT)-based knowledge management system actively supports task execution through workflow support or supporting diagnosing, problem solving, and decision-making. Two typical examples of systems for these respective purposes are *workflow management systems* and *knowledge-based systems* (see Definition; also referred to as expert systems).

Workflow management systems

Workflow management systems contain knowledge about how the process should be executed: it knows about the sequence of steps and what needs to be done in these steps (Alavi and Leidner 2001; Becerra-Fernandez and Sabherwal 2014). In other words, process knowledge is embedded in the system and actively supports the user in executing the right steps at the right time. A typical example of a workflow are the steps involved in handling an insurance claim or requesting reimbursement for travel expenses. The process in both examples consists of a number of steps that need to be executed in a particular order and in each step the system provides directions about what is needed from the user in terms of input. Based on the input of the user the system might also choose alternative paths, for example completing a reimbursement form for (inter)national travel. Because the workflow system contains knowledge about the sequence and rules, less experienced users can also execute the process since they are guided by the system throughout the process. Furthermore, it ensures consistency in process execution because every user is guided through the process in the same way.

DEFINITION **Knowledge-based system**

A computer-based system containing knowledge about a particular domain and that can use this knowledge to diagnose or solve problems in that domain. Such systems are also referred to as expert systems since they intend to mimic the capability of an expert to diagnose or solve a particular problem.

Knowledge-based systems

Another way of supporting employees in their tasks is to assist in the actual execution of the task rather than telling the employee which steps to follow. This requires that the IT-based knowledge management system contains domain knowledge concerning the particular task at hand. Such knowledge-based systems (see Illustration 9.2) can reason using domain knowledge and support the employee in taking a decision or solving a particular problem (cf. Tarekegn 2016; Joram, Harrison, and Joseph 2017). A simple example is a glue advisor you can find in a 'Do It Yourself' (DIY) store. Such an advisor helps customers in the DIY store to select the right glue for a particular job. The system typically gets input from the user by asking questions about the application and the materials involved. Then it uses rules to determine what glue is the best choice for the job. Another example is the rules-based system for finding oil drilling locations that was described in the introduction to the Part 4. Rule-based systems are just one type of knowledge-based system; other variants are *case-based*, *model-based*, and *constraints-based systems* (Becerra-Fernandez and Sabherwal 2014).

Case-based systems are common in the legal domain and they can support lawyers in finding similar cases when preparing for a new case. Similar cases are useful because the specifics of that case (e.g. the applied strategy) might also be applicable in the new case. A well-known example of a *model-based system* is the weather forecast system used by meteorologists. It contains models about the Earth's atmosphere which enable them to make weather forecasts. Another example is a neural-network-based approach to detect credit card fraud (Quah and Sriganesh 2008). *Constraints-based systems* can be found in the scheduling domain such as making a work schedule for maintenance engineers. Typically there are multiple solutions to this problem and the system proposes a solution by applying constraints (e.g. working days, holidays etc.).

The goal of knowledge-based systems is to support professionals in executing their work. They can potentially improve decision-making and increase consistency in judgement across cases or situations. However, professionals also need to accept that knowledge-based systems take over part of their work. They might consider the system as an infringement of their expertise and status and therefore might not want to use it. Also they might not trust the outcome of the system or not understand why the system provides a particular recommendation. As a result the adoption of knowledge-based systems is not always successful in organizations. An important factor to improve adoption is when the knowledge-based system offers the possibility to explain how it arrived at the outcome (Arnold et al. 2004). But having an explanation facility in the knowledge-based system in itself is not enough. Giboney et al. (2015) demonstrated that there needs to be a cognitive fit between how the system explains its decision and the preferred information format of the user. Additionally, in the case of a cognitive fit the user would spent more time on reading the explanation and hence the explanation is more influential.

 Illustration 9.2 Design of a knowledge-based system

The components of a knowledge-based system are to some extent similar to that of a knowledge repository. In its core there is a knowledge base containing knowledge about a particular domain. There are different ways in which this domain knowledge is being captured in the knowledge base: rules, models, cases, or constraints (see also main text). To enter and update knowledge in the knowledge base there needs to be a user interface. This interface is used by an expert or by a specialist who elicits the knowledge from the expert. On top of the knowledge base there is a reasoning engine which can apply the knowledge from the knowledge base to the problem at hand. But before the reasoning engine can do its job it needs input from a user or sensors, for example in the weather forecast example the model needs sensor inputs such as temperature and humidity readings. Data from the user is collected through the user interface, which also presents the result to the user. Finally, there can be an explanation facility, which can explain to the user how it arrived at its results.

Questions

1. Compare a knowledge repository system with a knowledge-based system and describe how these systems differ in how they store knowledge and how knowledge is made accessible to the user.

2. In case a company wants to provide employees access to knowledge for troubleshooting problems with a network printer, would you recommend a knowledge repository or a knowledge-based system? Provide arguments why.

Sensor-based approach to ICT-based knowledge management

The third role for ICTs is in creating knowledge from the vast amount of data that is collected by organizations through their transaction-based information systems, intelligent sensors, website, social media, etc. As outlined in Table I this relates to Newell's sensor-based approach and to Earl's system-based approach. With this approach the focus is on applying data analytics techniques to generate new insights and knowledge from data. This approach of IT-enabled knowledge creation is a result of increased digitalization of business processes and society itself. Everything an organization or individual does leaves a digital trace in some sort of computer-based information system. Furthermore, devices and equipment that organizations and individuals use are increasingly connected to the Internet, resulting in an 'Internet of Things' where massive amounts of data are exchanged and stored (Uden and He 2017).

> **DEFINITION   Big data**
>
> Big data refers to a massive amount of data being analysed, where the amount of data is typically characterized by four 'v's: volume, variety, velocity, and veracity.

The volume and variety of data that is available, and the speed at which new data is created, means that it is referred to it as big data (Watson 2014; see Definition). It is only recently that organizations started to realize the value of big data and the knowledge that might be hidden in it. By using big data analytics, organizations can explore the data and generate knowledge by analysing relations, patterns, and clustering in the data. In terms of the SECI (socialization, externalization, combination, and internalization) model discussed in Chapter 7, this can be considered as a IT-enabled 'combination'.

Data analytics techniques are also known as data mining techniques and can be divided in two groups: supervised and unsupervised methods (Provost and Fawcett 2013). *Supervised methods* have a clear target such as finding customers that are likely to default on their loan or detecting fraud with credit cards. This requires having a data set from which it is known which customers default so that the algorithm (e.g. classification tree, random forest, neural network) can be trained to detect these customers using other data about the customer (e.g. combination of age, duration of loan, and calls to helpdesk). *Unsupervised methods* are lacking such a target and there is no data set needed for training the algorithm. An example is using a clustering algorithm to detect if the customers of an organization can be clustered in groups sharing similar characteristics (e.g. a combination of age, education, income, buying pattern) to identify particular customer segments. In other words, with supervised methods there is a clear outcome of the analysis while with unsupervised methods it is not always clear what one is looking for and what one might find. (See Time to reflect.)

Applying big data analytics sets requirements on the data as well as the technological infrastructure. Typically, the data comes from different sources (i.e. information systems, website, sensors) so this data needs to be brought together so that it can be analysed. This requires that formats are compatible and that data definitions are aligned. Furthermore, the quality of the data should be good because the 'garbage in is garbage out' principle also applies in this context. Data governance practices can help organizations to manage their data properly and to guarantee the quality of the data (Otto 2011). Regarding the technological infrastructure it is important that it can handle the volume and variety of the data as well as the velocity in which it is created. This sets special requirements for the databases, networks, and applications used to capture, store, and process this data. Today, such services are also offered in the cloud.

Once the infrastructure is in place organizations also need a process to systematically harvest knowledge from the data. The first process descriptions already stem from the early 1990s when the field was still referred to as 'knowledge discovery from databases' (KDD). An overview of KDD models is provided by Mariscal et al. (2010) and is based on a literature review. It shows that most of these models follow the same steps and one of the most used models up till today is the CRISP DM model[1]. The steps distinguished in this model are: data understanding, business understanding, data preparation, model building, model evaluation, and model deployment. In this process it is important to have experts with knowledge of data analytics and these experts are also referred to as data scientists.

 Time to reflect   Big data: dawn of the algorithms

There is an increase of artificial intelligence algorithms in business applications. A downside of many of these algorithms is that they cannot explain how they derived a certain outcome or conclusion. Now imagine that you want to buy a new health insurance policy. Would you consider it ethical if an algorithm decided on your being accepted as a new customer (by comparing your profile to that of existing customers) but could not explain why you had been accepted or rejected? Would it be more acceptable if you knew what data had been used for the decision? Would you consider buying a health insurance policy at a company if you knew that gender and nationality were being used by the algorithm in its decision to accept you or not?

---

[1] CRISP DM stands for 'cross-industry standard process for data mining' and was developed by a consortium of companies in the mid-1990s. The standard has seen several revisions and the most active proponent of CRISP DM is IBM who incorporated the ideas in their SPSS product.

Critical reflection of objectivist approaches on ICTs and knowledge management

Over time, a growing number of people have challenged the assumptions of the objectivist perspective. One of the criticisms concerns the assumption that the majority of knowledge can be codified and thus captured in a computer-based system. A simple example can already demonstrate that there is a lot of knowledge that cannot be codified or is at least very hard to codify. The example concerns codifying knowledge on how to ride a bike. You can try this for yourself by making a description of how to ride a bike (assuming you know how to ride yourself). Hence, you will experience the difficulty of codifying this knowledge. If codifying knowledge on how to ride a bike is already difficult, one can imagine that is also difficult to codify knowledge about best practices in an organizational context. Therefore, setting up a knowledge repository for sharing best practices in an organization is not a trivial task and there is no guarantee for success.

Another criticism concerns the assumption that once knowledge is codified, it is also understandable for others. In other words, if codified knowledge is made available to others it can be easily used by them. However, this depends on how well the knowledge has been documented as well as on the context and knowledge of the receiver. For example, a non-trained doctor will not be able to interpret the results from an expert system that supports doctors in diagnosing diseases because of a lack of domain knowledge and not understanding the domain-specific terminology.

Both criticisms also explain why many knowledge management projects, based on the objectivist approach, fail in organizations. Hence, organizations should carefully check these two assumptions before considering the use of objectivist approaches of IT-enabled knowledge management. The outcome of this check depends on the particular application that the organization has in mind. For a particular application it is important to determine if knowledge can be codified and if the targeted users of the system are able to interpret/use this knowledge when it is made available to them. Even if both conditions are met, there are several reasons why an objectivist approach towards IT-enabled knowledge management might fail. Reasons have been mentioned throughout this section and include willingness to share one's knowledge, trust in the knowledge being shared, accessibility of the knowledge, and transparency of reasoning in knowledge-based systems.

 ## Conclusion

One of the key objectives of the chapter has been to highlight different approaches on the use of ICT to support knowledge management in the objectivist perspective. In the objectivist perspective knowledge is regarded as a discrete object that can exist separately from the people who possess and use it. Furthermore, it is assumed that most knowledge can be codified and that it can be shared using a transmitter–receiver model. The objectivist conceptualization of knowledge typically argues that ICTs can have an important and direct role in the knowledge processes.

This chapter discussed three different approaches of IT-enabled knowledge management that support the objectivist perspective on knowledge management. The repository-based approach towards IT-enabled knowledge management is about creating a library of organizational knowledge to stimulate re-use of knowledge and learning in the organization. The process and domain knowledge model approach towards IT-enabled knowledge management concerns actively supporting employees in following the right process or using expert knowledge in their task. Finally, the sensor-based approach towards IT-enabled knowledge management relates to the new trend of big data and the potential to discover and create new knowledge from the massive amount of data that is captured by organizations today.

The different approaches towards IT-enabled knowledge management have been discussed separately for the sake of clarity. A separate discussion results in a better understanding of the features of each approach. Furthermore, each of the approaches provides a conceptual description of IT-enabled knowledge management support and do not necessarily match one on one with software solutions offered by vendors. In practice, the different approaches can be combined into one software solution or knowledge management platform. Take for instance the Microsoft SharePoint platform which is often used by organizations to support knowledge management. This platform integrates both the repository-based approach and the process model-based approached (i.e. workflow management).

The IT-enabled knowledge management approaches discussed in this section show only one part of the spectrum of IT-enabled knowledge management approaches, in other words those that relate to the objectivist perspective on knowledge management. The other part of the spectrum of IT-enabled knowledge management approaches are discussed in the next chapter and relate to the practice-based perspective on knowledge management. Due to the different take on knowledge and knowledge sharing, this perspective results in a different range of IT-enabled knowledge management approaches, which can be considered complementary to the objectivist approaches discussed in this section.

 Case study Wiki as tool to share knowledge in an SME

InfoNet Solutions is a small company of thirty employees which is located in the Northeast of Italy. It offers several ICT services to its clients and is specialized in: cloud computing, data centres, virtualization, and business continuity. Knowledge management at the organization focuses on knowledge transfer concerning the systems that they install at their clients. In the process of installing a new system there are mainly three departments involved: sales/marketing, delivery, and after-sales support. Sales and marketing is typically responsible for acquiring new projects and clients. When acquiring new projects it is important to know about installed systems with other clients so they can exploit the knowledge from previous projects. Delivery is responsible for design, development, and implementation of a system at a client. They need access to knowledge about any problems or other experiences with installed systems. Once a system is installed, the after-sales department is responsible for maintenance and updates of the system. In turn, the support people need knowledge about the components and configuration of the installed system and why it was designed that way.

To meet their knowledge management needs, the company started to create a written report for each new installed system (a 'libretto di impianto'). In 2003, the company started to use a file server for storing documents and e-mails for each installed system. This knowledge management system was mainly used by the technical department and soon they found it was difficult to locate, classify, and retrieve a particular piece of knowledge. To overcome these problems the company started to use intranet software but once again found that it did not adequately support the knowledge flows in the company. Therefore, in 2009, the company adopted a wiki-based knowledge management system for exchanging knowledge about installed systems. In 2013, the knowledge management system was extended to all three departments involved in delivering a new system to their clients. Key requirements in the design of the wiki were content that is really needed by the employees and usability of the system. The result is a wiki that is composed of two sub-portals, one intended for commercial staff and the other for technical staff. Every employee has access and can contribute to the system. Any addition of new content or editing of existing content is logged by the versioning management function. Colleagues can discuss these changes and hence collaboratively create and edit content. Besides text other kinds of content can also be uploaded to the wiki (e.g. photos and software code). To support the easy and quick insertion of new content the company uses predefined templates. Furthermore, in addition to full text search, a pre-defined structure of sections is used for easy location of knowledge in the wiki. One of the future plans of the company concerning the wiki is to use it on mobile devices.

Research by Scarso and Bolisani (2016) showed that the wiki is used daily by many of its employees, showing that it really meets the needs of their employees. However, it is not the only system that the employees use, they also still rely on the exchange of tacit knowledge by means to telephone calls or informal talks. The wiki is therefore complementary to others systems that support knowledge management at InfoNet. In realizing the wiki, it was found that organizational and cultural factors were more decisive than technical factors. It was for instance found that a combination of a bottom-up approach (i.e. initiated by users) with a top-down approach (i.e. initiated by management) during the implementation was a key factor. Another important factor was that it integrated very well with the daily work of people, which was why they saw a clear benefit from using and contributing to the wiki.

Source: Scarso, E., and Bolisani, E. (2016). 'Factors Affecting the Use of Wiki to Manage Knowledge in a Small Company', *Journal of Knowledge Management*, 20(3): 423–43.

Questions

1. Why do you think the InfoNet Solutions employees still rely on the exchange of tacit knowledge? How is it complementary to the knowledge shared through their wiki?

2. What are the benefits of using wiki technology to build a knowledge repository in terms of ease of use and implementation effort?

 ## Review and Discussion Questions

1. When introducing a knowledge repository, organizations face the 'chicken and egg' problem. Users will not use the system unless there is something on the system, and contributors will not contribute if the repository is not used. What can organizations do to stimulate contributions to the knowledge repository? What are the positive and negative side effects of stimulating knowledge contributions?

2. Neural networks are a type of artificial intelligence that has been used to build knowledge-based systems to detect credit card fraud. A disadvantage of neural networks is that it cannot show how it arrived at its conclusions (e.g. why it suspects fraud). For a bank employee using a knowledge-based system of this kind, what might be the effect of the lack of explanation on the user's acceptance of recommendations made by the system? Would it make any difference if the users were knowledgeable about credit card fraud themselves? Would you expect inexperienced users to be more likely to accept the recommendation of the knowledge-based system? Note: a user in this context refers to a bank employee using the system.

3. Increased computer power and big data make it possible to analyse large amounts of data to search for new insights and knowledge. One way of doing this is an unsupervised search that uses regression techniques to find possible relations between data items in the data set. What are possible downsides of this method of data exploration? Under what conditions would you recommend it to organizations? After discussing these questions have a look at https://goo.gl/3BQNd5.

Suggestions for Further Reading

K. J. Fadel and A. Durcikova (2014). 'If It's Fair, I'll Share: The Effect of Perceived Knowledge
    Validation Justice on Contributions to an Organizational Knowledge Repository', *Information and
    Management*, 51/5: 511–19.
Knowledge that is contributed to a repository needs some validation to ensure quality of knowledge
in the repository. This paper studies the effect of fairness of the validation process on the willingness
to contribute.

J. S. Giboney, S. A. Brown, P. B. Lowry, and J. F. Nunamaker (2015). 'User Acceptance of Knowledge-
    Based System Recommendations: Explanations, Arguments, and Fit', *Decision Support Systems*, 72:
    1–10.
Studies the user's acceptance of recommendations from knowledge-based systems. It shows that
fit between the user's own explanation and that of the knowledge-based system increases the
acceptance.

S. Ransbotham (2016). 'Knowledge Entrepreneurship: Institutionalising Wiki-Based Knowledge-
    Management Processes in Competitive and Hierarchical Organisations', *Journal of Information
    Technology*, 31: 226.
Critical review on the value of wikis for knowledge sharing. Although there are many positive stories,
the article shows that critical challenges remain in competitive and hierarchical organizations.

L. Uden and W. He (2017). 'How the Internet of Things Can Help Knowledge Management: A Case
    Study from the Automotive Domain', *Journal of Knowledge Management*, 21/1: 57–70.
Case study on the application of Internet of Things and big data in the automotive domain. It
describes a knowledge management system that provides real-time knowledge to car owners and
vendors.

 *To further your understanding of knowledge management in organizations explore the book's
accompanying online resources at* **www.oup.com/uk/hislop4e/**

10 Practice-Based Perspectives on ICT-Enabled Knowledge Management

Introduction

Even over the short space of time that knowledge management has been regarded as an important topic there has been a significant evolution in the role that information and communication technologies (ICTs) are conceptualized as being able to play in such processes. Broadly speaking, this has seen practice-based perspectives on knowledge become more fully embraced. As will be seen, the practice-based perspective regards ICTs as having a less direct, but equally important role in supporting and facilitating the social interactions that underpin inter-personal knowledge processes. This involves dealing with the concepts of 'transactive memory systems' (TMSs; see Definition), 'crowd sourcing', and the use of social media.

This chapter links to and builds on the earlier Introduction to Part 4. The specific focus in this chapter is on examining the diverse ways in which ICTs can be used to facilitate knowledge management processes which are compatible with the practice-based perspective on knowledge (see Chapter 3). Table I in the introduction to Part 4 identified three separate ways to utilize ICTs to facilitate knowledge management activities utilizing this perspective. Each of these is examined in more depth here. The chapter begins by revisiting the key features of the objectivist perspective on knowledge, focusing on their implications regarding the role that ICTs can play in knowledge processes. After this, the chapter then examines each of the three approaches to knowledge management compatible with the practice-based perspective that were identified in Table I.

Epistemological assumptions and ICTs

Most fundamentally, due to the way those writing from a practice-based perspective conceptualize knowledge, they believe that the codification and storage of knowledge in ICT-based repositories is unlikely to result in useful knowledge. This is because these processes of codification typically produce a denuded form of knowledge, as the tacit assumptions and values which underpin it are lost (Hislop 2002b; Walsham 2001). Thus, effectively, what is codified is only part of the knowledge people possess and its utility, on its own, is limited.

Further, as outlined in Chapter 3, those adopting a practice-based epistemology assume that the transmitter–receiver metaphor of knowledge sharing is inappropriate, as the sharing of knowledge does not involve the simple transferral of a fixed entity (i.e. explicit knowledge) between two people. Instead, the sharing of knowledge involves two people actively inferring and constructing meaning from a process of interaction (Hislop 2002b; Bosua and Scheepers 2007). This relates to the processes of perspective making and taking which were described in Chapter 3, where those interacting develop an understanding of the values, assumptions, and tacit knowledge which underpin each other's knowledge base (Walsham 2001). Communication processes in such interactions, to be successful, are required to be relatively rich, open, and based on a certain level of trust.

The role which those writing from a practice-based perspective believe that ICTs can play in knowledge processes is thus somewhat indirect, being related to facilitating and supporting the social relationships and communication processes which underpin knowledge processes. Walsham (2001: 599) usefully summarized this by arguing that 'computer based systems can be of benefit in knowledge based activities . . . to support the development and communication of human meaning'.

Practice-based perspectives on knowledge and the three roles for ICTs in knowledge management

As outlined in Table I, despite the diversity of approaches to knowledge embedded in the three typologies of knowledge examined in Chapter 4, there are three ways that those utilizing a practice-based perspective on knowledge consider ICTs can be used to facilitate organizational knowledge management activities. First, a network-based approach can be used to produce 'expertise maps', allowing people looking for help to identify others with relevant knowledge and expertise, which is where the concept of TMSs is relevant. Second, they can be used as tools to facilitate rich forms of communication and collaboration between people who are physically dispersed, which is where the use of social media is examined (Panahi et al. 2012). Third, the crowd sourcing concept opens up traditional organization boundaries (Newell 2015). Here the assumption is that an organization has limitations in what it can possibly know, but that there are people outside the organization that can extend the knowledge of the organization. ICT platforms can assist in reaching those people to tap into their knowledge (Von Krogh 2012).

Network-based approach to ICT-based knowledge management

The use of ICTs for mapping expertise fits closely with Earl's cartographic school of knowledge management. From this perspective, ICTs can be used to support knowledge management activities by allowing people to search for and identify other people with expertise that they are looking for. Where this approach to ICT-enabled knowledge management differs from the library/repository approach is that no attempt is made to codify knowledge and expertise. Instead, knowledge is shared via inter-personal communication and interaction, which can occur once someone looking for a particular type of expertise has found someone who possesses it. The benefit of this approach to knowledge management is that it allows people to establish and develop contacts with strangers who have relevant knowledge which would have been difficult to achieve by other means. Such a facility has the potential to be of particular use in geographically dispersed teams or multinational organizations.

DEFINITION Transactive memory system

Knowledge relating to the distribution of expertise within teams whereby team members have an understanding of who possesses what specialist knowledge.

The importance of knowing where expertise is located within the context of geographically dispersed teams helps to explain why the concept of TMSs has largely been developed and researched in this context, with research interest in the topic developing over a decade (Kanawattanachai and Yoo 2007; Jarvenpaa and Majchrzak 2008; Oshri et al. 2008; Choi et al. 2010; Mell et al. 2014; Hood et al. 2016). Choi et al. (2010) formally define TMSs as 'a specialized division of cognitive labour that develops within a team with respect to the encoding, storage and retrieval of knowledge from different domains' (p. 856). More informally, they say that in TMSs 'team members know who knows what and who knows who knows what' (p. 856). Thus, it is a concept that is closely linked to the idea of expertise mapping. Research on TMSs suggests that their existence is linked to and can facilitate the sharing and joint creation/ application of knowledge within teams (see Illustration 10.1). But, vice versa, knowledge sharing in online communities also helps to build the TMS. And especially the more experienced people in the community are better at locating expertise in the organization through their developed understanding of the TMS (Hwang et al. 2015).

 Illustration 10.1 The relationship between IT support, TMSs, and the sharing and application of knowledge within teams

Choi et al. (2010) examined the impact of information technology (IT) support and TMSs on knowledge processes and team performance in the context of two large South Korean firms, one an oil company and one a steel company, both of which had well-developed knowledge management systems. Research data were collected via surveys, with over 740 useable surveys involving people from 139 teams being analysed. The focus here is narrowly on the relationship between IT support, TMSs, and the sharing and application of knowledge. In terms of the relationship between IT support and TMSs, a positive relationship was found, which suggests that one effective way of developing transactive memory within teams is through investing effectively in IT systems. Second, a positive relationship was found to exist between both IT support and the sharing and application of knowledge, and between TMSs and the sharing and application of knowledge. This therefore suggests that if investments in IT support lead to the development of transactive memory, this can be an effective way to facilitate the sharing and application of knowledge.

Question

This presents a very positive view of the relationship between IT investment, TMSs, and knowledge sharing. In terms of the relationship between TMSs and knowledge sharing, can you identify factors which may inhibit the relationship?

Knowing who the expert is, or being able to locate the expert using an expertise map, is however not a guarantee that employees will approach the expert. Research by Helms et al. (2011) shows that there are multiple reasons why employees prefer to ask a colleague for advice rather than an expert who is more knowledgeable on the particular topic for which advice is being sought. One of the reasons is that it feels safer to ask a colleague than an expert. Furthermore, a colleague is easy to approach (also in terms of proximity) and might be more willing to make time to give advice. Further, experts might receive many requests for advice and therefore might not be available. Experts might also use jargon or lack the skills to communicate effectively, which are also reasons for not approaching them.

ICTs that support the network-based approach focus on providing information on 'who knows what' so that experts can be located and contacted for help. Before the social media era, this was achieved by producing databases of expertise also referred to as electronic yellow pages or knowledge maps (Cheung et al. 2007). An expertise database consists of the profiles of employees, which describe their expertise, as well as general information such as function, location, and contact details. However, filling a database with profiles of experts and keeping it up-to-date can be an enormous challenge for large organizations. It requires discipline of the employees to visit the expertise databases and to update their profile regularly.

The social media era has created new solutions and also an environment where it is common to have a profile and to update it. The main functionality of these social networks is creating a profile page, establishing online relationships, and interacting with other users. Well-known enterprise social networks (ESNs) are Facebook, LinkedIn, and Yammer, which can be used for expertise location (Skeels and Grudin 2009; Mäntymäki and Riemer 2016; Hacker 2017). A potential issue with using such profiles to identify suitable sources of expertise is that they represent a 'stage' via which people can present themselves to the world. Thus, they may be as much a mechanism for 'strategic self-presentation' as they are a source of objective knowledge (Leonardi and Treem 2012).

But in addition to traditional expertise databases, users can also establish relationships (e.g. follow the updates of an expert) and experts can be contacted directly. Furthermore, interaction with experts takes place online so that it is visible for others who might also learn from it (Riemer et al. 2011). An additional advantage is that the digital traces on social networking platforms can be used to detect experts and communities using social network analysis (Trier and Richter 2014). This is achieved by building a network between the users of the network based on the relationships and interactions between them. In this network, central people might be an indication of experts and clusters of people might be an indication of communities (Zhang et al. 2007).

Collaboration tools to facilitate ICT-based communication and knowledge sharing

The second practice-based use for ICTs in knowledge management activities is to facilitate inter-personal communication and collaboration. This type of usage fits with Earl's organizational and spatial schools of knowledge management. Here ICTs, via a wide range of virtual/web-based platforms, forums, and conduits, such as e-mail, instant messaging, discussion boards, intranets, chatrooms, (micro)blogs, etc., create conditions where rich inter-personal interactions can take place between people who are geographically dispersed and who have limited opportunities for face-to-face interaction. One example of how this can be done is through the creation of virtual spaces or 'cafes' whose primary purpose is to stimulate and facilitate informal interactions and processes of knowledge sharing between people. The knowledge management initiatives studied by McKinlay (2002) and Alavi et al. (2005–6) both had such features to them. Second, the creation of online communities of practice also represents a means of developing and encouraging rich forms of communication and knowledge sharing that are ICT-mediated (McClure Wasko and Faraj 2000; Chua 2006; Fahey et al. 2007; Usoro et al. 2007; Hwang et al. 2015). However, by the late 2000s one of the most common ways that ICTs were being argued as facilitating knowledge management initiatives was via the use of social media (Li and Poon 2011; Matschke et al. 2012; Helms et al. 2017). Thus, in considering ICTs as a tool to facilitate communication and collaboration, the focus here is on social media.

Before considering the role that social media can play in knowledge management processes it is necessary to define the term. Social media refers to web-based platforms and applications that are collectively created via ongoing user contributions (see Definition). Two more formal definitions of social media are those of Kaplan and Haenlein (2010) and Kietzmann et al. (2011), and relate to the underlying Web 2.0 technology that form the platform on which social media are build. Kaplan and Haenlein (2010: 61) define social media as: 'a group of Internet-based applications that build on the ideological and technological foundations of Web 2.0, and that allow the creation and exchange of user-generated content'. Web 2.0 refers to a collection of technologies (e.g. RSS, Ajax, Javascript, Dynamic HTML) that made the World Wide Web more interactive, enabling the end user to contribute knowledge to platforms such as Wikipedia (Knol et al. 2008). Compared to first-generation websites and platforms (e.g. Web 1.0), where interaction between the user and the site was largely one way, with users taking content from sites, with Web 2.0 platforms, users have a greater degree of interactivity and play a more active role in contributing knowledge and the creation of the Web 2.0 platform (Allen 2010). It is in this context also that the term 'user-generated content' is used because Web 2.0 allows users to generate and publish content and to react and add to the contents of others, resulting in a collaborative World Wide Web. Similarly, Kietzman et al. (2011: 241) define social media as applications that 'employ mobile and web-based technologies to create highly interactive platforms via which individuals and communities share, co-create, discuss, and modify user-generated content'. Also here the focus is on a new type of applications enabled by mobile and web-based technologies. The applications that social media refer to are web-based and mobile applications including wikis (e.g. Wikipedia), (micro) blogs (e.g. WordPress, Twitter), social bookmarking (e.g. AddThis, Delicious), social networking (e.g. LinkedIn, MySpace, Facebook, Yammer), instant messaging (e.g. Whatsapp, WeChat), and media sharing (e.g. YouTube, Instagram) (adapted from Helms 2013).

DEFINITION **Social media**

A web-based service or platform, based on Web 2.0 technology, that enables the sharing, co-creation, discussion, and modification of user-generated content (Werder et al. 2014: 3).

In relation to knowledge management, social media are argued to have positive benefits for the workers who utilize them and for the organizations that employ them. In terms of worker benefits, the interactivity of social media is argued to help empower workers through creating opportunities for them to participate in dialogue and discussion and share their knowledge in inter-personal and community discussions (Levy 2009; Li and Poon 2011). It is even suggested that social media can be useful to overcome traditional barriers in knowledge sharing relating to the contribution and retrieval of knowledge (Leonardi 2017).

Two typical characteristics (i.e. affordances) of social media that make them so useful for knowledge management are the visibility and persistence of content on these platforms (Treem and Leonardi 2012). Content is potentially visible to a large audience who then can participate in the discussion. Leonardi (2017) uses a nice metaphor in this context by describing the communication on social media as 'communication through a leaky pipe'. It illustrates that communication on social media has a large, unintended audience and that it stimulates knowledge spill-overs in the organization (Von Krogh 2012). Furthermore, the persistence of content makes it a great archive for searching for answers and solutions—something that is much more difficult to achieve when knowledge is exchanged in person or through e-mails.

The use and value of social media for knowledge sharing is empirically researched by Mäntymäki and Riemer (2016). They studied the use of Yammer (an ESN) in five Australian companies. Their qualitative pre-study showed that Yammer was used for ideas and work discussion, problem solving, task management, events, and updates. Especially, the first two uses directly relate to knowledge sharing and creation in the organization, while messages about events and updates keep people informed and hence contribute to developing the TMS. The quantitative part of the study by Mäntymäki and Riemer (2016) showed that sharing knowledge and discussing ideas with colleagues are key contributors to value as experienced by the users of the ESN.

Further, the web-based nature of these technologies means that people can participate in knowledge sharing communities irrespective of their geographic location. Although it is technologically feasible to cross geographic boundaries, knowledge sharing across boundaries does not happen spontaneously as is shown by Hwang et al. (2015). They studied the knowledge sharing behaviour of employees of an IT consulting firm in the Fortune 500, in an online knowledge sharing community. The results showed that a traditional barrier for knowledge sharing, in other words sharing knowledge more readily with similar others (e.g. based on location, age, or education), also exists in an online context. This behaviour is explained by risk avoidance because with similar others people tend to feel more safe to ask what might be considered dumb questions. Especially in a global online knowledge sharing community where a post is publicly visible and also archived, people might show risk avoiding behaviour (Ellison et al. 2015). Although ESNs provide users the functionality to limit the audience who can see their posts, organizations might encourage their employees not to use these because it is in the interest of the company that knowledge is shared broadly (Ellison et al. 2015). But the study of Hwang et al. (2015) showed that the risk avoiding behaviour can be overcome when employees get more experienced in the online knowledge sharing community. They found that over time the preference of the employees shifted to sharing knowledge with others who have similar expertise rather than a similar background. Consequently, making a global online knowledge sharing community successful takes time. People need time to get to know each other and to learn about each other's expertise before true global knowledge sharing will take place.

Besides all the benefits that are ascribed to the use of social media for knowledge management purposes, there are also risks involved that relate to spill-over of knowledge when it is shared on social media (Von Krogh 2012). Although knowledge spill-over is considered useful when it happens within the organizational boundaries, it is typically considered a risk when knowledge spills-over to parties outside the organizational boundary, in other words to competitors (Von Krogh 2012). Spill-over of knowledge becomes a potential risk when employees have difficulty in distinguishing between organizational and public use of social media. This might be particular difficult for the new generation of 'digital natives' whose lives are intertwined with social media and who bring their own mobile devices to the workplace.

A second risk of using social media for knowledge sharing is the watering-down of knowledge (Von Krogh 2012). In this case, the problem is when knowledge from outside the organizational boundary flows into the organization. Social media are ideal for searching for knowledge outside the organization, especially since these tools are more user-friendly than the tools that organizations offer for storing and retrieving knowledge. The problem of using knowledge found on social media is that it might not be checked (i.e. of low quality) and that it is also freely available for competitors so it is difficult to gain a competitive advantage from such knowledge. Furthermore, internal knowledge might be watered-down because it is not used anymore or it is polluted with knowledge from outside the organization. In summary, social media can have unwanted effects of knowledge spill-over and watering-down of knowledge which might directly affect the competitive position of the organization.

Crowd-based approach to ICT-based knowledge management

The third practice-based use for ICTs in knowledge management activities is to facilitate the sourcing of knowledge outside the organization. This type of usage fits with both Earl's strategic school and Newell's crowd-based approach. It is based on the concept of crowd sourcing what has been defined by Howe (2006) as: 'the act of a company or institution taking a function once performed by employees and outsourcing it to an undefined (and generally large) network of people in the form of an open call'. The function that is being outsourced can be anything from a simple task (e.g. on Amazon's Mechanical Turk) to more complex R&D tasks on the InnoCentive platform (Ghezzi et al. 2017). From a knowledge management perspective the outsourcing of knowledge-intensive tasks is of interest. This is because of the potential such strategies provide to tap into knowledge outside the organizational boundaries. This is also in line with the ideas of open innovation: that organizations cannot only rely on their own research and development anymore and need to collaborate with other companies with complementary knowledge and skills—see Chapter 7 (Chesbrough 2003). Therefore, the potential of a crowd-based approach is that organizations can source ideas and engage in collaborative knowledge creation with parties outside the organizational boundary.

Another key element in crowd-sourcing is that it is outsourced to an 'undefined (and generally large) network of people' also referred to as the crowd (Howe 2006). The idea here is that the crowd knows more than a few individual experts, is more creative, and is better in decision-making. A well-known example of the capabilities of the crowd is Wikipedia, an online encyclopaedia that is created and edited by the crowd. The fact that this encyclopaedia contains much more information than traditional encyclopaedias ever had demonstrates that the crowd knows much more than a small group of expert people. Organizations have also discovered the wisdom of the crowd and try to tap into this knowledge. One specific group is of special interest to them, namely the users of their products and services. Users do have extremely valuable knowledge for organizations that stem from the use of their products (Von Hippel 1986). In the case of very large organizations (e.g. HP), their own workforce is sometimes also considered as the crowd. With hundreds or thousands of employees it is impossible to know everyone (that's why they also say 'If only HP knew what HP knows' (Davenport 1993)) and therefore this is also considered as a crowd that can generate creative and new ideas.

There are several approaches in which the crowd can be involved in the innovation process to make use of their knowledge. The following typology by Helms and Booij (2012) identifies five distinct approaches: (1) general community engagement; (2) ideas competitions; (3) interactive value creation; (4) participatory design; (5) product design. It is ordered based on increasing levels of user participation (going from 1 to 5). Each of these five approaches can be supported by social media, with the particular type of social media platform utilized being dependent on the specific goals of the organization and how the affordances of different social media can support this (Helms and Booij 2012). Of the five approaches, general community engagement and ideas competitions are most widely adopted. General community engagement involves a community approach where the company tries to engage (potential) customers in an online forum where they share experiences and provide feedback. A good example is the brand communities on Facebook of organizations such as StarBucks and Coca-Cola (Gallaugher and Ransbotham 2010). Ideas competitions are more focused and are aimed at generating new ideas for products or to solve problems. In the literature they have been studied extensively and examples include: SAPiens (Ebner et al. 2009), Dell IdeaStorm (Bayus 2013), MyStarBucksIdea (Bayus 2013), Accenture GrapeVine (O'Leary 2013), and IBM Thinkplace (Majchrzak et al. 2009). The process of an idea competition consists of five distinct phases and at its core it consists of idea generation and evaluation (Ebner et al. 2009). Idea generation is supported by mobile or web-based applications (http://www.ideastorm.com) where people can submit ideas. Depending on the design of the competition, users and/or experts can rate the ideas by 'liking' them, for example. Finally, a few ideas may lead to actual implementation by the organization. The ideas of so-called 'serial ideators' are more likely to be implemented by the organization than those of others, but once one of their ideas is implemented serial ideators lose interest in the competition (Bayus 2013). A potential problem with ideas competitions can be the posting of useless content (e.g. complaints), but by making the whole process visible to everyone such diversions are typically responded to by other users (Majchrzak and Ives 2009). In other words, the crowd will filter out such responses and therefore discourage users from posting useless content. An ideas competition is not necessarily hosted by the organization itself; it can also decide to use an innovation exchange platform such as InnoCentive (Feller et al. 2012). This is a third party platform that offers organizations the possibility to organize idea storms or challenges (i.e. for problem solving).

The other approaches with higher levels of user interaction focus on more close forms of collaboration between organizations and their users. An example of *participatory design* is Nike, which tapped into user innovation communities discussing basketball shoes (Füller et al. 2007). These were in-depth discussions focusing on the design of the shoes or improving shortcomings that the users experienced. In some cases, users also included detailed drawings of improved shoe designs to which Nike responded. Such communities clearly contain a wealth of knowledge for Nike because they are in direct contact with engaged users of their products and learn about user preferences concerning the design and possible improvements concerning comfort or performance of the shoes. The online communities were supported by message boards and online discussion forums. Users on the forum participated because of need (i.e. wanting better products) or out of excitement. Furthermore, the users were willing to share their knowledge free of charge, even knowing that the companies could make millions of dollars with this knowledge (Füller et al. 2007). The highest form of user participation is when users are directly involved in collaborative product design. In this case users need to have good design/engineering skills and in fact be professionals. Because of the intense collaboration required here, this usually does not take place through social media. It is however possible to use social media to recruit such professionals on a temporary or permanent basis. In the example of the basketball communities, companies occasionally recruited new designers from the community.

 ## Conclusion

This chapter has looked at the role that ICTs can play in facilitating knowledge management processes when a practice-based epistemology is utilized. One of the key aspects of this perspective is the assumption that there are significant limits involved in attempting to codify knowledge. Thus, in contrast to the way ICTs are used to manage knowledge when adopting an objectivist perspective (see Chapter 9), when a practice-based perspective is utilized, ICTs are not used for this purpose. Instead, from a practice-based perspective, the role of ICTs in knowledge processes is more concerned with facilitating the inter-personal communication processes which are essential to knowledge sharing. Linking back to the Table I, in the Introduction to Part 4, and also to Chapter 4 on knowledge management strategy, three distinct ways were identified and examined to use ICTs for this purpose. First, with a network-based approach, the role of ICTs is to provide a means for people to publicize their expertise and identify relevant experts, after which the social relations necessary to knowledge sharing can be developed. Second, using ICTs as collaboration tools, such as through the use of social media, various technologies are the medium via which people communicate and interact. Finally, with the crowd-based approach to knowledge management this logic is extended beyond the boundaries of the organization, to provide a mechanism via which organizations can use ICTs to access a diverse range of external expertise.

 ## Case study Yammer at Deloitte Australia

Deloitte is a well-known group of globally operating consulting firms with offices in almost any country in the world. All firms operating under this brand are a member of Deloitte Touche Tohmatsu, which is located in the UK. In total Deloitte employs 245,000 people worldwide who are active in tax, audit, and assurance, (technology) consulting, merger and acquisitions, and risk and advisory services. In such an organization it is important that employees can find each other when particular expertise is needed, to source ideas or to engage in collaborative problem solving. Many organizations take a top-down approach to such knowledge management initiatives and introduce applications and platforms to support the knowledge sharing needs of employees. However, at Deloitte they followed a bottom-up approach where the users took the lead in introducing a platform to support their needs. This is typical for new technologies such as social media that are easy to use and easily accessible in the cloud.

In 2008, employees in the Australian office started to use Yammer by creating an account and inviting other colleagues. Yammer is a web-based platform that can be characterized as an ESN platform. Its core functionality is similar to the more well-known Twitter platform. However, Yammer can also be used in a closed environment such as an organization, messages can be longer than on Twitter and can include documents, pictures, and links. Users can access Yammer through a web browser or by using the Yammer application (app) on their mobile device. Gradually the platform became more popular among employees, and between September 2008 and April 2011, 5,213 users participated in the platform by posting 44,588 messages in 1,275 threads (i.e. topics in which message are posted). In 2010, Deloitte decided to roll out the use of Yammer globally, and the CEO of Deloitte Australia was in charge of it.

Since the platform was adopted bottom-up, there was not a clear purpose defined for using it. Researching the threads provided Deloitte Australia with more insight into its purpose. The research was conducted in collaboration with researchers and students from the University of Sydney. Studying the topic of messages within threads showed that information sharing was by far the most popular use of the platform. Other uses of the platform include social conversation, praising other's work or contribution, discussion with colleagues, seeking advice, and problem solving.

Besides the knowledge management purposes of the platform, social conversation was also identified as being important in building the community and to increase trust. Yammer also has the feature to make specific groups and at Deloitte Australia such groups typically formed around service lines, regions, and industries (i.e. resembling the typical structure of a consulting firm). Messages in the groups were also analysed revealing that there were typically four different type of groups: conversational groups (i.e. virtual water cooler), solution oriented groups (i.e. innovation hot-spots), networks of expertise, and information sharing groups.

An important success factor in the use of the ESN platform is that users selected the platform themselves and also developed their own ways and purposes for using the platform. Too much management involvement in those early stages might have result in people turning away from the platform. In later stages management facilitated the use of the platform by understanding how the employees were actually using the system. This understanding was achieved by studying the groups and conversations that emerged on the platform.

Source: Riemer, K., and Tavakoli, A. (2013). 'The Role of Groups as Local Context in Large Enterprise Social Networks: A Case Study of Yammer at Deloitte Australia'. Report no. BIS WP2013, University of Sydney.

Question

1. In your opinion, how valuable is an enterprise social networking (ESN) platform (such as Yammer in this case study) in terms of appraising knowledge workers in knowledge-intensive organizations?

2. As with any social networking platform, there is often a group of users who are merely 'lurkers': i.e. they rarely contribute knowledge, but they know what is going on in the online groups they have joined. What would you as a manager do to turn 'passive lurkers' into 'active contributors' of knowledge in ESN forums and conversations?

 ## Review and Discussion Questions

1. Instead of building a proprietary social network platform to support expertise location, organizations can also decide to use an existing platform such as LinkedIn. To what extent do you think that LinkedIn is suitable for supporting expertise location in an organization? Does it contain the right information and functionality for expertise location? Are there any ethical considerations in asking employees to use a platform such as LinkedIn (i.e. can you ask them to share their personal details with the LinkedIn organization)?

2. As outlined, one risk with using social media profiles to identify sources of expertise is the issue of 'strategic self-presentation', where what people present is less an 'objective' perspective on their knowledge and expertise and is more a mechanism for self-publication. When looking for sources of expertise via this means, what, if anything, can be done to address this issue?

3. Despite the benefits of using social media there are also risks in using social media for knowledge sharing such as knowledge spill-over outside the organizational boundary and watering-down of knowledge. To what extent could a social media policy help, in your opinion, or are there other options you consider more effective?

4. An ideas competition can only be successful if people are motivated to share their ideas with an organization. This problem is similar to the problem of motivating people to share their knowledge discussed earlier in this book. What are possible incentives that an organization can use to stimulate the submission of ideas in an idea competition? What are the pros and cons of each of the incentives?

5. One challenge with using social media, and the Internet more generally, to identify knowledge and expertise is the question of the quality of the knowledge that is found. What is done to evaluate knowledge and information searches to minimise such risks?

 ## Suggestions for Further Reading

S. Newell (2015). 'Managing Knowledge and Managing Knowledge Work: What we Know and What the Future Holds', *Journal of Information Technology*, 30: 1-17.
Provides a succinct and up to date overview of the diverse ways in which ICTs can be involved in the management of knowledge and knowledge work.

M. Mäntymäki and K. Riemer (2016). 'Enterprise Social Networking: A Knowledge Management Perspective', *International Journal of Information Management*, 36/6: 1042–52.
In this paper the authors identity five main uses of ESNs and how this contributes to knowledge management in the organization. It also reveals that personal and work oriented ESNs are to some extent intertwined.

N. Oostervink, M. Agterberg, and M. Huysman (2016). 'Knowledge Sharing on Enterprise Social Media: Practices to Cope With Institutional Complexity', *Journal of Computer-Mediated Communication*, 21/2: 156–76.
This study of an organisation's use of enterprise social media (ESM) to share knowledge found that two dissimilar institutional complexities, namely logics of the corporation and logics of the profession, inform professionals' knowledge sharing behaviour. Professionals develop three coping practices in the form of connection management, reputation management, and information management to manage the ambiguities they face in engaging with ESM affordances.

A. Majchrzak, L. Cherbakov, and B. Ives (2009). 'Harnessing the Power of the Crowds with Corporate Social Networking Tools: How IBM Does It', *MIS Quarterly Executive*, 8/2: 151–6.
Describes the case of IBM and how it uses social media applications for crowd sourcing in their own organization and to identify experts networks based on the content they share and the relations that they have.

 To further your understanding of knowledge management in organizations explore the book's accompanying online resources at www.oup.com/uk/hislop4e/

PART 5

Socio-cultural Issues Related To Managing and Sharing Knowledge

While enormous numbers of organizations have implemented knowledge management initiatives, many of them have been either partial successes or outright failures. Research consistently reveals that some of the main obstacles to success in such initiatives are social and cultural factors. Thus, for those concerned with achieving an understanding of the dynamics of knowledge management initiatives, appreciating the significance of social and cultural factors is vital. The four chapters in this section of the book all deal with different aspects of this topic. While the early knowledge management literature arguably neglected socio-cultural aspects of knowledge management initiatives (Scarbrough and Swan 2001), this is not true of contemporary knowledge management literature. This is because, as the literature on knowledge management has evolved, greater recognition has been taken of such issues. Thus, there now exists a significant body of writing which highlights the crucial role that socio-cultural factors play in shaping the character and dynamics of knowledge management initiatives. The chapters in this section of the book make use of this work. Chapter 11 provides an overview of the important influence that a range of social and cultural factors (such as trust, conflict, differences in cultural background between collaborators) have on the character and dynamics of organizational knowledge management processes and why it can't be taken for granted that people will be willing to actively participate in such processes. Chapter 12 examines the dynamics of knowledge-related processes within a homogeneous group context, in communities of practice, a form of organizing and interaction that is argued to facilitate knowledge sharing. The chapter examines the positive and negative aspects of such forms of group work, which can involve both face-to-face and virtual collaboration. Chapter 13 builds from this by examining the dynamics of knowledge sharing in a totally different group context, where, unlike in communities of practice, people have limited common knowledge and only a weak sense of shared identity. This can include knowledge processes within multidisciplinary teams, or knowledge processes which span functional or organizational boundaries. Chapter 14 focuses on the topics of power, politics, and conflict, which, as will be seen, are under-researched areas in the knowledge management literature.

11

The Influence of Socio-cultural Factors in Motivating Workers to Participate in Knowledge Management Initiatives

Introduction

As the topic of knowledge management has matured and evolved, so has interest in the human, cultural, and social dimensions of the topic. There is now a substantial body of writing and research on how these factors influence the character and dynamics of knowledge management processes, and workers' willingness to become involved in them. The aim of this chapter is to provide an overview and introduction to this literature and the issues it addresses.

The importance of human, social, and cultural factors in shaping knowledge management processes is visible in a significant amount of case study evidence on knowledge management initiatives (see various examples presented throughout the chapter). This work shows that human, social, and cultural factors are often key in shaping the success or failure of knowledge management initiatives, and that a reluctance by workers to participate in knowledge management activities is not uncommon. The positive impact of workers' engagement in knowledge sharing activities, and the dysfunctional consequences of knowledge hoarding/ hiding, are visible in the way they can impact on individual and organizational performance. Thus, for example, Henttonen et al. (2016) identified a positive link between inter-personal knowledge sharing and individual performance, while Lee et al. (2010) and Cheung et al. (2016) identified a positive relationship between knowledge sharing within teams and team-level innovation performance. Conversely, Evans et al. (2015) found that levels of knowledge hoarding (and perceived hoarding) were negatively related to both team and organizational-level performance.

What is suggested here is that, whatever approach to knowledge management an organization adopts, the motivation of workers to participate in such processes will be key to their success. The importance of human agency to the success of knowledge management initiatives flows largely from the character of organizational knowledge. Primarily, much organizational knowledge, rather than being explicit in a disembodied form, is personal, tacit, and embodied in people. Ozlati (2015: 192) suggested that 'a significant amount of organizational knowledge resides in the minds of individuals.' Thus knowledge management activities require a willingness on the part of those who possess important organizational knowledge to participate in such processes. Or, as Rutten et al. (2016: 200) argue, 'accessing this knowledge is only possible through [the] active participation of the people carrying this knowledge.'

In exploring this topic the chapter begins by conceptualizing the decision workers face about whether to participate in knowledge management initiatives as being comparable to a 'public good dilemma'. After this, the next two sections examine how the context in which most knowledge management initiatives occur shapes workers' attitudes to knowledge management processes by influencing the nature of the relationship between employers/managers and workers, and also inter-personal relations between workers. The fourth and fifth sections look at the role of inter-personal trust and how a worker's sense of belonging to and identity with work groups shapes their willingness to codify and share knowledge with colleagues. The chapter closes by examining the literature which considers the influence that national culture and individual personality can have in shaping people's attitudes to participating in knowledge activities.

The share/hoard dilemma

The decision workers face about whether to participate in knowledge-related activities has been compared to a classical public good dilemma, with the knowledge workers have access to in their organizations being considered a public good (Cabrera and Cabrera 2002; Renzl 2008; Hau et al. 2016; Razmerita et al. 2016). A public good is a shared resource which members of a community or network can benefit from, regardless of whether they contributed to it or not, and whose value does not diminish through such usage. Collective organizational knowledge resources are thus a public good as anyone can utilize them, whether they have contributed to their development or not. In such situations there is thus the potential for people to 'free-ride' by utilizing such resources but never contributing to their development. The dilemma for the worker is that there are potentially positive and negative consequences to either sharing knowledge and contributing to the public good, or hoarding knowledge and acting as a free-rider (see Time to reflect). Thus in deciding how to act in such situations workers are likely to attempt to evaluate the potential positive and negative individual consequences of sharing or hoarding knowledge.

 Time to reflect   Knowledge as a public good?

If a public good is a shared resource whose value does not diminish through use, to what extent can knowledge be considered a public good? Does the use of shared knowledge diminish or affect its value? Is there a risk that sharing it with large numbers of people may reduce its value?

Some of the main potential benefits to workers of knowledge sharing are that doing so may be intrinsically rewarding (see for example Jeon et al. 2011; Ma and Chan 2014; Cavaliere et al. 2015), that there may be benefits at the group level (such as enhanced team or organizational

Table 11.1 The Potential Advantages and Disadvantages to Workers of Sharing their Knowledge

Knowledge Sharing	Advantages	Intrinsic reward of process of sharing
		Group/organizational-level benefits (such as improved group performance)
		Material reward (financial or non-financial)
		Enhanced individual status
	Disadvantages	Can be time-consuming
		Potentially giving away a source of power and expertise to others
Knowledge Hoarding (Free-Riding)	Advantage	Avoids risk of giving away and losing a source of power/status
	Disadvantage	Extent of knowledge may not be understood or recognized

performance), that there is some material reward (such as a pay bonus or a promotion), or that a person's status as an expert becomes enhanced (see Table 11.1). However, the negative consequences of contributing knowledge are that, first, doing so may be time-consuming. Second, there is the risk that workers are 'giving away' a source of individual power and status (see more later and also in Chapter 14). Finally, there are also the rewards/benefits of hoarding to be accounted for. While the benefit of hoarding knowledge (free-riding) is that the worker avoids the risk of giving away knowledge, and the power and status that may accompany it, a potential negative consequence is that by doing so they never receive full recognition for what they do know. There is now an extensive body of evidence in the knowledge management literature that considers such issues. The key aim of this chapter is to provide some insights into this literature, shedding light on the factors shaping people's knowledge sharing/hoarding decisions.

A potential limitation of this way of conceptualizing worker's knowledge sharing/hoarding decisions is that it presents an overrational view of how people think and act. Fundamentally, workers' behaviour and decisions are not only shaped by rational calculation. Spender (2003) develops an analysis which suggests that issues of emotion also shape people's decision-making processes. For Spender, emotions affect how people think and act when they have to deal with situations beyond their control and when uncertainty exists. The importance of the linkage between emotion and uncertainty is that uncertainty is argued to be a fundamental feature of organizational life. In studies of knowledge management initiatives, the emotion of fear has been highlighted by a number of writers as inhibiting people from participating in knowledge management initiatives, with the workers studied fearing a number of things, including a loss of status and power, the loss of their jobs, and a fear of ridicule related to concerns that sharing knowledge may reveal its limitations to others (Ardichvili et al. 2003; Newell et al. 2007; Renzl 2008; Hsu and Chang 2014; Matschke et al. 2014).

Van den Hooff et al. (2012) provide insights into the role that emotions can play in people's attitude to knowledge sharing. In a study of Dutch information technology (IT) workers they examined the extent to which the emotions of pride and empathy affected people's eagerness and willingness to share knowledge. Empathy is defined as a person's ability to sympathetically react to the experiences of others, and is linked to the sense of shared identity with others. Pride is defined as a positive self-evaluation of one's own capabilities and skills. They hypothesized that both emotions would be positively linked to people's willingness and eagerness to share knowledge. In the case of empathy it was assumed that the stronger a person's group identity and level of empathy, the more likely they would be to share knowledge. In relation to pride they argued that the greater the pride someone had in their knowledge, the happier they would be to share it with others. As hypothesized, they found that levels of both pride and empathy were positively related to people's willingness and eagerness to share knowledge (See also Illustration 11.1.).

 Illustration 11.1   Sharing knowledge via social media platforms: a social dilemma perspective

Razmerita et al. (2016) used the 'social dilemma' perspective to identify the enablers and barriers to knowledge sharing via social media among some Danish workers. They collected data via both an online survey and interviews. In doing so, they considered the extent to which a diverse range of individual, organizational, and technological factors acted to encourage or discourage the workers from sharing knowledge. For example, in terms of individual-level factors they examined whether people enjoyed helping others, or whether they received monetary reward for sharing knowledge among other things. In terms of organizational-level factors they examined a range of factors including whether knowledge sharing was encouraged or whether there was a lack of management support. Finally, in terms of technological factors, they considered factors such as whether IT systems were regarded as usable and whether people had received adequate training, etc.

Their analysis found that the most important factors which motivated and enabled knowledge sharing were when people enjoyed helping others, people regarded knowledge sharing as important, people recognized that their knowledge sharing was valuable to their organization, knowledge sharing was both encouraged and recognized by their employer, and knowledge sharing was an intrinsic part of the organizational culture. In term of barriers to knowledge sharing, the most significant was a lack of time, with other important inhibiting factors being the perception that colleagues were not engaging in knowledge sharing or that there was a lack of management support for knowledge sharing.

Question

On the basis of this analysis, what recommendations would you make to any organization wanting to encourage its workers to share knowledge?

In understanding the socio-cultural factors which shape workers' willingness to participate in organizational knowledge management initiatives it is also important to take account of the context in which such action takes place, as this shapes workers' relations with colleagues and their managers/employers, and as a consequence influences workers' knowledge sharing/hoarding decisions. The next section looks at the worker–manager relationship in the context of the employment relationship.

The context of the employment relationship: employer–employee relations in business organizations

The focus in this section is narrowly on one specific type of organization: private business organizations operating in capitalist markets. While the analysis here is of limited use in understanding the manager/employee relationship in other types of organization, such as public sector or voluntary organizations, it is arguable that the vast majority of knowledge management initiatives occur within private business organizations.

Much analysis in the knowledge management literature portrays the knowledge possessed by an organization's workforce as an economic asset which is owned by the employing organization, and which they have the power to manage. However, the knowledge that workers have can also be conceptualized as belonging to them rather than their employer. From this perspective, while workers may apply, develop, and use their knowledge towards the achievement of organizationally directed goals and objectives, the knowledge is fundamentally the workers', to use as, when, where, how, and if they want. This highlights the potential tension between workers and the organizations they work for over who owns and controls their knowledge, and points towards an important factor which may inhibit the willingness of workers to share their knowledge.

Arguably, the origin of this tension is the intrinsic character of the employment relationship in private business organizations. First, the employment relationship involves organizational management acting as the mediating agents of shareholders and typically places workers in a subordinate position, with no ability to shape corporate objectives and with one of management's key roles being to achieve their shareholders' objectives (for profit, market share, etc.) through controlling and directing workers' efforts (Tsoukas 2000; Contu and Willmott 2003). The issue of power in the employment relationship is returned to and examined in more detail in Chapter 14. Second, embedded in the employment relationship is the potential for conflict between the interests of managers/shareholders and workers.

In the context of workers' knowledge this tension relates not only to who 'owns' an employee's knowledge, but how and for what purposes such knowledge is used. Two examples of such conflict are examined by Kamoche and Maguire (2011) and Trusson et al. (2014). In both cases, conflicts emerged from workers' unhappiness regarding the way management expected them to utilize their knowledge. The Kamoche and Maguire paper is examined in more detail in Chapter 14. In the situation examined by Trusson et al. (2014), IT service workers resisted efforts by their managers to codify knowledge they generated in solving customer problems into an organizational database. Management's intention in this case was to improve organizational efficiency through creating a database of solutions that workers could utilize, which would speed up the problem solving process. However, the workers either felt unwilling or unable to do so (they regarded such codification efforts as difficult to achieve and time-consuming, and didn't feel they had the time available to invest in this activity as doing so would prevent them from meeting their ongoing performance targets).

While management may perceive that it is in the interests of the organization to encourage workers to codify their knowledge, workers may be reluctant to do so if they feel that such efforts will negatively affect them through diminishing their power and/or status. Such concerns can be illustrated by the findings of Serenko and Bontis's (2016) research into the antecedents of knowledge hiding from colleagues. This research was conducted with employees of credit unions in Canada and the USA. One cause of knowledge hiding by these workers was perceptions of job insecurity. Serenko and Bontis explain this by arguing that workers hid knowledge from each other as a way to protect their personal 'expert power' and demonstrate their individual value to their employer. These examples show that such concerns by workers mean that they may not participate in organizational knowledge management processes if they perceive there to be negative personal consequences from doing so.

It is also useful to acknowledge that a wide range of factors other than the immediate employment relationship can affect a worker's relationship with their employer and shape their knowledge sharing attitudes. This can include a manager's personality and management style (Yeo and Marquardt 2015), the nature of people's jobs, including the amount of autonomy they possess (Ozlati 2015; Stenius et al. 2016), or the extent to which they experience time pressures to undertake their normal work activities (see the Trusson et al. 2014 example immediately above, plus Vuori and Okkonen 2012; Matschke et al. 2014), and the character of an organization's structure (Cavaliere et al. 2015).

'Procedural justice' is another such factor (Kim and Mauborgne 1998). Procedural justice represents the extent to which organizational decision-making processes are fair, with fairness being related to how much people are involved in decision-making, the clarity of communication regarding why decisions are made, and the clarity of the expectations. Kim and Mauborgne (1998) suggest that, when all these factors are addressed, workers will feel valued for their intellectual capabilities and skills, and that experiencing such feelings can impact on workers' attitudes towards knowledge sharing: 'when they felt that their ideas and person were recognized through fair process, they were willing to share their knowledge and give their all' (1998: 332; see Time to reflect). Empirical support for these ideas are provided by Han et al. (2010), who present the findings of a study involving 260 knowledge-intensive Taiwanese companies. A key finding from this study was that employee participation in decision-making processes provided employees with a sense of psychological ownership over the decisions. Further, this sense of psychological ownership was positively linked to levels of employee organizational commitment, which was in turn positively related to levels of knowledge sharing. Huo et al (2016) reinforce these ideas, finding that when perceptions of procedural justice are low, workers are likely to hoard their knowledge in order to protect it.

 Time to reflect   Expectations of equity?

What level of equity do workers expect from the organizations they work in? For example, with regards to involvement in decision-making, what types of decisions and what levels of involvement do workers regard as fair?

The ubiquity of conflict in business organizations and its impact on knowledge processes

A general weakness of the mainstream knowledge management literature is that issues of conflict, power, and politics are generally neglected (see Chapters 1 and 14). However, such factors arguably can have a significant influence on the character and dynamics of knowledge processes in organizations. The purpose of this section is to highlight the important role that inter-personal and inter-group conflict can have on knowledge processes in organizations. Primarily, the actual or perceived differences of interest between individuals or groups in organizational life in general, or in knowledge management projects specifically, may affect attitudes to participating in such activities. The analysis of how such factors influence organizational knowledge processes is returned to and developed in Chapter 14 by adding the issue of power into the analysis.

The typical neglect of conflict (and power and politics) in the mainstream knowledge management literature is largely due to the assumptions of consensus and goal congruence in business organizations that exists in the majority of the knowledge management literature. For example, as outlined in Chapter 1, Schultze and Stabell (2004) suggest that one dimension against which the knowledge management literature can be characterized is the extent to which consensus in society and organizations is assumed, with their analysis suggesting that consensus represents the mainstream perspective in the knowledge management literature. This perspective has echoes of Fox's unitarist framework on organizations, where everyone in an organization is assumed to have common interests and shared values (Fox 1985).

However, such a perspective on organizations can be challenged by evidence and analysis which suggests the opposite, that conflict is an inherent and unavoidable feature of life in business organizations. A radical version of this argument, similar to that developed in the previous section, can be found in knowledge management literature adopting what Schultze and Stabell (2004) label a dissensus perspective (see Figure 1.2) and suggests that conflict between management and workers is an inevitable part of the employment relationship. A less radical version of this argument aligns with what Fox (1985) labelled the pluralist perspective on organizations, where organizations are regarded as a coalition of different interest groups acting in a coordinated way. Marshall and Brady (2001: 103), reflecting such a perspective, refer to the 'frequent organizational reality of divergent interests, political struggles and power relations'. Empirical support for this perspective can also be found in the work of Buchanan (2008), where political behaviour has been found to be a common feature of organizational life.

The contemporary knowledge literature contains numerous examples where such conflicts have affected attitudes to knowledge sharing (Hislop 2003; Currie and Kerrin 2004; Currie et al. 2008; Mørk et al. 2010; Heizmann 2011; Yeo and Marquardt 2015; Holten et al. 2016; Marin et al. 2016). Such conflicts can be due to factors such as personality differences (Chen et al. 2011b; Yeo and Marquardt 2015), inappropriate behaviour of people (Holten et al. 2016), historical antagonisms between different interest groups (Hislop 2003; Currie and Kerrin 2004; Currie et al. 2008), or competing and conflicting knowledge claims made by different individuals/groups (Mørk et al. 2010; Heizmann 2011; Marin et al. 2016). For example, Currie et al.'s (2008) analysis of an unsuccessful attempt to codify and share knowledge on risk and patient safety within National Health Service hospitals in the UK was affected by various conflicting interests. First, conflicts of interest existed between clinicians and managers regarding priorities, with clinicians regarded as being more focused on the quality of patient care, and management seen as being more focused on the efficient management of cost. Further differences existed between different professional groups regarding the core question of how to define the term 'risk', with various professional groups conceptualizing it in very different ways. These differences, along with various other factors, resulted in clinicians generally being unwilling to codify their knowledge as required.

 Illustration 11.2 The impact of task and relationship conflict on knowledge sharing

Chen et al. (2011) conducted research with staff in two Chinese software companies to examine how conflict was related to knowledge sharing. In looking at this topic they examined both task and relationship conflict. Task conflict is defined as conflict in relation to work activities and tasks, for example, relating to work procedures, resource allocation, etc. Personality conflict relates to conflict caused by significant differences in personality relating to issues such as inter-personal style or beliefs. In the paper, Chen et al. examine how both types of conflict impact on three psychological states (perceived meaningfulness of work, perception of safety to express dissenting views, perception of availability of resources to complete tasks), and how these psychological states impacted on people's level of work engagement and knowledge sharing. Crucially, they hypothesized that task conflict would have a positive impact on the three psychological states, as this type of conflict facilitates positive dialogue and information sharing related to the completion of work tasks. In contrast they hypothesized that personality conflict would be negatively related to each of the psychological states, as this type of conflict was likely to distract people from work and create negative situations which may be difficult to resolve.

Chen et al. found that all the hypothesized relationships in their model were supported. Thus task conflict had a positive impact on people's psychological stages, while personality conflict had a negative one, people's psychological state was positively related to levels of work engagement, and, finally, levels of work engagement were positively linked to knowledge sharing. Thus, conflict does not necessarily have a negative impact on knowledge sharing.

Question

Of these two types of conflict, which do you think is most common in organizations?

As per Illustration 11.2, and as was also found by Ferguson and Taminiau (2014—see Illustration 3.5 in Chapter 3), inter-personal or inter-group conflict does not always necessarily have a negative effect on knowledge processes, such as making people unwilling to share knowledge with certain others they disagree with. In some cases conflicts and differences of opinion may facilitate processes of knowledge sharing and knowledge creation. In these cases, differences of perspective or opinion result in dialogue where each group or individual attempts to understand the perspective of the other in order to attempt to resolve the differences and reach consensus via a process of negotiated discussion. However, such positive outcomes from conflict only occur when people or groups are willing to engage in such dialogue, which is not always the case (see Time to reflect).

 Time to reflect   Conflicts of interest in knowledge sharing

Can you think of an example from your own experience where there was inter-personal or inter-group conflict with regards to the sharing and utilization of some knowledge? What was the basis of the conflict?

The importance of taking account of how conflict (and power and politics) shapes people's willingness to participate in knowledge management processes is not just due to the fact that conflict is an inherent/common feature of organizational life. As will be shown in Chapter 14, it is also due to the close interrelationship that exists between power and knowledge.

Inter-personal trust

This section highlights the crucial role that inter-personal trust can have in shaping people's attitudes to participating in organizational knowledge processes. As will be seen, it has been generally found that the lower the level of trust a person has in someone else, the less willing they will be to share knowledge with them. However, this section also highlights the complexity of the concept of trust, and thus after providing a general definition of it and outlining how levels of trust affect attitudes to knowledge sharing, the concept will be unpacked through considering both the distinction between trust and a person's 'propensity to trust' as well as the typologies of distinctive types of trust that have been developed.

The crucial role of trust in shaping people's willingness to participate in knowledge-related processes has been recognized by an extensive number of writers (Andrews and Delahaye 2000; Abrams et al. 2003; Ardichvili et al. 2003; Levin and Cross 2004; Mooradian et al. 2006; Newell et al. 2007; Holste and Fields 2010; Zhou et al. 2010; Hsu and Chang 2014; Yeo and Marquardt 2015; Holten et al. 2016). Fundamentally, a lack of trust between individuals is likely to inhibit the extent to which they are willing to share knowledge with each other. To understand why this is the case it is useful to formally define what trust is and how it shapes the character of inter-personal relationships.

Trust can be defined as 'the willingness of a party to be vulnerable to the actions of another party based on the expectation that the other will perform a particular action important to the trustor' (Mooradian et al. 2006: 524; see Definition). Therefore, if trust exists, a person is likely to act on faith by the unilateral provision of resources, information, etc. (in this context giving knowledge), with the expectation that this action will be reciprocated at some point in the future. Thus trust involves an element of risk, where a person makes themselves vulnerable to another by providing knowledge prior to receiving anything in return, with one risk being that the other might act opportunistically and not provide anything in return (Cheung et al. 2016). The existence of trust helps mediate and reduce the perception of risk people experience and provides a level of confidence that their action will be reciprocated.

DEFINITION   Trust

The belief people have about the likely behaviour of others, and the assumption that they will honour their obligations (not acting opportunistically). A trusting relationship is based on an expectation of reciprocity or mutual benefit.

However, sharing knowledge on the basis of trust arguably involves an unavoidable element of uncertainty, and can thus be a process which produces and is shaped by emotion (see earlier section in this chapter for a discussion on the relationship between uncertainty and emotion). Knowledge sharing can be a time-consuming and uncertain process. Not only is there uncertainty on whether someone will reciprocate a trust-based action, but even when there is reciprocation there will be an element of uncertainty regarding the utility of the knowledge received. Acting on the basis of trust, due to the uncertainty involved, can therefore generate and produce strong emotions, both positive and negative, with, for example, someone feeling anger when their trust has been betrayed, or where someone feels a sense of happiness and joy when a trust-based action is effectively reciprocated.

Illustration 11.3   The impact of affect and cognitive-based trust on knowledge sharing

Rutten et al. (2016) examined the extent to which varying levels of both cognitive and affect-based trust (see Table 11.2) affected levels of knowledge sharing. This was done for both explicit codified knowledge and implicit knowledge, which they defined as knowledge that can be partially codified and is 'somewhere between tacit and explicit knowledge' (p. 200). Rutten et al.'s hypothesis was that increased levels of both forms of trust would be positively linked to levels of knowledge sharing. Rutten et al. collected data by distributing surveys to workers in various departments of one large financial organization in the Netherlands.

Rutten et al.'s hypotheses were supported, with increased levels of knowledge sharing, for both explicit and implicit knowledge, occurring when levels of both cognitive and affect-based trust were high. Further, when comparing the results for implicit and explicit knowledge, the relationship between levels of trust and knowledge sharing was stronger for implicit knowledge. Finally, they also made a similar comparison between the results for affect-based and cognitive-based trust, and found the relationship to be stronger with affect-based trust. Overall therefore, trust was positively linked to knowledge sharing, particularly in the case of implicit knowledge and affect-based trust. Thus, with respect to the sharing of implicit or tacit knowledge, strong, emotional-based trust between people is important.

Question

Why is trust more important for the sharing of implicit knowledge than for the sharing of explicit knowledge?

Research has found trust to be a complex concept. One aspect of this is the distinction that can be made between a person's general propensity to trust others and specific instances where trust exists in particular people (Mooradian et al. 2006). Mooradian et al. conceptualize a person's propensity to trust as being a relatively enduring predisposition they have which is a facet of the personality trait of 'agreeableness', one of the five dimensions in the five-factor personality model (see later section in this chapter on the five-factor model). Thus the propensity to trust is a 'general willingness to trust others' (Mooradian et al. 2006: 525) which can vary significantly between people. In contrast, the act of trusting is a specific instance in a particular context and at a particular time, where trust is extended to or developed in a particular entity (person, group, organization). Mooradian et al. argue that the greater a person's propensity to trust, the more likely they will be to extend trust to others in specific contexts. As will be discussed later, they examine how a person's propensity to trust is related to knowledge sharing attitudes and conclude that this personality variable can influence people's general willingness to share knowledge with others.

A number of analyses introduce another layer of complexity by suggesting that trust has multiple dimensions and that there is more than one type of trust. For instance Wang et al. (2006) distinguish between calculus-, knowledge-, and identification-based trust, while Lee et al. (2010) talk of reliance and disclosure-based trust. The most common typology utilized in the knowledge management literature (McAllister 1995; see Table 11.2) differentiates between cognitive and affect-based trust (see Illustration 11.3; see also for example Zhou et al. 2010; Holste and Fields 2010; and Rutten et al. 2016). Further, this work suggests that each type of trust is developed in quite different ways, and that they have a complex, mutually interdependent relationship. However, there is inadequate space here to fully describe, compare, and contrast these different typologies.

Table 11.2 McAllister's Two Types of Trust

Type of Trust	Description of Trust
Cognitive-based	Trust in a person's competence to carry out a particular activity, based on knowledge of person's past performance.
Affect-based	An emotional form of trust based on strength of personal relation between people, developed over time, where a sense of mutual care exists.

Source: McAllister (1995); see also Holste and Fields (2010); Rutten et al. (2016).

The final issue touched on here is the fact that trust can be developed not only in individual people, but also in groups, teams, or organizations, and that these types of trust can have an equally important influence on a person's willingness to share knowledge with others. For example, Renzl (2008) found evidence that the greater the extent to which workers trusted their managers the more likely they would be to have a positive attitude to sharing knowledge with colleagues. Ozlati (2015), based on a study of diverse R&D workers, also found that institutional-based trust (the ability of an organization to ensure that employees are trustworthy) positively moderated the relationship between autonomy and knowledge sharing. Ardichvili et al. (2003) reached similar conclusions with respect to people's willingness to sharing knowledge within the context of a virtual community of practice. Finally, Usoro et al. (2007)—see the next section and the communities of practice literature more generally (see Chapter 12)—suggest that the greater a person's level of trust in and identification with a particular work group or community, the more likely they will be to be willing to share knowledge with others in that community/group. Cheung et al (2016) reached similar conclusions with respect to knowledge sharing in diverse innovation teams, with low levels of team-based trust found to inhibit knowledge sharing.

The issue of trust links to themes examined in a number of the remaining chapters in this section of the book. First, it is relevant in Chapter 12 on communities of practice where the nature of inter-personal relations in communities of practice, in which groups of people have shared identity and values, facilitates the development of high levels of trust among community members, which has positive consequences for intra-community knowledge sharing. Trust is also examined in Chapter 13, on group-based working where people do not have shared values and identity, which makes the development of trust more difficult.

Group identity

This section examines how issues of personal identity can affect the extent to which and ways in which workers participate in organizational knowledge processes. As will be seen, research has shown that the extent to which people feel a part of and identify with their organization, a project team, a work group, or a community of practice can significantly shape their willingness to participate in knowledge processes. This links closely to the final parts of the previous section on how people's level of trust in a team or organization can affect their attitude to knowledge sharing. Rosendaal and Bijlsma-Frankema (2015), based on a study of team-based knowledge sharing, suggest that trust in team members facilitates the development of a common identity among team members. Further, Chapter 5 noted how knowledge-intensive workers can identify strongly with the clients they work for, with Ravishankar and Pan (2008) presenting an example from an Indian IT consultancy firm where the sense of identity some staff had with the client firm made them unwilling to participate in their employer's knowledge management initiative due to concerns that they would give away valuable client knowledge to colleagues. Rosendaal and Bijlsma-Frankema (2015) summarize these ideas succinctly by concluding that 'members who accept a team as part of their identity are better prepared to share their knowledge and thus tend to put in more effort to reach team goals' (p. 245).

Further, the extensive literature on communities of practice (see Chapter 12) suggests that when people feel a sense of identity with a community this facilitates the development of trust with other community members and is likely to create a positive attitude towards sharing knowledge with other community members. For example, Usoro et al. (2007), who examined a virtual, IT-mediated community of practice in a Fortune 500 global IT company, found that people's level of community trust was positively related to knowledge sharing.

Finally, a number of studies have shown how workers' identity with the particular functional group or business unit that they work in can influence their knowledge sharing patterns, with it being common for people who have a strong sense of identity with their function or business unit being relatively unwilling to share knowledge with people from outside of these areas (see e.g. Hislop 2003). For example, Rosendaal (2009) found that the more people identified with the teams they worked in, the more likely they were to share knowledge with other team members. Further, Currie and Kerrin's (2003) study of the sales and marketing business of a UK-based pharmaceutical company found that the existence of strong subcultures within the sales and marketing divisions created an unwillingness among staff to share knowledge across these functional boundaries.

All this research thus suggests that one of the key effects of a worker's sense of identity is to influence who they are and are not willing to share knowledge with. The issues touched on here will be examined more extensively in Chapter 12, which looks at the characteristics of knowledge processes within communities of practice where people have a strong sense of shared identity; and in Chapter 13, which examines knowledge processes where people do not have such a strong sense of shared identity, such as in cross-functional or multidisciplinary team working.

National culture

The extent to which national cultural characteristics shape people's attitude to participation in knowledge management activities is a subject on which knowledge is increasing (see for example Li et al.'s 2014 meta-analysis of relevant studies). Much of the analysis which links issues of national culture to knowledge management has come from studies of cross-national collaborations, where cultural differences have been found to play a significant role. For example, this was the case with Inkpen and Pien's (2006) study of Chinese–Singaporean collaboration, Li's (2010) study of IT-based communication between workers from the USA and China, Boh and Xu's (2013) study of knowledge sharing between workers in Norway and Vietnam, and Zimmermann and Ravishankar's (2014) study of knowledge sharing between German and Indian workers.

The assumption that a person's cultural background will shape their attitude to knowledge and knowledge management activities is something that is explicitly acknowledged within the practice-based epistemology (see Chapter 3; see also Illustration 11.4). Thus, as was outlined, this epistemology suggests that people's knowledge and understanding, what counts as valid types of knowledge, etc., will be shaped by cultural factors, including national cultural characteristics. This idea has been reinforced by a number of published studies which have looked specifically at how the characteristics of particular cultural values impact on people's knowledge management activities (see e.g. Huang et al. 2008; Tong and Mitra 2009; McAdam et al. 2012). Kanzler (2010) on German and Chinese scientists is a good example of such research, showing how the attitudes of the scientists from both countries to knowledge sharing appeared to be shaped by national cultural characteristics. For example, in the study it was found that concerns about a loss of power were negatively related to the intention to share knowledge of the German, but not the Chinese scientists. Kanzler argued that this was because German society is more individualistic than Chinese society and so concerns about a loss of power due to sharing and 'giving up' knowledge were greater for the German scientists.

Illustration 11.4 Factors influencing knowledge transfer in different cultural contexts

Li et al. (2014) undertook a meta-analysis of studies on knowledge transfer in different cultural contexts in order to understand the factors shaping these processes. In terms of cultural characteristics they utilized the work of Hofstede, which characterizes people from the same countries as having similar cultural characteristics, with a particular focus on the power distance and individualism–collectivism dimensions. In relation to the power distance dimension, in countries with high power distance scores, high levels of inequality are regarded as acceptable, and workers typically unquestioningly accept guidance and knowledge from their superiors as valid and legitimate, whereas in countries with low power distance scores, superiors are regarded more as equals, and their knowledge is not always accepted unquestioningly. In relation to the individualism-collectivism dimension, in countries where individualism is strong people are relatively self-centred, and primarily focus on the achievement of individual goals. In contrast, in countries where collectivist values are strong, people are more orientated towards collaboration with group members and focus on the goals of the groups they identify with.

Li et al.'s (2014) analysis found that these cultural characteristics affected the character of knowledge transfer processes in various ways. In countries which have low power distance scores and which are individualist in orientation (such as the UK, Denmark, or Germany) people are less likely to engage in knowledge transfer activities as they are more likely to be independent and autonomous, being happy to depend on their own knowledge. However, in such contexts people will engage in knowledge transfer activities if they regard it as being in their own best interests to do so (such as to access useful knowledge they do not possess). Second, when evaluating the credibility of a knowledge provider, due to the importance of authority, workers in high power distance cultures are more likely to assume the knowledge of senior managers as unquestioningly being legitimate, and are more likely to engage in uni-directional, top-down process of knowledge transfer. In contrast, in low power distance countries people are less deferential to hierarchy and will typically engage in knowledge transfer activities with anyone regarded as credible, irrespective of their hierarchical position. Finally, in high power distance countries, due to people's strength of affiliation to the groups they are a part of, high levels of within-group trust, and strong social relations are likely to exist, facilitating within-group knowledge transfer activity. Such strong levels of within-group relations are

> less common in individualist cultures, and thus the conditions for within-group knowledge transfer processes are weaker.
>
> ··
>
> Question
>
> Hofstede's work assumes that cultures are relatively homogeneous within a country. To what extent does culture vary within countries, particularly large countries such as the USA or Russia?

How national cultural factors influence cross-national collaborations and processes of knowledge sharing will be considered further in Chapter 13 on cross-community knowledge processes, as cross-national collaboration can be conceptualized as a cross-community form of collaboration.

Personality

The final factor considered which may shape workers' attitudes to participating in knowledge management processes is not related to the socio-cultural characteristics of the work environment, but is concerned with personality. Fundamentally, some research suggests that people with certain personality traits may have a more positive attitude to knowledge sharing than others. However, in general, this is a very underexplored topic in the knowledge management literature.

A number of studies in this area have concluded that certain personality traits did appear to be positively related to knowledge sharing attitudes. All the studies in this area (Cabrera and Cabrera 2005; Mooradian et al. 2006) make use of the five-factor personality model (see Illustration 11.5). This personality model, which is becoming the dominant way of conceptualizing personality, suggests that human personality can be understood to be made up of five broad traits: openness, conscientiousness, extraversion, agreeableness, and neuroticism (see Table 11.3).

Table 11.3 Characteristics of the Traits in the Five-Factor Personality Model

Trait	Characteristics
Openness (or openness to change)	The extent to which someone is imaginative, creative, and curious.
Extraversion	The extent to which someone is sociable, talkative, enthusiastic, and assertive.
Neuroticism	The extent to which someone experiences negative emotions such as anxiety, anger, or guilt.
Conscientiousness	The extent to which someone is careful, self-disciplined, hard-working, dependable, and reliable.
Agreeableness	The extent to which someone is generous, trustful, cooperative, and forgiving.

Source: Matzler et al. (2011).

However, despite these studies using the same personality model, they come to different conclusions about which personality traits are related to positive knowledge sharing attitudes. Thus, Cabrera and Cabrera's (2005) research found that the 'openness to change' personality variable was related to a positive knowledge sharing attitude. By contrast, Mooradian et al.'s (2006) study found a link between 'agreeableness' and positive knowledge sharing attitudes. Further, all these studies are based on surveys conducted in single organizations, so their findings cannot be regarded as generalizable. Therefore research in this area is in its infancy and is inconclusive regarding exactly how personality relates to a person's propensity to share knowledge or their willingness to participate in any organizational knowledge processes.

 Illustration 11.5 Personality traits and attitude to knowledge sharing

Matzler et al. (2011) found that the personality variables of agreeableness and conscientiousness were positively linked to knowledge sharing activities. Matzler et al.'s analysis is based on a study of 150 workers from within an Austrian utility company. The conceptual model they tested suggested that agreeableness would be positively linked to levels of affective commitment to the organization, while conscientiousness would be positively linked to the extent to which people document their knowledge. The model also suggested that levels of affective commitment and the extent to which people document their knowledge would be positively linked to the extent to which people share knowledge. The statistical analysis the researchers undertook of the survey data collected supported all the hypotheses that were tested, and provided support for the conceptual model. Thus, this study supports the idea that the personality variables of agreeableness and conscientiousness are linked to knowledge sharing.

Question

How generalizable are these findings, given they are based on a survey of workers from one Austrian organization?

 Conclusion

Fundamentally this chapter has shown that human, social, and cultural factors are typically key to the success of knowledge management initiatives. This is because they have a significant influence on the extent to which workers are willing to participate in such initiatives, and without such willingness the knowledge management initiatives are unlikely to succeed, as the resource they are focused on managing and sharing, workers' knowledge, will remain locked in the worker's head.

The chapter conceptualized the decision workers face about whether to participate in such initiatives as being comparable to a public good dilemma, where people's actions are shaped by how they evaluate the potential consequences of the various options they have. However, a caveat was added by suggesting that account needs to be taken of emotion in decision-making as it was problematic to conceptualize workers as purely rational decision-makers.

The chapter highlighted a number of key socio-cultural factors which can play a crucial role in shaping workers' motivation to participate in knowledge management initiatives. First, the nature of the employment relationship means that in relation to knowledge management initiatives the interests of workers and their employers may not always be compatible. Second, the typically conflictual nature of intra-organizational relations was also found to shape the character of organizational knowledge management initiatives. Third, inter-personal trust was found to be important, with a lack of trust likely to inhibit the extent to which people are willing to share knowledge with each other. Fourth, the role of personal identity was also found to be important, with a person's identity often shaping who they were and were not willing to share knowledge with. Fifth, national cultural characteristics have been found to shape people's attitudes to knowledge processes. Finally the role of personality in shaping people's general proclivity to share knowledge was also highlighted.

This chapter to some extent has acted as a springboard to the remaining chapter in this part by giving an introduction to key socio-cultural issues. Many of the factors examined here can be influenced by how management in an organization act. These issues have been deliberately avoided here as they are examined in Chapters 15 and 16 which consider the role that human resource management, culture management, and leadership practices can play in dealing with these issues and encouraging workers to participate fully in organizational knowledge management initiatives.

 Case study ParcelCo: a case study of factors inhibiting knowledge sharing

Aziz and Sparrow's (2011) analysis provides insights into a range of factors which influenced knowledge sharing patterns within a single organization, a UK-based express parcel delivery company (referred to here as ParcelCo). Their focus was on one type of knowledge, knowledge about customers, as this is argued to be a crucial source of knowledge for any organization, and its effective utilization is argued to be a potentially important source of competitive advantage. Further, they argue that a crucial source of customer knowledge is possessed by workers who have extensive, direct, personal interactions with customers. In ParcelCo three type of worker possessed such knowledge. These were delivery drivers, who developed their knowledge via dropping off and collecting deliveries at customer sites; sales staff, who developed their knowledge of customers via their sales activity; and customer service staff, who dealt directly with existing customers, dealing with queries and complaints.

Aziz and Sparrow collected an extensive amount of research data on the organization via a range of methods including direct observation, interviews, and surveys. In examining patterns of knowledge sharing and the reasons for them, Aziz and Sparrow differentiated between formal knowledge (equivalent to explicit or codified knowledge) and informal knowledge (equivalent to tacit knowledge).

In broad terms, ParcelCo did *not* represent an exemplar of good practice with respect to the sharing of customer knowledge. The key reason for this was that culture in ParcelCo was very performance driven, with all staff primarily focused on meeting personal KPIs (key performance indicators) set for them as part of their jobs, with knowledge sharing not being a measureable KPI. This was summed up by Aziz and Sparrow as follows: 'everybody has a weekly target and tried to achieve it to satisfy his or her line manager . . . the target is mainly expressed in sales or volume terms and this is the core of the company culture' (p. 37). Much of the knowledge sharing identified, where it did occur, was linked to the meeting of KPIs.

When analysed in detail, noticeable differences in knowledge sharing patterns existed for each type of worker. First, customer service workers were more likely to share informal (tacit) knowledge rather than formal (codified) knowledge, which may have been due to the nature of their work, where it can be difficult to fully codify knowledge from their customer interactions. Further, the sharing of formal knowledge was also uncommon for delivery drivers, with a key reason being that they didn't have access to any of the IT systems that would allow them to codify any knowledge they possessed. The drivers also reported that time constraints affected their ability to both collect and share knowledge on customers. First, the demands of the targets they were set meant that time to interact with and talk to customers was limited and brief. Further, they also found that due to the time pressures they experienced, it was virtually impossible to share any knowledge they did possess.

One noticeable difference between the teams examined was that levels of knowledge sharing among sales staff were higher than among customer service staff or delivery workers. This was linked to the nature of their work, and the type of KPIs they were set, with the sharing of formal knowledge being linked to KPIs for the sales staff, but not the drivers or customer service staff. With both these type of worker, people typically worked very individually, and had little need to interact with and share knowledge with peers.

Apart from a culture focused on (individual) performance targets, Aziz and Sparrow identified a number of other overarching factors which inhibited the sharing of knowledge within ParcelCo. First, the highly structured nature of the organization, where seven to eight layers of management separated workers who directly interacted with customers from senior management, inhibited the upward, vertical flow of knowledge. Another factor inhibiting the upward flow of knowledge was that many senior managers had worked for the company for a long time and had been promoted from within. While this was positive in terms of offering career paths it inhibited senior management from learning from junior staff. This was because senior staff felt that they already had a good knowledge of the company, with little need to understand the knowledge and experience of other workers. Aziz and Sparrow summed this up by arguing, 'the senior managers are proud of their experience and believe they know whatever they need to know in order to manage their business' (p. 38).

Finally, two other general factors acted to inhibit knowledge sharing within ParcelCo. First, the performance focus of the culture meant that workers were unwilling to share knowledge about any negative experience due to a fear that doing so was 'considered as a symbol of inefficiency and ineffectiveness' (p. 38). Finally, for all three types of worker examined, who had extensive direct interaction with customers, staff turnover levels were high, and the customer knowledge possessed by these workers was lost when they left the organization.

Source: Aziz, N., and Sparrow, J. (2011). 'Patterns of Gaining and Sharing of Knowledge about Customers: A Study of an Express Parcel Delivery Company', *Knowledge Management Research and Practice*, 9: 29–47.

Question

1. Aziz and Sparrow have identified a number of factors affecting and inhibiting knowledge sharing patterns within ParcelCo. Assuming the role of a consultant tasked with helping them increase levels of knowledge sharing, what advice would you offer them and what issues would be your main, initial priority?

 ## Review and Discussion Questions

1. Based on your own experience, what has been the attitude of work colleagues to sharing their knowledge? Have you found them to be willing to share, or has hoarding been more typical? What are the most important factors which explain this behaviour?

2. How compatible have you and your employing organization's interests been with regard to how you have used your knowledge? Have the organization's goals and your own always been harmonious, or has there been any conflict and tension over how you use your knowledge?

3. Have you found trust to be an important factor underpinning attitudes to knowledge sharing? Have you had any experiences where a lack of trust has inhibited knowledge sharing, or where the existence of trust has facilitated it?

4. To what extent is people's behaviour at work (whether concerned with knowledge sharing or not) shaped by rationality and decision-making, and to what extent is it shaped by emotion and subjective feelings?

Suggestions for Further Reading

C. Trusson, N. F. Doherty, and D. Hislop (2014). 'Knowledge Sharing Using IT Service Management Tools: Conflicting Discourses and Incompatible Practices', *Information Systems Journal*, 24: 347–71.
A study that highlights various factors which shape workers attitudes towards the codification and sharing of knowledge, which included conflicts between workers and managers.

J-H. Li, X-R. Chang, L. Lin, and L-Y. Ma (2014). 'Meta-Analytic Comparison of the Influencing Factors of Knowledge Transfer in Different Cultural Contexts', *Journal of Knowledge Management*, 18/2: 278–306.
A review and analysis of academic studies examining knowledge transfer in different cultural contexts, which highlights the role that national cultural characteristics can play in shaping such processes.

J. Evans, M. Hedron, and J. Oldroyd (2015). 'Withholding the Ace: The Individual- and Unit-Level Performance Effects of Self-Reported and Perceived Knowledge Hoarding', *Organization Science*, 26/2: 494–510.
A case study of the performance effects resulting from actual and perceived levels of knowledge hoarding.

L. Razmerita, K. Kirchner, and P. Nielsen (2016). 'What Factors Influence Knowledge Sharing in Organizations? A Social Dilemma Perspective of Social Media Communication', *Journal of Knowledge Management*, 20/6: 1225–46.
Uses a social dilemma perspective to investigate the diverse range of factors influencing workers' social-media-related knowledge sharing activities.

 To further your understanding of knowledge management in organizations explore the book's accompanying online resources at www.oup.com/uk/hislop4e/

Communities of Practice

Introduction

In the vast literature on knowledge management that has been produced, the concept of 'communities of practice' has been one of the most popular. This is evident in the large quantity of academic articles and books that have been published on the topic (see e.g. Amin and Roberts 2008; Hughes et al. 2008; Cranefield et al. 2015). The popularity of the term is largely because communities of practice are argued to facilitate inter-personal knowledge sharing (e.g. allowing information technology (IT) professionals who work in different companies to share knowledge and ideas—see Moran 2010), can support and underpin innovation processes in organizations (Bertels et al. 2011), and have the potential to help improve organizational performance (Schenkel and Teigland 2008; Bradley et al. 2011). Thus, a growing number of writers suggest that developing communities of practice can provide an effective means for people and organizations to manage and share knowledge. There seems to be no limitation in terms of industry or situation, since communities of practice are broadly adopted. Recently, there is much attention in the literature for the application of communities in the healthcare (e.g. Cantillon et al. 2016) and education domains (e.g. Kwong et al. 2016).

Communities of practice are informal groups of people who have some work-related activity in common. As will be seen, the communities of practice literature is most closely associated with the practice-based perspective on knowledge, as it assumes that the knowledge people have is embedded in and inseparable from the (collectively based) activities that people carry out. The informality of these communities stems from the fact that they emerge from the social interactions that are a necessary part of the work activities that people undertake. Further, while most of the literature on communities of practice focuses on organizationally specific communities, communities can span organizational boundaries (see Illustration 12.1). For example, Gittelman and Kogut (2003) conceptualize the researchers involved in the biotechnology industry in the USA as constituting a community of practice.

This chapter has a very specific focus, discussing and analysing the *internal dynamics* of communities of practice as well as the different types of communities of practice, and how and if they can be managed. It starts with defining communities of practice and describing the term's origins, features, and dynamics. After that it discusses the intra-community knowledge processes that take place inside a community of practice and it introduces different types of communities of practice. Special attention is given to online communities which are very common in today's digitized world. Given the benefits that communities of practice can bring to organizations, it is discussed to what extent they can be managed and stimulated by the organization. In this context, it is also discussed how social network analysis can help to visualize the network sharing relations in a community and how it can be used to probe problems that need attention. The section is concluded by some critical perspectives on communities of practice.

The character and dynamics of inter-community knowledge processes are explored in Chapter 13. Chapters 12 and 13 can therefore be read together, as they both examine the dynamics of group-based knowledge processes. The reason for doing this in two chapters rather than one is that, as will be discussed more fully in Chapter 13, the character and dynamics of intra- and inter-community knowledge processes are qualitatively different.

Defining communities of practice

DEFINITION Community of practice

A group of people who have a particular activity in common, and as a consequence have some common knowledge, a sense of community identity, and some element of a shared language and overlapping values.

Communities of practice (see Definition) are groups of individuals who have some form of practice or activity in common, for example, an informal group of IT staff within an organization which has responsibility for designing and maintaining similar IT systems. These groups are typically informal and ad hoc in nature, developing out of the communication and interaction which is a necessary part of most work activities. Unlike formalized work groups and teams, they do not represent a part of the formal organizational structure and therefore typically do not appear on organization charts (see Table 12.1 or Wenger and Snyder 2000). They

Table 12.1 Difference between a Community of Practice and Formal Work Groups

	Community of Practice	Organizational Work Group/Team
Objective	Evolving Shaped by common values Internally negotiated	Clear, formally defined Externally determined
Focus of Efforts	Collective practice/knowledge	Provide specific service and/or product
Membership	Voluntary	Typically formalized and delegated (though occasionally voluntary)
Government of Internal Structure	Consensually negotiated Non-hierarchical	Formalized division of labour Hierarchical structure Individualized roles and responsibilities
External System of Management and Control	Self-managing Informal, inter-personal relations	Formalized relations defined by organizational hierarchy Performance monitoring against specific targets, goals
Time Frame	Indefinite, internally negotiated	Permanent, or with finite timeframe/objective

thrive on personal, informal relations between people through which knowledge is shared and created (Cross et al. 2001). Such informal relations result in a network structure as opposed to the hierarchical structure of the formal organization. The informal network of relations between employees of the organization is also referred to as the *social capital* of the organization. Through these social relations employees can access knowledge or mobilize resources for purposive action (Lin 2011). Consequently, social capital provides organizations an advantage in developing intellectual capital—see also Chapter 5 (Nahapiet and Ghoshal 1998).

Historically, such informal groups have been treated with hostility by senior management, who may be concerned about how these groups may undermine formal structures and systems (Brown and Duguid 1991). However, due to the increasing acknowledgement of the role they can play in facilitating knowledge sharing, organizations have been attempting more and more often to deliberately support and develop communities of practice (see examples later, such as Borzillo et al. 2011). By their very nature, however, communities of practice are not easily amenable to deliberate management and control. The contradictions of attempting to formalize such inherently informal interactions are not insignificant, and will be discussed later.

 Illustration 12.1   A community of practice among designers in Turin

Bettiol and Sedita (2011) describe the characteristics of a community of practice that developed in Turin among graphic/industrial designers and architects in the city. The community started in the mid-2000s in the immediate aftermath of the Winter Olympics, and after Turin was nominated to be the first World Design Capital. Some designers in Turin decided to try and build/sustain the city's reputation for design that these events had stimulated. A number of people were key in developing the community, which by 2009 involved fifty-three design studios and 119 designers. The aims of the community were to both help sustain Turin's reputation for design and allow individual designers and studios to share knowledge and ideas with each other. One potential benefit to individual designers of participation in the community was that they could find out about job opportunities in different studios. Knowledge was shared among community members via formal events organized by community members; and also, informally, when community members met up individually or in groups at non-community events. The community helped forge a sense of identity among the designers, with Bettiol and Sedita (p. 476) concluding that the community became a 'hotbed for sensemaking and building of meaningful relationships among people who share a common identity'.

....

Question

The authors describe a community of designers that emerged in Turin after the Winter Olympics. Please explain why this should be considered a community of practice rather than a formal work group (see also Table 12.1).

Communities of practice: origins, features, and dynamics

The term communities of practice (see Definition) was popularized by Lave and Wenger (1991) and Brown and Duguid (1991). In those early days it represented a new view on learning, which was situated in the workplace rather than in the classroom. Communities of practice therefore typically refer to people who share the same profession: an iconic example given by Lave and Wenger is a group of midwives. Communities of practice have also been compared to medieval guilds that were established to train apprentices in a certain profession. However, another important reason why the medieval guilds existed was to protect the profession and trade, a characteristic which is not commonly associated with today's communities of practice.

Lave and Wenger (1991) used the term 'legitimate peripheral participation' to characterize the process by which people learn and become socialized into being a member of a community. This process is based on 'triadic' group relations involving masters (or 'old timers'), young masters (or 'journeymen'), and apprentices (or 'newcomers'), for example in a group of midwives, firemen, or consultants. Apprentices learn from watching and communicating with the master and other members of the community, and start as peripheral members, participating initially in relatively straightforward tasks. However, over time, as the apprentices become competent in these basic skills, they gradually become introduced to more complex tasks. Legitimate peripheral participation is thus the process by which newcomers to a community acquire the knowledge required to be a community member, through gradually increasing levels of *participation* in community activities, during which time they simultaneously move from being *peripheral* members of the community to become more central and *legitimate* members of it. Informal learning from other group members is a key element of this process, or as Trowler and Turner (2002: 242) suggest, 'learning to become an organizational member is far more a question of socialization than of formal learning'.

Over time the concept of communities of practice has been adopted by many different disciplines and slowly moved away from the traditional definition of communities of practice (see Time to reflect). A more contemporary definition is: a group of people who have a particular activity in common, and as a consequence have some common knowledge, a sense of community identity, and some element of a shared language and overlapping values (see also Definition feature earlier). This community of practice concept is based on two central premises: the practice-based perspective on knowledge and the group-based character of organizational activity. The primary relevance of the practice-based perspective on knowledge stems from the assumption in the communities of practice literature that knowing and doing are inseparable, as undertaking specific tasks requires the use and development of embodied knowledge. The second major premise is that organizational activities are typically collective, involving the coordinated interaction of groups of workers. Thus, one common feature of virtually every type of work imaginable, from office cleaning to management consulting, is that they involve an element of coordination and interaction with co-workers, subordinates, and/or supervisors.

Therefore, while the knowledge that members of a community of practice have and develop is highly personal, there is an extent to which much of this knowledge is simultaneously shared within a community. From an objectivist perspective on knowledge, the common knowledge shared by the workers in a community of practice is collective/group knowledge (with both tacit and explicit elements: see Table 2.2).

Communities of practice can be seen to have three building blocks (Brown and Duguid 1991; Lave and Wenger 1991), all of which flow from the community members' involvement in some shared activities (Table 12.2). First, participants in a community possess and develop

Table 12.2 Building Blocks of Communities of Practice

Building Blocks of a Community of Practice
Body of common knowledge/practice
Sense of shared identity
Some common or overlapping values

a stock of common, shared knowledge. Second, communities typically also develop shared values and attitudes, a common 'world-view'. Finally and equally importantly, members of communities also possess a sense of communal identity (Brown and Duguid 2001; Bettiol and Sedita 2011). These elements of a community develop not only through the physical activities involved in collectively carrying out the communities' tasks, but also through language and communication. Thus, for example, stories or specialist jargon can be regarded as a part of the collective knowledge of the group, whose use by group members contributes to their sense of collective identity and shared values.

A useful way to illustrate these characteristics is through an example. Trowler and Turner (2002) illustrate how the deaf studies group of an English university constitutes a community of practice. This group consisted of three hearing academics (who are fluent in sign language) and three deaf academics. The shared practice of this community constituted both the teaching of the deaf studies curriculum and research conducted by the group on a range of issues affecting deaf people. This group had a strong sense of collective identity as well as a belief in a common goal (contributing to the education of deaf people and their integration in society, raising awareness of the social issues affecting deaf people, and furthering knowledge on the issues which affect deaf people through carrying out research).

 Time to reflect 'Is Twitter a community of practice?'

This question was asked to Etienne Wenger on his Twitter account. What is your opinion? Is Twitter a community of practice? In formulating an answer to this question go back to Table 12.2, which describes the building blocks of a community of practice. Can you see all these building blocks in Twitter?

You can also check on Twitter what Etienne Wenger replied on 11 April 2011.

Communities of practice are highly dynamic, evolving as new members become absorbed into a community, existing members leave, and the knowledge and practices of the community adapt with changing circumstances (e.g. Mørk et al. 2012). Learning and knowledge evolution are therefore inherent and fundamental aspects of the dynamics of communities of practice, which helps explain why one of the main contexts in which the community of practice concept originated and developed was in the organizational learning literature.

Communities of practice and intra-community knowledge processes

Almost universally, the communities of practice literature considers communities of practice to be advantageous for both individuals and organizations. Thus they provide workers with a sense of collective identity and a social context in which they are argued to have the potential to effectively develop and utilize their knowledge. For organizations, they can provide a vital source of innovation. The knowledge management literature, which has utilized the communities of practice concept, argues that they can facilitate organizational knowledge processes. The rest of this section considers the potential benefits in terms of knowledge processes that communities of practice can provide.

Communities of practice have the potential to provide benefits in two broad areas. First, communities of practice can underpin levels of organizational innovativeness through supporting and encouraging the creation, development, and use of knowledge. Thus, Orr (1990) showed how the community of practice that existed amongst Xerox's photocopy repair engineers allowed these workers to develop their knowledge and understanding through solving problems that could not be corrected by simply following the knowledge encoded in instruction manuals. Second, the common knowledge possessed by members of a community of practice, combined with their sense of collective identity and system of shared values, means they have the potential to facilitate individual and group learning, and the sharing of knowledge within the community.

The advantages of communities of practice in enabling such knowledge processes are closely related to the elements that members of a community share (see Figure 12.1). As outlined earlier, members of a community of practice not only have a stock of common knowledge, but also have a shared sense of identity and some overlapping, common values. The simultaneous existence of these elements enables knowledge processes, as they simplify the communication of knowledge that is inherently sticky: tacit knowledge. First, the existence of these three elements make appreciating the taken-for-granted assumptions and values which underpin tacit knowledge easier to understand. Second, the existence of these elements is likely to produce and sustain trust-based relations, creating social conditions that are conducive to knowledge sharing (see Chapter 11 for a discussion of how identity and group-based identities can affect people's knowledge sharing behaviours).

Types of communities of practice

The generic way in which the concept of communities of practice is defined means it can be applied to an enormous range of different contexts. The growing popularity and use of the term suggests that communities of practice exist almost everywhere. At the same time, this has led to all kinds of alternative names for communities of practice. Examples of other names include: informal networks (Krackhardt and Hanson 1993; Allen et al. 2007), advice networks (Cross et al. 2001; Nebus 2006), knowledge networks (Hansen 2002; Helms and Buysrogge 2006; Akgün et al. 2006), networks of practice (Baalen et al. 2005; Hustad and Teigland 2005; Wasko and Faraj 2005), and online communities (Preece 2000; Faraj and Johnson 2011). These terms are sometimes used as synonyms for

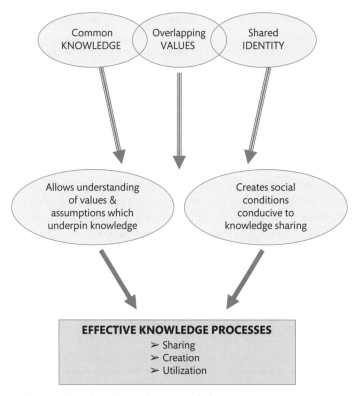

Figure 12.1 How Communities of Practice Underpin Knowledge Processes

communities of practice or they refer to a different type of knowledge sharing community. One of the reasons might be that their purpose is different from traditional communities of practice. For example, advice networks are about seeking advice from peers concerning task- or job-related aspects, and not about apprenticeship as is the case for traditional communities of practice. Another reason might be because a group has different characteristics such as different geographic dispersion characteristics or different modes of interaction. An example is online communities which are about knowledge sharing in geographically dispersed and technology enabled communities.

Due to this heterogeneity in the definition and use of communities of practice, a number of writers (Handley et al. 2006; Roberts 2006; Amin and Roberts 2008) suggest that it is becoming increasingly important to differentiate between types of community as they may have different characteristics and dynamics. For example, communities can vary in size from involving small numbers of people to involving hundreds and even thousands of people (see e.g. Fahey et al. 2007; Borzillo et al. 2011). Further, communities can also differ in terms of their geographic spread and means of interaction, from communities where everyone is collocated on the same site and communicates extensively via face-to-face interaction, to globally dispersed communities where people interact largely via IT (in virtual communities of practice—see Ardichvili et al. 2003; Usoro et al. 2007). Finally, communities can vary from being based within a single organization to spanning a whole industrial/business sector (such as the biotechnology community in the USA examined by Gittelman and Kogut 2003).

In an attempt to classify communities of practice using empirical data, Verburg and Andriessen (2011) performed an analysis of thirty-eight networks in large organizations. In their study they included twelve different characteristics of networks including: purpose, formalization, boundary, reciprocity, and size. For each of the thirty-eight networks the characteristics were collected, after which categorical principal component analysis was performed on the twelve variables. This revealed that the variables were related and that two different clusters of variables could be distinguished. The first cluster was named 'proximity' and refers to the interaction between members and their geographical dispersion. The second cluster was named 'institutionalization' and refers to the level of formalization and support of the community within the organization. Proximity and institutionalization were then used as dimensions for further analysis and each of the thirty-eight networks were mapped onto these two dimensions. A detailed analysis then suggested that the networks can be divided into four clusters: informal networks, question and answer (Q&A) networks, strategic networks, and online strategic networks (see Figure 12.2).

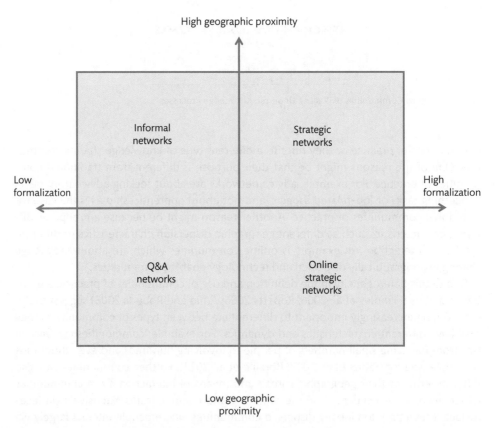

Figure 12.2 Verburg and Andriessen's (2011) Types of Community of Practice

Source: Verburg and Andriessen (2011).

Informal networks are characterized by high proximity and low institutionalization and come closest to the traditional communities of practice we discussed before. The members of informal networks share a similar practice, have much interaction due to their close proximity, and appear spontaneously from a need to share knowledge and learn. Q&A networks are characterized by low proximity and low institutionalization and are loosely connected, large networks of people with various backgrounds. In the network the members post questions and seek answers for certain practical problems, like in company intranets and discussion forums. Strategic networks are characterized by high proximity and high institutionalization and consist of experts that are brought together to perform a strategic task for the organization. The purposes for bringing them together and to support them with organizational resources could be innovation or organizational transformation. Last, online strategic networks are characterized by low proximity and high institutionalization. They are similar in nature to the strategic networks but the interaction in these networks is exclusively through electronic means.

Online communities

Since its development in the early 1990s, the World Wide Web has provided new ways of communicating digitally. This also led to a new phenomenon called online communities. Rheingold (1993) defined online communities as 'cultural aggregations that emerge when enough people bump into each other often enough in cyberspace'. After Rheingold there were many other authors who defined the concept of online community and an overview of these definitions is provided by Iriberri and Leroy (2009). These definitions show that online communities can be considered as an online variant of 'communities of interest' or 'communities of practice'.

An early example of online communities are the mega-communities at Shell, which used e-mail distribution lists as the underlying technology. Hundreds or even thousands of engineers could be on the distribution list, which was used to ask for assistance in solving technical problems. Other technologies from the early Internet era are bulletin board services (bbs) and Usenet lists enabling electronic communication and the exchange of messages. Later these were replaced by more modern tools such as discussion forums. An example is StackOverflow, a community of 6.7 million programmers who share their knowledge and learn from each other. Today social media are used as the main technology platform for online communities and especially social networking sites (SNS) such as Facebook are very popular (Helms et al. 2017). But the use of such platforms is not limited to the general public only, as organizations have discovered SNS also. Organizations use social media to create communities around their brand or product, for example (Helms and Werder 2013).

Research has revealed that online communities have specific characteristics and do not necessarily behave the same as offline communities. A good example is reciprocity, which is typically found in offline communities. This theory implies that when you help a colleague, s/he will return the favour in the future when you need his help. In online communities this expectation is generalized to the network level (Wasko and Faraj 2005). Instead of expecting a particular person to return the favour, one will trust that at least somebody in the network will return the favour in the future. Another difference is the strength of ties; in offline communities there are often strong bonds between people because they meet personally and hence develop strong relations. On the other hand, in online communities there is tendency to develop weaker relations, also referred to as weak ties (Trier and Richter 2014). This behaviour is directly influenced by the design and features of online platforms (Kane et al. 2014). Search capabilities on social networking platforms make it, for instance, possible to find people one might not have met otherwise and it is possible to follow updates of many people one does not meet in person. Therefore, when applying online communities in an organizational context, one should be aware that a different approach might be needed for online communities than for offline communities. Furthermore, one can invoke preferred behaviour through the design and features of the social networking platform that is supposed to support the online community.

So far, one might get the impression that online communities are simply the successors of offline communities. However, this is not true since both can perfectly well co-exist and even strengthen each other. For example, a group of experts in an organization might occasionally meet in person, say, around the coffee machine. But they can continue their conversation on an online platform in which other colleagues may also join, whom they cannot meet in person because they are located on another continent. Additionally, they might involve experts from outside the organization because the introduction of online social network platforms has blurred traditional boundaries of communities (Zablith et al. 2016). The co-existence of offline and online communities adds another dimension to understanding communities in an organizational context and makes it a complex phenomenon to understand. For practitioners who want to improve knowledge sharing and learning in their organization, it is important to understand that both cannot be considered in isolation and that also the selection of a particular online networking platform might influence the behaviour in both offline and online communities.

Managing communities of practice

In discussing how to explicitly manage communities of practice, the difficulties, contradictions, and risks of doing (or attempting to do) this need to be highlighted. The contradictions and difficulties related to managing communities of practice stem from their fundamentally informal, emergent, and somewhat ad hoc nature (see Table 12.1). These characteristics mean that communities of practice are not easily amenable to top-down control. Communities of practice are autonomous, self-managing systems, which can exist and flourish without the need for any senior management support (Baumard 1999). Managerial attempts to control and influence communities of practice may therefore conflict with a community's system of self-management. The risk in attempting to explicitly manage communities of practice is that such attempts may in fact have adverse effects on the community, and the very knowledge processes that such efforts are intended to support and develop can become undermined (see e.g. Thompson 2005; Anand et al. 2007). For example, attempts to formalize a community may introduce rigidities which inhibit its innovativeness or adaptability.

However, despite these difficulties and potential problems, more and more organizations are attempting to develop and support communities of practice as part of their knowledge management initiatives. This section considers the ways in which this can be done. Due to the narrow focus of this chapter, only issues related to managing and supporting individual communities and intra-community knowledge processes are examined. The managerial implications of coordinating inter-community relations and knowledge processes are discussed separately, in Chapter 13.

The literature typically suggests that management should not play a role in initiating communities of practice, as this is contradictory to their fundamental character, but that there is scope to facilitate and manage communities that do already exist. In general terms, the knowledge management literature advocates two main ways in which communities of practice, once formed, can be managed and supported. First, it is argued that their management should be done with a 'light touch'. Second, all management interventions should reinforce the essential attributes of communities that make them so effective at facilitating knowledge processes.

Advocates of the 'light touch' approach to managing communities of practice include McDermott (1999), Ward (2000), and Anand et al. (2007). Thus, McDermott suggests that organizations should 'develop natural knowledge communities without formalizing them' (p. 110). Ward, utilizing a garden metaphor, argues that communities of practice require to be 'tended and nurtured rather than commanded and controlled' (p. 4). The gardening metaphor, suggesting that communities of practice have organic qualities and are continually adapting and evolving, usefully captures the informal and emergent aspect of communities of practice. For example, Thompson (2005) suggests that managerial initiatives that are too directive or controlling of workers may inhibit communities. The limitation of this managerial advice is that it is often somewhat vague and lacking in detail. Thus, the analyses that advocate such an approach typically fail to provide specific details on what the 'light touch' management approach looks like or consists of.

More concrete is the second type of advice, to reinforce the best attributes of communities of practice. This advice covers a range of issues including:

- Emphasize practice-based, peer-supported learning methods rather than formalized, classroom-based methods as this reinforces the existing ways that communities learn and share knowledge (Brown and Duguid 1991; Stamps 2000).

- Have specific people within a community undertaking organizing roles which have the objective of sustaining and developing the community (see Illustration 12.2).

- Due to the significant length of time required for communities of practice to develop (to allow the creation of a common perspective and a stock of common knowledge, as well as a sense of collective identity) continuity is important (Baumard 1999). Overly discontinuous social relations are thus likely to hamper their development.

- Find, nurture, and support existing communities (Borzillo et al. 2011; see Time to reflect). McDermott (1999) suggests that the best way to do this is to reinforce each community's systems of self-management, for example strengthening their existing mechanisms for social interaction, and providing them with adequate autonomy to allow them to decide and control both what knowledge is important, as well as how it should be organized and shared.

Illustration 12.2 Managing and supporting communities of practice

Borzillo et al. (2011) examined nine communities of practice within seven multinational corporations. While they varied in terms of the degree of management support provided, and also in terms of their size and characteristics (the smallest had forty members and the largest 400), Borzillo et al. develop a general model of how people's relationships to and involvement with communities evolved over time. However, the focus here is on the various ways in which these communities were managed. Arguably, the main way that these communities were managed was via key community members (defined as 'core members') taking on organizing roles within the communities. These roles were community leaders, facilitators, content coordinators, and community supporters.

Specific roles played by facilitators include the advertising of community events to community members and non-members, as well as mentoring new members, and helping to network and link together community members who may have some specific shared interests. Content coordinators played the role of subject-matter experts, and provided knowledge and information in response to questions and queries. Finally, the community support role involved organizing or providing resources that facilitated community activities, such as IT resources. The most demanding and time-intensive role was that of community leader, with a community leader taking a lead in any activity deemed useful for sustaining or developing the community.

Borzillo et al. also found that communities that were supported by organizational management tended to integrate and involve new members more quickly than voluntary communities. This was for a number of reasons, including that management more actively marketed and advertised sponsored communities, the financial resources provided to sponsored communities facilitated their development, and with sponsored communities there were greater expectations placed on people to participate in them. However, Borzillo et al. conclude by suggesting that, for management, getting the balance right between providing autonomy to communities and managing/controlling is not straightforward. Therefore, a significant amount of advice exists on how communities of practice can best be supported. Ironically, much of this advice suggests that the best way to manage communities is to provide them the autonomy to manage themselves.

Questions

Borzillo et al. show that management support helps to grow the community. However, at the same time they warn that management should provide enough autonomy to community of practice. Discuss with other students: should management be involved in choosing the topic for the community? Also, should management be involved in membership decisions of the community? Based on the discussion try to describe where support of the community ends and where control starts.

 Time to reflect   Managing communities

The literature suggests that management should not try to command and control communities of practice but should nurture them. One way of facilitating communities of practice is to allow employees to spend some of their work time on communities of practice and to take on active community roles. In what other ways can management facilitate communities of practice in the organization, in your opinion?

Finally, it is worth concluding this section by highlighting how some of the features in many contemporary organizations create conditions which make developing and sustaining communities of practice difficult (Roberts 2006). First, Roberts, drawing on Bauman (2007), suggests that the contemporary trend in society towards an increasing sense of individualism, and away from collective and community forms of identity and action, may make people unlikely to develop community-based forms of identity at work. Roberts further suggests that the high level of dynamism and turbulence in many contemporary business and market sectors means the organizations which have to compete in them have to constantly change and adapt, which again may make it difficult to generate and sustain the type of long-term inter-personal relations and sense of community identity necessary for communities of practice to develop.

Visualizing and analysing communities of practice: social network analysis

The previous section concluded that communities of practice are hard to manage and control, and that at best they can be nurtured and facilitated by the organization. To be able to nurture and facilitate them it is necessary to know which communities are present in the organization, which people are part of these communities, and what knowledge sharing relationships exist between these people. Visualizing the communities of practice in the organization is a powerful tool to better understanding communities of practice and to learning what is needed to let them flourish. Visualizing the community of practice is realized by mapping the network of relations between the members of the community of practice using social network analysis (see Figure 12.3).

Social network analysis is part of social network theory, which stems from the sociology domain where it is used to study the relationships between people. Studying social relations has resulted in many different social network theories and many of them are also useful to

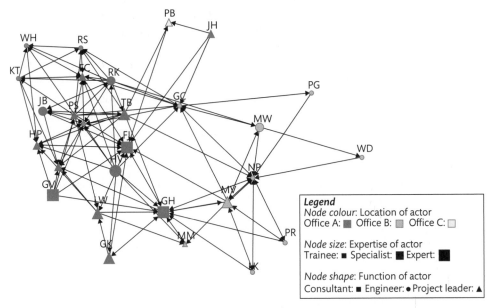

Figure 12.3 Example of the Visualization of a Knowledge Sharing Network

Source: Helms (2007).

explain knowledge sharing in communities of practice. Examples include weak tie theory (Granovetter 1973), structural holes theory (Burt 1992), and homophily theory (Zenger and Lawrence 1989).

The methods and techniques used for visualizing and analysing social networks are based on graph theory. Graphs are mathematical structures to model the relations between objects. A well-known example of graph theory is calculating the shortest path between two locations. The shortest path between two points in a network is useful for understanding knowledge sharing in networks (Helms 2007; Huffaker 2010). It might for example be an indicator of how many people are between you and an expert. Therefore, it provides information on how easy it is to tap into knowledge available in the organization. Analysing the network of a community of practice can therefore lead to the conclusion that experts are too isolated in the community of practice. In that situation the organization can facilitate the community of practice by stimulating the formation of new knowledge sharing relations that better embed the experts in the community.

Another frequently used measure is centrality and measures the central position of a person in a network. In social network theory a central position is equivalent to having power and in knowledge management theory it is equivalent to having an advantageous position in terms of access to knowledge. In contrast, non-central people in a network depend on more central people to have access to knowledge. According to knowledge management theory, the possession of expertise is a possible explanation for a central position in the network. Experts are often sought after by others for their advice and opinion (Borgatti and Cross 2003; Helms et al. 2011). Central people can also be considered as brokers when they are on the shortest path between two other people in the network. In that situation a person cannot reach another person without going through the broker. When this brokering relation spans a certain boundary, for example two departments in an organization, it is also referred to as a boundary spanning position or a bridge (see Chapter 13 for more on this). Centrality can thus be a measure that organizations can use to identify the brokers in or between communities of practice. Organizations can facilitate this important role by giving the brokers more time to spend on their broker role in the community of practice.

There are many different tools available to visualize and analyse social networks (e.g. Net-Miner, Gephi, UCINET). Creating network visualizations using these tools is relatively simple and does not require much expertise. Analysing the network requires a basic understanding of graph theory in order to be able to interpret the results of the analysis. Collecting the network data that is needed as input for these tools can be challenging, as is demonstrated in Illustration 12.3.

 Illustration 12.3   The challenges of collecting knowledge sharing network data

Applying social network analysis requires the availability of network data and hence the collection of this data. How network data is collected depends on the size of the network and if the participants of the network can be identified a priori. In small networks (up to fifteen to twenty people), where all the participants are known (e.g. a department of an organization), one can conduct interviews and ask every person about their relations with others in the network. In large networks this might become too labour intensive and therefore a survey might be more appropriate. There are mainly two strategies for setting up such a survey. The first strategy asks respondents to name the five or ten other people with whom they have contact, and it works with very large groups. The other strategy presents a full list of the members in the network and asks with whom they have relations, which works only with networks up to approximately a hundred members.

There are also situations imaginable where not all members of the network are known beforehand. An example might be a community of practice which emerged bottom-up or another example is a group of criminals. In both cases there is no administration or record of persons who are part of the network. Consequently, it is not possible to interview, or send a survey, to all members of the network. In such a situation snowballing can be used to discover the network. Snowballing starts with a few persons, but at least one, you know are part of this network. These persons are the so-called seed nodes and they are asked to give the names of their relations. Once you have the names of the relations of seed nodes, these relations are approached in a second round of data collection. This process is repeated a few times until the researcher is satisfied with the collected data.

In the current digital age, there are also other options for collecting network data because people leave digital footprints in many different systems. One can think of e-mail systems containing data about who communicates with whom, discussion fora keeping records of conversations, and social network platforms containing data about friendship relations. Mining such systems provides a wealth of network data for research. However, the question is whether it really provides the data one is looking for. Research showed that network data from e-mail or phone conversations does not provide the same outcomes as knowledge sharing network data collected by a survey (Reijsen and Helms 2009). This is because e-mail is used for much more than sharing knowledge with others. Still, collecting digital data is attractive since it is much easier to collect data this way compared to more traditional methods of data collection. Furthermore, it provides longitudinal data while interviews and surveys typically provide data about one snapshot in time. Longitudinal data provide the opportunity to study how networks evolve over time which provides more fundamental insights into how knowledge sharing networks function.

Questions

Are there any ethical or privacy issues that need to be addressed before collecting network data at an organization?

Critical perspectives on communities of practice

As outlined earlier, much of the communities of practice literature presents communities in a very positive light, suggesting that in relation to knowledge processes they are largely or exclusively beneficial for organizations. The limitation of this idealistic characterization of communities is that it creates a blindness to their potential negative features and the range of ways in which they may inhibit organizational knowledge processes. Arguably much of the communities' literature has thus provided a somewhat one-sided and unbalanced analysis of communities of practice. However, increasingly, a number of writers are examining the ambiguities, problems, and difficulties with both the way communities of practice are conceptualized and their role in organizational knowledge processes.

Two specific issues are examined here. First, how issues of power and conflict can shape the internal dynamics of communities is considered. Second, this section closes by considering the way that communities may develop 'blinkers' which can inhibit innovations and inter-community interaction.

Power, conflict, and the internal dynamics of communities

As will be seen in this chapter, one of the major criticisms of the majority of the mainstream knowledge management literature is the neglect of issues of power and conflict. The communities of practice literature is no exception in this and, thus, issues of power and conflict within communities are typically either downplayed or ignored. In *Situated Learning*, Lave and Wenger (1991) do discuss these issues, but their appeal for future analyses to take greater account of 'unequal relations of power' (p. 42) within communities has generally been neglected by subsequent writers (the most notable exceptions being Fox 2000; Contu and Willmott 2003; and Mørk et al. 2010). Further, these issues have also been downplayed in some of their own later work, such as Wenger (1998), where, as Fox makes clear, issues of power and conflict are largely relegated to footnotes. While Wenger et al. (2002) devote a whole chapter to the 'downside of communities', issues of power are ignored. One manifestation of this neglect of power and politics in the communities of practice literature is that it typically portrays them as idealistic communities of equals where conflict is rare and where homogeneity exists and consensus is the norm.

However, such perspectives arguably downplay the extent to which communities of practice have inherent tensions built into them which unavoidably result in them possessing an 'unequal distribution of power' (Lave and Wenger 1991: 42), and where what Fox (2000) described as 'power conflicts' are likely. The uneven distribution of power results from the, by definition, greater amount of community knowledge masters have compared to newcomers (Contu and Willmott 2003). While communities of practice do not have a formal hierarchical structure, this does not mean that all members of the community are equal. This uneven distribution of knowledge creates potential conflicts in processes of legitimate peripheral participation. For example, Lave and Wenger (1991: 57) argue that 'There is a fundamental contradiction in the meaning to newcomers and old-timers of increasing participation by the former; for the centripetal development of full participants . . . implies the replacement of old timers'.

Legitimate peripheral participation thus requires the 'old timers' to help develop the knowledge of the 'newcomers' who will, over time, take their place. The contradictions inherent in such a process are fundamental, and unavoidable (see Lave and Wenger 1991: 113–17). Another source of conflict within communities of practice relates to the 'contradictory nature of collective social practice' (Lave and Wenger 1991: 58). Although the members of a community work together collectively and cooperate, they are also simultaneously, to some extent, competing with each other inside their organizations, for example, for promotion opportunities (see Illustration 12.4).

 Illustration 12.4 Innovation, change, and power dynamics within a community of practice

Mørk et al. (2010) examined two cases where innovation in medical practices in Norway challenged some existing communities of practice, which resulted in conflict and power dynamics developing. The innovation examined was laparoscopic (keyhole) surgery, where surgical procedures are carried out via inserting a laparoscope and other surgical instruments into patients via small incisions. The advantage of laparoscopic surgery is that it is significantly less invasive than conventional open surgery. However, laparoscopic surgery requires the learning of special surgical techniques, and may thus be seen as threatening the established authority and knowledge of existing surgeons.

One of the cases examined was the use of laparoscopic surgery for treating prostate cancer. The treatment of prostate cancer had traditionally been the responsibility of urologists. However, the development of laparoscopic surgical techniques in this domain was initially done by a non-urological medical team based at the University Hospital in Oslo. To develop their knowledge and expertise in this surgical procedure, the plan was to collaborate with urologists from a range of hospitals. However, the urologists at one of the hospitals involved in initial collaborations with the laparoscopic team suddenly withdrew from the collaborative project, primarily because they wanted their hospital to become a national centre of excellence in this new procedure. This effectively ended the collaboration with the non-urological team from the University Hospital in Oslo. Mørk et al. argue that the urologists did this as they regarded the non-urological laparoscopic team from Oslo to be challenging their authority, knowledge, and expertise within the established urological community of practice, which they decided to resist, in order to retain a degree of control over knowledge and practice in this area.

Questions

The urologists decided to hoard their knowledge in order to protect their status. Do you think that they can protect their knowledge forever? Are there other options (than hoarding knowledge) that the urologists could consider and that would be beneficial for both the urologists and the non-urologists?

The power conflicts that are an inherent aspect of communities take on greater importance when communities are faced with change, which over time they inevitably are. Change that requires a community's practices/knowledge to adapt threatens the status quo (the reproduction of existing knowledge/practices), and can have contradictory implications for different members of a community of practice (Fox 2000). Thus old-timers may see such change as a threat to their status (see Illustration 12.4), power, and knowledge, whereas other members of a community may see it as an opportunity to develop and increase their own power, knowledge, and status (Handley et al. 2006). These insights have two implications with regard to how communities of practice respond to change, which are both neglected by the mainstream literature. First, communities of practice are as likely to resist as to support change; and, second, it cannot be assumed that all the members of a community will respond in the same way to change.

Blinkered and inward-looking communities

While the collective sense of identity and values that exist between members of a community can create a bond that may facilitate the development of trust and knowledge sharing, there are potential negative consequences if such bonds are too strong. For example, where too strong a sense of community identity exists this may provide a basis for exclusion, where those not part of the 'community' are ignored, and their knowledge not considered to be relevant or important to the community (Baumard 1999; Alvesson 2000). This can cause communities to become inward-looking, and unreceptive to ideas generated outside the community (Brown and Duguid 1998). In such circumstances a community's search processes may be limited rather than extensive, with consequent negative implications for the community's innovativeness (Leonard and Sensiper 1998). Moreover, the type of competency traps outlined in the unlearning and forgetting chapter (Chapter 8) can develop, where a community can fail to innovate, change, and adapt, with the risk that its ideas and practices eventually become outdated.

Such communities may neglect not only external ideas but also people. Communities with a strong sense of identity may become exclusive clubs or 'cliques' (Wenger et al. 2002), where membership is tightly controlled, and the factors that define a community's identity are used to exclude entry to others. Just as with the neglect of external ideas, such practices can result in communities becoming poor at absorbing new external knowledge and ideas (see Time to reflect).

 Time to reflect   'Not invented here' syndrome

Have you worked as part of a team or community where there has been a hostility or blindness to ideas generated outside of it? If so, did this have any effect on group or organizational performance?

 Conclusion

Communities of practice have been defined as informal groups that have some work activities in common. As a consequence, these communities develop:

1. A shared body of common knowledge

2. A shared sense of collective identity

3. Some overlapping values.

The mainstream knowledge management literature portrays communities of practice as being effective vehicles for knowledge sharing and knowledge creation. Consequently, the existence of effectively operating communities of practice is typically argued to underpin individual- and organizational-level learning processes as well as supporting high levels of organizational innovativeness. The effectiveness of communities of practice in this respect is because:

● The existence of common knowledge and a shared system of values makes sharing tacit knowledge easier, as group members have insights into the implicit assumptions and values embedded in each other's knowledge

● The shared knowledge, values, and identity which exist also facilitate the development and maintenance of trust-based relations, which, as outlined in Chapter 11, create social conditions conducive to knowledge sharing.

However, the chapter also concluded that the mainstream literature on communities of practice portrays an overly optimistic image of them. To understand why communities of practice have the potential to inhibit as much as facilitate knowledge processes, account needs to be taken of issues of power and conflict within communities, as well as the way that too strong a sense of community identity may inhibit inter-community processes of knowledge sharing. This last conclusion points towards the dynamics of inter-community interaction, which is the topic dealt with in Chapter 13.

Case study Communities of practice as means to implement agile software development at Ericsson

Ericsson is a multinational that was founded in 1876 in Stockholm, Sweden, and specializes in telecommunication and networking equipment. It employs approximately 110,000 people working on different continents. The products of Ericsson are used in the technology infrastructure of many telecom and Internet service providers worldwide.

Due to fierce competition in the telecom industry, Ericsson believed that agile and lean principles would help the organization to reduce lead times and respond faster to customer requests. Between 2009 and 2010 Ericsson changed its research and development (R&D) unit by implementing cross-functional scrum teams.

The organization used communities of practices to support the implementation of cross-functional teams on a large scale, involving about forty scrum teams in the development of a complex product across three sites: Finland, Hungary, and the US. The use of communities of practices was based on the advice of consultants and suggestions from practitioners' literature on scaling the implementation of agile working. Initial attempts to create communities through managers failed because communities emerge voluntarily when needed. Over time, as the organization and its members grasped the idea behind communities of practice, the first communities started to emerge as people holding the same roles in different teams met to share experiences.

The communities of practice that developed over time at Ericsson can be categorized based on the different purposes they served (Paasivaara and Lassenius 2014). First, the typical knowledge sharing and learning communities that were the first to emerge were especially among scrum masters/coaches due to the need to share knowledge and solve problems related to agile development. Later on, a second type of community developed from the need to coordinate work. Following the failure of organization-wide scrum-of-scrum meetings to achieve cross-team coordination, communities of practice emerged between cross-functional teams working on common features of the product. Third, communities of practice were created among developers from the different product areas with the intention to share knowledge and integrate their tools. And, fourth, a community of practice emerged with the aim to improve the product development flow through the whole organization. According to Paassivaara and Lassenius (2014), this community clearly showed the characteristics needed for a community of practice to successfully achieve its purpose.

The experiences at Ericsson provided insights on eight factors that led to the successful implementation and functioning of the communities of practice. For instance, the organization of communities around specific topics relevant to employees' daily work was identified as one of the essential success factors for participation. Related to this point, two other factors that affected participation and the good functioning of a community were the creation and use of a clear and relevant agenda for each community meeting and an appropriate rhythm of these meetings (i.e. frequency and duration). A fourth aspect that characterized successful communities at Ericsson was the presence of an engaged leader or facilitator, especially when s/he was an expert in the topic or knowledge domain of the community. A fifth element that ensured good working communities was the use of tools to keep everyone informed on meetings, agendas, and decisions. Two important success factors were related to the organizational culture of these communities of practice: the authority to take decisions and their openness. Finally, the possibility to organize site-specific and cross-site communities was also seen as a positive point for discussing common issues.

Source: Paasivaara, M. and Lassenius, C. (2014). 'Communities of Practice in a Large Distributed Agile Software Development Organization—Case Ericsson', *Information and Software Technology*, 56: 1556–77.

Questions

1. Do you think that these types of communities are exclusive to software development organizations?

2. To what extent do the mentioned success factors differ from the characteristics of good management?

Acknowledgement: Thanks to Dr Montserrat Prats López, Assistant Professor at Open University of the Netherlands, for contributing this case.

 ## Review and Discussion Questions

1. If you are or have been a member of a community of practice, how were you socialized? How did you develop the knowledge, values, and identity that characterize membership? Did your socialization closely resemble the process of legitimate peripheral participation described by Lave and Wenger?

2. What if anything can be done to prevent an offline community communities developing a sense of identity that is so strong that it inhibits members of the community from accepting ideas generated outside of it? And would this approach also be valid for online communities?

3. To what extent is it possible to formalize legitimate peripheral participation and the socialization of new community members? Are there any potential risks for a community of formalizing such processes?

4. Based on any organizational experience you have had, what effect have communities of practice had on organizational knowledge processes? Have they been largely or purely positive and beneficial? Have there been any negative aspects to them (such as knowledge hoarding)?

5. How can social network analysis be useful to analyse knowledge sharing in organizations? Are there any ethical/privacy issues involved when performing such an analysis? And how could these issues be encountered?

 ## Suggestions for Further Reading

G. C. Kane, M. Alavi, G. Labianca, and S. P. Borgatti (2014). 'What's Different about Social Media Networks? A Framework and Research Agenda', *Management Information Systems Quarterly*, 38(1), 274–304.
Presents an overview of why online communities are different from offline communities and what research is still needed in this area to better understand the behavior of online communities.

B. Mørk, T. Hoholm, G. Ellingsen, B. Edwin, and M. Aanestad (2010). 'Challenging Expertise: On Power Relations within and across Communities of Practice in Medical Innovation', *Management Learning*, 41/5: 575–92.
An interesting case which highlights the power dynamics that can develop as communities evolve over time.

J. Roberts (2006). 'Limits to Communities of Practice', *Journal of Management Studies*, 43/3: 623–39.
Provides a comprehensive analysis of the limitations and criticisms of the community of practice concept.

J. Cranefield, P. Yoong, and S. L. Huff (2015). 'Rethinking Lurking: Invisible Leading and Following in a Knowledge Transfer Ecosystem', *Journal of the Association for Information Systems*, 16(4), 213–47.
People on the periphery of a community of practice have often been referred to as lurkers or free-riders. This paper sheds further light on the position of the lurker and demonstrates how lurkers can have value.

 To further your understanding of knowledge management in organizations explore the book's accompanying online resources at **www.oup.com/uk/hislop4e/**

13 Boundary-Spanning Knowledge Processes in Heterogeneous Collaborations

Introduction

The focus of this chapter is on knowledge processes in group contexts that are distinct from those examined in Chapter 12: communities of practice. Within communities of practice, as has been outlined, people have a shared sense of identity, values, and some common practice/knowledge. Thus, in such contexts, collaboration is within relatively homogeneous groups, where people have much in common. What is distinctive about the group contexts examined here is that they involve collaboration between people who are more diverse and heterogeneous, and who may have only a limited sense of shared identity and common knowledge. These contexts are referred to as boundary-spanning situations as they involve collaboration between people who have divergent identities, and whose collaboration thus involves the spanning of the boundaries between these groups or communities (see Definition). A boundary is defined as a 'border that divides one group from another' (Hwang et al. 2015). Similarly, Hsaio et al. (2012) define a boundary as a 'demarcation . . . that marks the limit of an area' (p. 463). Importantly, boundaries can be highly diverse, referring to geographic boundaries, which physically separate groups of people, as well as social boundaries, which distinguish between groups with separate and distinct identities, and which may differentiate people in terms of organizational identity, hierarchical position, professional background, or social status, etc. Thus, as will be illustrated via various examples, boundary-spanning knowledge processes are found in an enormous variety of contexts. While, as outlined in Chapter 12, there has been much interest within the knowledge management literature on communities of practice, what are here referred to as boundary-spanning collaborations represent a more common form of group working in contemporary organizations.

> **DEFINITION Boundary-spanning collaboration**
>
> A form of heterogeneous group collaboration involving people who have distinct differences between them such as knowledge base, sense of identity, native language spoken, etc.

The reason why these group contexts are examined separately from the knowledge processes within homogeneous communities of practice examined in Chapter 12 is that the lack of much common knowledge and limited shared identity that exist in the type of boundary-spanning collaboration involving heterogeneous people makes them distinctive from the group dynamics and knowledge processes that are typical within communities of practice. For example, in terms of the knowledge dimension, Carlile (2002: 442), in the context of cross-functional working, argued that 'the characteristics of knowledge that drive innovative problem solving within a function actually hinder problem solving and knowledge creation across [functional] boundaries'. In relation to the identity dimension, the different identities that people have in boundary-spanning contexts, as was highlighted in Chapter 11, can have a significant impact on the character and dynamics of inter-personal relations (such as the extent to which trust exists or can be developed), which influences the dynamics of inter-personal knowledge processes. Ultimately, due to such factors, boundary-spanning knowledge processes are typically more complex and difficult to manage than those that occur within communities of practice.

This topic has been addressed by people adopting both objectivist and practice-based epistemologies. For example, Easterby-Smith et al. (2008) and all the contributors to the special issue of the *Journal of Management Studies* on knowledge sharing in intra- and inter-firm knowledge transfer processes broadly adopt an objectivist perspective (see also Harzing et al. 2016). This is visible in the way Easterby-Smith et al. model the character of inter-firm knowledge processes (see Figure 13.1), which utilizes the transmitter–receiver model of knowledge sharing outlined in Chapter 2. By contrast, other writers, such as Carlile (2002, 2004), Oborn and Dawson (2010), Bresnen (2010), and Hsiao et al. (2012), examine this topic utilizing a practice-based epistemology.

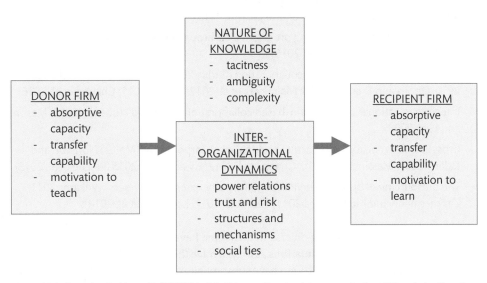

Figure 13.1 Easterby-Smith et al.'s (2008) Model of Factors Shaping Inter-organizational Knowledge Transfer

Source: Adapted from Easterby-Smith et al. (2008).

In looking at this topic, the chapter has a relatively narrow focus, being concerned with how the nature of knowledge and the character of inter-personal dynamics shape the character of micro-level knowledge processes in boundary-spanning contexts. Thus, the chapter has some, but only limited, engagement with the vast literature that exists on joint ventures and inter-firm alliances. Much of the writing in this area has adopted an organization-level analysis, looking at how firm performance is affected by participation in such alliances, and how the structuring of these alliances at the firm level shapes their likelihood of success. Such issues are not considered here.

In the following section, we consider why boundary-spanning collaboration is so important and widely used, as well as the benefits that can be derived from this form of collaboration. After this, the chapter examines the character of boundary-spanning knowledge processes, outlining how the lack of common knowledge and shared identity shape their dynamics. Next, Carlile's (2002, 2004) influential work is used to distinguish between the types of boundaries that can be involved in boundary-spanning working, before considering the way that boundary-spanning knowledge processes can be facilitated and managed, such as through the use of boundary objects and the management of cross-boundary social relations via the activities of brokers and boundary-spanners.

The significance of boundary-spanning collaboration

Consider the following situations:

- Inter-organizational collaboration on the development and/or production of complex and high-technology products (Tallman and Phene 2007; Harryson et al. 2008; Hsiao et al. 2012).
- Collaborative working that spans significant cultural boundaries (Chen et al. 2010; Li 2010; Boh and Xu 2013; Klitmøller and Lauring 2013).
- Cross-project knowledge sharing processes (Scarbrough et al. 2004; Cacciatori et al. 2012; Frank et al. 2015; Mueller 2015).
- Cross-occupational/functional collaboration (Carlile 2002, 2004; McGivern and Dopson 2010; Oborn and Dawson 2010; Majchrzak et al. 2012; Tasselli 2015; Cheung et al. 2016).
- Inter-organizational supply-chain-based collaboration (Dyer and Nobeoka 2000; Mason and Leek 2008).
- Cross-business collaboration *within* multinational corporations (MNCs) (Jonsson and Kalling 2007; Massingham 2010; Chang et al. 2012; Hwang et al. 2015; Reiche et al. 2015).
- The outsourcing of business services to third-party, external providers (Williams 2011; Zimmermann and Mayasandra 2011; Betz et al. 2012; Kotlarsky et al. 2014).

All these situations, while being diverse in character, have one thing in common: they all represent boundary-spanning situations as they involve the sharing, development, or creation of knowledge among people who have substantially different knowledge bases as well as distinctive identities. One of the reasons why examining the dynamics of boundary-spanning knowledge processes is so important is that the type of working practices outlined in these examples are becoming more and more common (Hsiao et al 2012; Kotlarsky et al. 2014). The reason for their growing significance relates to the benefits that can be derived from this form of collaboration. Most fundamentally, collaboration between people with diverse and distinctive knowledge bases creates the potential for knowledge creation and innovation to occur through the insights that can be developed through bringing together and combining diverse bodies of knowledge. For example, Taselli (2015) argues that inter-professional knowledge sharing between doctors and nurses can facilitate innovation and the diffusion of best practices. Further Chang et al. (2012) considers the organizational benefits multinationals can derive from sharing knowledge via the effective use of expatriate workers.

Another factor that signals the importance of boundary-spanning knowledge processes is the growing acknowledgement that the knowledge bases of all organizations are to some extent fragmented into separate, specialized knowledge domains. This led Brown and Duguid (1991: 53) to refer to organizations as being comparable to a 'community-of-communities'. Further, Tasselli (2015: 843) talked about how organizations often resemble 'small worlds of variable segregated groups'. Finally, Carlile (2002, 2004), utilizing a practice-based epistemology, makes a similar argument in talking about the localized nature of knowledge that develops within particular functions of organizations (due to their focus on specific, distinctive problems, and the use of particular, localized practices), and argues that cross-functional collaboration constitutes a boundary-spanning process. Thus, the knowledge base of all organizations can be considered as being made up of a diversity of localized communities which have some overlapping knowledge in common, but which also possess much specialized and specific knowledge.

From this perspective one of the general tasks of management is to coordinate these diverse internal communities, integrating, diffusing, and combining fragmented internal knowledge as necessary (Blackler et al. 2000; Brown and Duguid 2001; Kotlarsky et al. 2014). Thus, if the knowledge base of all organizations is constituted by a diverse collection of specialized knowledge domains, intra-organizational processes which require collaboration across these domains can be conceptualized as boundary-spanning situations as much as inter-organizational collaborations.

Global MNCs represent a good example of an organization type consisting of a 'community-of-communities'. Within such organizations the knowledge in different functional areas, and different business units/divisions, is relatively specialized and distinct, and the people who work in such organizations often have a strong sense of identity with the function/business unit/division that they are part of (see Time to reflect). Thus knowledge sharing across such boundaries within these organizations represents an example of the type of boundary-spanning collaboration examined here, as will be illustrated via various examples. Further, such forms of knowledge sharing within MNCs can provide an important source of innovation and competitive advantage, where knowledge and learning from one part of the organization is shared more widely (Paraponaris and Sigal 2015).

 Time to reflect   Fragmented organizational knowledge bases

Is the level of fragmentation in an organization's knowledge base likely to be proportional to organizational size? Further, if so, are the difficulties of managing such a fragmented knowledge base likely to be greatest for large, global multinationals?

Characterizing boundary-spanning knowledge processes

As illustrated by Figure 12.2, knowledge processes within communities of practice are facilitated by the high degree of common knowledge, overlapping values, and shared sense of identity that community members typically possess. This is because in such circumstances it is likely that the tacit assumptions underpinning people's knowledge, which are key to effective knowledge sharing, are likely to be well understood or commonly shared. Also, the level of trust and mutual understanding between people in this context is likely to be conducive to effective knowledge sharing. However, in boundary-spanning collaborations, as has been outlined, the situation is somewhat different (see Table 13.1). In these circumstances people may only have a weak sense of shared identity or may have separate and distinct identities; are likely to possess a limited amount of shared, common knowledge; and, finally, may have fundamentally different value and belief systems. Thus, the social relations between people who are not members of the same group/community are much less conducive to effective knowledge sharing.

The following two sub-sections consider in detail how the lack of a shared identity and/or differences in knowledge can inhibit knowledge processes in boundary-spanning contexts.

Identity

People from different teams, departments, organizations, sites, or functions who work together may have either a weak sense of common identity or distinctive and separate identities. For example, Massingham (2010) found that collaboration across business units within one Australian multinational was influenced by the differences in identity that existed between host country nationals and parent country nationals (see Illustration 13.2). Further, Zimmermann and Ravishankar's (2014) study of IT offshoring between German and Indian workers found that some German workers were reluctant to share knowledge due to the weak sense of shared identity they had with Indian workers. However, such a weak sense of shared identity between workers is not exclusive to international collaborations. For example, similar issues occur in workplaces employing a range of different professions, such as healthcare (Oborn and Dawson 2011; Tasselli 2015). Thus, Tasselli's (2015: 844) study of interprofessional knowledge sharing in the UK's National Health Service talked about how the existence of 'distinct occupational groups', 'cliques', and 'cohesive sub-groups' significantly shaped knowledge sharing patterns.

This potentially weak sense of common identity arguably complicates knowledge processes through the potential for conflict this creates, as people with differing senses of identity may

Table 13.1 Factors Making Boundary-Spanning Knowledge Processes Difficult

- Weak shared identity or different sense of identity
- Knowledge-related differences:
   1. Lack of common knowledge
   2. Tacitness and context specificity of knowledge make transferability difficult
   3. Epistemic differences: knowledge based on different assumptions, values, and world-view

perceive differences of interest to exist between themselves and others. As was made apparent in Chapter 11 via a number of different examples, conflict or perceptions that differences of interest exist between people/groups have been found to play a crucial role in shaping whether, with whom, and how people are prepared to share knowledge. Further, people's identity can be aligned to different types of group, including particular business units, organizations, professions, or functions. Another type of identity that has to be considered is more culturally based—national forms of identity—as such forms of identity can affect the character and dynamics of boundary-spanning knowledge processes.

As was outlined in Chapter 3, those adopting a practice-based epistemology build on the assumption that all knowledge is culturally embedded, and that everyone's knowledge thus to some extent reflects the values, assumptions, and worldviews which predominate in the cultures they were socialized into (Inkpen and Pien 2006; Jonsson and Kalling 2007; Chen et al. 2010). For example, Chen et al. (2010)'s study of cross-cultural training found that cultural differences between Chinese and American workers significantly affected the character and effectiveness of the training that was undertaken. According to Hofstede, culture in the US is highly individualistic, while in China there is a more collectivist or group orientation to culture. These culture differences shaped people's approach to training. Thus, the US trainers preferred to facilitate two-way training and communication where trainees were active in the learning process through asking questions and taking the initiative. This contrasted with the preferred learning style of the Chinese trainees which was more passive and one-way, with it being assumed that trainers provided all relevant knowledge and trainees passively accepted/learnt it without challenging, probing, or questioning the knowledge (see Chapter 11 for more detail on how national culture can affect knowledge processes in organizations).

At a more basic level, cross-cultural communication and knowledge sharing can also be slowed down and inhibited by a lack of a shared language, misinterpretations due to variable language skills, or concerns about limitations in people's language competencies (see Li 2010; Klitmøller and Lauring 2013; Shoemaker and Zaheer 2014; see Illustration 13.1). Such problems can be particularly acute when cross-cultural communication is largely information technology (IT)-mediated (Newell et al. 2007; Klitmøller and Lauring 2013; Pinjani and Palvia 2013). For example, Peltokorpi (2006) found that knowledge sharing between some Nordic managers working in Japan and the Japanese people they worked with were inhibited by the lack of a shared language with which to communicate. Peltokorpi further found that the knowledge sharing behaviours of the Japanese workers were heavily influenced by their cultural values, so the strong respect they had for status hierarchies inhibited lower level workers from interacting with the Nordic managers.

 Illustration 13.1 Shared language, identity, and knowledge transfer in multinationals

Reiche et al. (2015) examined how the existence of a common language between staff from the headquarters (HQ) and subsidiaries of MNCs affected the development of a shared identity, as well as the transfer of knowledge from the HQ to the subsidiary. Their research was based on a survey-based study of workers from 800 subsidiaries from nine different countries. They utilized social identity theory to argue that the sense of personal identity people possess and develop can strongly influence who they are willing to collaborate and share knowledge with. Further, they argue that possessing a common language can provide the basis for a shared sense of identity between people. Their research found that a shared language between staff from the HQ and subsidiaries was positively related to knowledge flows from the HQ to the subsidiary. The reason for this was that having a common language did provide people with a shared sense of identity, and engaging in a process of knowledge sharing between HQ and subsidiary strengthened this sense of identity. However, a shared language on its own was not found to be a sufficient condition for successful knowledge flows. The transfer of knowledge from HQ to subsidiaries was also affected by the extent to which staff in subsidiaries shared the visions and goals of their HQs, and also the extent to which HR decision-making processes were centralized. They found that knowledge flows from HQ to subsidiaries was more likely when subsidiary staff shared the vision of the HQs, and when HR decision-making was centralized.

Question

What are the managerial implications of this research for MNCs wanting to facilitate knowledge sharing between their HQ and subsidiaries?

Knowledge

The difficulties of knowledge sharing in boundary-spanning contexts, as outlined, are related to more than just the sense of identities that individuals possess. An equally important factor complicating such processes is the nature of the knowledge possessed by people in these situations. These difficulties stem from three interrelated factors (see Table 13.1).

First, as in any context, the sharing of knowledge may be inhibited by its tacitness. However, the sharing of tacit knowledge in boundary-spanning contexts is made more difficult and complex by two other knowledge-related factors: the limited amount of common knowledge that can exist; and the significant epistemological differences that can exist in the knowledge people possess (i.e. their knowledge is based on different underpinning assumptions and values). Thus, for example, Taselli (2015) argues that the challenges of inter-professional knowledge sharing among the medical staff that were observed were related to the fact that the distinct professional groups that existed represented 'distinct sub-cultures with their own inherent norms and values' (p. 844). Equally, Zimmermann and Ravishankar (2014) found that the transfer of knowledge between German and Indian workers in an IT offshoring project was inhibited by the fact that these workers did not possess the same contextual knowledge (such as on HQ strategies or customer requirements). Further, the tacitness of such knowledge made it both difficult for the German workers to communicate, and difficult for the Indian workers to translate and understand.

The issue of epistemological differences is worth elaborating on, as such differences can have a profound effect on attempts to share or collectively utilize knowledge. Brown and Duguid (2001: 207) argue that, while the advantage of communities of practice is that 'common . . . practice . . . creates social-epistemic bonds', conversely '[p]eople with different practices have different assumptions, different outlooks, different interpretations of the world around them, and different ways of making sense of their encounters'. Thus, in boundary-spanning contexts people may not only have limited amounts of common, shared knowledge, but the knowledge they possess may be based on a fundamentally different system of values and assumptions (Majchrzak et al. 2012). Carlile (2002), in a similar vein, and adopting a practice-based epistemology, argued that such epistemic differences will always exist in boundary-spanning contexts because people's knowledge is localized, being developed around and focused on the particular problems and issues in their day-to-day work. Carlile's analysis also suggests that the scope for conflict in such situations can be related to such knowledge-based differences. He suggests that this is because people's knowledge becomes 'invested in practice'. People's sense of competence relates to the knowledge they possess and the way it allows them to do their work. Thus, people can become committed and attached to particular types of knowledge and ways of doing things, and may be reluctant to adapt and change them due to the negative impact such change may have on their sense of individual competence. Further, Hwang et al. (2015) suggest that conflict and disagreements may simply arise out of misunderstandings resulting from the limited amounts of 'mutual knowledge' people possess in such contexts.

The complexity of knowledge sharing in such circumstances stems from the fact that epistemological differences between people or groups can inhibit the development of even a fundamental understanding of the basic premises and values on which the knowledge of others is based (see Illustration 13.2). For example, Li (2010) found that online knowledge sharing between American and Chinese workers was inhibited by different logics related to the significance of context. Chinese workers were more concerned about the contextual nature of knowledge, and were less willing than American workers to share knowledge across contexts, or use knowledge developed in other contexts. Further, in the example of cross-functional collaboration examined by Majchrzak et al. (2012), the knowledge differences that existed between people meant that effective collaboration took a significant amount of time and resources, and required extensive dialogue between people to 'transcend' the differences in knowledge that existed.

The embeddedness of knowledge in language means that epistemological differences in boundary-spanning contexts can stem from national cultural and linguistic differences as much as from differences in people's work practices. For example, Peltokorpi's (2006) research suggested such differences had a significant negative impact on the ability of Norwegian managers to communicate and share knowledge with the Japanese people they worked with. First, Japanese is argued to be a 'high context' language (where non-verbal, tacit, and shared meanings are important) and meaning is determined as much by how things are said as by the words used, while Western languages are 'low context' and meaning is determined more by what is said than how it is said. One illustration of how such factors inhibited communication and knowledge sharing was that the Nordic managers said they were often unclear what their Japanese subordinates meant when they said 'yes'.

 Illustration 13.2 The impact of 'knowledge gaps' on the transfer of knowledge within a multinational between 'parent' and 'host' country staff

For all multinationals, the transfer of knowledge across and between divisions, and between the corporate centre and different divisions, is important to their ongoing competitiveness and success. Massingham (2010) examined problems with the transfer of knowledge between parent and host country staff within a single Australian multinational company in the building materials sector, which had divisions in six Asian countries.

Massingham found that gaps between the knowledge of parent and host country staff inhibited the sharing of knowledge in four distinctive ways. One of these situations was where host country staff lacked sufficient knowledge to learn how to do a particular task that was being taught to them by parent country staff. One example of this was the inability of host country staff to make large-scale investment decisions. The knowledge on how to do this was transferred from parent country staff in the form of codified market research reports. However, host country staff lacked the tacit knowledge to utilize the knowledge in these reports to make effective investment decisions. Parent country staff interpreted this inability as incompetence on the part of host country staff—such tasks were routine to them due to the implicit and intuitive nature of the tacit knowledge they drew on in carrying out this work.

Massingham argued that the tacit knowledge required to make these investment decisions involved combining external market knowledge with internal knowledge of the company, which was knowledge that parent country staff had built up over time, through experience. The tacit nature of the knowledge used by parent country staff in making these decisions, combined with the lack of confidence they had in the ability of host country staff to learn how to carry out these tasks, meant that parent country staff were either unable or unwilling to share the necessary tacit knowledge with host country staff.

Question

What can be done to facilitate the sharing of such deeply tacit knowledge?

In conclusion, boundary-spanning knowledge processes are inhibited by the differences in the knowledge possessed by the people involved in such processes. In general terms, the greater the degree of common knowledge that exists, the more straightforward knowledge processes are likely to be. Further, the character of knowledge processes in such circumstances are also affected by the degree of epistemological difference in the assumptions and values underpinning the knowledge bases involved, with a high level of epistemological difference likely to significantly increase the difficulty and complexity of such knowledge processes.

Identity, knowledge, trust, and social relations

One of the major conclusions to emerge from the previous section was that, where the common knowledge base is limited, or where people have a limited sense of shared identity, this means that the social relationship between parties is unlikely to be strong, and that the foundations for the existence of trust are relatively weak. Thus in such circumstances not only is the existence of strong trust unlikely, but the development of trust will typically be complicated and difficult (Newell et al. 2007; Janowicz-Panjaitan and Noorderhaven 2009). This section thus examines the topic of trust in boundary-spanning contexts, which links back to Chapter 11, where the topic of trust was introduced and conceptualized.

At the most general level, and somewhat unsurprisingly, trust in these contexts has been found to significantly affect knowledge sharing, with levels of knowledge sharing typically being found to be directly related to levels of trust (Jonsson and Kalling 2007; van Wijk et al. 2008; Cheung et al. 2016—see Illustration 13.3). Becerra et al. (2008) found that trust was more closely related to the sharing of tacit, rather than explicit, knowledge. Becerra et al., whose analysis is based on surveys of Norwegian firms involved in inter-firm alliances, argue that, as was suggested in Chapter 11, trust is closely and inversely related to perceptions of risk. One of Becerra et al.'s main findings was that trust was related to the extent to which a partner was prepared to take a risk, as perceptions of trust reduce the risk that people perceive they are taking.

Illustration 13.3 Functional diversity, innovation, knowledge sharing, and trust within R&D teams

Cheung et al. (2016) examined the complex interrelationship between functional diversity, innovation, knowledge sharing, and trust within research and development (R&D) teams. The R&D teams studied were in a single, large, Chinese IT company. The team's work involved a range of activities including designing hardware and software, product testing, and product quality improvement. Research data was collected via surveys, with almost 450 workers from ninety-six different teams completing the survey.

Functional diversity was argued to have potential benefits for innovation levels, but only if people within the teams were motivated to share knowledge with each other. Without such motivation, people will not share knowledge with people who are different, and are likely to either hoard knowledge from other team members or only share knowledge with people who are similar. In such circumstances innovation levels of teams is likely to suffer. Levels of affect-based trust in team members was argued to positively influence people's willingness to share knowledge in diverse teams.

The research hypotheses tested by Cheung et al. (2016) were supported. Thus the relationship between functional diversity and knowledge sharing was negative when levels of affect-based trust were low, and became less negative as levels of affect-based trust increased. Further, knowledge sharing was positively related to levels of innovation. In practical terms, to ensure that functionally diverse teams are innovative and share knowledge effectively it is necessary to develop levels of affect-based trust among team members.

Question

As Cheung et al.'s analysis is based on the study of teams which work face-to-face, and where workers are from the same country, how generalizable are their findings to other types of team, which may also involve international diversity, or where workers may have to collaborate extensively via ICTs rather than face-to-face?

What is of particular interest here is how strong trust-based relations develop in boundary-spanning contexts, which can be illustrated via various examples. First, Inkpen and Pien's (2006) study of the long-term collaboration between Singaporean and Chinese workers in the development of the Suzhou Industrial Park found that knowledge sharing in the early stages of the collaboration was inhibited to some extent due to low levels of trust. Despite the formalization of the collaboration in a number of written contracts, even levels of commitment-based trust were initially low, as Singaporean staff were unhappy with the level of ambiguity that existed in the written contracts. However, over time, through face-to-face interaction and close collaboration between Chinese and Singaporean workers, levels of cognitive- and affect-based trust developed significantly as these workers developed not only personal relationships (affect-based trust) with each other, but also a confidence in each other's abilities (cognitive-based trust). Zimmerman and Ravishankar (2014)'s study of collaboration between German and Indian workers identified a virtuous circle involving levels of trust and a sense of team-based identity, people's willingness to transfer knowledge, and their knowledge sharing efforts. Thus, the higher the level of trust that existed, the more willing people were to engage in knowledge sharing activities, and the more people engaged in knowledge sharing activities, the more levels of trust in team members increased (see Time to reflect).

Time to reflect   Face-to-face communication and trust

How important is face-to-face interaction for the development of trust and an effective working relationship between people from significantly different cultures? Can cross-cultural working relations be developed without any face-to-face interaction?

Harryson et al.'s (2008) study of the development of Volvo C70, which involved intensive collaboration between Swedish and Italian engineers, found that informal socialization provided another means via which trust-based working relations could be developed. The types of events that project team members participated in included attending football matches together, having wine-tasting events, regularly going out to dinner together, and weekend snowboarding trips. Thus trust-based working relations can be developed via collaboration on work-related activities and also through interacting and socializing at non-work events. Similarly, Williams (2011) found that, with the offshoring of IS development work to India, the sharing of more tacit knowledge through what was referred to as 'client embedment' (developing an understanding of the client through either social interaction with client staff or spending time working at client sites). Finally, Ertug et al. (2013) found that perceptions of trustworthiness in international joint ventures was related to the general propensity to trust a partner's home country.

A classification of boundary types

Thus far, while boundary-spanning contexts have been acknowledged as being highly diverse, no effort has been made to systematically differentiate between the different types of boundary that exist, and how the character of these boundaries influences the nature and dynamics of boundary-spanning knowledge processes. This topic is addressed here through using Carlile's (2002, 2004) framework of boundary types. The empirical focus of Carlile's work is predominantly on cross-functional working within single organizations. Adopting a practice-based perspective Carlile characterized such situations as involving boundary-spanning in that the knowledge possessed by staff working in different functional areas, even within the same organization, is understood to be quite different. For Carlile this is because the knowledge of staff in these functional areas is localized, being concerned with addressing the particular problems and being embedded in the particular work practices that each function is involved in and responsible for.

Carlile developed a typology distinguishing between three distinctive types of boundary: syntactic, semantic, and pragmatic (see Table 13.2), with the degree of novelty of the collective tasks being undertaken varying from low (syntactic boundaries) to high (pragmatic boundaries). Syntactic boundaries are assumed to be the easiest to work across as people share a common logic, set of values, and worldview. Thus, working across a syntactic boundary involves the relatively straightforward process of transferring knowledge and information from one community to the other. Semantic boundaries are more difficult to work across, as with them people do not have a shared logic or set of values. Instead, in such contexts people will have different understandings and interpretations of

Table 13.2 Carlile's (2002, 2004) Boundary Types and their Characteristics

	Syntactic	Semantic	Pragmatic
Degree of Novelty in Collaborative Activity	Low	Medium	High
Type of Activity Involved in Facilitating Boundary Activity	Common syntax/language/ understanding exists. Focus on sharing and transferral of knowledge/information across boundary.	Existence of differing interpretations across boundary requires development of mutual understanding.	Dealing with conflicting interests which requires one party to adapt/change their knowledge.
Dominant Knowledge Process Involved	Transfer	Translation	Transformation

the same knowledge. In such contexts, successfully working across a semantic boundary involves people developing an understanding of and sensitivity to other people's understandings and interpretations.

Finally, pragmatic boundaries are the most complex and difficult type of boundary to work successfully across. In such contexts not only do people have different interpretations and understandings of issues/events, they also have different interests, and working successfully across a pragmatic boundary thus involves both developing some common, shared interests and (at least) one group/community being prepared to change and transform their knowledge. Due to the extent to which people and groups develop a sense of investment in and commitment to their knowledge/practices (see earlier), doing so is typically never straightforward.

A fundamental element in Carlile's typology is the role of boundary objects in facilitating cross-boundary working. Carlile suggests that to successfully work and share knowledge across each boundary type requires the use of appropriate boundary objects. This element in his analysis is examined and illustrated in the following section.

Facilitating/managing knowledge between communities

Up to this point the chapter has emphasized the not insignificant difficulties in sharing knowledge in boundary-spanning contexts. However, these difficulties are to some extent manageable. There is much that can be done to address them and facilitate boundary-spanning knowledge processes. In general terms, this involves improving the level of mutual understanding and developing the social relationship between relevant people.

From a practice-based perspective, developing such an understanding involves the sort of perspective making and taking processes outlined in Chapter 3. While the practice-based perspective on knowledge assumes that processes of perspective making and taking are necessary for the sharing and communication of knowledge in *all* circumstances, the lack of common knowledge in boundary-spanning contexts raises the importance of such processes. These perspective making and taking processes do not result in the integration of the different knowledge bases into a coherent whole, but should instead involve a process of dialogue, where 'each community maintains its own voice while listening to the voice of the other' (Gherardi and Nicolini 2002: 421). Thus, perspective making and taking occurs through a process of talking, listening, acknowledging, and being tolerant to any differences identified.

Current writing suggests two broad ways in which this can be achieved. First, work can be invested in managing the social relationship between people; and, second, the existing areas of overlap between people can be developed by means of boundary objects.

Relationship management

Relationship management actively involves key, strategic individuals in developing the social relationship between the people involved in a boundary-spanning work situation. A range of different, but overlapping, labels have been used for the people undertaking such roles. Thus Brown and Duguid (1998) differentiated between the roles of broker and translator, while Haas (2015) identified three roles including boundary-spanner, gatekeeper, and broker. As Haas outlines, there are a diversity of definitions used by different writers for all these different roles, many of which are overlapping. The two most commonly used labels are broker and boundary-spanner, so the focus here is on them. In terms of brokering, Brown and Duguid (1998) define a broker as someone who is a member of multiple communities, and uses their knowledge and understanding of both to facilitate the development of mutual understanding between other members of the communities. Gherardi and Nicolini (2002) argue that a broker is someone who has the ability to 'transfer and translate certain elements of one practice to another'. Klitmøller and Lauring's (2013) study of a global virtual team involving workers from Denmark and India talked about the important brokering role played by an Indian worker who had a long-term presence working in Denmark. This person, who was Indian, but worked face-to-face with Danish workers, had links to both groups of workers, and acted as a mediator in communication between Indian and Danish workers, which many workers felt improved the effectiveness of communication. Castro's (2015) study of a Parisian innovation hub concerned with sustainable cities, which involved a large number of small companies, government agencies, and academics, found that the brokering activities undertaken by the hub's director to liaise between different participants was also important in facilitating the hub's activity.

While a broker is someone who has a sense of identity as being part of more than one community, a boundary-spanner, by contrast, is someone who is primarily embedded with and identifies with one community, but who plays a strategic role developing relations with, and sharing knowledge with people from other, relevant external communities (Haas 2015; Roberts and Beamish 2017). This is a role which has relevance not only for processes of knowledge sharing, but also innovation more generally, and the management of change (see for example Levina and Vaast 2005). In the context of MNCs, expatriates, people who work at the corporate HQ and are transferred to work at subsidiary divisions, can be conceptualized as boundary-spanners (Barner-Rasmussen et al. 2010, 2014). Such workers can play a crucial role in sharing knowledge within MNCs (Chang et al. 2015—see Illustration 13.4; Kane and Levina 2017; Roberts and Beamish 2017).

Illustration 13.4 The role of expatriate boundary-spanners in sharing knowledge within MNCs

Chang et al. (2012) examine the factors influencing the extent to which expatriate workers facilitate knowledge sharing between the HQ and subsidiary of Taiwanese MNCs based in the UK. They found that expatriates did play a positive role in the transferral of knowledge to subsidiaries, and that when this happened there was a positive impact on subsidiary performance. However, for this boundary-spanning role to facilitate knowledge sharing expatriates must have the willingness, motivation, and opportunity to engage in knowledge sharing activities. In specific terms, they must be willing to accept the loss of power/status that results from transferring their knowledge to subsidiary staff; to cope with the cultural challenges involved in expatriate work; and, finally (as relational skills), to actively develop social relations with subsidiary staff during their expatriation.

Question

What are the implications of these findings for the recruitment and training of expatriates?

Boundary objects

The final method discussed by Brown and Duguid (1998) to facilitate knowledge sharing in boundary-spanning contexts involves the development and utilization of boundary objects, a concept initially developed by Star (1989, 2010). Boundary objects are entities that are common to a number of communities and can be either physical or linguistic/symbolic in character. An example of a digital boundary object was a three-dimensional virtual workspace examined by Alin et al. (2013) which facilitated the sharing of knowledge in engineering design projects. An example of linguistic/epistemic boundary objects is provided by McGovern and Dawson (2010). In their study of attempts to translate genetics knowledge and science into medical practices that could be used to treat patients, the projects concerned were conceptualized as epistemic/knowledge objects, with control over them being a significant source of dispute among the various epistemic communities involved in the projects.

Boundary objects provide a focus for negotiation, discussion, or even shared activity between people from different communities, and thus can be utilized to help develop and improve the working relationship between people, and the mutual understanding they have of each other (Bresnen 2010). The boundary object concept has proved popular and has been used by an increasing number of analysts to understand change processes (Fenton 2007; Windeck et al 2015), biomedical innovation (Swan et al. 2007; McGivern and Dopson 2010), and the sharing of project-specific knowledge (Sapsted and Salter 2004; Swan et al. 2007; Bresnen 2010).

A more systematic analysis of the concept of boundary objects is developed by Carlile, as alluded to earlier. Carlile (2002) outlined a typology of distinctive types of boundary objects that was adapted from Star's (1989) work (see Table 13.3), and links this to his typology of boundary types (see Table 13.2) to suggest that successfully working across boundaries requires the use of boundary objects appropriate to the type of boundary being crossed (see Table 13.4). In the space available here it is only possible to sketch out the complex model developed over two detailed academic papers (Carlile 2002, 2004).

Table 13.3   Carlile's Boundary Object Types

Boundary Object Type	Boundary Object Characteristics
Repository	Common data or information that provide shared reference point for groups involved in cross-boundary work.
Standardized forms/ methods	Shared forms and methods of working allow differences of opinion across a boundary to be acknowledged, accounted for, and understood.
Objects/models	Complex representations (such as drawings, computer simulations) which can be observed, shared by groups involved in cross-boundary situations.
Maps	Representation of dependencies between groups involved in cross-boundary working.

Source: Carlile (2002, 2004).

To successfully span syntactic boundaries, the fact that people have a shared syntax and language means repository type boundary objects, in the form of common data and information, can facilitate cross-boundary working. Thus, the primary knowledge process involved in spanning syntactic boundaries is knowledge sharing, where repository type boundary objects are developed via the transferral and sharing of knowledge to allow the development of a common knowledge base, agreed upon and understood by all communities.

Successfully spanning semantic boundaries, where people do not have a shared syntax and language, and where people may have divergent interpretations and understandings, is more complex. To do this involves the development and use of boundary objects which facilitate a

Table 13.4   Carlile's Boundary Types and Appropriate Boundary Objects

Type of Boundary	Characteristics Required for Cross-Boundary Collaboration	Boundary Objects that Allow Successful Cross-Boundary Working
Syntactic	Shared system and common set of data/ information.	Repository
Semantic	Provide a means for people to specify and learn about cross-boundary differences and dependencies.	Standardized form and methods Objects/models Maps
Pragmatic	Provide a means whereby people develop a common sense of shared interests and a willingness to transform their knowledge to achieve them.	Objects/models Maps

Source: Carlile (2002, 2004).

process of perspective making and taking, where people develop an increased understanding of the perspective of others. Carlile suggests that this can be achieved via the use of three types of boundary object. First, standardized forms and models can be used, where people gain insights into the perspective of others via understanding the different ways that common forms are used. Second, objects/models can be used, as the use of shared drawings, etc., provides a way in which people's differences in perspective can be communicated and discussed. Finally, maps, which outline the interdependencies between communities, can also be used, as they allow groups to understand how people's perspectives are shaped by their community interests and co-dependencies. Thus, with the spanning of semantic boundaries, the primary knowledge process is one of translation.

Finally, pragmatic boundaries are the most difficult and complex to span, due to the differences of interest that exist between communities, with Carlile arguing that both object/models and maps are appropriate boundary objects for this context. This is because the development and use of maps allow people to better understand and appreciate the differences of interest that exist, while the use of objects/models can provide a resource which not only allows people to develop a sense of shared interests and common endeavour, but also to transform their knowledge to achieve a collective goal. Thus, with the spanning of pragmatic boundaries, the primary knowledge process is one of transformation.

Carlile (2002) illustrated the role of boundary objects in facilitating boundary-spanning via the analysis of a specific issue that developed and was eventually resolved in his ethnographic study of the development of a new car valve. While the development process involved collaboration among staff from four functions/communities (sales, manufacturing engineering, production, and design engineering), the focal issue involved the manufacturing and design engineering functions. A manufacturing engineer, who was responsible for transforming the design engineers' work into a manufacturable product, had a concern about the design that would potentially require a significant redesign to be undertaken. Thus, the boundary being spanned was a pragmatic one, requiring the transformation of knowledge. The manufacturing engineer's initial efforts at communicating his concerns to the design engineers failed, largely because, Carlile argued, the boundary object used, some out-of-date design drawings, represented an inappropriate boundary object that the design engineers couldn't effectively relate to—the drawings didn't reflect the latest version of the design they were familiar with. However, when the same manufacturing engineer later expressed the same concerns to the designers with up-to-date drawings, his efforts were successful, and the design engineers agreed to change the design. Carlile argued that the up-to-date drawings were a suitable boundary object as they allowed effective boundary-spanning dialogue and communication. The outcome of these efforts was an effective boundary-spanning collaboration, as all concerned took account of the manufacturing engineer's concerns and undertook to change the design, even though this involved utilizing some new design principles and ideas that were novel to the company.

Conclusion

This chapter has narrowly focused on boundary-spanning knowledge processes involving collaboration within heterogeneous groups, where people have different knowledge bases, identities, and/or language skills. Arguably, the relevance and importance of boundary-spanning knowledge processes has increased due to the changes in working practices that have emerged from the contemporary restructuring of work organizations. The difference between the social dynamics and knowledge processes that occur within boundary-spanning knowledge processes and those that occur within communities of practice relate to the sense of shared identity and typically high level of common knowledge which exists within communities, but which tends to be absent from boundary-spanning contexts (see Chapter 12). It may also be the case that not only are there limited amounts of common, shared knowledge between parties, but that there may be epistemic differences in the knowledge of the people and communities involved, where their knowledge is based on fundamentally different assumptions and values.

Typically, as illustrated by a number of examples, boundary-spanning knowledge processes are likely to be more complex and difficult to make successful than those occurring within more homogeneous group contexts such as communities of practice. This is due to both the differences in identity, which may induce boundary-spanning conflict, and the lack of common knowledge. Somewhat simplistically, the less common knowledge that exists, and the greater the level of epistemic difference, the more complicated and difficult the knowledge sharing process will be.

Knowledge sharing across communities was shown to require two primary and closely interrelated elements, both of which are developed through a process of social interaction and communication. First, boundary-spanning collaborations are facilitated by people acting as brokers and/or boundary-spanners, who play the crucial role of bridging and communicating between people from different communities. Finally, boundary-spanning knowledge processes can be facilitated through the use of boundary objects. However, Carlile's analysis suggests, for boundary objects to be effective, the type of boundary object has to be appropriate to the type of boundary being worked across.

 Case study Cross-functional knowledge sharing in R&D via co-location: the case of Novartis

Corradi et al. (2015) analysed a pilot study into how the organization of physical workspace was managed to facilitate cross-functional working within Novartis. This pilot study was conducted within part of the biomedical research division.

Novartis is a Swiss-based pharmaceutical company, and is one of the world's largest pharmaceutical companies employing almost 120,000 workers worldwide. One key element of its business involves the development of new drugs and medicines. This R&D work is multidisciplinary, involving a range of scientists with different technical backgrounds and knowledge bases. Thus, such work can be conceptualized as an example of boundary-spanning work.

In order to facilitate and improve this work via encouraging inter-personal knowledge sharing between workers, Novartis undertook what was labelled a 'co-location pilot' project, which involved redesigning the physical workspace that some R&D staff worked in. Almost 200 workers were involved in the pilot project, including people from the R&D and marketing divisions. The project involved three floors of one building, which were custom designed, and which were inter-connected by an integrated, internal staircase. The space in these three floors was carefully designed to be multifunctional and support the type of work activities involved; it included a mixture of different types of rooms and areas, and designated spaces for project teams to work, meeting rooms, research labs, open public spaces, and a large kitchen area for all. All workers had access to all space, and the space was designed to create physical proximity, where all workers were closely located to each other. Further, while there were a number of discrete meeting rooms and labs, the general design philosophy was to create an open-plan space where it was easy for people to see each other, with free movement of people.

The co-location project was deemed successful by the workers involved in it, as it was perceived to positively improve cross-functional collaboration among workers. One of the benefits of the workspace was that it facilitated informal, spontaneous interaction between staff. Prior to the pilot, cross-functional collaboration had typically occurred via the organization of formal meetings. Such meetings affected and restricted communication, as not all people were able to attend formal meetings, and the formality of the meeting format shaped communication patterns. Further, prior to the pilot study, when people were located in different buildings, opportunities for face-to-face interaction was limited. In these circumstances, much inter-personal, cross-functional communication also occurred via e-mail.

The co-location pilot project changed this, creating more opportunities for face-to-face interaction and more informal communication. This can be illustrated via a number of interview quotations from people involved in the project, who said, 'communication has become much easier, more spontaneous and faster', 'there is a lot of passive diffusion of information from other line functions into my head. When other line functions next to my desk discuss topics, I pick them up', and 'I meet people I would not otherwise have met if they were in a different building. I'm developing social relations with widely differing associates'. One consequence of the increase in informal communication and face-to-face interaction was that the quantity of e-mails people sent and received decreased. Finally, the kitchen area also provided a space where spontaneous informal interactions and social relations were developed. For example, some people said, 'in the coffee zone, and while passing the desks I meet a lot of people', and 'the spot to start unplanned discussions with people from other functions is at the coffee machine'.

Overall, therefore, the co-location pilot had a significant impact on knowledge sharing patterns, increasing levels of cross-functional knowledge sharing, reducing the extent of e-mail-based communication, and increasing the extent to which knowledge was shared face-to-face, via informal mechanisms.

Source: Corradi, A., Heinzen, M., and Boutelier, R. (2015) 'Designing Workspaces for Cross Functional Knowledge Sharing in R&D: The "Co-location Pilot" of Novartis', *Journal of Knowledge Management*, 19/2: 236–56.

Questions

1. While the pilot project was regarded as successful, what are the potential negative consequences of this method of organizing workspace? For example, is it possible that people may find it harder to have uninterrupted time where they can focus intensely on a particular task, such as writing a report?

2. This case shows how the design of physical workspace can facilitate informal, spontaneous interaction between people, and the development of social relations across functions by people who were previously unfamiliar with each other. Is it possible to replicate such interaction patterns via ICTs, when it is not possible to co-locate all workers in the same space?

 ## Review and Discussion Questions

1. The prevalence of inter-organizational networking can be gauged by a simple piece of research. Examine the business section from any serious daily newspaper and you are likely to find relevant examples. However, is this type of working practice likely to be more common in some business sectors more than others? What factors affect the extent to which inter-organizational networks are developed and utilized?

2. Reflect on any work experience that you have had. What, if anything, did you and your work colleagues most strongly feel a sense of identity with: your immediate work group, the function you worked in, the division you worked for, or the overall corporate group? Are these senses of identity likely to inhibit the development of an effective working relationship and the sharing of knowledge with people from different parts of the organization?

3. When collaboration involves geographically dispersed workers, does the successful sharing of tacit knowledge need to involve some level of face-to-face interaction?

4. To what extent does having a shared language create a common sense of identity? Is the benefit of a shared language relate more to the ability to communicate than to any sense of shared identity it creates?

 ## Suggestions for Further Reading

B. Reiche, A-W. Harzing, and M. Pudelka (2015). 'Why and How Does Shared Language Affect Subsidiary Knowledge Inflows? A Social Identity Perspective', *Journal of International Business Studies*, 46: 528–51.

An interesting case study of how shared language and social identity shape knowledge flows within MNCs.

S. Tasselli (2015). 'Social Networks and Inter-professional Knowledge Transfer: The Case of Health Professionals', *Organization Studies*, 36/7: 841–72.

A case study of inter-professional knowledge sharing patterns among healthcare professionals.

S. Cheung, Y. Gong, M. Wang, L. Zhou, and J. Shi (2016). 'When and How Does Functional Diversity Influence Team Innovation? The Mediating Role of Knowledge Sharing and the Moderation Role of Affect-based Trust in Teams', *Human Relations*, 69/7: 1507–31.

A quantitative study of trust and knowledge sharing affecting innovation performance in functionally diverse teams.

A. Klitmøller and J. Lauring (2013). 'When Global Virtual Teams Share Knowledge: Media Richness, Cultural Difference and Language Commonality', *Journal of World Business*, 48: 398–406.

A case study of communication medium, culture, and language differences affecting knowledge sharing between Danish and Indian workers collaborating in global virtual teams.

 To further your understanding of knowledge management in organizations explore the book's accompanying online resources at **www.oup.com/uk/hislop4e/**

14 Power, Politics, Conflict, and Knowledge Processes

Introduction

One of the defining characteristics of the vast majority of the writing on knowledge management is that discussions of power are typically marginalized, if not completely absent (Kärreman 2010). Such an omission is puzzling, as a cursory glance outside the narrow confines of the knowledge management literature reveals both the need to understand issues of power in explaining organizational dynamics and the close relationship between knowledge and power. However, the neglect of this topic is not total, because, as has already been shown in Chapters 12 and 13, a number of writers do take such issues seriously. What this chapter argues is that despite the general neglect of this topic in the knowledge management literature, understanding the relationship between power and organizational knowledge processes is of fundamental importance, and the task of doing so is magnified by the general absence of such an analysis.

While power has not been adequately dealt with in the knowledge management literature there has been a growing acknowledgement, as was outlined in Chapter 11, that conflict in relation to knowledge processes is not uncommon, and that such conflict can play an important role shaping such processes, for example influencing who a person is willing and unwilling to share knowledge with. These issues are raised again here, but are explicitly linked to the topics of power and politics. Arguably, a missing link in the knowledge management literature that does examine such issues is that it does not address the fundamental causes of such conflicts. To do so requires power to be accounted for, which reveals not only the inherent potential for conflict that exists in organizations but how power is structurally embedded in the employment relationship and the basis for all knowledge practices.

In the analysis presented, power and knowledge will be seen to be extremely closely interrelated, which is another reason why issues of power require to be accounted for in attempting to understand the dynamics of organizational knowledge processes. However, there isn't a consensus around either how power should be defined or how its relationship to knowledge should be conceptualized. This is accounted for by examining two different perspectives on power, and linking them to the two dissensus-based perspectives on knowledge management research identified by Schultze and Stabell (2004).

The chapter is structured into three major sections. The first section provides an overview of the two perspectives on power, and outlines how they link with Schultze and Stabell's framework. The following two sections then separately examine the two perspectives on power considered. First to be examined is the 'power as a resource' perspective, which links back to the topics of the employment relationship and intra-organizational conflict discussed in Chapter 11. The second perspective examined is Michel Foucault's (1980) distinctive perspective on power/knowledge. While the former sections concentrate on power and conflict within organizational boundaries, a final section is added that elaborates on power, politics, and conflict that develop *across organizational boundaries* and problems that may arise as a result of this, and the need to balance knowledge development and knowledge protection.

Two perspectives on power and the power/knowledge relationship

It should not really be a surprise that two contrasting perspectives on power that have been articulated in the knowledge management literature, as power is one of the most contested concepts in social theory. This section provides an overview of these two perspectives on power and power/knowledge relations, and links them with the two 'dissensus' perspectives in Schultze and Stabell's (2004) framework on knowledge management research articulated in Chapter 1 (see Figure 1.2).

In Schultze and Stabell's (2004) framework of knowledge management research there were two dimensions: epistemology and social order. In terms of the social order dimension they differentiated between the consensus- and dissensus-based views. In Chapters 2 and 3, where the characteristics of the two epistemological perspectives that dominate in the knowledge management literature were presented, the focus was deliberately confined to epistemologies linked to the consensus-based perspective on social order (what Schultze and Stabell labelled the constructivist and neo-functional discourses). Part of the rationale for doing so was that the two consensus-based perspectives have been more extensively utilized, and interest in and use of either of the dissensus-based perspectives has been comparatively marginal and limited. However, in considering how power and politics link to knowledge processes in organizations, it is necessary to make use of the two epistemologies/discourses on knowledge management that link to the dissensus-based perspective on social order (in Schultze and Stabell's terms, the dialogic and critical discourses). Thus the neglect of them is addressed here, in the chapter in which they are most fully articulated.

Before outlining the two perspectives on power, what differentiates them and how they map onto the two dissensus-based perspectives on social order in Schultze and Stabell's framework, it is worth, briefly, (re)articulating what the two dissensus-based epistemologies/discourses have in common. Their primary common feature is that in contrast to the consensus-based perspective which assumes that harmonious social relations typically predominate, the two epistemologies linked to the dissensus-based perspective on social order assume that antagonistic relations are an inherent feature of social dynamics both in business organizations and in society more widely. From this perspective societies are made up of groups whose interests are often oppositional and conflicting, where political behaviour motivated by the pursuit of such interests is common. Further, one of the features common to both of the epistemologies/discourses linked to the dissensus-based perspective, and the reason they are both examined here, is that power and knowledge are conceptualized as

Table 14.1 Mapping of Two Perspectives of Power onto Critical and Dialogic Perspectives on Knowledge Management Research

	Critical Discourse	Dialogic Discourse
Character of knowledge	A stable entity/resource that can exist independently of people.	Knowledge largely tacit and provisional, being embodied by people and embedded in the activities they undertake.
	Power as Resource	**Foucault's Power/Knowledge**
Character of power	A stable resource (that has diverse forms) which exists independently of people, and which can be utilized by actors to influence people and/or events with the aim of achieving particular goals.	A phenomenon which is embedded within and inseparable from social relationships and the discourses people articulate which people can utilize, but not possess, and which shapes (and legitimates) particular ways of acting and thinking.
Relationship between power and knowledge	Knowledge is an important type of power resource that people can utilize in pursuit of particular interests.	Power and knowledge are inseparable and mutually constituted.

Source: Schulze and Stabell (2004).

being closely interrelated. Thus, from these perspectives, in examining the character and dynamics of organizational knowledge processes it is fundamentally important and necessary to take account of power.

The primary reason why the two perspectives on power examined here map neatly onto the two dissensus perspectives in Schultze and Stabell's framework (the critical and dialogic discourses) is that they conceptualize power in almost identical ways to how knowledge is conceptualized in these discourses (see Table 14.1). The 'power as resource' perspective (which maps onto the critical discourse perspective in Schultze and Stabell's framework) links to the influential resource-based tradition in the analysis of power (Dahl 1957; French and Raven 1959; Bacharach and Baratz 1963), as well as the more radical perspective on power developed by Lukes (1974). The alternative power/knowledge perspective (which maps onto the dialogic discourse) is embedded in the work of Foucault, whose distinctive understanding of power has grown in influence, and has been utilized and adopted by a number of writers to understand organizational knowledge processes.

As seen in Table 14.1, and as will be outlined more fully in subsequent sections, what differentiates these perspectives on power is not only how they define power, but how they conceptualize the relationship between power and knowledge. Thus the 'power as resource' perspective regards knowledge as a power resource that people can utilize politically, where conflict exists, in the pursuit of particular self-interested goals. By contrast the Foucauldian perspective on power, and the reason why the term power/knowledge is used, is that power and knowledge are regarded as being completely inseparable, with all acts of power being embedded in and to some extent perpetuating particular ways of understanding (knowledge), while all statements of knowledge involve the exercise of power (by implicitly and unavoidably privileging a particular perspective and simultaneously questioning the legitimacy of other claims to knowledge).

An important topic from both perspectives which links power and politics to knowledge is the process via which certain forms and types of knowledge come to be regarded as legitimate, while other knowledge claims become marginalized and regarded as having less legitimacy. Thus each of the following sections outlines how this process occurs from the viewpoint of the two perspectives on power examined.

Power as a resource and the critical discourse on knowledge management

As already highlighted, the perspective on power associated with the critical discourse on knowledge management aligns with the resource-based view on power (see Definition and Table 14.1). This perspective on power was first articulated over fifty years ago, in the late 1950s, and has been highly influential since then.

Theorizing power and power/knowledge relations

From this perspective, power is a resource that individuals can develop and utilize to influence the attitudes, values, and behaviour of others in the pursuit of particular objectives. Thus, Hales (1993: 20) defines power resources as 'those things which bestow the means whereby the behaviour of others may be influenced', while Liao (2008: 1882) similarly defines power as 'the ability of an agent to change or control the behaviours, attitudes, opinions, objectives, needs, and values of another agent'. The key feature of these definitions is that power is conceptualized as a discrete resource/entity that people can possess or have access to. Hales argues that power resources have this ability through three specific properties they possess (see Table 14.2). First, they are relatively scarce and only available to some. Second, they are desired because they can satisfy certain wants. Finally, there are no alternatives available, in that the only way to satisfy these wants is via the use of particular power resources. Thus knowledge has the potential to be a power resource if it has these characteristics. For

Table 14.2 Properties of Power Resources which Make Them Influential

Property	Expert Power-Based Example
Scarcity	Specialist knowledge/expertise which only a limited number of people possess.
	Knowledge which may be highly tacit and which requires to be developed though experience.
Satisfy wants	Knowledge which may satisfy individual wants through its possession or use (such as status or rewards).
	Knowledge which satisfies organizational goals and objectives through its possession or use (such as providing organizations with status, profits, market share, or product/market innovations).
No alternatives	Where there are no alternative sources of knowledge which can satisfy important wants (see earlier).

Source: Hales (1993).

example, the specialist technical knowledge built up over time that an experienced engineer possesses will be a power resource available to the engineer who possesses it if it is scarce and only possessed by a small number of people, if it is important and useful to their employer, and if there are no alternative sources of similar expertise.

DEFINITION **Power (resource-based perspective)**

Power is a (scarce) resource whose use allows people to shape the behaviour of others.

This perspective assumes that there are five distinct types of power resources that people can utilize (see Table 14.3 and Illustration 14.1). The first two types of power represent contrasting ways of attempting to influence others. First, reward power utilizes a person's ability to offer rewards as a way of influencing behaviour. Rewards can take a variety of forms, from monetary to non-monetary (such as an award, praise, or recognition). This power resource is thus available to anyone who has access to such rewards. However, the ability to shape someone's behaviour in this way is limited by the extent to which the latter desires the reward that is offered. Fundamentally, the more desirable the reward is to a person, the more likely his/her behaviour is to be influenced by being offered it. In contrast, coercive power utilizes the ability to punish non-compliance as a way of influencing behaviour. As with rewards, such punishments can take a variety of forms including witholding a reward, providing a negative report on a person, or even the extreme of using physical threats. However, the ability to influence someone in this way is affected by the extent to which s/he regards the potential punishment as serious and important. Legitimate power refers to the ability to influence someone via his/her view of a person as being someone who has a legitimate right to give commands and control behaviour. The most obvious example of this is the authority possessed by a manager, due to his/her formal position, roles, and responsibilities in the organizational hierarchy. However, simply possessing managerial authority does not guarantee that someone will have legitimate power. For example, if it is deemed that someone achieved his/her position by unfair means (such as favouritism), or that s/he is unfairly abusing his/her authority (such as via bullying and threatening people), s/he may not be deemed as having legitimate power

Table 14.3 Types of Power

Power Resource	Nature/Source of Influence
Reward	Influencing others via the ability to administer rewards for particular behaviours.
Coercive	Influencing others via the ability to administer a punishment for non-compliance with requests.
Legitimate	Influencing others via persuading them of the legitimacy of someone's right to define and control behaviour.
Reference	Influencing others via possessing and developing their admiration and desire to gain approval.
Expert	Influencing others via the possession or use of particular knowledge, expertise, or skill.

and may not be able to use his/her position to effectively influence others. The fourth type of power is reference power. This source of power is based not on hierarchical position in an organization, but is instead based on the extent to which people admire and respect someone and wish to gain his/her approval.

Of most relevance to the topic of knowledge management is the fifth and final type of power: expert power. A person has access to this type of power if s/he possess or utilizes what are regarded as important and legitimate knowledge and skills. However, simply possessing knowledge and skills is not necessarily a source of expert power as the legitimacy of someone's knowledge may be open to dispute, or someone's competence in utilizing knowledge and skills may be questioned or compromised.

 Illustration 14.1 Resource-based power and knowledge sharing

Liao (2008) uses the resource-based model of power to examine the extent to which and ways in which managers are able to influence their subordinates' knowledge sharing behaviours. Empirical data was collected from a survey of research and development (R&D) staff in three Taiwanese computer companies. The theoretical model they tested considered both the direct effect that the five types of power available to managers had on employees' knowledge sharing, and also the indirect effect when the relationship between the types of power and employee knowledge sharing was mediated by trust.

In terms of the direct effect, it was found that only reward and expert power had a direct influence on employees' knowledge sharing. In terms of the indirect relationship it was found that only reference and expert power had a positive relationship with employees' trust in their managers. Perhaps unsurprisingly, coercive power had neither a direct nor an indirect relationship with employee' knowledge sharing.

These findings have significant organizational implications. First, in terms of the direct relationship between power and knowledge sharing, the importance of reward power suggests that rewarding employees may be a useful way to motivate them to share knowledge. Second, in terms of the indirect relationship between power and knowledge sharing, the importance of reference and expert power in the development of trust suggests that managers should develop both types of power, through managing employees so that they both respect the expert knowledge of managers and also respect them as individuals.

Questions

1. To what extent does this illustration reinforce the idea that the use of coercive power is unlikely to be a successful way to influence people as its use is never likely to be regarded as legitimate?

2. Can you think of situations where the use of coercive power may be considered legitimate?

Linking power and knowledge to conflict and politics

To fully understand the role that power resources can play in organizational knowledge processes, it is necessary to consider the complex relationship that exists between power, knowledge, politics, and conflict in organizations. Figure 14.1 sums this relationship up diagrammatically. However, before explaining it more fully it is necessary to define what is meant by politics. Political acts are those actions whereby people deliberately attempt to influence others through the use of power resources with the aim of achieving particular goals (which may be in conflict with the goals of others).

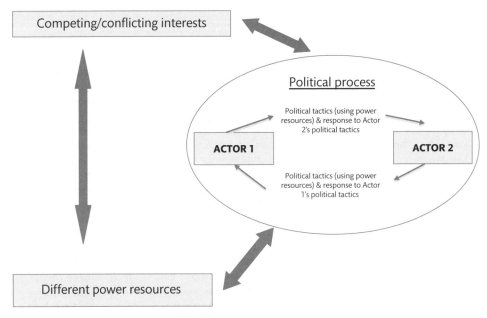

Figure 14.1 Linking Power, Politics, and Conflict

The political process in Figure 14.1 is a dynamic social situation where different actors (individuals or groups) who have competing or conflicting interests draw upon particular power resources, which are used as political tools aimed at achieving each group's objectives. The political process is a dynamic situation as it can evolve over time, with actors having scope to change what interests they pursue, what power resources they draw upon in pursuit of their aims, and the particular political tactics they utilize. For example, in relation to expert power, there are a diverse range of political tactics with which this source of power can be utilized in attempting to influence others. Some could choose to share or hoard their expert knowledge, or they might choose to selectively share it with only certain people. Thus, with every source of power, a diverse range of political tactics can be utilized.

A key part of the model outlined in Figure 14.1 is how the dynamics of political processes are shaped by the way actors respond to the political tactics and power resources of others. As outlined earlier in describing the character of power resources, the ability of people to use their power resources to influence others depends on the extent to which they are regarded as important and legitimate by people. Such judgements have important implications for how actors behave, because if someone's power is deemed legitimate, then people are more likely to comply than if it is regarded as being of dubious legitimacy. Thus while managerial power is, to some extent, a function of organizational position it is one of the problematic aspects of management that such power can't be assumed to be *automatically* deemed as legitimate by workers (Hislop et al. 2000). For example, behaviour such as verbally abusing workers or not adequately consulting them may undermine the extent to which power related to managerial position is deemed legitimate by workers (see Illustration 14.2).

Illustration 14.2   Disputed knowledge: 'pit sense' and the bureaucratization of risk assessment in coal mines

Kamoche and Maguire (2011) examined a political dispute within the UK coal industry regarding how risk assessment should be carried out which centred on a dispute regarding the legitimacy of 'pit sense', a form of sense-based, tacit knowledge developed by miners which they had traditionally used to evaluate risk. This tacit knowledge was developed over time, through working in mines, was never codified in any way, was regarded by miners as being fundamentally important to safe working, and was knowledge that management had little understanding of or control over. Thus, in terms of the resource-based view of power, this was a dispute regarding the 'expert power' possessed by the miners in the form of specialized knowledge on risk assessment that was not possessed by management.

'Pit sense' involved being aware of unusual and suspicious noises or smells that might suggest a problem in a mine. This knowledge was defined as being concerned with 'how to look after yourself in a mine, knowing what to do and what not to do' (p. 732). However, over time, with the development of new, mechanized work practices and the development of more rule-based, bureaucratic working practices, management increasingly came to question the validity and legitimacy of 'pit sense'. Fundamentally, management wanted risk assessment to be more focused on using standardized health and safety procedures and to be less driven by 'pit sense'. To help do this they implemented new health and safety procedures and simultaneously attempted to undermine the legitimacy of 'pit sense'. For example, it began to be referred to by some managers as 'old wives tales' (p. 736). However, due to both the miners' reluctance to give up 'pit sense' and to the lack of control that management had over the miners' working practices, they weren't able to eliminate the use of 'pit sense'.

Instead, an uneasy compromise was reached by the miners and management whereby the miners used the new rules, but had discretion to ignore them when they chose to do so. An illustration of this was provided by one miner who said,

> you're supposed to wear ear muffs while you're bolting. Now if something is going to come over, usually it gives you a warning, you can hear something. When you've got ear muffs on you can't hear it coming. So more often than not we don't wear our ear muffs. (p. 736)

The compromise made by management was to accept that this was done, but ignore it, as long as productivity levels were maintained at an acceptable level.

Questions

1. Analyse this case using the political model outlined earlier in the chapter and summarized in Figure 14.1. How would you characterize the political tactics utilized by both management and the miners?

2. Could the dispute have been resolved differently if either management or the miners had utilized different sources of power or used different political tactics?

Yanow (2004), in examining the nature of the knowledge possessed by bakery workers, found that formal codified knowledge ('expert' knowledge) was typically privileged over the tacit knowledge possessed by bakery drivers ('local' knowledge). This privileging of codified knowledge (and simultaneous marginalization of tacit, 'local' knowledge) was a consequence of the greater legitimacy accorded formal, codified knowledge and the reduced legitimacy that was typically accorded more tacit, contextual, and local knowledge. Analysed in the context of the issues examined here, this process of privileging codified expert knowledge and marginalizing local, tacit knowledge is the outcome of a political process whereby the legitimacy of these different forms of knowledge has been disputed and resolved in a particular way. Overall, from a resource-based perspective on power, an actor's knowledge-based power resources are never automatically regarded as legitimate by others, and the extent to which they are, will influence how others respond to them.

The critical discourse on knowledge management and the inevitability of power and conflict in business organizations

In examining the importance of power to knowledge processes from the perspective of a critical discourse on knowledge management and from a resource-based perspective on power it is necessary to return to two issues discussed in Chapter 11: the employment relationship and the potential for conflict that exists between workers in organizations. It is due to both of these factors that those adopting a critical discourse on knowledge management believe knowledge processes in organizations typically produce conflict both between workers and management and between different workers (and groups of workers). As suggested previously and in Figure 14.1, issues of conflict, power, and politics are intimately interrelated. Thus, acknowledging that organizational knowledge processes often create conflict suggests that power and politics is also an unavoidable element of such processes.

In terms of the employment relationship, while Chapter 11 highlighted the potential conflict between workers and organizational management that knowledge management processes can induce, what was only touched on was the extent to which the employment relationship is also a relationship of power. Thus, this section highlights issues of power embedded in the employment relationship.

As outlined in Chapter 11, there are contradictory tensions between workers and their employing organization over the ownership and control of workers' knowledge (Contu and Willmott 2003). On the one hand, their interests may be compatible through the potential mutual benefits that workers and their employers may derive from the employer supporting and facilitating the workers' knowledge activities. On the other hand, simultaneously, the requirement of organizations to extract economic value from their workers' knowledge may conflict with their workers' individual objectives in this respect. Such tensions are amplified by the (potential) fragility of the employment relationship resulting from the ability of both parties to easily terminate the relationship, the worker through leaving or the employer through making workers redundant.

However, only when the employment relationship is located within the socio-economic context of capitalist relations of production does a structurally embedded power relationship become visible. For example, Tsoukas (2000), developing a realist conception of the employment relationship, referred to the 'structural basis of managers' power' (p. 34), which places workers in a typically subordinate relationship to managers/superiors. From this perspective, management are the mediating agents of capital owners and shareholders, where organizations are shaped by demands to make profit and accumulate capital. This requires managers/superiors to control and simultaneously achieve the cooperation of workers in order to turn their labour power into actual, productive work effort. Such a perspective on the employment relationship is developed by Contu and Willmott (2003), who talk of the hierarchical organization of the employment relationship and how this places workers in a typically subordinate position to management.

At this point, a significant caveat is required when considering the situation of knowledge workers. The power of management over workers is contingent upon the specific characteristics of the organizational context, and the power of management can be diminished or enhanced by shifts in societal power relations (Tsoukas 2000). For knowledge workers, two factors imbuing them with power are, first, the typical importance of their knowledge to the organizations they work for; and second, the general scarcity of their skills in labour markets, which makes many knowledge workers highly sought after (Flood et al. 2001; Beaumont and Hunter 2002). These factors are thus likely to provide knowledge workers with significant amounts of power and may mean they are likely to be in a less subordinate position to management than other types of workers (see Time to reflect).

 Time to reflect　The power of knowledge workers

How unique is the situation of knowledge workers? Are they the only type of workers whose knowledge is important and valued? Can you think of other types of workers who have important knowledge that provides them with a source of power?

As also outlined in Chapter 11, for those adopting a dissensus-based perspective on social order, the potential for conflict in organizations emanates from more than just the nature of the employment relationship. This potential flows from the different interests that exist within organizations between both individuals and groups. So, from this perspective the social dissensus, conflict, and antagonism that is assumed to exist within societies also exists within organizations. Thus, both the dissensus-based perspectives on knowledge management adopt, as outlined in Chapter 11, what Fox (1985) labelled a pluralist perspective, which assumes organizations can be conceptualized as being made up of a coalition of different interest groups acting in a coordinated way. This divergence of interests may come from individuals/ groups competing over scarce organizational resources or through clashes between the personal objectives and strategies that individual employees may pursue in order to sustain and develop their careers, such as receiving recognition for particular efforts/knowledge, receiving financial rewards, or gaining promotions.

 Time to reflect　The nature of organizations

What does your own experience say about the nature of organizations? Is conflict inevitable? Are power imbalances inherent?

As outlined in Chapter 11, despite the general neglect of issues of power, politics, and conflict in much knowledge management literature, there is a significant and growing body of empirical evidence which reinforces this perspective, as conflict or perceived conflict between individuals and groups has been found to play an important role in shaping the character and dynamics of organizational attempts to manage knowledge. (See Time to reflect.)

Power/knowledge and the dialogical discourse on knowledge management

It is impossible to examine the relationship between power and knowledge (see Definition) without taking account of the work of the French philosopher Michel Foucault, as arguably he is the single most influential author in this area. Further, both in the general business and management literature and in the area of human resource management his work and ideas have become relatively influential (Townley 1994; McKinlay and Starkey 1998; Barratt 2002; Motion and Leitch 2009; Introna et al. 2010; McKinlay et al. 2010). As will be seen, Foucault's (1980) conceptualization of power, and characterization of the relationship between power and knowledge, is quite different from the resource-based perspective on power just elaborated. This section begins by giving a brief overview on the way Foucault theorizes power and its relationship with knowledge before subsequent sections elaborate some of the key ways in which his work is relevant to the topic of knowledge management. As has been alluded to earlier in the chapter, only a small amount of writing on the topic of knowledge management draws on Foucault's work. Examples of studies on knowledge processes which explicitly utilize Foucauldian concepts include Hayes and Walsham (2000); McKinlay (2000, 2002); Marshall and Rolinson (2004); Sewell (2005); Heizmann (2011); Heizmann and Olsson (2015).

Conceptualizing power/knowledge

In understanding Foucault's (1979) particular way of conceptualizing power it is worth quoting him directly:

> the power exercised on the body is conceived not as a property, but as a strategy . . . this power is exercised rather than possessed; it is not the 'privilege', acquired or preserved, of the dominant class, but the overall effect of its strategic positions—an effect that is manifested and sometimes extended by the position of those who are dominated.
>
> (Rabinow 1991: 174, quoting Foucault 1979)

Thus Foucault suggests that power, rather than being a discrete resource that social actors can utilize, is something which is produced and reproduced within and through the dynamics of evolving social relationships. This therefore resonates with the practice-based epistemology's conceptualization of knowledge as being embedded in particular contexts and work practices. Thus, power isn't a resource that can be utilized at will by an actor, but is instead something that is embedded in the way people act, talk, and interact with others. In more simple terms, power isn't a resource that actor A can use autonomously to influence actor B (as with the resource-based view of power), but is instead something that is constituted by actors A and B through how they interact with each other. Both actors play an equally fundamental role in the constitution of power.

Further, Foucault suggests that power and knowledge are so inextricably interrelated that they are fundamentally inseparable, and coined the phrase 'power/knowledge' to symbolize this (Foucault 1980). Further, the term power/knowledge symbolizes that not only are power and knowledge mutually constituted, but also that neither element should be privileged over the other. To properly appreciate Foucault in this respect, it is again worth quoting him directly:

> Power produces knowledge . . . power and knowledge directly imply one another; that there is no power relation without the correlative constitution of a field of knowledge, nor any knowledge that does not presuppose and constitute at the same time power relations.
>
> (Rabinow 1991: 17, quoting from Foucault 1979)

The implication of this insight for understanding the dynamics of knowledge processes are therefore profound, as all uses of knowledge, or attempts to shape and manage knowledge within organizations, inevitably involve the use of power.

> **DEFINITION** **Power (power/knowledge perspective)**
>
> Power is produced and reproduced through the evolution of social relations. Power is embedded in language and is implicated in struggles over truth claims whereby the veracity of certain knowledge or truth claims are negotiated.

Discourse, power/knowledge, and the legitimation of truth claims

A further consequence of the way power/knowledge is conceptualized is the importance of language and discourse. Fundamentally, power/knowledge claims are embedded in and expressed through language, as truth claims. Styhre (2003: 88) thus argues that 'discourses are always based on power, and are manifestations of power'. For Foucault, this is the case with all truth claims, and is evidence of a Nietzschean-inspired scepticism with the apparent absolute truth claims that are based in taken-for-granted belief systems such as religion. For Foucault, as with Nietzsche, there is a rejection of all essentialisms as there is argued to be no basis on which absolute truth can be established.

Thus, the process via which certain claims to knowledge become established as legitimate and others become marginalized and regarded as having limited legitimacy is a collaborative social process of negotiation and struggle over meaning between actors articulating different truth claims. While in the resource-based perspective power resources are seen as relatively fixed and stable entities that actors utilize and draw upon in attempting to resolve political dynamics in a way favourable to them, from a Foucauldian perspective, power/knowledge claims have no such stable status, with the extent to which they are regarded as legitimate being an outcome of the process of negotiation over meaning that actors engage in. Such a process of negotiation is examined by both Marshall and Rollinson (2004), who examine the dynamics of conflict during a problem solving situation, and Heizmann (2011), who analysed power/knowledge disputes between human resources (HR) practitioners within a single multinational corporation (described in the extended case study at the end of this chapter).

Sewell (2005) reinforces these ideas in his conceptual paper which outlines the character of a Foucauldian perspective on knowledge management. For Sewell such an approach would involve the three equally important processes of elicitation (identifying useful knowledge), representation (the codification of useful knowledge), and finally, legitimation (the process via which some knowledge claims come to be regarded as legitimate—and simultaneously the legitimacy of other knowledge claims becomes reduced). Sewell further makes transparent his commitment to a dissensus-based perspective on organizations, by placing at the centre of his analysis the idea that workers and managers are likely to have competing interests, and that a key part of the struggle produced by this conflict is the process via which management attempt to control how workers think and act through discursive strategies aimed at establishing the legitimacy of managerial truth claims.

Power/knowledge and conflict across organizational boundaries

The prior sections concentrated on the resource-based and Foucault perspectives of power, and its impact on knowledge processes within organizational boundaries. However, power, politics, and conflict can also arise across organizational boundaries, which impact the relationship between organizations and its externals. Examples include firms that provide consultancy services to clients, and strategic alliances and multinational companies (MNCs) that operate remotely from headquarters (HQ) as a result of offshoring and outsourcing activities (Pozzebon and Pinsonneault 2012; Hong et al. 2016). In each of these instances, external parties or entities develop knowledge structures and expertise as a result of their own political sense making and sense giving activities that relate to a specific context. This context exists in the form of *localized situated knowledge* and includes best practices applied through consulting services in a specific niche market, or unique expertise that underpins the culture of MNCs in a foreign country. For example, knowledge sharing practices embedded in the work practice of a Chinese MNC may be vastly different to those in the US, India, or Africa due to local routines, cultural norms, and idiosyncratic behaviour that shape knowledge processes in its local context. These concentrated localized entities of knowledge may create power/knowledge conflicts between the HQ, alliances, and its remote multinationals, or between firms and their external consultants.

Pozzebon and Pinsonneault's (2012) case study on client-consultant relationships explored the interaction between power and knowledge associated with these relationships when implementing configurable technologies. They analysed three classic types of client-consultant relationships: *dependency*, whereby consultants are expert authorities who hold control and responsibility for results; *autonomy*, where clients hold the control and responsibility for results; and *cooperation*, where clients and consultants cooperate through the sharing of control and responsibilities. This study confirms the inseparable nature of socio-political and technical knowledge and skills of information technology (IT) consultants, and highlights clients' reliance on this knowledge. However, this reliance creates a tension between knowledge possession and practice epistemologies of clients and consultants. In reality, possession and practice epistemologies can be complementary and yield far greater benefits through collaboration that is built upon mutual trust and understanding. Pozzebon and Pinsonneault propose unilateral and bilateral mechanisms, for example brainstorming and training sessions during different stages of the client-customer relationship to reinforce or transform the power/knowledge balance.

Other examples that relate to power/knowledge relationships across organizational boundaries is collaboration and cooperation between MNCs and their HQ (Hong et al. 2016; Whittle et al. 2016). MNCs that are present in host countries assimilate and blend their own knowledge with locally situated knowledge through socially constitutive processes that translate, legitimize, and operationalize socially meaningful knowledge. Localized expertise may serve as a barrier that negatively impacts on the legitimization of knowledge and result in HQ or expatriates viewing their knowledge as 'superior' to those of MNC employees. As a result cross-cultural conflict and tensions may arise between HQ and MNC employees. In their study, Hong et al. explored knowledge assimilation stages between two China-based subsidiaries of different Japanese MNCs. Findings describe many challenges associated with cultural differences that impacted on learning, sense making, execution of procedures, management, and leadership styles. Findings also indicate that employees in host countries felt subordinate and that their locally generated ideas and knowledge management practices were overlooked and unacknowledged. Despite geopolitical asymmetry, employees in host countries gained significant power through locally situated knowledge, while staff at the HQ side perceived host country employees' sense making practices oppositional and counter-productive. The findings indicate that expatriate managers need to be cognizant of and value the high level of knowledge that MNCs develop as a result of locally situated expertise. In addition, host country employees need to be encouraged and supported to develop host country knowledge and situated practices, in other words getting time to develop new ideas, build localized models, and test them.

A final point to consider relates to strategic management of intellectual capital (Erickson and Rothberg 2010). While the extension of firm operations (i.e. consulting, outsourcing, and offshoring across organizational boundaries) impacts the relationship between power and organizational processes, this extension challenges the protection of knowledge assets across organizational boundaries. Competitive intelligence (CI) as a discipline concentrates on activities that gather, analyse, and distribute intelligence about products, consumers, and competitors to support strategic decision-making for an organization. On the one hand the development of knowledge in its situated context is necessary to build competitive advantage, however greater development of competitive organizational knowledge assets makes it more difficult to defend these assets from incursions by competitors (Erickson and Rothberg 2009). In particular, the digital storage of codified knowledge assets in firm repositories and its distribution via digital networks may open up more opportunities for CI infiltration. Organizations should therefore determine whether the development and sharing of its knowledge assets could be risked in view of the competitive environment. Erickson and Rothberg (2010) suggest a balance between the development of competitive knowledge assets and investment in protecting these assets.

A firm's institutional capabilities to effectively protect its competitive knowledge assets from imitation and expropriation has been promoted as early as 1996 by Liebeskind (see also Chapter 8 on unlearning, loss, and the protection of knowledge). Three institutional capabilities to protect firms' proprietary knowledge are proposed in the form of, first, *incentive alignment capabilities* to control transactions that include knowledge between firms; second, *employment capabilities* in the form of contracts and rules that prohibit the leakage of knowledge between firms and outsiders; and, third, *re-ordering capabilities* that increase the future value of incentives for employees, which reduces their mobility and the lateral flow of knowledge to competitors. As a result of the growth in digitization and firms' increased use of boundary spanning technologies to collaborate and network globally, strategies are required to ensure that any localized situated CI is adequately protected from leakage to competitors.

Conclusion

While two contrasting perspectives on power have been examined, they both point to the conclusion that to analyse and effectively understand the full dynamics of organizational knowledge processes, power requires to be accounted for. The chapter has identified two key reasons why this is the case. From a resource-based perspective, the importance of taking account of power is due to the extent to which conflict shapes organizational knowledge processes, and the role that power and politics play in shaping them. From a Foucauldian perspective, power requires to be accounted for in knowledge management processes, as power and knowledge are inseparable and mutually constituted. In addition, organizations also need to be conscious of power/knowledge relationships that evolve across organizational boundaries and invest in mechanisms that positively transform challenges associated with these.

As a consequence, one of the most general conclusions of this chapter is that the centrality of power to knowledge processes means that any analyses of such processes that neglects to account for power are relatively impoverished. For example, taking account of power helps to explain and understand the human/social dimension of knowledge processes, such as whether people are willing or reluctant to participate in organizational knowledge processes. Thus, Walsham suggests (2001: 603):

> what we know affects how influential we are [thus] . . . there may be good reasons why individuals may not wish to participate in, or may modify some aspect of their sense-giving activities, for reasons related to organizational politics.

Knowledge management was also shown to be concerned with more than simply managing all the knowledge that exists in organizations. Taking account of power helps reveal and make visible how knowledge management processes involve certain claims to knowledge becoming legitimated (and others marginalized), which often involves disputes and negotiations over competing knowledge claims. Thus, taking account of power helps address the typically neglected topic of why certain types and forms of knowledge become the focus of knowledge management initiatives. Finally, firms require an analysis of environmental conditions to balance the development of knowledge with its protection.

 Case study Power matters: the importance of Foucault's power/ knowledge in knowledge management research

Heizmann and Olsson (2015) highlight Foucault's power/knowledge lens as a vehicle for knowledge management researchers and practitioners to investigate the role of power in organizational knowledge cultures. The authors illustrate the value of the power/knowledge lens by drawing on empirical insights from two diverse knowledge cultures—a large insurance corporation and a theatre company—to explain how practitioners' knowledge practices are subject to modalities of power. This paper adds value by exposing the relational character of dysfunctional or collaborative relations among organizational members and ways in which these are linked to their communication practices.

The first case study is of a large Australian insurance company, which is a branch of a multinational insurance firm that has a silo mentality that suggests the presence of underlying power/knowledge relations. HR professionals wanted to change this environment and in doing so promoted a shift to a 'high performance culture' that valued knowledge sharing and collaboration behaviour. This change specifically targeted: changing the behaviour of business unit managers, distributing brochures on the role of leadership, facilitating leadership workshops, and conducting individual coaching sessions with managers.

Initiatives to change and modernize the organization's knowledge sharing behaviour and culture was met with resistance while the HR and marketing functions were considered as having subordinate roles to business functions. This resistance manifested as power dynamics in the knowledge sharing relations between HR practitioners and business unit managers. These managers openly resisted and challenged HR knowledge and practices. As a result, HR practitioners had to find new ways to frame HR issues as enablers of 'high performance' to justify and legitimate their unit's perspective. PowerPoint presentations, strategic documents, and quantitative survey data were used as hard evidence that justified their initiatives. One of the HR participants mentioned a need to 'communicate in a manner consistent with the communication style of the organization' and commented how the organizational culture survey has been a great tool for the HR department in this process. The same participant stated: 'Now we can say "according to your team's engagement results you need to pick up your game"'. Practitioners' framing and tying in of new ideas with existing power/knowledge relations proved to be useful in promoting the cultural changes that were envisaged. Hence, the communication strategies of HR professionals increased their influence.

The second case described in Heizmann and Olsson's paper focuses on Burbage Shakespeare, a successful international classical theatre company. This company seems to epitomize the harmonious, consensus-based knowledge culture idealized in the knowledge management literature (Schultze and Stabell 2004). Notably, a collegial and cooperative environment for productions is important and one production in which the director adopted an 'auteur-like' approach was received with frustration and discontent by company members. A common discursive framework resulting from agreed-upon strategies and decisions was required to evaluate, contest, and confirm arguments. 'Authenticity' and 'creativity' discourses guided all work and decisions, and while these were competing discourses, the company's shared goal in each production was to balance the competing claims of these discourses. Participants were therefore able to draw on each discourse at different times in different situations. In fact, the paper mentions that it was 'the creative tensions between their competing claims that make each new production both unique and connected to tradition'. The Burbage example therefore indicates that its productive knowledge culture resulted from its dialogic nature, which offered a space for 'open conversation'. This space allowed for the discussion and evaluation of multiple narratives and arguments to achieve a shared purpose. This case study illustrates that an organization's knowledge culture is shaped by the interaction of a specific context and broader discursive practices and traditions.

Questions

1. Who would be best placed to evaluate claims and negotiate a resolution in an environment where there is tension between authenticity and creativity discourses as in the Burbage case study?

2. Imagine there are different regions and a head office—to what extent are the types of regional versus head office disputes found in the case study relatively unavoidable in geographically dispersed organizations, and common to all multinational corporations?

 ## Review and Discussion Questions

1. In general, how compatible are the interests of workers and their employers over how workers' knowledge is used? Does the requirement by organizations to derive economic value from it mean conflict is likely or inevitable?

2. The chapter assumed that power and knowledge are closely related, if not inseparable. Can you think of any ways in which knowledge can be used in organizations that do not involve the use of power?

3. Foucault's (1980) perspective on power/knowledge suggests that all power/knowledge claims are open to dispute, and that it is never possible to establish any form of ultimate, objective 'true' knowledge. What implications does such an assumption have for the possibility of resolving disputes which occur within organizations?

 ## Suggestions for Further Reading

L-F. Liao (2008). 'Knowledge Sharing in R&D Departments: A Social Power and Social Exchange Theory Perspective', *International Journal of Human Resource Management*, 19/10: 1881–95.
Explicitly utilizes the resource-based perspective on power to consider the way in which managers can influence the knowledge sharing behaviours of subordinates.

H. Heizmann and M. R. Olsson (2015). 'Power Matters: The Importance of Foucault's Power/
Knowledge as a Conceptual Lens in KM Research and Practice', *Journal of Knowledge Management*,
19/4: 756–69.

Highlights the importance of a Foucauldian perspective on power and uses this lens to examine
the central role of power in two different knowledge cultures: a large insurance organization and a
theatre company.

A. Willem and H. Scarbrough (2006). 'Social Capital and Political Bias in Knowledge Sharing: An
Exploratory Study', *Human Relations*, 59/10: 1343–70.

Case study analysis of two Belgian companies which examines how politics moderates the
relationship between social capital and knowledge sharing and can produce a very selective form of
self-interested knowledge sharing.

B. Mørk, T. Hoholm, G. Ellingsen, E. Maaninen-Olsson, and M. Aanestad (2012). 'Changing Practices
Through Boundary Organizing: A Case from Medical R&D', *Human Relations*, 65/2: 263–88.

An interesting empirical case which examines the politics involved in 'boundary organizing' activities
related to the implementation of changes in knowledge and practice.

 *To further your understanding of knowledge management in organizations explore the book's
accompanying online resources at* **www.oup.com/uk/hislop4e/**

PART 6

The Management of Knowledge Work (and Workers)

The book concludes in Part 6 by considering the various strategies that can be used by organizational managers to (indirectly) manage knowledge, via managing and motivating those who possess valuable organizational knowledge, organizational workers, to participate in knowledge management activities. This is done in two separate chapters.

Chapters 15 considers the role that a range of human resource management practices such as reward systems or training and development systems can have in shaping the dynamics of knowledge management processes. It also considers what can be done to develop organizational loyalty and commitment, which can help organizations retain workers who possess valuable organizational knowledge that they may lose if such people leave.

The book then concludes in Chapter 16 by considering the impact that organizational culture and leadership can have on knowledge management processes. These topics are looked at together, due to the close interrelationship that can exist between leadership styles and strategies, and organizational culture. With respect to the topic of organizational culture, it is assumed that organizational culture is something that can be managed, and that workers' engagement in knowledge management activities can be facilitated via the development and use of particular types of culture. Equally, with respect to the section on leadership, it is assumed that various leadership practices and styles can motivate workers to participate in knowledge management activities.

15

Facilitating Knowledge Management via the Use of Human Resource Management Practices

Introduction

As the introduction to Part 5 and Chapter 11 detail, social and cultural issues have been found to play a key role in affecting the dynamics and likely success of knowledge management initiatives. This is primarily because such factors have increasingly been recognized as playing a fundamental role in determining whether workers will be willing to actively participate in knowledge management initiatives. Inevitably, this has led to organizations deliberately attempting to use different types of managerial practices to encourage workers to participate in knowledge management activities and initiatives. The focus of this chapter is on how different human resource management (HRM) practices can impact on workers' attitudes towards, and participation in, knowledge management activities.

In broad terms the attitudes and behaviours that are relevant to knowledge management initiatives are outlined in Table 15.1. Thus, the use of HRM practices can be seen to be concerned not only with attempting to create a positive attitude towards, and a willingness to participate in, organizational knowledge management activities, but also with making workers committed and loyal to their employer. This is fundamentally because, if workers are not committed and loyal to their organizations, there is a risk that organizations will lose any tacit knowledge these workers possess through staff turnover (Eckardt et al. 2014). As was touched on in Chapter 5, the problem of knowledge loss through staff turnover is a common issue experienced by knowledge-intensive firms. Thus HRM practices concerned with supporting organizational knowledge management efforts should be concerned as much with developing the commitment and loyalty of workers as they are with persuading workers to share, codify, or create knowledge.

The chapter begins by outlining two distinct reasons why HRM practices can be used to support organizational knowledge management activities. The next main section examines how a range of specific HRM practices such as job design, recruitment and selection, and training can all be used to reinforce and support organizational knowledge management efforts. The third and final major section considers the importance

Table 15.1 Attitudes and Behaviours Relevant to Knowledge Management Initiatives

Attitudes	Behaviours
• Positive attitude towards knowledge management initiatives	• Active participation in knowledge management initiatives
• Level of loyalty and commitment to the organization and the goals it is pursuing	• Having continuous employment for significant periods

of staff loyalty and retention to organizational knowledge management activities and considers a range of ways that organizations can attempt to develop the loyalty of their staff and thus help to prevent the loss of potentially vital sources of knowledge through the loss of staff.

Why HRM practices are important to knowledge management

This section considers two separate reasons why HRM practices can help produce the type of behaviours and attitudes that are necessary to make knowledge management initiatives successful. First, making links between the share/hoard dilemma outlined in Chapter 11, and the concept of motivation, HRM practices can be used to motivate workers to participate in knowledge management activities through positively influencing the type of socio-cultural factors which have been shown to be crucial to employee participation in knowledge management activities. The second potential way in which HRM practices can be utilized to support and facilitate organizational knowledge management activities is through developing employee's organizational commitment, with it being suggested that commitment may be an important variable which mediates the relationship between HRM practices and knowledge management activities.

In considering the first explanation regarding the motivational role of HRM practices it is useful to link back to the share/hoard dilemma, which was outlined in Chapter 11 (see Table 11.1). This dilemma suggested that the willingness of workers to participate in organizational knowledge management activities depends on what they perceive the positive and negative consequences of doing so are likely to be. If they perceive that the positive benefits are likely to outweigh the negative ones, then they are likely to participate in knowledge management activities. If they feel the opposite, that the negative consequences are likely to outweigh the positive ones, they are more likely to 'hoard' their knowledge and not participate in knowledge management activities. Chapter 11 highlighted some of the most important factors that the knowledge management literature has found can influence workers' share/hoard decisions, which include the extent to which they perceive their interests to be in conflict with their employers, the extent of group and community identity they feel, and the extent to which they trust colleagues. HRM policies have the potential to play a crucial role influencing how workers resolve such share/hoard decisions through providing positive motivation for participating in knowledge management activities. For example the development of good trust-based social relations, or the development of a strong sense of team identity, could be achieved via providing train-ing which bring employees together to learn collectively, or via designing jobs requiring inter-personal collaboration.

In talking about motivation, it is necessary to distinguish between intrinsic and extrinsic motivation. Intrinsic motivation refers to the pleasures and positive feelings people can derive from simply carrying out a task or activity, rather than for any reward derived from doing so. Thus if a software engineer derives pleasure from the process of writing com-puter code which is efficient and effective, they are intrinsically motivated to carry out this activity. In contrast, extrinsic motivation refers to the external rewards people derive from carrying out a task, such as money. Thus, a software engineer is extrinsically motivated to write computer code if the main reason they do it is for the salary they are paid. In terms of linking HRM practices, motivation, and knowledge management, HRM practices can be utilized to provide both intrinsic and extrinsic motivations for undertaking knowledge management activities. For example, as will be shown later, in terms of intrinsic moti-vation, HRM practices can be used to design jobs that are intrinsically interesting and challenging, and which thus encourage and motivate workers to utilize and share their knowledge. In contrast, HRM practice such as reward systems can be used to extrinsically motivate workers to participate in knowledge management activities through offering financial incentives for doing so.

The second way to understand why HRM practices can positively influence worker's knowledge-related attitudes and behaviours is via linking to the concept of organizational commitment (see Definition). As has been highlighted in Chapters 11, 12, and 13, people's sense of identity as being part of a group, team, or organization can significantly influence their willingness to participate in knowledge management activities. In broad terms, the greater the strength of a person's identity with a team or group, the more likely they are to participate in knowledge management activities which involve other group/team members, or which are perceived to benefit the group. Thus, the more a worker identifies with and is committed to the organization they work for, the more likely they will be to participate in organizational knowledge management activities. In this context, the role of HRM practices is therefore to help develop employees' levels of organizational commitment.

> **DEFINITION Organizational commitment**
>
> The sense of emotional attachment that people feel to the organizations they work for, which may be reflected in the alignment of individual and organizational values and objectives.

A number of writers suggest that the level of commitment workers feel for the organizations they work in may affect both their knowledge sharing attitudes and behaviours as well as their level of loyalty (Byrne 2001; Storey and Quintas 2001; Hislop 2002a; O'Neill and Adya 2007; see Illustration 15.1). There have also been a number of empirical studies that have provided evidence in support of these arguments. Thus, Robertson and O'Malley Hammersley (2000) found that levels of organizational commitment affected employee retention levels and at-titudes to knowledge processes. Second, Han et al. (2010) in a study involving staff working in eight high technology Taiwanese companies found this to be the case with employees' participation in organizational decision-making processes. Thus, they found that levels of participation in decision-making processes was positively related to the sense of psychological ownership workers felt over such decisions, with levels of psychological ownership being positively linked to employees levels of both organizational commitment and knowledge sharing. Finally, Camelo-Ordaz et al. (2011) found that a range of high-involvement HRM practice (included recruitment and selection practices intended to select people on the basis of their fit with the organization, team-based reward and appraisal systems, reward systems which encouraged knowledge sharing, and the provision of extensive training and development opportunities) influenced employee's levels of knowledge sharing indirectly by affecting their levels of organizational commitment. An alternative way of developing workers' organizational commitment is by managing an organization's culture, which is a topic examined in Chapter 16.

 Illustration 15.1 High-involvement work practices, knowledge sharing, and service performance

Flinchbaugh et al. (2016) examined the impact of high-involvement work practices within teams on levels of knowledge sharing and team performance. They studied teams within non-profit organizations responsible for providing residential care and support to young people with significant mental health problems. In this context, team working and communication was an important component in the provision of effective care. The high-involvement work practices studied included providing routine feedback on work performance, involvement in key work decision-making processes, and being provided information on the organization's financial performance. The analysis of their survey results found that the use of high-involvement work practices was positively related to level of team-based knowledge sharing, and also that levels of team-based knowledge sharing were positively linked to team service performance levels. They also found that levels of perspective taking, the extent to which people are sensitive to and aware of the perspective of others, moderated the relationship between high-involvement work practices and levels of knowledge sharing. In practical terms, Flinchbaugh et al. (2016) concluded that utilizing high-involvement work practices represents a potentially useful way to enhance levels of knowledge sharing and team performance. In relation to the importance of perspective taking, they also found that employee awareness of high-involvement work practices was variable, suggesting that management communication regarding such activities is important to ensure effective employee awareness.

Questions

1. What other means, apart from those outlined here, could be utilized to create a sense of employee involvement?

2. In terms of perspective making, what could management do to increase employees' awareness of their high-involvement work practices?

HRM practices and knowledge management

This section examines how some specific HRM practices can be used to shape attitudes and behaviours towards organizational knowledge management activities, with a number of relevant examples being used to illustrate and support the points being made.

Recruitment and selection

The knowledge management literature suggests a number of ways in which recruitment and selection processes can be utilized to support knowledge management activities. First, they can be used to recruit people whose values are compatible with those of the existing organizational culture; and, second, they can be used to select people with personalities that are conducive to knowledge sharing. Finally, the importance of language in effective communication in multinationals (see Chapter 13) suggests that in such contexts recruitment and selection processes should take account of language competencies and skills.

In relation to the first topic both Swart and Kinnie (2003) and Robertson and Swan (2003) suggest that recruiting people whose values are aligned with those of the company was an important factor in the success of the companies they examined. Both papers presented analyses of a single successful knowledge-intensive firm which was successful not only in narrow economic and business terms but also in terms of having happy and committed workers, which meant neither organization had significant turnover problems. The way such forms of recruitment reinforces and sustains organizational knowledge activities is that by recruiting people whose values and norms are compatible with those that exist in an organization this means new recruits are likely to be able to develop a strong sense of identity with their employer and work colleagues, and that a good foundation for the development of strong trust-based relations between new recruits and their colleagues should exist. Another empirical study which has examined this topic and which did find a positive link to exist between 'fit' based recruitment and attitudes to knowledge sharing was conducted by Chen et al. (2011a)—see Illustration 15.2. Similar findings were reached by Camelo-Ordaz et al. (2011), as outlined earlier in the chapter.

As outlined in Chapter 11, the way in which personality relates to knowledge sharing attitudes is a topic that is significantly underresearched, with very few empirical studies being done into this topic. Further, as outlined in Chapter 11, while all the studies in this area (Cabrera and Cabrera 2005; Mooradian et al. 2006; Matzler et al. 2011) use the five factor personality model, they reach different conclusions about which personality traits are related to positive knowledge sharing attitudes. Another weakness of these studies, which limits their generalizability, is the fact that they are all studies of a single organization. Thus, to more effectively test the generalizability of the findings of these studies, the same research questions would need to be tested on a wider population.

 Illustration 15.2 HRM practices to facilitate intra-team knowledge sharing

Chen et al. (2011a) investigated how a range of different HRM practices affected the willingness of people within research and development (R&D) teams in Taiwan to share knowledge. All the R&D teams surveyed were in high technology industries (electronics, communications, precision machinery, semiconductors, and optoelectronics). They analysed the surveys of over 200 employees from fifty separate R&D teams. Overall they found that most of the HRM practices examined did affect people's knowledge sharing behaviours.

First, they found that recruiting people who fitted with the existing culture and values of the teams promoted knowledge sharing. Second, they found that people's willingness to share knowledge was also positively related to the extent to which they perceived that their employer paid attention to their long-term career development. Finally they found that performance appraisals which were focused on the individual inhibited people's willingness to share knowledge within teams. Thus, in the type of team-based contexts that they examined, team-focused rather than individually focused performance appraisals are likely to facilitate knowledge sharing. Finally one hypothesis they tested that was not supported by the study was that the use of reward systems would increase people's willingness to share knowledge. Thus this study undermines the argument that financial rewards can be used to motivate people to share knowledge.

Question

This case suggests that in team-based work contexts individually focused rewards and appraisal systems can inhibit people's willingness to share knowledge. Can you identify jobs where work is not team-based and collaborative, and where individually focused rewards and appraisal systems may motivate people to share knowledge?

If the premise of these studies is accepted (that personality traits can influence people's general attitudes to knowledge sharing, making certain types of people generally more open to doing so than others) then attempting to recruit people with appropriate personality traits may represent another way in which recruitment and selection processes can be used to support organizational knowledge activities. However, the scarcity of research on this topic, and the contradictory findings of the studies that have been done, means that at the moment using personality tests to identify positive knowledge sharing attitudes is something that needs to be done with caution.

The final recruitment and selection issue addressed relates to the context of multinationals where, unavoidably, employees who are required to communicate and share knowledge have different native languages and have variable skills speaking in non-native languages. The importance of language to knowledge sharing in this context was considered previously, in Chapter 13 on cross-community collaboration. Peltokorpi and Vaara (2014) examined the impact of language sensitive recruitment on processes of knowledge transfer in multinationals. Language sensitivities relate to both the language competence of staff from the parent company headquarters in the language of subsidiary divisions and the language competence of staff in subsidiaries of the core language used at the corporate headquarters. Peltokorpi and Vaara (2014) found that language sensitive recruitment in multinationals was positively related to levels of knowledge transfer. This was not only because it facilitated effective inter-personal communication, but also that it made it easier for people to develop internationally diverse networks and to have a stronger sense of common identity with other staff within the organization who did not share the same native language. Thus, in this context, recruitment for language skills and competencies is a potentially important mechanism to facilitate intra-organizational knowledge transfer and collaboration.

Job design

In the area of job design there is a strong consensus about the best way to structure jobs to facilitate appropriate knowledge sharing attitudes. In general terms, work should have three key features: it should be interesting and challenging; second, workers should have high levels of autonomy with regard to decision-making and problem solving; and, finally, it should encourage and require inter-personal collaboration. For example, Chen et al.'s (2011b) study into the link between conflict and knowledge sharing conducted in Chinese software companies recommended that inter-personal knowledge sharing would be encouraged if workers had challenging and meaningful work tasks along with high levels of autonomy. In terms of the first feature, not only should work be challenging and fulfilling, providing opportunities for workers to effectively utilize their existing skills and knowledge, but it should also provide opportunities for workers to continuously develop their knowledge and skills (Robertson and O'Malley Hammersley 2000; Swart and Kinnie 2003). For example Monks et al. (2016) found a positive relationship between learning enhancement opportunities and people's willingness to engage in processes of knowledge exchange. The importance to knowledge workers of having interesting and challenging work is supported by the findings of Horowitz et al.'s (2003) study of Singaporean knowledge workers, which found that providing challenging work was ranked as the most important factor by managers for helping to retain their knowledge workers. Relatedly, Han et al. (2010), as outlined earlier, found that involvement in decision-making was positively linked to levels of organizational commitment and knowledge sharing.

In terms of autonomy, available evidence also suggests that knowledge workers place a lot of importance on having high levels of autonomy at work (Khatri et al. 2010). Thus, in the scientific consultancy examined by Robertson and Swan (2003), autonomy was found to be important to the consultants, and extended to the projects they worked on (the consultants had the autonomy to freely choose which project they worked on so long as they reached their annual revenue targets), the selection of the training and development activities they undertook (consultants identified their own development needs and funding was available for virtually all training requests), and being able to choose their work clothing and work patterns. Further, a number of studies have found a positive link between levels of autonomy in work and motivation to share knowledge (Ozlati 2015; Stenious et al. 2016). Finally, Kuo and Lee's (2011) study into empowering leadership concluded that providing workers with high levels of autonomy was likely to help with the development of a knowledge sharing culture.

The third feature of work tasks argued to encourage worker's participation in knowledge management activities is that they should require and/or encourage collaboration among people. This is because collaborative working makes knowledge sharing a central feature of work activities but also because close collaborative working is likely to facilitate the development of the type of strong inter-personal relations which are conducive to inter-personal knowledge sharing (Kase et al. 2009; Holste and Fields 2010; Monks et al. 2016). Caligiuri (2014) suggests that this can be done within the context of multinationals through designing international assignments and global, cross-site teams, with the aim of facilitate knowledge exchange.

Training

While, as outlined, providing opportunities for self-development can be integrated into the way people's work activities are organized, it can also be achieved through providing appropriate opportunities to undertake formal training. Thus, research suggests that knowledge workers regard the provision of such opportunities by their employers to be crucially important (Robertson and O'Malley Hammersley 2000; Hunter et al. 2002). For example, Yalabik et al. (2017) suggest that providing appropriate training to knowledge workers may be one key way to help develop their commitment and loyalty. While the provision of such opportunities is a potentially double-edged sword for employers (as supporting such activities potentially makes it easier for staff to leave), without supporting continuous development, staff may be likely to leave anyway. Garvey and Williamson (2002) suggest that the most useful sort of training to support a culture of learning and knowledge development is not investing in 'narrow' skills-based training, but training with a broader purpose to encourage reflexivity, learning through experimentation, and how to conduct critical dialogues with others. This is reinforced by the empirical study of Monks et al. (2016), who found that providing learning enhancement opportunities, such as training, was positively linked to both reflexivity and a willingness to engage in knowledge exchange processes. Hansen et al. (1999) suggest that the type of training provided should reflect the particular approach to knowledge management an organization adopts (see Chapter 4). For example, in relation to their distinction between codification- and personalization-based approaches to knowledge management they argue that the provision of IT-based training is relevant for organizations pursuing a codification-based strategy, whereas training to develop inter-personal skills and team working is most appropriate for organizations pursuing a personalization-based knowledge management strategy.

Reinforcing this point about linking the type of training provided to the approach to knowledge management adopted, a number of the studies into the role of Web 2.0 technologies to facilitate knowledge management (see Chapter 10) suggest that the provision of training on the use of these technologies is likely to encourage workers to utilize them for knowledge sharing (Paroutis and Al Saleh 2009; Teo et al. 2011). Finally, Kase et al. (2009) suggest that one of the knowledge-related benefits of training is that it facilitates the development of good inter-personal relations between those undertaking it, which may encourage such people to share knowledge with each other in the future.

Coaching and mentoring

A growing body of literature also suggests that the use of coaching and mentoring in organizations can facilitate the informal sharing of knowledge (Garvey and Williamson 2002; Harrison and Kessels 2004; Kets de Vries 2005; Karkoulian et al. 2008; Caligiuri 2014). What coaching and mentoring have in common is that they are both concerned with the sharing of knowledge between a relatively experienced person, the mentor or coach, and someone less experienced, the mentee (Wilson and Elman 1990). However, they can be distinguished from each other on a number of levels. First, while mentoring typically has an indefinite time-scale, coaching is usually undertaken for a set duration. Second, coaching is typically more structured in the way it is organized, for example, occurring at set regular times, for specific time periods. Finally, while coaching is typically concerned with the development of relatively narrow and specific skills and knowledge, mentoring is less focused.

However, both coaching and mentoring can take many forms. For example, mentoring can be done in highly formalized ways, or relatively informally. Further coaching can be done on a one-to-one basis or in groups. The knowledge sharing benefits of mentoring and coaching can be provided by a number of brief examples. First, Kets de Vries (2005) in evaluating a single, intensive group coaching activity found that the development of trust among participants in this activity facilitated inter-personal knowledge sharing. Second, Karkoulian et al. (2008) in a study of mentoring in Lebanese banks found that informal mentoring had a positive impact on knowledge sharing behaviours. Third, Monks et al. (2016) classified mentoring as one aspect of 'learning enhancement opportunities' which were found to be positively related to people's willingness to engage in processes of knowledge exchange. Finally, in the study of leadership undertaken by Lee et al. (2010), which is examined in Chapter 16, one of the ways team leaders developed intra-team trust and knowledge sharing was via a process of mentoring that involved linking experienced team members with less experienced ones. Thus, setting up and facilitating both coaching and mentoring activities represents another way via which inter-personal knowledge sharing can be facilitated by organizational management.

Reward and performance appraisal

In the area of reward, there isn't a consensus regarding how reward systems can best be used to support knowledge management activities. Some suggest that rewarding people for appropriate knowledge-related behaviours and embedding knowledge-related attitudes and behaviours in performance appraisal processes represents a potentially important way to use HRM practices to underpin organizational knowledge management efforts (Cabrera and Cabrera 2005; Oltra 2005). Thus, Lin and Lo's (2015) study of healthcare workers in Taiwan found that financial rewards were positively linked to people's willingness to share knowledge. Further it is also agreed that such reward systems should reflect the particular knowledge management strategy adopted by an organization and the type of knowledge processes associated with it. For example, Hansen et al. (1999) argue that if a codification strategy is pursued, the pay and reward systems should acknowledge employee efforts to codify their knowledge and search for the knowledge of others, while with a personalization strategy, pay and reward systems should recognize the efforts of workers to share their tacit knowledge with each other.

However, this perspective is challenged by a number of writers who suggest that there may be negative consequences to directly linking individual financial rewards to knowledge behaviours. For example, Osterloh and Frey (2000), in distinguishing between extrinsic forms of motivation (largely financial) and intrinsic forms of motivation (motivation related to the benefits derived from carrying out an activity itself), conclude that financial rewards may inhibit the sharing of tacit knowledge (see also Illustration 15.3). Further, Fahey et al. (2007) and Milne (2007) both reach a similar conclusion and argue that directly linking individual rewards to knowledge sharing may mean people develop instrumental attitudes to such processes whereby they only participate in knowledge processes when they derive some form of financial reward from doing so, which may inhibit knowledge sharing when such rewards are not available. Further support for such ideas is provided by Stenius et al. (2015) who found that people's motivation to share knowledge was negatively related to financial rewards, while Ozlati (2015) found that financial rewards were unrelated to knowledge sharing motivation.

Another area of debate concerns whether individual- or group-based rewards provide the best way to facilitate positive knowledge-related attitudes and behaviours. Thus, some research suggests that individually focused financial rewards can play a positive role. For example, Horowitz et al.'s (2003) survey of Singaporean knowledge workers found that providing a 'highly competitive pay package' (p. 32) was ranked as the second most effective way to help retain knowledge workers. Further, Kankanhalli et al. (2005) and Huang et al. (2008) also found that individually focused reward systems support participation in knowledge management activities.

 Illustration 15.3 The contradictory effects of intrinsic and extrinsic motivation in facilitating knowledge sharing

Andreeva and Sergeeva (2016) investigated the impact of a range of extrinsically and intrinsically motivating human resource (HR) practices on people's willingness to share knowledge. The extrinsic HR practices included both financial and non-financial rewards, and the intrinsic HR practices related to the character of people's jobs, referring specifically to the level of autonomy and variety people had to carry out their jobs. The survey-based study was conducted with teachers in St Petersburg, Russia. Their findings are interesting as they did not find a simple relationship between either extrinsically or intrinsically motivated HR practices and knowledge sharing. They found that the impact of both types of HR practice varied depending on the extent to which people had opportunities to share knowledge, for example via meetings/workshops/events where people could interact, where people have time to share knowledge, or where jobs required collaboration, etc. When opportunities to share knowledge were low, knowledge sharing was positively linked to extrinsically motivating HR practices, and intrinsic HR practices had no impact. In contrast, when opportunities to share knowledge were plentiful, the opposite occurred, with intrinsic HR practices being directly related to knowledge sharing, and extrinsic HR practices having no impact.

Question

From a managerial perspective, what conclusions can be drawn from this study about how to use HRM practices to encourage knowledge sharing?

However, in contradiction with this, others suggest that such individually focused rewards can inhibit knowledge sharing not only through creating an instrumental attitude to knowledge sharing but also through the way such reward mechanisms may undermine people's sense of team or community spirit (Nayir and Uzunçarsili 2008). For example, in the organization studied by Lam (2005) the use of individually focused rewards contributed importantly to the individualistic culture which existed, which meant that people were unwilling to codify and share knowledge with colleagues. Thus some suggest that the best way to develop group focused knowledge sharing is through making knowledge-related rewards group- rather than individual-based (Cabrera and Cabrera 2005). The research of Chen et al. (2011a—see Illustration 15.2) also reinforces these conclusions.

Finally a growing number of writers suggest that non-financial rewards such as recognition can play an important role in facilitating and encouraging appropriate knowledge behaviours in people (O'Dell and Hubert 2011; Teo et al. 2011; Yeo and Marquardt 2015; Razmerita et al. 2016). While Huang et al. (2008) found that financial rewards did encourage knowledge sharing among the Chinese workers they studied, they found that people's attitude to knowledge sharing was more strongly influenced by non-financial rewards. Paroutis and Al Saleh's (2009) study of what motivates people to share knowledge using Web 2.0 technology concluded that:

> companies involved in implementing Web 2.0 should consider introducing soft rewards like praise and recognition to encourage employee participation. For instance having a recognition programme where 'the most active blog', 'top-rated blog post' or 'best wiki contribution' is publicized on the company's intranet or newsletter is one effective way to recognize employees' contributions.

HRM, staff retention, and knowledge management

Retaining workers who possess valuable knowledge should arguably be as important an element in an organization's knowledge management strategy as motivating workers to participate in knowledge activities. This is because the tacit and embodied nature of much organizational knowledge means that when employees leave an organization, they take their knowledge with them. Thus staff turnover can result in a leakage and loss of knowledge of importance to the organization (Schmitt et al. 2012; Eckardt et al. 2014). As Byrne (2001: 325) succinctly put it, 'without loyalty knowledge is lost'. However, paradoxically, while many writers comment on the importance of retention, very few knowledge management studies examine the topic of retention in any detail (Martins and Meyer 2012). Some of the key studies which do look at this issue are considered here.

This raises the question of what organizational management can do to induce high levels of commitment and loyalty among their workers. Developing high levels of commitment is generally not simple and straightforward. However, empirical evidence suggests a number of factors within managerial control can affect commitment levels including: employee voice and employee trust in management (Farndale et al. 2011); the provision of training (Bulut and Culha 2010); and levels of organizational support (He et al. 2011).

In general, the literature on knowledge workers and knowledge-intensive firms (see Chapter 5) suggests that developing the loyalty of knowledge workers is particularly problematic. This is to a large extent because labour market conditions, where the skills and knowledge of knowledge workers are typically relatively scarce, creates conditions for knowledge workers which are favourable to mobility. In relation to knowledge workers, Joo (2010) found that, in a study of South Korean companies, organizational commitment was facilitated by workers having strong and supportive supervision from managers, and from the organization having a learning culture. One of the most comprehensive study of factors influencing employee commitment levels was undertaken by Giauque et al. (2010), who studied workers in small knowledge-intensive firms in Switzerland. Their study found that the three most important factors influencing commitments among workers was the quality of the organization's reputation, the extent to which procedural justice was seen to exist (in terms of fairness of decision-making, etc.), and the extent to which the organization provided support for people's non-work commitments, such as in offering flexible working to facilitate parenting responsibilities.

Ilustration 15.4 The impact of knowledge workers' variable commitments and their impact on people's intention to quit

Yalabik et al. (2017) conducted a study into the impact that some of the various types of commitment that knowledge workers possessed had on their intention to quit their organizations, which gives an indication of loyalty levels. Their study was conducted among UK knowledge workers who worked for a global outsourcing and consultancy firm. They found that workers' organizational- and team-level commitment was negatively related to their intention to quit and positively related to their level of professional commitment. The relationship between client-level commitment and intention to quit was not found to be significant. Based on these findings, Yalabik et al. made the following suggestions to reduce people's intention to quit and develop their loyalty. First, to develop organizational commitment, employers should design jobs to be intrinsically interesting through making work challenging and providing good levels of autonomy. To develop team-level commitment, employers should develop a strong culture of team-based collaboration. Finally, to reduce the impact of professional commitment on people's intention to quit, employers should provide the sort of training opportunities that workers can get from their professional associations.

Questions

1. Of the various types of loyalty that knowledge workers possess, which is the most important?

2. Further, from an HRM perspective, in order to increase people's levels of commitment and reduce their intention to quit, which type of commitment should organizations prioritize in developing?

Having a high turnover rate is a potentially significant problem for knowledge-intensive firms (Alvesson 2000; Flood et al. 2001; Beaumont and Hunter 2002). First, this is a potential problem because the knowledge possessed by knowledge workers is typically highly tacit. Therefore, when they leave an organization, they take their knowledge with them. For example, one key source of knowledge possessed by knowledge workers is social capital—their knowledge of key individuals. The need for knowledge workers to work closely with client organizations means that they often develop close relations with important client staff. Thus, when such workers leave, there is a risk for their employer that they will lose their clients as well. The second main reason why poor retention rates may be a problem for knowledge-intensive firms is that the knowledge, skills, and experience possessed by knowledge workers is often a crucial element in organizational performance. For example, Eckardt et al.'s (2014) study of the impact of staff turnover on firm performance found that this relationship was stronger in service firms compared to manufacturing firms.

 Time to reflect The weakness of instrumental loyalty?

Instrumental-based loyalty derived through pay and financial rewards is argued to be a weak form of loyalty. Do you agree? How significant is pay and related financial reward in the development of organizational loyalty and commitment?

Table 15.2 Types of Loyalty and Strategies for Developing Them

Type of Loyalty	Strategy for Development	Means of Development
Instrumental-based	Financial	Providing employees with good pay and fringe benefits.
Identification-based	Institutional-based	Developing a vision and set of values and encouraging employees to identify with them.
		Achieved through culture management, vision building, use of stories.
	Communitarian-based	Developing a sense of community and social bonding among workers.
		Achieved through use of social events and meetings which bring people together and allow them to develop strong relations with, and knowledge of, each other.
	Socially integrative	A combination of the institutional- and communitarian-based strategies.

Source: based on Alvesson (2000).

Alvesson (2000) argues that one of the best ways to deal with the turnover problem is to create a sense of organizational loyalty in staff, particularly through developing their sense of organizational identity. Alvesson identifies two broad types of loyalty and four strategies for developing them (see Table 15.2). The weakest form of loyalty is argued by Alvesson to be instrumental-based loyalty, which is when a worker remains loyal to their employer for as long as they receive specific personal benefits, with one of the most effective ways of developing such loyalty being through pay and working conditions (see Time to reflect). The second, and what Alvesson argues is a stronger form of loyalty, is identification-based loyalty, which is loyalty based on the worker having a strong sense of identity as being a member of the organization, and where the worker identifies with the goals and objectives of their organization. The three strategies for developing identification-based loyalty are illustrated in Table 15.2. This type of loyalty is typically not developed through financial rewards and is instead built through developing a culture that workers can buy into, through creating a sense of community among staff, or both.

 ## Conclusion

The central focus of this chapter has been on how HRM practices have the potential to facilitate and support organizational knowledge management activities. The chapter began by presenting various explanations for why they have this potential which relate to their role in motivating workers to behave in certain ways or developing people's level of organizational commitment. Broadly, however, organizational management can use HRM practices to facilitate knowledge management initiatives by dealing with the problems and challenges that can often make workers unwilling to participate in knowledge management activities (see Chapter 11). The chapter also illustrated the role that specific HRM practices such as reward systems, job design, or training can having in shaping the attitudes and behaviours of workers to knowledge initiatives. In general terms, with the exception of reward systems, where evidence is contradictory and opinion is divided, there is a broad consensus regarding specifically how HRM practices should be utilized to support knowledge management initiatives.

Finally, the chapter also showed how attempting to develop the commitment and loyalty of workers can be a key part of an organization's knowledge management strategy. This is because not only does the typically tacit and embodied nature of knowledge mean that when workers leave an organization they take much of their knowledge with them, but also the level of commitment a worker feels towards their employer is likely to affect their willingness to participate in knowledge management initiatives. However, developing such commitment and attitudes is by no means straightforward.

 Case study Rethinking the role of HRM practices in facilitating knowledge exchange: a case study of CERN, a knowledge-intensive organization

Mabey and Zhao (2017) use a study of CERN, which is classified as a knowledge-intensive organization, to suggest ways in which HR practices can be used to facilitate knowledge sharing that challenge some conventional logic. CERN is the European organization for nuclear research located near Geneva, Switzerland. CERN can be classified as a knowledge-intensive organization as its key employees are highly qualified and experienced scientists who collaborate on cutting-edge research. Within CERN, Mabey and Zhao focused on one very large particle physics collaboration which involved over 3,500 scientists who worked at 178 separate institutions located in thirty-eight different countries. Thus, the collaboration examined was a highly dispersed international collaboration project. Further, knowledge sharing between scientists is key to the success of all CERN's collaborative projects. They found levels of knowledge exchange between scientists to be high, and argue that how this was achieved can provide lessons for other organizations.

The HRM implications for knowledge sharing they derive from their study are organized around five paradoxes they identified. The first paradox they articulate is that the more knowledge is formally managed, the less likely it is that knowledge exchange will occur. They resolve this paradox by suggesting that rather than try to manage knowledge in a top-down way, via a formal initiative, it is more effective to do it via the way work is designed. Fundamentally, they suggest that jobs should be designed to develop high levels of trust between collaborators, which can be done by designing jobs to require and involve interdependence, which then allows for the development of mutual goals.

The second paradox is that the more democratic that processes of knowledge sharing should be, the more there is a need for intentional leadership. This paradox is resolved by suggesting the need for decentralized leadership which is sensitive to and utilizes the political realities of organizations. With top-down hierarchical leadership a potential problem is that messages communicated to workers are shaped by social relations, politics, and how people interpret management intent. To address this astute political leadership is necessary at middle management level, which doesn't ignore but embraces the political reality of organizational life, and which utilizes knowledge of this to mobilize support for management initiatives.

The third paradox is that the more knowledgeable people are, the less likely they will be to lead others. This paradox is resolved by suggesting a need to reward knowledge generosity. This is done via a number of means. First, it is necessary to identify those senior colleagues willing to share knowledge with those who are less experienced. Then, such people should be provided adequate time to engage in appropriate mentoring and knowledge sharing. Second, workers should also be appropriately rewarded and provided with suitable resources from HR to develop the type of social networks they feel are appropriate to their particular type of work.

The fourth paradox is that the more pervasive the use of information technology (IT) systems for knowledge sharing, the more isolated workers can potentially become. This paradox is addressed by supporting the development of communities of practice. In globally dispersed organizations such as CERN, this will inevitably involve some element of virtual communication and knowledge sharing. However such remote communication should be accompanied by regular face-to-face meetings between collaborators to allow the development of social relations and the exchange of more tacit knowledge. Further, with respect to the technologies used for virtual collaboration, decisions on this should not be made in a top-down way by IT departments. Instead the users of such systems should be involved in choosing which systems they regard as most appropriate and user friendly.

Finally, the fifth paradox identified was that the more informal knowledge exchange processes are, the more likely discrimination is to occur. This paradox is resolved by HR recognizing and embracing the potential knowledge sharing benefits from social and cultural diversity, such as how embracing different perspectives and alternative viewpoints can lead to a healthy questioning of taken-for-granted assumptions. This can be facilitated by, first, developing an organizational culture which recognizes and celebrates cultural richness and diversity. Second, it can also be facilitated by relevant diversity awareness training, which both helps people recognize the benefits of self-questions that can emerge from collaboration with diverse others and trains people with the skills to manage such differences in social situations.

Question

1. These findings are based on a study of a distinctive type of non-business organization. To what extent are they transferrable to the business world, for example in facilitating knowledge exchange within multinationals?

 ## Review and Discussion Questions

1. The research presented suggests that having interesting and challenging work is more likely than pay in motivating people to participate in knowledge in organizational knowledge activities. To what extent do you agree with this?

2. In Giauque et al.'s (2011) study organizational support was found to be one of the factors linked to levels of commitment. What types of support for non-work commitments and responsibilities are likely to be most attractive to employees?

 ## Suggestions for Further Reading

P. Caligiuri (2014). 'Many Moving Parts: Factors Influencing the Effectiveness of HRM Practices Designed to Improve Knowledge Transfer within MNCs', *Journal of International Business Studies*, 45: 63–72.
An overview of some the key factors shaping how HRM practices impact on knowledge sharing within multinational corporations

J. Nieves, A. Quintana, and J. Osorio (2016). 'Organizational Knowledge and Collaborative Human Resource Practices as Determinants of Innovation', *Knowledge Management: Research and Practice*, 14: 237–45.
An empirical study into how HRM practices can affect the knowledge processes key to innovation.

Z. Yalabik, J. Swart, N. Kinnie, and Y. Van Rosenberg (2017). 'Multiple Foci of Commitment and Intention to Quit in Knowledge Intensive Organizations (KIOs): What Makes Professionals Leave?', *International Journal of Human Resource Management*, 28/2: 417–47.

An empirical study into how different types of commitment affect the extent to which knowledge workers remain loyal to their employers.

E. Martins and H. Mayer (2012). 'Organizational and Behavioural Factors that Influence Knowledge Retention', *Journal of Knowledge Management*, 16/1.

Highlights a range of factors which influence the extent to which organizations are able to retain important knowledge.

 To further your understanding of knowledge management in organizations explore the book's accompanying online resources at **www.oup.com/uk/hislop4e/**

16 Leadership, Organization Culture Management, and Knowledge Management

Introduction

This chapter examines the closely interrelated topics of leadership and organizational culture, and how they can impact on knowledge management initiatives. The vast majority of the literature on these topics argues that certain leadership styles or types of organizational culture can support and facilitate knowledge management activities. Thus, as with Chapter 15, which examines the use of human resource management practices, the primary focus here is relatively practical, considering the way that leadership and culture management activities can be utilized to persuade workers to take part in knowledge management activities.

There are two fundamental reasons why these topics are considered together in the same chapter. First, they are topics that are closely interrelated in that the attitudes, values, and behaviours of organizational leaders can have a significant impact on the type of culture that exists within an organization. This is particularly true within small companies, where the leader and/or founder of the organization can have a profound impact in shaping the nature of organizational culture (Illustration 16.1). The second reason why leadership and organizational culture are examined in the same chapter is that the adoption of certain leadership styles and attempts to manage organizational cultures have some characteristics in common. Thus, in contrast to the types of human resource management processes examined in the previous chapter, which are broadly focused on short-term timescales and the management of workers' day-to-day (knowledge-related) behaviours, both leadership and culture management activities can be regarded as relatively strategic in nature and medium-term in their focus, being concerned with the development of visions and values that will inspire and motivate workers to behave in certain ways.

 Illustration 16.1 Leadership, culture, and knowledge management within Australian small to medium-sized enterprises

Nguyen and Mohamed (2011) examined the extent to which leadership was positively related to knowledge management activities. They also investigated the extent to which organizational culture moderated this relationship. They conceptualized leadership in terms of the transformational/transactional framework (see subsequent sections for definitions). They hypothesized that both forms of leadership would be positively related to knowledge management activities. Further, they argue that due to the close interrelationship that exists between leadership and organizational culture, with them being 'two sides of the same coin' (p. 209), organizational culture will moderate the relationship between both leadership styles and knowledge management activities.

Nguyen and Mohamed tested these hypotheses in a survey-based study of some Australian small to medium-sized enterprises (SMEs), with surveys being distributed to SMEs involved in a wide range of industries. In terms of the hypotheses tested, the researchers did find that a positive relationship existed between both leadership styles and knowledge management activities. Thus both leadership styles were found to facilitate people's participation in knowledge management activities. However, while organizational culture was found to moderate the relationship between transactional leadership and knowledge management activities, it was not found to moderate the relationship between transformational leadership and organizational culture. A potential explanation put forward for these findings was that organizational culture moderates the relationship between transactional leadership and knowledge management, as this style of leadership operates within, and is linked with, the existing organizational culture and is not concerned with or focused on developing or changing organizational culture, which transformational leadership is.

Questions

1. Is the relationship between leadership, culture, and knowledge management found by Nguyen and Mohamed likely to be particularly strong due to the fact that they conducted their research on SMEs?

2. Is the moderating effect of culture on the relationship between leadership and knowledge management activities likely to be less in larger organizations?

Both topics have been the focus of a significant amount of research and debate, with a vast academic literature existing on both. While the development of interest in the topic of organizational culture management has been relatively recent, becoming a topic of great interest in the early 1980s, the study of leadership by contrast has a much longer heritage, with academic interest in the topic beginning in the first decades of the twentieth century. While brief links are made to both of these literatures, the central focus here is on the contemporary knowledge management literature that examines the impact of leadership and organizational culture on knowledge management activities.

The chapter begins by examining the topic of organizational culture and its relationship to knowledge management before then considering the impact the leadership can have on knowledge processes. There are two separate sections on the topic of organizational culture, with the first one focusing on the relationship between organizational culture and knowledge management processes; and the second examining the different perspectives on the debate regarding the extent to which knowledge-based cultures can be created within organizations. The topic of leadership is also divided into two sections, with the first giving a brief overview of the way in which the conceptualization of leadership has evolved over time; and the second section looking more narrowly at the relationship between leadership and knowledge management activities.

The impact of organizational culture on knowledge management activities

This section both defines organizational culture and gives insights into the impact that organizational culture can have on knowledge management activities. An enormous quantity of the knowledge management literature that examines the topic of organizational culture argues that it can significantly influence organizational knowledge management activities (Al-Alawi et al. 2007; Donate and Guadamillas 2010; Stock et al. 2010; Rai 2011; Chang and Lin 2015; Razmerita et al. 2016). While in many papers such statements are made without the support of empirical evidence (De Long and Fahey 2000; Cabrera and Cabrera 2005; Milne 2007; du Plessis 2008), in an increasing number of papers detailed and strong empirical data is presented to illustrate how organizational culture can impact on people's willingness to participate in knowledge management and innovation activities (Lam 2005; Chang and Lee 2007; Sanz-Valle et al. 2011; Suppiah and Singh Sandhu 2011; Liao et al. 2012). For example, Serenko and Bontis (2016) found that the more positive an organizational culture is (open, altruistic, and collaborative), the less likely people will be to hoard knowledge. Finally, while the vast majority of this literature suggests that organizational culture can positively influence knowledge management activities and initiatives, there have been a number of studies, as will be shown later, which have highlighted the negative impact that certain types of organizational culture can have on knowledge management activities (Lam 2005; Rai 2011; Sanz-Valle et al. 2011; Suppiah and Singh Sandhu 2011).

Before proceeding any further it is necessary to define what organizational culture is (see Definition). While every piece of writing on culture typically gives its own specific definition, a useful one is that provided by Schein, one of the most influential writers on the topic. He defined a group's culture as consisting of 'the basic tacit assumptions about how the world is and ought to be that a group of people share, and that determines their perceptions, thoughts, feelings, and their overt behavior' (Schein 1996).

This definition is useful as it highlights two key features of organizational culture. First, it emphasizes the collective nature of organizational culture, as for culture to be organizational it is something that needs to be shared by a significant proportion of organizational staff. Second, the definition makes explicit that culture exists both at the level of ideas and values (such as the importance of good customer service, being innovative and creative) and at the level of behaviours (such as the particular ways that work processes are carried out, how and when team meetings are organized, how people are rewarded and recognized, etc.).

DEFINITION **Organizational culture**

The beliefs and behaviours shared by an organization's members regarding what constitutes an appropriate way to think and act at work.

While there are debates within the organizational culture literature regarding the nature of organizational culture and the extent to which it can be managed (Harris and Ogbonna 2002; Mathew and Ogbonna 2011) there is a significant proportion of literature which argues that organizational culture can be managed and that there are a number of benefits that can be derived from having a strong, clear organizational culture. First, at the level of values and ideas, having a strong, clear culture means that employees should clearly understand what the key organizational values are. Further it is argues that if employees accept the validity and importance of the values of the culture this may mean that employees will be loyal and committed to the company and it also has the potential to create among staff a strong sense of collective organizational or team/group identity. Second, at the level of behaviour, if employees believe in and accept an organization's culture it is argued that this will help make them behave in ways which support and reinforce the culture (Michailova and Minbaeva 2012). For example if the culture of the organization emphasizes the importance of innovation and creativity, if employees believe in these values they are likely to behave in innovative and creative ways, such as collaborating with people to produce new products or services.

Two of the factors identified in Chapter 11 that influence the attitudes of workers regarding their participation in organizational knowledge management activities are the relationship between workers and management and the extent to which workers have a sense of group identity. Culture management activities are argued to support organizational knowledge management efforts by addressing both these issues, through developing workers' trust in and commitment to management in their organization and to the organization more generally; and, second, through helping develop the workers' sense of team and/or group identity.

A general weakness of much of the literature which examines the link between culture and knowledge management is that it is often relatively vague regarding the characteristics of organizational culture which facilitate knowledge management activities. Thus, for example, O'Dell and Hubert (2011) simply talk about a 'knowledge sharing' culture, while Donate and Guadamillas (2010) talk about a 'knowledge-centred' culture. Within this literature, however, there is a broad consensus on the general characteristics of an organizational culture likely to facilitate knowledge management activities. These characteristics are that, first, knowledge sharing is regarded as a norm; second, that organizational staff have a strong sense of collective identity; third, that colleagues have a high level of trust in and respect for each other; fourth, that organizational processes are regarded as fair; and, finally, that staff have high levels of trust in and commitment to management.

However, by the late 2000s a number of writers on knowledge management had begun to be more specific regarding the characteristics of 'good' and 'bad' organizational cultures. This has typically been done through using academic typologies of organizational culture to identify which best support knowledge management activities. While various typologies of organizational culture exist, the one that has been used most frequently in the knowledge management literature is that developed by Cameron and Quinn (see for example Stock et al. 2010; Sanz-Valle et al. 2011; Suppiah and Sandhu 2011; Cavaliere and Lombardi 2015). Thus, before looking at the research into the impact of these culture types on knowledge management and learning, it is necessary to give a brief overview of Cameron and Quinn's organization culture typology.

Cameron and Quinn's (2006) typology uses two dimensions to develop a typology which distinguishes between four distinctive organizational culture types (see Figure 16.1). In this framework, one dimension is flexibility/adaptability versus stability/continuity, while the other dimension examines whether the culture is focused internally within the organization, or whether its primary focus is external, on the market and general business environment. Using these dimensions Cameron and Quinn distinguish between what they refer to as a

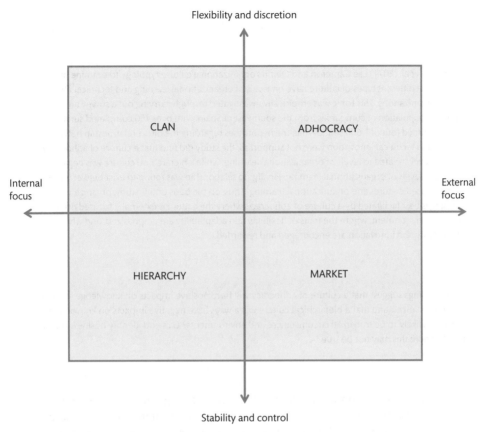

Figure 16.1 Cameron and Quinn's Organizational Culture Typology

Source: Cameron and Quinn (2006).

'clan culture', a culture of adhocracy, a hierarchical culture, and a market focused culture. The characteristics of a clan culture is that it is a culture which is flexible and adaptable and which is primarily internally focused, being concerned with facilitating collaboration among staff and the development of a strong sense of group and team identity among staff. A culture of adhocracy is also flexible and adaptable, but it is more focused on the market and the external business environment. This type of culture is suited to companies that operate in dynamic markets and it emphasizes values of creativity and innovation. A hierarchical culture is one that is both internally focused, and concerned with stability and continuity. The characteristics of this culture are a focus on adhering to organizationally defined rules and norms within organizations that have clearly defined authority structures. Finally, a market-based culture is one which is externally focused, but where the emphasis is on stability and continuity. This culture is appropriate to business environments which are not characterized by high levels of change, and where the focus of the culture is with factors such as consistency, incremental innovation or change, and maintaining or developing levels of competitiveness in business markets.

Illustration 16.2   Organizational culture types and organizational learning

Sanz-Valle et al. (2011) use Cameron and Quinn's organizational culture typology to examine the impact that different types of culture have on levels of organizational learning and technical innovation within organizations. This topic was empirically investigated through carrying out a survey among a diverse population of companies from the southeast of Spain, with over 450 completed surveys being returned (out of 1,600 sent). While the hypotheses regarding the direct relationship between culture and technical innovation were not supported, the study did find that a culture of adhocracy was positively related to levels of organizational learning, while a hierarchical culture was negatively related to levels of organizational learning. Finally, no relationship was found to exist between clan- or market-based cultures and organizational learning. Thus, on the basis of this study, organizational learning is best facilitated by a culture of adhocracy, where the culture is externally focused on the business environment, where the traits of flexibility and adaptability are emphasized, and where values of creativity and innovation are encouraged and rewarded.

Questions

These findings suggest that a culture of adhocracy will have positive impacts on knowledge sharing in all circumstances, and that a hierarchical culture will always have negative impacts on knowledge sharing. Is this likely to be true in all circumstances and environments? Can you identify business environments where this may not be true?

Recent writing on organizational culture types shows a significant degree of consensus regarding both the types of organizational culture that facilitate and inhibit knowledge processes in organization. This research has been done on a heterogeneous range of different types of organization, including seven public and private sector Malaysian organizations (Suppiah and Sandhu 2011), hospitals in the USA (Stock et al. 2010), Taiwanese banks and insurance companies (Liao et al. 2012), large manufacturing firms based in Tuscany (Cavaliere and Lombardi 2015), and firms in southeast Spain (Sanze-Valle et al. 2011—see Illustration 16.2). The type of culture which most strongly facilitates knowledge management activities is a culture of adhocracy, with Sanz-Valle et al. (2011) finding this culture type to be positively related to levels of organizational learning, while Liao et al. (2012) found a culture of adhocracy to be positively related to levels of organizational innovation. The type of organizational culture which inhibits knowledge management activities is generally found to be a hierarchical or bureaucratic culture, with Stock et al. (2010) finding this culture type to be negatively related to levels of knowledge dissemination within organizations, Sanz-Valle et al. (2011) finding it to be negatively related to levels of organizational learning, Liao et al. (2012) finding it to be negatively linked to levels of organizational innovation, and Suppiah and Sandhu (2011) finding it to be negatively related to the sharing of tacit knowledge among employees. However, one of the most recent studies using the competing values framework by Cavaliere and Lombardi (2015) found quite different results, with the hierarchical culture being most positively linked to processes of donating and collecting knowledge.

Creating and managing an organizational culture to support knowledge management activities

A general limitation of much of the literature on this topic is that it provides little indication of either what organizations require to do to achieve such cultures or what barriers may exist to their development. In the literature which does consider how appropriate cultures can be created, there is disagreement on whether organizational cultures should be changed to create appropriate knowledge behaviours and values, or whether knowledge management efforts should be designed to reflect an organization's existing cultural values.

The mainstream perspective in the knowledge management literature is that organizational cultures can be changed to produce appropriate knowledge-related behaviours and values (see, for example, Teo et al. 2011). Analysis based on this assumption therefore argues that one of the key tasks likely to underpin the success of knowledge management initiatives is the modification of an organization's culture in ways that encourage and support desired knowledge behaviours and attitudes (De Long and Fahey 2000; Ribiere and Sitar 2003). Pan and Scarbrough (1999) argue that appropriate knowledge cultures can be developed, but admit that doing so is a complex, daunting, and time-consuming process. Their argument is based on a detailed examination of one organization, Buckman Laboratories. (See Time to reflect.)

An alternative perspective is supported by McDermott and O'Dell (2001), who suggest that organizations which are successful with their knowledge management initiatives 'build their knowledge management approach to fit their culture' (2001: 77). This is because organizational cultures are much more resilient than any knowledge management initiative, thus organizations which attempt to shape the culture to fit with their knowledge management initiative, rather than vice versa, are likely to find that their knowledge management initiatives fail (see also O'Dell and Hubert 2011). Further, the success of such initiatives is also predicated on organizations having suitable knowledge cultures already in place. Thus, embedded in McDermott and O'Dell's analysis is a pessimistic view that large scale culture change cannot be achieved, and that if appropriate knowledge behaviours are not a part of the existing culture, then it is likely to be very difficult to change the culture to make them so.

 Time to reflect How controllable is organizational culture?

Do management have the power to control and influence organizational culture, or is culture something beyond the control of management?

To align a knowledge management initiative with the organization's culture they argue that it is necessary to link it to both the visible and the invisible elements of the culture (see Table 16.1). In terms of visible elements, the knowledge management initiative needs to be focused on addressing existing business problems, matching the existing 'style' of the organization (such as the degree of bureaucratic rigidity), and ensuring that reward and appraisal systems make visible the importance of appropriate knowledge behaviours. In terms of the invisible aspects of an organization's culture, knowledge management initiatives should

Table 16.1 Linking Knowledge Management Initiatives to Organizational Culture

Visible Elements of Culture	Invisible Elements of Culture
Knowledge management initiatives should:	Knowledge management initiatives should link to:
• link to existing business problems	• core organizational values
• reflect existing organizational style.	• existing networks of social relations.
HR practices should link to appropriate knowledge behaviours.	

Source: McDermott and O'Dell (2001).

reflect existing core values and should link into existing networks of social relations. In a similar vein, Schultze and Boland (2000) argue that knowledge management initiatives are likely to fail if they involve the development and use of work practices which are incongruent with existing work practices.

These two perspectives on the manageability of knowledge-related cultures reflect similar debates in the wider culture literature (Harris and Ogbonna 2002; Mathew and Ogbonna 2011). Finally, again reflecting a theme in the wider culture management literature, some analysis acknowledges that organizations may not have coherent and unitary cultures, and that distinctive sub-cultures may exist which shape the characteristics and dynamics of organizational knowledge sharing processes (De Long and Fahey 2000; Alavi et al. 2005–6). For example, Currie and Kerrin's (2003) case study of a pharmaceuticals company found that the existence of strong sub-cultures within the sales and marketing divisions inhibited the sharing of knowledge between staff in them, despite a number of management initiatives aimed at changing this knowledge sharing/hoarding pattern. Finally, the literature on boundary spanning knowledge processes (see Chapter 13) that considers intra-company situations, such as cross-functional collaboration or collaboration between business units within the same company, also suggests that significant differences can exist in the culture of different parts of an organization. However, in the literature which examines the relationship between organizational culture and knowledge management, this does not represent the mainstream perspective, with this literature typically assuming, implicitly, that organizations have unitary and coherent cultures. Thus the link between the existence of organizational sub-cultures and knowledge management processes is significantly underresearched.

The conceptualization of leadership in the academic business and management literature

Before examining the knowledge management literature that deals with the topic of leadership it is useful to begin by providing some context to this work through, briefly, engaging with the general academic literature on leadership. Given both the amount of writing that has been produced on the topic of leadership and the diversity of perspectives and theories on leadership that have been developed, it is impossible in the space available here to provide a comprehensive overview of this literature. Thus, all that is provided here is the presentation of a schematic outline of how the theorization of leadership has historically evolved and some detail on what represents the mainstream contemporary perspective on leadership.

Serious interest in the topic of leadership in the academic business literature dates back to the early twentieth century. At this time, what is characterized as the 'trait' theory of leadership dominated (see Table 16.2). This perspective suggested that great and successful leaders possess particular personality traits and characteristics that distinguished them from others, such as high levels of charisma. Thus from this perspective, great leaders are people born with particular traits that distinguish them from 'ordinary people'. However, over time, this perspective became subject to a number of criticisms, not least that empirical evidence has provided questionable support for it. Since then a number of different perspectives on leadership were developed (see Table 16.2), which themselves became subject to a number of criticisms. A useful starting point for those interested in gaining a more detailed understanding of how the theorization of leadership has evolved is to read relevant books or book chapters on the topic (see for example Northouse 2007; Densten 2008; Yukl 2008).

Table 16.2 Historical Overview of Diverse Perspectives on Leadership

Leadership Theory	Assumptions about Leadership	Contemporary Status/Relevance
Trait approach	Great leaders are born, not created, and possess particular inherent characteristics that distinguish them from other people—such as charisma, the ability to communicate effectively, emotional intelligence.	Most popular in 1930s and 1940s but re-emerged in 1970s. Discredited as empirical studies found no agreed relationship between particular traits and successful leadership. Also criticized for neglecting context.
Behaviour-based theories	Focus on what leaders do— attempt to identify behaviours of successful leadership.	Developed in 1950s but still utilized by some researchers. Have been criticized for lacking adequate theorization and empirical methodologies used to measure and investigate behaviours.
Contingency approach (including Fiedler's contingency theory and path-goal theory)	What constitutes appropriate leadership is shaped by the nature of the organizational context.	Developed in late 1960s with general growth in popularity of contingency theory. Has been criticized on a number of issues including lack of consistent empirical support.
'New leadership' theories (including charismatic leadership theory and transformational/transactional leadership theory)	Concerned with how leader's action and talk motivates followers to act.	Developed in late 1970s and have grown in popularity since. Have been criticized for universalistic assumptions which neglect importance of context.

As suggested in Table 16.2, 'new leadership' theories represent the most popular contemporary perspective on leadership in the academic business literature. It is worth elaborating on this perspective in a little depth, not only because of its contemporary popularity but also because, as will be seen later, it represents one of the perspectives on leadership most widely used by writers on knowledge management.

 Time to reflect   Applying leadership theories

Think of an example of a high profile and successful leader (either from a business organization or from some other context, such as a sports team or political party). Which leadership theory best explains their success?

Arguably Burns's (1978) development of the concept of transformational leadership (see Definition) represents the starting point of what has subsequently been labelled 'new leadership'. However, various terms such as strategic leadership, charismatic leadership, and visionary leadership have been utilized by others to refer to a very similar style of leadership. Thus, typically, all these concepts are categorized as together representing 'new leadership' theory (Vera and Crossan 2004). Arguably, one of the key features of transformational leadership (and all 'new leadership' theories) is that it represents a form of leadership and people management that is distinctive from more traditional forms of management. Thus, transformational leadership is often defined in parallel with, and as the virtual opposite of, management (what might be referred to as micro-management, which is referred to by various writers on instrumental leadership, for example Nadler and Tushman 1990; and on transactional leadership, for example Burns 1978). As outlined in Table 16.3, transformational leadership is fundamentally concerned with motivating and inspiring followers by developing long-term strategic visions and persuading people to buy into them and work towards their achievement. Transformational leaders thus motivate workers through providing them with intellectual stimulation and inspiring them to work towards these corporate visions and values.

Table 16.3 Distinguishing Leadership from (Micro-)Management

	Leadership	(Micro-) Management
Focus of Timescales	Long-term	Short-term
Primary Role	Strategic	Operational
Key Task	Development and communication of long-term vision.	Day-to-day management of people towards work objectives.
People Management Role	Motivate by providing inspiring vision and providing intellectual stimulation.	Day-to-day management of people towards short- and medium-term work objectives though goal setting and reward management.
Impact on Culture, Values, and Structure	Develop new values and vision with aim of sustaining long-term competitiveness.	Reinforce existing culture, values, and structures through operating within them.

> **DEFINITION** **Transformational leadership**
>
> A mode or style of leadership focused on the development of long-term visions, values, and goals which also involves persuading workers to become attached to them and to work towards achieving them.

While this literature places a central emphasis on the strategic importance of transformational leadership, there is also an acknowledgement that this form of leadership is not enough on its own to successfully motivate and manage workers. Thus, it is usually argued that transformational leadership needs to be used in parallel with other forms of leadership and management that are more focused on the day-to-day management of workers and operational issues. Thus, for example, Burns talked of transformational and transactional leadership, and Nadler and Tushman (1990) refer to charismatic and instrumental leadership.

However, while there is an enormous corpus of writing on the topic of leadership, and while it represents a relatively mature subject area, there is a lack of consensus on the question of what leadership fundamentally consists of, and whether and how links can be made between the leadership styles and behaviours of key individuals, and organizational performance (see for example Northouse 2007; Kelly 2008). Further, the mainstream literature on leadership has been criticized on such fundamental issues as making universalist assumptions about the relevance of certain leadership styles which neglect to adequately account for context, being weakly theorized, making use of questionable research methods, and providing weak empirical support for the claims that are made (Barker 2001; Güldenberg and Konrath 2006; Yukl 2008). Despite this lack of consensus the vast majority of knowledge management literature, as will be seen in the following section, adopts a relatively uncritical stance to contemporary perspectives on transformational leadership. (See Time to reflect.)

Knowledge management and leadership

There now exists a reasonable body of writing on the relationship between leadership and knowledge management processes. Thus, for example, von Krogh et al. (2012) undertook a systematic literature review of the literature on leadership and knowledge management, and identified forty-eight published journal articles on the topic that were published between 1997 and 2009. Further, since then a number of other papers have also been published—see for example Lee et al. 2010; Kuo and Lee 2011; Nguyen and Mohamed 2011; Zhang and Cheng 2015; Argyris and Ransbotham 2016; Fischer et al. 2016; Kwon and Cho 2016. While the dominant perspective on leadership adopted by the knowledge literature is the strategic/transformational leadership perspective (see for example von Krogh's 2012 review of literature on leadership and knowledge management), as will be seen, a diversity of other perspectives on leadership are also utilized.

This literature can be characterized by two features: first, the claims it makes with regard to the relationship between knowledge management or learning and leadership; and, second, the claims made regarding the type of style of leadership necessary to facilitate knowledge management and learning. With regards to the link between leadership and knowledge management this literature typically makes a relatively strong claim that effective leadership can play an important role in facilitating learning and knowledge management activities in organizations. For example, a range of studies have found that various leadership roles were positively related to knowledge sharing in organizations (Yang 2007; Huang et al. 2008; Cavaliere et al. 2015; Zhang and Cheng 2015; Argyris and Ransbotham 2016). Further, due to the assumptions made in this literature regarding the importance of knowledge processes to organizational performance, effective leadership is also assumed to help contribute to competitive advantage and organizational performance. Thus, Hinterhuber and Stadler (2006: 237) argue that 'leadership and strategy are the immaterial competencies which contribute most to a company's value'. Empirical studies which substantiate the relationship between leadership, knowledge management, and team performance is provided by Lee et al. (2010—see Illustration 16.3) and Srivastava et al. (2006), while Kwon and Cho (2016) found that leadership was positively related to organizational level innovation.

 Illustration 16.3 Leadership, trust, knowledge sharing, and team performance

Lee et al. (2010) examined the relationship between a certain type/style of leadership and the level of knowledge sharing within teams, as well as team performance. The empirical study they undertook was carried out within one Australian automotive company. The type of team leadership behaviours they examined was quite specific, being labelled as the 'knowledge builder role'. The behaviours associated with this leadership role include providing technical advice to team members, developing expertise within the team, searching beyond the team for new ideas, monitoring the quality of the team's work, and initiating the development and implementation of new working practices. The following interview quotation from a team leader also illustrates the nature of this role: 'I try to encourage them to challenge each team member's input into the design work and not just accept what they're told. I try and bring to the table different ways for them to look at things and to look outside their functions' (p. 483).

The conceptual model that they tested hypothesized that the team knowledge builder role was potentially directly related to levels of knowledge sharing within teams. The model also hypothesized that the relationship between knowledge builder behaviours and knowledge sharing in teams was also mediated by either trust in the team leader or trust in the team. Further, with both leadership and team-based trust, they suggested that two forms of knowledge-based trust existed. These forms of trust were reliance trust, where people are willing to rely on the knowledge of others; and disclosure trust, where people are willing to sharing sensitive knowledge or information with other team members.

Lee et al.'s (2010) model was tested via a survey based study of thirty-four project teams within the automotive company, with almost 200 team members and leaders completing the survey. In testing their theoretical model, Lee et al. found that knowledge builder behaviours were positively linked to knowledge sharing in teams, but that the relationship was mediated by team-based trust (but not leadership-based trust). Thus Lee et al. (2010) conclude that knowledge builder behaviours, by developing levels of reliance and disclosure-based trust in team members, are indirectly but positively related to levels of team-based knowledge sharing. Finally, the hypothesis that levels of knowledge sharing in teams was positively related to team performance was also supported.

Question

The knowledge builder style of leadership seems a particularly appropriate leadership style for relatively small teams/groups. To what extent is this style of leadership relevant to organizational level leadership?

With regards to the style of leadership argued to be necessary to facilitate knowledge management activities, a range of perspectives are utilized, with the strategic/transformational perspective on leadership being the dominant one. This literature talks about the importance of leaders who are concerned with developing long-term strategy and vision. Second, in relation to people management this literature emphasizes the ability of the leader to inspire and motivate rather than to micro-manage workers. For example, Nonaka et al. (2006: 1192) talk about leadership as being concerned with 'interpreting, nurturing and supporting the knowledge vision', and that in relation to their SECI (socialization, externalization, combination, and internalization) model of knowledge creation (see Chapter 7) should be about 'enabling knowledge creation—not controlling and directing it'. However, a number of papers have examined other styles/forms of leadership, and found them to facilitate knowledge management activities. Thus, for example, Lee et al. (2010) examine leadership concerned with 'knowledge building' in teams (see Illustration 16.3). Further, others have also examined the impact of empowering leadership on knowledge management activities (see for example, Srivastava et al. 2006; Kuo and Lee 2011), while Cavaliere et al. (2015) examine supportive leadership, and Kwon and Cho (2016) use the concept of developmental leadership. Finally, a number of writers simply talk about knowledge leadership, or knowledge entrepreneurship, without linking to any existing conceptualization of leadership (Zhang and Cheng 2015; Argyris and Ransbotham 2016; Fischer et al. 2016—see Illustration 16.4).

 Illustration 16.4 The effect of knowledge leadership on knowledge sharing in engineering design teams

Zhang and Cheng (2015) examined the impact of knowledge leadership on knowledge sharing within small engineering project design teams. Their research was conducted by surveying engineering design teams in the construction industry. They examined the relationship between knowledge leadership, social capital, and knowledge sharing within teams using surveys. In examining knowledge leadership they didn't utilize any existing perspective on leadership. Instead they conceptualized knowledge leadership as having a number of key roles. These are, first, to develop a sense of shared purpose/objective between team members; second, to establish a collaborative culture between team members; and, third, to facilitate learning and knowledge sharing between team members. Social capital was defined in conventional terms, referring to the actual and potential resources embedded within people's networks of social relations. As defined by Nahapiet and Ghosal (1998) this has structural, cognitive, and relational dimensions.

Zhang and Cheng (2015) found that knowledge leadership was positively related to social capital, which was directly and positively related to levels of knowledge sharing within teams. Thus Zhang and Chen conclude that the key way in which knowledge leaders can enhance knowledge sharing in teams is to develop levels of social capital by developing relations between team members and creating a sense of shared objectives within teams.

Question

Assuming the role of a leader with an engineering design team, list some methods that can be used to develop social relations and a sense of common purpose between team members.

Conclusion

This chapter has been concerned with providing an overview of how organizational culture and leadership in organizations can impact on organizational knowledge management activities. As outlined, the assumption that typically underpins much of the literature on this topic is that both can have a very positive role in facilitating and supporting knowledge management activities.

The culture of an organization was shown to be an important factor shaping the attitudes of workers to knowledge management initiatives, and the extent to which they are prepared to use and share their knowledge. In general terms, cultures of adhocracy are found to facilitate knowledge management, whereas bureaucratic or hierarchical cultures were generally found to inhibit knowledge management activities. However, it was also shown that there is an active debate on this topic, with some writers raising questions regarding the extent to which effective knowledge cultures can be achieved through culture management initiatives. Thus, while the majority of writers suggest that knowledge management activities can be facilitated by the development of appropriate cultures, McDermott and O'Dell (2001) suggest that attempting to modify an organization's culture to fit in with the objectives of a knowledge management initiative is likely to be a recipe for failure.

In terms of leadership, while transformational leadership is the dominant perspective in the knowledge management literature, there are also a number of papers that consider the relationship between other leadership styles and knowledge management. The transformational leadership perspective makes a relatively sharp distinction between leadership and management, arguing that while management is focused upon operational issues and is concerned with the day-to-day management of people and resources, transformational leadership by contrast is more focused on strategic issues and is concerned with more long-term matters such as developing and communicating a future vision that people can be inspired and motivated by. As has been shown here, a growing body of empirical evidence suggests that various leadership styles are positively related to the level of knowledge sharing within organizations, which suggests that knowledge management initiatives can be facilitated by effective and appropriate leadership.

 Case study The impact of organizational culture on knowledge sharing: the case of Danisco

Michailova and Minbaeva (2012) examined the impact of organizational values, which are a core element of a corporate culture, on knowledge sharing among employees. This was done within the multinational corporation Danisco, which is one of the world's leading producers of food ingredients and is based in Denmark. The research was conducted in fourteen sites based in eleven separate countries dispersed across the world.

In examining organizational culture, Michailova and Minbaeva focus on organizational values which are relatively tangible and identifiable, and which constitute a core element of organizational culture. Organizational values are defined as

beliefs regarding the means and ends that management 'ought to' identify in the running of an enterprise . . . . are relatively stable over time . . . [and] . . . are decisive in determining the type of paradigm that is in use within the organization . . . and reveal 'how people communicate, explain, rationalize, and justify what they say and do as a community'. (p. 60)

From a management and control perspective, advocates of managing organizational culture believe that if employees can be persuaded to internalize an organization's culture, they will behave in ways compatible with the culture. From a knowledge sharing perspective, if knowledge sharing is part of an organization's culture and employees internalize it, then organizational culture can shape people's knowledge sharing behaviours.

In examining organizational values Michailova and Minbaeva distinguish between espousement, enactment, and internalization. Espoused values are values that are articulated in words by organizations and managers, for example in corporate documentation such as mission statements, internal communication documents, etc. The enactment of organizational values occurs when they are acted upon directly by management, through making changes to governance mechanisms, organizational processes, etc., in ways designed to ensure their utilization within the organization. Finally, internalization is the process which occurs after processes of espousement and enactment, by which individual workers accept those values as valid and relevant, and begin to act in ways which are compatible with and reinforce the organizational values. This involves a process of value alignment between individual and organizational values resulting in a process of self-discipline, where people manage their actions in line with the individual/organizational values.

In the case of Danisco, Michailova and Minbaeva studied Danisco in the early 2000s and identified five values that were articulated as part of its culture. These were about creating value for customers, being innovative, taking responsibility, the importance of dialogue and open communication, and building competences. From the analysis of corporate literature the three of these values that were most important were about innovation, dialogue, and competences. In Michailova and Minbaeva's study, the focus was purely on the value of 'dialogue'. This value was about the importance of open and honest dialogue and communication, both within the organization and externally. Following the espousement of these values in a range of corporate communications, they were enacted via a range of mechanisms including being embedded into people's annual performance appraisal and being displayed in high profile ways within corporate buildings. Most significantly, thirty knowledge management teams were set up in different parts of the organization with the aim of embedding the value of dialogue and knowledge sharing in corporate processes. The knowledge management teams communicated with staff via face-to-face meetings, interactive workshops, and also a range of virtual/online communication tools. Further, the induction process for new employees communicated the values to people, and mentoring and expatriation systems were utilized to embed the value of dialogue and knowledge sharing within the company.

Michailova and Minbaeva believed that organizational values would only affect people's knowledge sharing behaviours if the value of dialogue has been internalized by people. To test this hypothesis they distributed a survey to a diverse range of Danisco workers after the values had been enacted. The statistical analysis of the survey data supported their hypothesis and found that the internalization of the organizational value of dialogue was positively linked to the extent to which people were willing to share knowledge.

The results also revealed some more detailed patterns in knowledge sharing between employees. For example, knowledge sharing was more likely between staff within the same departments than it was between staff from different departments. Further, communication across/between different hierarchical levels within the organization seemed to be relatively weak. Thus existing processes were regarded as not helping the dialogue between hierarchical levels, and people didn't regard the learning opportunities from staff at lower levels in the organizational hierarchy as being significant.

Questions

1. Are there other mechanisms, apart from those outlined, that Danisco could have utilized to better enact the value of dialogue?

2. Is the finding about knowledge sharing being more extensive within departments rather than across departments something that is likely to be typical in most organizations, in part due to the fact that proximity and a need to collaborate for work means intra-departmental communication is likely to be common?

3. What, if anything, can be done to improve knowledge sharing across hierarchical levels?

Review and Discussion Questions

1. One critique of much of the leadership literature, including the concept of transformational leadership that is widely used in the knowledge management literature, is that it makes universalistic assumptions that such forms of leadership are appropriate in all contexts and situations. Thus, much of the knowledge management literature on leadership implies that transformational leadership is appropriate to all knowledge intensive firms and the management of all knowledge workers. Do you agree with this argument or do you think that context matters and that, while transformational leadership may be useful in some contexts, different types of situation require different styles of leadership?

2. Can leadership capabilities be taught and learned, or is the ability to lead effectively something that cannot be taught?

3. If an organization does *not* have a culture of collaboration and knowledge sharing, how easy is it likely to be to develop such a culture?

4. Is the existence of distinctive sub-cultures within an organization likely to be related to organizational size or the extent to which people in the organization are geographically dispersed?

 Suggestions for Further Reading

R. A. Wiewiora, B. Trigunarsyah, G. Murphy, and V. Coffey (2013). 'Organizational Culture and Willingness to Share Knowledge: A Competing Values Perspective in Australian Context', *International Journal of Project Management*, 31: 1163–74.

A study which uses Cameron and Quinn's typology of organizational cultures to examine the relationship between different types of culture and processes of knowledge sharing.

H. Nguyen and S. Mohamed (2011). 'Leadership Behaviours, Organizational Culture and Knowledge Management Practices: An Empirical Investigation', *Journal of Management Development*, 30/2: 206–21.

Examines how transformational and transactional styles of leadership affect knowledge management activities in Australian SMEs and also examines the extent to which organizational culture moderates these relationships.

Y. Argyris and S. Ransbotham (2016). 'Knowledge Entrepreneurship: Institutionalizing Wiki-Based Knowledge-Management Processes in Competitive and Hierarchical Organizations', *Journal of Information Technology*, 31: 226–36.

An in-depth empirical case study examining the effect that knowledge-based leadership had on knowledge sharing via the use of a wiki-based social media platform.

G. Von Krogh, I. Nonaka, and L. Rechsteiner (2012). 'Leadership in Organizational Knowledge Creation', *Journal of Management Studies*, 49/1: 240–77.

A review of the literature on leadership and knowledge management (up to 2009), which provides a comprehensive overview.

 To further your understanding of knowledge management in organizations explore the book's accompanying online resources at www.oup.com/uk/hislop4e/

References

Abrams, L., Cross, R., Lesser, E., and Levin, D. (2003). 'Nurturing Interpersonal Trust in Knowledge-Sharing Networks', *Academy of Management Executive*, 17/4: 64–77.

Agarwal, R., Campbell, B., Franco, A., and Ganco, M. (2016). 'What Do I Take With Me? The Mediating Effect of Spin-Out Team Size and Tenure on the Founder–Firm Performance Relationship', *Academy of Management Journal*, 59/3: 1060–87.

Ahmad, A., Bosua, R., and Scheepers, R. (2014). 'Protecting Organizational Competitive Advantage: A Knowledge Leakage Perspective', *Computers and Security*, 42/1: 27–39.

Ahn, J. H., and Chang, S. G. (2004). 'Assessing the Contribution of Knowledge to Business Performance: The KP 3 Methodology', *Decision Support Systems*, 36/4: 403–16.

Akgün, A. E., Byrne, J., Keskin, H., Lynn, G. S., and Imamoglu, S. Z. (2005). 'Knowledge Networks in New Product Development Projects: A Transactive Memory Perspective', *Information and Management*, 42/8: 1105–20.

Akgün, A., Byrne, J., Keskin, H., and Lynn, G. (2006). 'Transactive Memory System in New Product Development Teams', *IEEE Transactions on Engineering Management*, 53/1: 95–111.

Akgün, A., Lynn, G., and Byrne, J. (2006). 'Antecedents and Consequences of Unlearning in New Product Development Teams', *Journal of Product Innovation Management*, 23/1: 73–88.

Akgün, A., Byrne, J., Lynn, G., and Keskin, H. (2007a). 'Organizational Unlearning as Changes in Beliefs and Routines in Organizations', *Journal of Organizational Change Management*, 20/6: 794–812.

Akgün, A., Byrne, J., Lynn, G., and Keskin, H. (2007b). 'New Product Development in Turbulent Environments: Impact of Improvisation and Unlearning on New Product Development', *Journal of Engineering Technology Management*, 24/3: 203–30.

Al-Alawi, A., Al-Marzooqi, N., and Mohammed, Y. (2007). 'Organizational Culture and Knowledge Sharing: Critical Success Factors', *Journal of Knowledge Management*, 11/2: 22–42.

Alavi, M., and Leidner, D. (2001). 'Review: Knowledge Management and Knowledge Management Systems: Conceptual Foundations and Research Issues', *MIS Quarterly*, 25/1: 107–36.

Alavi, M., and Tiwana, A. (2003). 'Knowledge Management: The Information Technology Dimension', in M. Easterby-Smith and M. A. Lyles (eds), *The Blackwell Handbook of Organizational Learning and Knowledge Management*. Oxford: Blackwell, pp. 104–21.

Alavi, M., Kayworth, T., and Leidner, D. (2005–6). 'An Empirical Examination of the Influence of Organizational Culture on Knowledge Management Practices', *Journal of Management Information Systems*, 22/3: 191–224.

Alin, P., Iorio, J., and Taylor, J. (2013). 'Digital Boundary Objects as Negotiation Facilitators: Spanning Boundaries in Virtual Engineering Project Networks', *Project Management Journal*, 44/3: 48–63.

Allen, J. (2010). 'Knowledge-Sharing Successes in Web 2.0 Communities', *IEEE Technology and Society Magazine*, Spring: 58–64.

Allen, J., James, A. D., and Gamlen, P. (2007). 'Formal Versus Informal Knowledge Networks in R&D: A Case Study Using Social Network Analysis', *R&D Management*, 37/3: 179–96.

Alvesson, M. (1995). *Management of Knowledge Intensive Firms*. London: de Gruyter.

Alvesson, M. (2000). 'Social Identity and the Problem of Loyalty in Knowledge-Intensive Companies', *Journal of Management Studies*, 37/8: 1101–23.

Alvesson, M. (2001). 'Knowledge Work: Ambiguity, Image and Identity', *Human Relations*, 54/7: 863–86.

Alvesson, M. (2011). 'De-essentializing the Knowledge Intensive Firm: Reflections on Sceptical Research Going Against the Mainstream', *Journal of Management Studies*, 48/7: 1640–661.

Alvesson, M. (2014). *The Triumph of Emptiness: Consumption, Higher Education and Work Organization*. Oxford: Oxford University Press.

Alvesson, M., and Kärreman, D. (2001). 'Old Couple: Making Sense of the Curious Concept of Knowledge Management', *Journal of Management Studies*, 38/7: 995–1018.

Alvesson, M., and Spicer, A. (2016). *The Stupidity Paradox: The Power and Pitfalls of Functional Stupidity at Work*. London: Profile Books.

Alvesson, M., and Willmott, H. (2001). 'Identity Regulation as Organizational Control: Producing the Appropriate Individual', *Journal of Management Studies*, 39/5: 691–744.

Amara, N., Landry, R., and Doloreux, D. (2009). 'Patterns of Innovation in Knowledge-Intensive Business Services', *Service Industries Journal*, 29/4: 407–30.

Amin, A., and Roberts, J. (2008). *Community, Economic Creativity, and Organization*. Oxford: Oxford University Press.

Anand, N., Gardner, H., and Morris, T. (2007). 'Knowledge-Based Innovation: Emergence and Embedding of New Practice Areas in Management Consulting Journals', *Academy of Management Journal*, 50/2: 406–28.

Andreeva, T., and Ikhilchik, I. (2011). 'Applicability of the SECI Model of Knowledge Creation in Russian Cultural Context: Theoretical Analysis', *Knowledge and Process Management*, 18/1: 56–66.

Andreeva, T., and Kianto, A. (2012). 'Does Knowledge Management Really Matter? Linking Knowledge Management Practices, Competitiveness and Economic Performance', *Journal of Knowledge Management*, 16/4: 617–36.

Andreeva, T., and Sergeeva, A. (2016). 'The More the Better . . . or is it? The Contradictory Effects of HR Practices on Knowledge-Sharing Motivation and Behaviour', *Human Resource Management Journal*, 26/2: 151–71.

Andrews, K., and Delahaye, B. (2000). 'Influences on Knowledge Processes in Organizational Learning: The Psychosocial Filter', *Journal of Management Studies*, 37/6: 797–810.

Antonocopoulou, E. (2006). 'The Relationship Between Individual and Organizational Learning: New Evidence from Managerial Learning Practices', *Management Learning*, 37/4: 455–73.

Antonacopoulou, E. (2009). 'Impact and Scholarship: Unlearning and Practising to Co-create Actionable Knowledge', *Management Learning*, 40/4: 421–30.

Ardichvili, A., Page, V., and Wentling, T. (2003). 'Motivation and Barriers to Participation in Virtual Knowledge-Sharing Communities of Practice', *Journal of Knowledge Management*, 7/1: 64–77.

Argyris, C. (1990). *Overcoming Organizational Defences*. Needham Heights, MA: Allyn and Bacon.

Argyris, C., and Schön, D. (1996). *Organizational Learning II: Theory, Method, and Practice*. Reading, MA: Addison-Wesley.

Argyris, Y., and Ransbotham, S. (2016). 'Knowledge Entrepreneurship: Institutionalising Wiki-Based Knowledge Management Processes in Competitive and Hierarchical Organizations', *Journal of Information Technology*, 31/2: 226–39.

Arnold, V., Clark, N., Collier, P. A., Leech, S. A., and Sutton, S. G. (2004). 'Explanation Provision and Use in an Intelligent Decision Aid', *Intelligent Systems in Accounting, Finance and Management*, 12/1: 5–27.

Aziz, N., and Sparrow, J. (2011). 'Patterns of Gaining and Sharing of Knowledge about Customers: A Study of an Express Parcel Delivery Company', *Knowledge Management Research and Practice*, 9/1: 29–47.

Baalen, P., van Bloemhof-Ruwaard, J., and van Heck, E. (2005). 'Knowledge Sharing in an Emerging Network of Practice: The Role of a Knowledge Portal', *European Management Journal*, 23/3: 300–14.

Bacharach, P., and Baratz, M. (1963). 'Decisions and Non-Decisions: An Analytical Framework', *American Political Science Review*, 57: 632–42.

Bain, R., and Mueller, C. (2016). 'Understanding Practice(s) and Practicing', in K. Orr, S. Nutley, S. Russell, R. Bain, B. Hacking, and C. Moran (eds), *Knowledge and Practice in Business and Organizations*. London: Routledge, pp. 30–42.

Ball, B., Karrer, B., and Newman, M. E. (2011). 'Efficient and Principled Method for Detecting Communities in Networks', *Physical Review E*, 84/3: 036103.

Barker, R. (2001). 'The Nature of Leadership', *Human Relations*, 54/4: 469–94.

Barner-Rasmussen, W., Ehrnrooth, M., Koveshnikov, A., and Mäkelä, K. (2010). 'Functions, Resources and Types of Boundary Spanners Within the MNC', *Academy of Management Proceedings*, 1: 1–6.

Barner-Rasmussen, W., Ehrnrooth, M., Koveshnikov, A., and Mäkelä, K. (2014). 'Cultural and Language Skills as Resources for Boundary Spanning within the MNC', *Journal of International Business Studies*, 45/7: 886–905.

Barratt, E. (2002). 'Foucault, Foucauldianism and Human Resource Management', *Personnel Review*, 31/2: 189–204.

Baskerville, R., and Dulipovici, A. (2006). 'The Theoretical Foundations of Knowledge Management', *Knowledge Management Research and Practice*, 4/2: 83–105.

Baskerville, R., and Pries-Heje, J. (1999). 'Grounded Action Research: A Method for Understanding IT in Practice', *Accounting, Management and Information Technologies*, 9/1: 1–23.

Bauman, Z. (2007). *Liquid Modernity*. Cambridge: Polity Press.

Baumard, P. (1999). *Tacit Knowledge in Organizations*. London: Sage.

Baumard, P., and Starbuck, W. (2005). 'Learning from Failures: Why it May Not Happen', *Long Range Planning*, 38/3: 281–98.

Bayus, B. L. (2013). 'Crowdsourcing New Product Ideas over Time: An Analysis of the Dell IdeaStorm Community', *Management Science*, 59/1: 226–44.

Beaumont, P., and Hunter, L. (2002). *Managing Knowledge Workers*. London: CIPD.

Beazley, H., Boenisch, J., and Harden, D. (2002). *Continuity Management: Preserving Corporate Knowledge and Productivity when Employees Leave*. London: John Wiley & Sons.

Becerra, M., Lunnan, R., and Huemer, L. (2008). 'Trustworthiness, Risk and the Sharing of Tacit and Explicit Knowledge Between Alliance Partners', *Journal of Management Studies*, 45/4: 691–713.

Becerra-Fernandez, I., and Sabherwal, R. (2014). *Knowledge Management: Systems and Processes*. London: Routledge.

Becker, K. (2008). 'Unlearning as a Driver of Sustainable Change and Innovation: Three Australian Case Studies', *International Journal of Technology Management*, 42/1–2: 89–106.

Becker, K. (2010). 'Facilitating Unlearning During Implementation of New Technology', *Journal of Organizational Change Management*, 23/3: 251–68.

Becker, K., Hyland, P., and Acutt, B. (2006). 'Considering Unlearning in HRD Practices: An Australian Study', *Journal of European Industrial Training*, 30/8: 608–21.

Bell, D. (1973). *The Coming of Post-Industrial Society*. Harmondsworth: Penguin.

Berends, H., and Lammers, I. (2010). 'Explaining Discontinuity in Organizational Learning: A Process Analysis', *Organization Studies*, 31/8: 1045–68.

Berman, S. L., Down, J., and Hill, C. W. L. (2002). 'Tacit Knowledge as a Source of Competitive Advantage in the National Basketball Association', *Academy of Management Journal*, 45/1: 13–31.

Bertels, H., Kleinschmidt, E., and Koen, P. (2011). 'Communities of Practice versus Organizational Climate: Which One Matters More to Dispersed Collaboration in the Front End of Innovation?', *Journal of Product Innovation Management*, 28/5: 757–72.

Berthoin Antal, A., Dierkes, M., Child, J., and Nonaka, I. (2001). 'Organizational Learning and Knowledge: Reflections on the Dynamics of the Field and Challenges for the Future', in M. Dierkes, A. Bertoin Antal, J. Child, and I. Nonaka (eds), *Handbook of Organizational Learning and Knowledge*. Oxford: Oxford University Press, pp. 921–40.

Bettiol, M., and Sedita, S. (2011). 'The Role of Community of Practice in Developing Creative Industry Projects', *International Journal of Project Management*, 29/4: 468–79.

Bettis, R., and Prahalad, C. (1995). 'The Dominant Logic: Retrospective and Extension', *Strategic Management Journal*, 16/1: 5–14.

Betz, S., Oberweis, A., and Styephan, R. (2012). 'Knowledge Transfer in Offshore Outsourcing Software Development Projects: An Analysis of the Challenges and Solutions from German Clients', *Expert Systems*, 31/3: 282–97.

Bierly, P., and Chakrabarti, A. (1996). 'Generic Knowledge Strategies in the U.S. Pharmaceutical Industry', *Strategic Management Journal*, 17/S2: 123–35.

Blackler, F. (1995). 'Knowledge, Knowledge Work and Organizations: An Overview and Interpretation', *Organization Studies*, 16/6: 1021–46.

Blackler, F., Crump, N., and McDonald, S. (2000). 'Organizing Processes in Complex Activity Systems', *Organization*, 7/2: 277–300.

Bock, G., Kankanhalli, G., and Sharma, S. (2006). 'Are Norms Enough? The Role of Collaborative Norms in Promoting Organizational Knowledge Seeking', *European Journal of Information Systems*, 15/4: 357–67.

Bogner, W., and Bansal, P. (2007). 'Knowledge Management as the Basis of Sustained High Performance', *Journal of Management Studies*, 44/1: 165–88.

Boh, W., and Xu, Y. (2013). 'Knowledge Transfer Across Dissimilar Cultures', *Journal of Knowledge Management*, 17/1: 29–46.

Boland, R., and Tenkasi, R. (1995). 'Perspective Making and Perspective Taking in Communities of Knowing', *Organization Science*, 6/4: 350–72.

Bolisani, E., and Scarso, E. (2000). 'Electronic Communication and Knowledge Transfer', *International Journal of Technology Management*, 20/1–2: 116–33.

Bolisani, E., Scarso, E., and Zieba, M. (2015). 'Emergent Versus Deliberate Knowledge Management Strategy: Literature Review and Case Study Analysis', in *Proceedings of European Conference on Knowledge Management*. London: Academic Conferences International Limited.

Bontis, N., Crosan, M., and Hulland, J. (2002). 'Managing and Organizational Learning System by Aligning Stocks and Flows', *Journal of Management Studies*, 39/4: 437–69.

Borgatti, S. P., and Cross, R. (2003). 'A Relational View of Information Seeking and Learning in Social Networks', *Management Science*, 49/4: 432–45.

Borzillo, S., Aznar, S., and Schmitt, A. (2011). 'A Journey Through Communities of Practice: How and Why Members Move from the Periphery to the Core', *European Management Journal*, 29/1: 25–42.

Bosch-Sijtsema, P., Ruohomäki, V., and Vartiainen, M. (2010). 'Multi-Locational Knowledge Workers in the Office: Navigation, Disturbances and Effectiveness', *New Technology, Work and Employment*, 25/3: 183–95.

Bosua, R., and Venkitachalam, K. (2013). 'Aligning Strategies and Processes in Knowledge Management: A Framework', *Journal of Knowledge Management*, 17/3: 331–46.

Bosua, R., and Scheepers, R. (2007). 'Towards a Model to Explain Knowledge Sharing in Complex Organizational Environments', *Knowledge Management Research and Practice*, 5/3: 93–109.

Bouty, I. and Gomez, M-L. (2010). 'Dishing Up Individual and Collective Dimensions of Organizational Knowing', *Management Learning*, 41/4: 545–59.

Bradley, K., Mathieu, J., Cordery, J., Rosen, B., and Kukenberger, M. (2011). 'Managing a New Collaborative Entity in Business Organizations: Understanding Organizational Communities of Practice Effectiveness', *Journal of Applied Psychology*, 96/6: 1234–45.

Bresnen, M. (2010). 'Keeping it Real: Constituting Partnering Through Boundary Objects', *Construction Management and Economics*, 28/6: 615–28.

Brown, J., and Duguid, P. (1991). 'Organization Learning and Communities of Practice: Towards a Unified View of Working, Learning and Innovation', *Organization Science*, 2/1: 40–57.

Brown, J., and Duguid, P. (1998). 'Organizing Knowledge', *California Management Review*, 40/3: 90–111.

Brown, J., and Duguid, P. (2001). 'Knowledge and Organization: A Social Practice Perspective', *Organization Science*, 12/2: 198–213.

Buchanan, D. (2008). 'You Stab My Back, I'll Stab Yours: Management Experience and Perceptions of Organization Political Behaviour', *British Journal of Management*, 19/1: 49–64.

Bui, H., and Baruch, Y. (2011). 'Learning Organizations in Higher Education: An Empirical Evaluation within an International Context', *Management Learning*, 43/5: 515–44.

Bulgurcu, B., Cavusoglu, H., and Benbasat, I. (2010). 'Information Security Policy Compliance: An Empirical Study of Rationality-Based Beliefs and Information Security Awareness', *MIS Quarterly*, 34/3: 523–48.

Bulut, C., and Culha, O. (2010). 'The Effects of Training on Organizational Commitment', *International Journal of Training and Development*, 14/4: 309–22.

Bunderson, J., and Reagans, R. (2011). 'Power, Status and Learning in Organizations', *Organization Science*, 22/5: 1182–94.

Bunker Whittington, K., Owen-Smith, J., and Powell, W. (2009). 'Networks, Propinquity, and Innovation in Knowledge-Intensive Industries', *Administrative Science Quarterly*, 54/1: 90–122.

Burns, J. (1978). *Leadership*. New York: Harper and Row.

Burrell, G., and Morgan, G. (1979). *Sociological Paradigms and Organisational Analysis: Elements of the Sociology of Corporate Life*. London: Heinemann Educational.

Burt, R. S. (1992). *Structural Holes*. Cambridge, MA: Harvard University Press.

Byrne, R. (2001). 'Employees: Capital or Commodity?' *Career Development International*, 6/6: 324–30.

Cabrera, A., and Cabrera, E. (2002). 'Knowledge Sharing Dilemmas', *Organization Studies*, 23/5: 687–710.

Cabrera, E., and Cabrera, A. (2005). 'Fostering Knowledge Sharing Through People Management Practices', *International Journal of Human Resource Management*, 16/5: 720–35.

Cacciatori, E., Tamoschus, D., and Grahber, G. (2012). 'Knowledge Transfer Across Projects: Codification in Creative, High-tech and Enginering Industries', *Management Learning*, 49/3: 309–31.

Caligiuri, P. (2014). 'Many Moving Parts: Factors Influencing the Effectiveness of HRM Practices Designed to Improve Knowledge Transfer within MNCs', *Journal of International Business Studies*, 45/2: 63–72.

Camelo-Ordaz, C., García-Cruz, J., Sousa-Ginel, E., and Valle-Cabrera, R. (2011). 'The Influence of Human Resource Management on Knowledge Sharing and Innovation in Spain: The Mediating Role of Affective Commitment', *International Journal of Human Resource Management*, 22/7: 1442–63.

Cameron, K., and Quinn, R. (2006). *Diagnosing and Changing Organizational Culture: Based on the Competing Values Framework*. Reading, MA: Addison-Wesley.

Cannon, M., and Edmondson, A. (2005). 'Failing to Learn and Learning to Fail (Intelligently): How Great Organizations Put Failure to Work to Innovate and Improve', *Long Range Planning*, 38/3: 299–319.

Cannon, R. L., Moore, P., Tansathein, D., Strobel, J., Kendall, C., Biswas, G., and Bezdek, J. (1989). 'An Expert System as a Component of an Integrated System for Oil Exploration', *Proceedings: Energy and Information Technologies in the Southeast*. London: IEEE, pp. 32–5.

Cantillon, P., D'Eath, M., De Grave, W., and Dornan, T. (2016). 'How Do Clinicians Become Teachers? A Communities of Practice Perspective', *Advances in Health Sciences Education*, 21/5: 991–1008.

Carleton, K. (2011). 'How to Motivate and Retain Knowledge Workers in Organizations: A Review of the Literature', *International Journal of Management*, 28/2: 459–68.

Carlile, P. (2002). 'A Pragmatic View of Knowledge and Boundaries: Boundary Objects in New Product Development', *Organization Science*, 14/4: 442–55.

Carlile, P. (2004). 'Transferring, Translating and Transforming: An Integrative Framework for Managing Knowledge Across Boundaries', *Organization Science*, 15/5: 555–68.

Carroll, J., Hatakenaka, S., and Rudolph, J. (2006). 'Naturalistic Decision Making and Organizational Learning in Nuclear Power Plants: Negotiating Meaning Between Managers and Problem Investigation Teams', *Organization Studies*, 27/7: 1037–57.

Casillas, J., Acedo, F., and Barbero, J. (2010). 'Learning, Unlearning and Internationalisation: Evidence from the Pre-Export Phase', *International Journal of Information Management*, 30/2: 162–73.

Castells, M. (1998). *The Rise of Network Society*. Oxford: Basil Blackwell.

Castro, L. (2015). 'Strategizing Across Boundaries: Revisiting Knowledge Brokering Activities in French Innovation Clusters', *Journal of Knowledge Management*, 19/5: 1048–68.

Cavaliere, V., and Lombardi, S. (2015). 'Exploring Different Cultural Configurations: How Do They Affect Subsidiaries' Knowledge Sharing Behaviours?' *Journal of Knowledge Management*, 19/2: 141–63.

Cavaliere, V., Lombardi, S., and Giustiniano, L. (2015). 'Knowledge Sharing in Knowledge-Intensive Manufacturing Firms: An Empirical Study of its Enablers', *Journal of Knowledge Management*, 19/6: 1124–45.

Cegarra-Navarro, J-G., Wensley, A., and Sanchez-Polo, M-T. (2010). 'An Application of the Hospital-in-the-Home Unlearning Context', *Social Work and Healthcare*, 49: 895–918.

Cegarra-Navarro, J-G., Sánchez-Vidal, M., and Cegarra-Leiva, D. (2011). 'Balancing Exploration and Exploitation of Knowledge Through an Unlearning Context: An Empirical Investigation in SMEs', *Management Decision*, 49/7: 1099–119.

Cegarra-Navarro, J-G., Eldridge, S., and Sanchez, A. (2012). 'How an Unlearning Context Can Help Managers Overcome the Negative Effects of Counter-Knowledge', *Journal of Management and Organization*, 18/2: 981–1005.

Cegarra-Navarro, J-G., Martinez-Martinez, A., Gutierrex, J. O., and Rodriguez, A. L. L. (2013). 'Environmental Knowledge, Unlearning, and Performance in Hospitality Companies', *Management Decision*, 51/2: 341–60.

Cerchione, R., and Esposito, E. (2017). 'Using Knowledge Management Systems: A Taxonomy of SME Strategies', *International Journal of Information Management*, 37/1: 1551–62.

Cha, H., Pingry, D., and Thatcher, M. (2008). 'Managing the Knowledge Supply Chain: An Organizational Learning Model of Information Technology Offshore Outsourcing', *MIS Quarterly*, 32/2: 281–305.

Chang, C., and Lin, T-C. (2015). 'The Role of Organizational Culture in the Knowledge Management Process', *Journal of Knowledge Management*, 19/3: 433–55.

Chang, S., and Lee, M. (2007). 'The Effects of Organizational Culture and Knowledge Management Mechanisms on Organizational Innovation: An Empirical Study in Taiwan', *The Business Review*, 7/1: 295–301.

Chang, Y., Gong, Y., and Peng, M. W. (2012). 'Expatriate Knowledge Transfer, Subsidiary Absorptive Capacity, and Subsidiary Performance', *Academy of Management Journal*, 55: 927–48.

Chang Lee, K., Lee, S., and Kang, I. W. (2005). 'KMPI: Measuring Knowledge Management Performance', *Information and Management*, 42(3): 469–82.

Chen, J., Sun, P., and McQueen, R. (2010). 'The Impact of National Culture on Structured Knowledge Transfer', *Journal of Knowledge Management*, 14/2: 228–42.

Chen, W-Y., Hsu, B-F., and Lin, Y-Y. (2011a). 'Fostering Knowledge Sharing Through Human Resource Management in R&D Teams', *International Journal of Technology Management*, 53/2-3-4: 309–30.

Chen, Z., Zhang, X., and Vogel, D. (2011b). 'Exploring the Underlying Processes Between Conflict and Knowledge Sharing: A Work-Engagement Perspective', *Journal of Applied Social Psychology*, 41/5: 1005–33.

Chesbrough, H. W. (2003). 'The Era of Open Innovation', *MIT Sloan Management Review*, 44/3: 35–41.

Cheung, C. F., Li, M. L., Shek, W. Y., Lee, W. B., and Tsang, T. S. (2007). 'A Systematic Approach for Knowledge Auditing: A Case Study in Transportation Sector', *Journal of Knowledge Management*, 11/4: 140–58.

Cheung, S., Gong, Y., Wang, M., Zhou, L., and Shi, J. (2016). 'When and How Does Functional Diversity Influence Team Innovation? The Mediating Role of Knowledge Sharing and the Moderation Role of Affect-Based Trust in a Team', *Human Relations*, 69/7: 1507–31.

Child, J. (2001). 'Learning Through Strategic Alliances', in M. Dierkes, A. Bertoin Antal, J. Child, and I. Nonaka (eds), *Handbook of Organizational Learning and*

Knowledge, Oxford: Oxford University Press, pp. 657–80.

Chiravuri, A., Nazareth, D., and Ramamurthy, K. (2011). 'Cognitive Conflict and Consensus Generation in Virtual Teams During Knowledge Capture: Comparative Effectiveness of Techniques', *Journal of Management Information Systems*, 28/1: 311–50.

Chiva, R., and Allegre, J. (2005). 'Organizational Learning and Organizational Knowledge: Towards the Integration of Two Approaches', *Management Learning*, 36/1: 49–68.

Choi, S., Lee, H., and Yoo, Y. (2010). 'The Impact of Information Technology and Transactive Memory Systems on Knowledge Sharing, Application and Team Performance: A Field Study', *MIS Quarterly*, 34/4: 855–70.

Chua, A. (2006). 'The Rise and Fall of a Community of Practice: A Descriptive Case Study', *Knowledge and Process Management*, 13/2: 120–8.

Coakes, E., Amar, A., and Grandos, M. (2010). 'Knowledge Management, Strategy, and Technology: A Global Snapshot', *Journal of Enterprise Information Management*, 23/3: 282–304.

Cohen, W., and Levinthal, D. (1990). 'Absorptive Capacity—A New Perspective on Learning and Innovation', *Administrative Science Quarterly*, 35/1: 128–52.

Collins, H. (2007). 'Bicycling on the Moon: Collective Tacit Knowledge and Somatic-Limit Tacit Knowledge', *Organization Studies*, 28/2: 257–62.

Conner, K. R., and Prahalad, C. K. (1996). 'A Resource-Based Theory of the Firm: Knowledge versus Opportunism', *Organization Science*, 7/5: 477–501.

Contu, A., and Willmott, H. (2003). 'Re-embedding Situatedness: The Importance of Power Relations in Learning Theory', *Organization Science*, 14/3: 283–96.

Contu, A., Grey, C., and Örtenblad, A. (2003). 'Against Learning', *Human Relations*, 56/8: 931–52.

Cook, S., and Brown, J. (1999). 'Bridging Epistemologies: The Generative Dance Between Organizational Knowledge and Organizational Knowing', *Organization Science*, 10/4: 381–400.

Cook, S., and Yanow, D. (1993). 'Culture and Organizational Learning', *Journal of Management Enquiry*, 2/4: 373–90.

Coopey, J. (1995). 'The Learning Organization, Power, Politics and Ideology', *Management Learning*, 26/2: 193–213.

Coopey, J. (1998). 'Learning the Trust and Trusting to Learn: A Role for Radical Theatre', *Management Learning*, 29/3: 365–82.

Coopey, J., and Burgoyne, J. (2000). 'Politics and Organizational Learning', *Journal of Management Studies*, 37/6: 869–85.

Corradi, A., Heinzen, M., and Boutelier, R. (2015). 'Designing Workspaces for Cross Functional Knowledge Sharing in R&D: The "Co-location Pilot" of Novartis', *Journal of Knowledge Management*, 19/2: 236–56.

Corradi, G., Gherardi, S., and Verzelloni, L. (2010). 'Through the Practice Lens: Where is the Bandwagon of Practice-Based Studies Heading?', *Management Learning*, 41/3: 265–83.

Costa, V., and Monteiro, S. (2016). 'Knowledge Processes, Absorptive Capacity and Innovation: A Mediation Analysis', *Knowledge and Process Management*, 23/3: 207–18.

Cranefield, J., Yoong, P., and Huff, S. L. (2015). 'Rethinking Lurking: Invisible Leading and Following in a Knowledge Transfer Ecosystem', *Journal of the Association for Information Systems*, 16/4: 213–47.

Cross, R., Borgatti, S. P., and Parker, A. (2001). 'Beyond Answers: Dimensions of the Advice Network', *Social Networks*, 23/3: 215–35.

Cross, R., Parker, A., Prusak, L., and Borgatti, S. P. (2001). 'Knowing What We Know: Supporting Knowledge Creation and Sharing in Social Networks', *Organizational Dynamics*, 30/2: 100–20.

Crossan, M., and Apaydin, M. (2010). 'A Multidimensional Framework of Organizational Innovation: A Systemic Review of the Literature', *Journal of Management Studies*, 47/6: 1154–91.

Crossan, M., Lane, H., and White, R. (1999). 'An Organizational Learning Framework: From Intuition to Institution', *Academy of Management Review*, 24/3: 522–37.

Crossan, M., Maurer, C., and White, R. (2011). 'Reflections on the 2009 AMR Decade Award: Do We Have a Theory of Organizational Learning?', *Academy of Management Review*, 36/3: 446–60.

Cruz, N., Pérez, V., and Cantero, C. (2009). 'The Influence of Employee Motivation on Knowledge Transfer', *Journal of Knowledge Management*, 13/6: 478–90.

Cuervo-Cazurra, A., and Un, A. (2010). 'Why Some Firms Never Invest in Formal R&D', *Strategic Management Journal*, 31: 759–79.

Currie, G., and Kerrin, M. (2003). 'Human Resource Management and Knowledge Management: Enhancing Knowledge Sharing in a Pharmaceutical Company', *International Journal of Human Resource Management*, 14/6: 1027–45.

Currie, G., and Kerrin, M. (2004). 'The Limits of a Technological Fix to Knowledge Management', *Management Learning*, 35/1: 9–29.

Currie, G., Waring, J., and Finn, R. (2008). 'The Limits of Knowledge Management for UK Public Services Modernization: The Case of Patient Safety and Service Quality', *Public Administration*, 86/2: 363–85.

Cutcher-Gershenfeld, J., Nitta, M., and Barrett, B. (1998). *Knowledge-Driven Work*. Oxford: Oxford University Press.

Cyert, R., and March, J. (1963). *A Behavioural Theory of the Firm*. Englewood Cliffs, NJ: Prentice Hall.

Dahl, R. (1957). 'The Concept of Power', *Behavioural Scientist*, 2: 201–15.

Dalkir, K. (2005). *Knowledge Management in Theory and Practice*. Oxford: Elsevier Butterworth Heineman.

Davenport, T. H. (1993). *Process Innovation: Reengineering Work Through Information Technology*. Boston, MA: Harvard Business Press, Addison-Wesley.

Davenport, T. H. (2005). *Thinking for a Living: How to Get Better Performance and Results from Knowledge Workers*. Boston, MA: Harvard Business School Press, Addison-Wesley.

Davenport, T. H., and Prusak, L. (1998). *Working Knowledge: How Organizations Manage What They Know*. Boston, MA: Harvard Business Press.

Davenport, T. H., De Long, D. W., and Beers, M. C. (1998). 'Successful Knowledge Management Projects', *Sloan Management Review*, 39/2: 43.

Dawes, S., Cresswell, A., and Pardo, T. (2009). 'From "Need to Know" to "Need to Share": Tangled Problems, Information Boundaries, and the Building of Public Sector Knowledge Management Networks', *Public Administration Review*, 69/3: 392–402.

Deetz, S. (1998). 'Discursive Formations, Strategized Subordination and Self-Surveillance', in A. McKinlay and K. Starkey (eds), *Foucault, Management and Organization Theory*. London: Sage, pp. 151–72.

DeFillippi, R., Arthur, M., and Lindsay, V. (2006). *Knowledge at Work: Creative Collaboration in the Global Economy*. London: Blackwell.

De Holan, P., and Phillips, N. (2004). 'Remembrance of Things Past? The Dynamics of Organizational Forgetting', *Management Science*, 50/11: 1603–13.

De Long, D., and Fahey, L. (2000). 'Diagnosing Cultural Barriers to Knowledge Management', *Academy of Management Executive*, 14/4: 113–27.

Denford, J. S., and Chan, Y. E. (2011). 'Knowledge Strategy Typologies: Defining Dimensions and Relationships', *Knowledge Management Research and Practice*, 9/2: 102–19.

Densten, I. (2008). 'Leadership: Current Assessment and Future Needs', in S. Cartwright and C. Cooper (eds), *The Oxford Handbook of Personnel Psychology*. Oxford: Oxford University Press.

Dixon, B., McGowan, J., and Cravens, G. (2009). 'Knowledge-Sharing Using Codification and Collaboration Technologies to Improve Health Care: Lessons from the Public Sector', *Knowledge Management Research and Practice*, 7: 249–59.

Donate, M., and Guadamillas, F. (2010). 'The Effect of Organizational Culture on Knowledge Management Practices and Innovation', *Knowledge and Process Management*, 17/2: 82–94.

Dovey, K. (1997). 'The Learning Organization and the Organization of Learning: Learning, Power, Transformation and the Search for Form in Learning Organizations', *Management Learning*, 28/3: 331–49.

Driver, M. (2002). 'The Learning Organization: Foucauldian Gloom or Utopian Sunshine?', *Human Relations*, 55/1: 33–53.

Drucker, P. (1999). 'Knowledge-Worker Productivity: The Biggest Challenge', *California Management Review*, 41/2: 79–94.

Duda, R., Gaschnig, J., and Hart, P. (1979). 'Model Design in the Prospector Consultant System for Mineral Exploration', *Expert Systems in the Microelectronic Age*, 1234: 153–67.

Dul, J., Ceylan, C., and Jaspers, F. (2011). 'Knowledge Workers' Creativity and the Role of the Physical Work Environment', *Human Resource Management*, 50/6: 715–34.

du Plessis, M. (2008). 'What Bars Organisations from Managing Knowledge Successfully?', *International Journal of Information Management*, 28: 285–92.

Durcikova, A., and Gray, P. (2009). 'How Knowledge Validation Processes Affect Knowledge Contribution', *Journal of Management Information Systems*, 25/4: 81–107.

Dyer, J., and Nobeoka, K. (2000). 'Creating and Managing a High-Performance Knowledge-Sharing Network: The Toyota Case', *Strategic Management Journal*, 21/3: 345–67.

Earl, M. (2001). 'Knowledge Management Strategies: Towards a Taxonomy', *Journal of Management Information Systems*, 18/1: 215–33.

Easterby-Smith, M. (1997). 'Disciplines of Organizational Learning: Contributions and Critique', *Human Relations*, 50/9: 1085–113.

Easterby-Smith, M., and Lyles, M. (2011). 'In Praise of Organizational Forgetting', *Journal of Management Inquiry*, 20/3: 311–16.

Easterby-Smith, M., and Lyles, M. (2015). *Handbook of Organizational Learning and Knowledge Management*. London: John Wiley.

Easterby-Smith, M., Crossan, M., and Nicolini, D. (2000). 'Organizational Learning: Debates Past, Present and Future', *Journal of Management Studies*, 37/6: 783–96.

Easterby-Smith, M., Lyles, A., and Tsang, E. (2008). 'Inter-Organizational Knowledge Transfer: Current Themes and Future Prospects', *Journal of Management Studies*, 45/4: 677–90.

Ebbers, J., and Wijnberg, M. (2009). 'Organizational Memory: From Expectations Memory to Procedural Memory', *British Journal of Management*, 20: 478–90.

Ebner, W., Leimeister, J. M., and Krcmar, H. (2009). 'Community Engineering for Innovations: The Ideas Competition as a Method to Nurture a Virtual Community for Innovations', *R&D Management*, 39/4: 342–56.

Eckardt, R., Skaggs, B., and Youndt, M. (2014). 'Turnover and Knowledge Loss: An Examination of the Differential Impact of Production Manager and Worker Turnover in Service and Manufacturing Firms', *Journal of Management Studies*, 51/7: 1025–57.

Eisenberg, H. (1997). 'Reengineering and Dumbsizing: Mismanagement of the Knowledge Resource', *Quality Progress*, 30/5: 57.

Elias, P., and Gregory, M. (1994). *The Changing Structure of Occupations and Earnings in Great Britain 1975–1990: An Analysis Based on the New Earnings*. Warwick: Institute for Employment Relations.

Elkin, G., Zhang, H., and Cone, M. (2011). 'The Acceptance of Senge's Learning Organization Model among Managers in China: An Interview Study', *International Journal of Management*, 28/4: 354–64.

Ellison, N. B., Gibbs, J. L., and Weber, M. S. (2015). 'The Use of Enterprise Social Network Sites for Knowledge Sharing in Distributed Organizations: The Role of Organizational Affordances', *American Behavioral Scientist*, 59/1: 103–23.

Empson, L. (2001). 'Fear of Exploitation and Fear of Contamination: Impediments to Knowledge Transfer in Mergers between Professional Service Firms', *Human Relations*, 54/7: 839–62.

Erickson, G. S., and Rothberg, H. N. (2009). 'Knowledge Asset Potential vs. Vulnerability: Balancing Risks', *Electronic Journal of Knowledge Management*, 7/5: 559–66.

Erickson, S., and Rothberg, H. (2010). 'Strategic Knowledge Management in a Low Risk Environment', *Proceedings of the European Conference on Knowledge Management*. London: ECKM, pp. 369–74.

Ertug, G., Cuypers, I., Noorderhaven, N. G., and Bensaou, B. (2013). 'Trust Between International Joint Venture Partners: Effects of Home Countries', *Journal of International Business Studies*, 44/3: 263–82.

Evans, J., Hendron, M., and Oldroyd, J. (2015). 'Withholding the Ace: The Individual- and Unit-Level Performance Effects of Self-Reported and Perceived Knowledge Hoarding', *Organization Science*, 26/2: 494–510.

Fadel, K. J., and Durcikova, A. (2014). 'If It's Fair, I'll Share: The Effect of Perceived Knowledge Validation Justice on Contributions to an Organizational Knowledge Repository', *Information and Management*, 51: 511–19.

Fahey, R., Vasconcelos, A., and Ellis, D. (2007). 'The Impact of Rewards Within Communities of Practice: A Study of the SAP Online Global Community', *Knowledge Management Research and Practice*, 5/3: 186–98.

Falkowski, T., and Bartelheimer, J. (2005). 'Applying Social Network Analysis Methods to Explore Community Dynamics', *Applications of Social Network Analysis*, 189: V212.

Faraj, S., and Johnson, S. (2011). 'Network Exchange Patterns in Online Communities', *Organization Science*, 22/6: 1464–80.

Faraj, S., Jarvenpaa, S., and Majchrzak, A. (2011). 'Knowledge Collaboration in Online Communities', *Organization Science*, 22/5: 1224–39.

Farndale, E., Van Ruiten, J., Kelliher, C., and Hope-Hailey, V. (2011). 'The Influence of Perceived Employee Voice on Organizational Commitment: An Exchange Perspective', *Human Resource Management*, 50/1: 113–29.

Fayyad, U., Piatetsky-Shapiro, G., and Smyth, P. (1996). 'From Data Mining to Knowledge Discovery in Databases', *AI Magazine*, 17/3: 37.

Feller, J., Finnegan, P., Hayes, J., and O'Reilly, P. (2012). '"Orchestrating" Sustainable Crowdsourcing: A Characterisation of Solver Brokerages', *The Journal of Strategic Information Systems*, 21/3: 216–32.

Felstead, A., Ashton, D., and Green, F. (2000). 'Are Britain's Workplace Skills Becoming More Unequal?', *Cambridge Journal of Economics*, 24/6: 709–27.

Fenton, E. (2007). 'Visualizing Strategic Change: The Role and Impact of Process Maps as Boundary Objects in Reorganization', *European Management Journal*, 25/2: 104–17.

Ferguson, J. E., and Taminiau, Y. (2014). 'Conflict and Learning in Inter-organizational Online Communities: Negotiating Knowledge Claims', *Journal of Knowledge Management*, 18/5: 886–904.

Fischer, M., Dopson, S., Fitzgerald, L., Bennett, C., Ferlie, E., Ledger, J., and McGivern, G. (2016). 'Knowledge Leadership: Mobilising Management Research by Becoming the Knowledge Object', *Human Relations*, 69/7: 1563–85.

Fisher, D., Smith, M., and Welser, H. T. (2006). 'You Are Who You Talk To: Detecting Roles in Usenet Newsgroups', *Proceedings of the 39th Annual Hawaii International Conference on Systems Sciences*. New York: IEEE publishing.

Fleming, P., Harley, B., and Sewell, G. (2004). 'A Little Knowledge is a Dangerous Thing: Getting Below the Surface of the Growth of "Knowledge Work" in Australia', *Work, Employment and Society*, 18/4: 725–47.

Flinchbaugh, C., Li, P., Luth, M., and Chadwick, C. (2016). 'Team-Level High Involvement Work Practices: Investigating the Role of Knowledge Sharing and Perspective Taking', *Human Resource Management Journal*, 26/2: 134–50.

Flood, P., Turner, T., and Hannaway, C. (2000). *Attracting and Retaining Knowledge Employees: Irish Knowledge Employees and the Psychological Contract*. Dublin: Blackhall.

Flood, P., Turner, T., Ramamoorthy, N., and Pearson, J. (2001). 'Causes and Consequences of Psychological Contracts Among Knowledge Workers in the High Technology and Financial Services Industry', *International Journal of Human Resource Management*, 12/7: 1152–65.

Foray, D. (2004). *Economics of Knowledge*. Cambridge, MA: MIT Press.

Fosstenløkken, S., Løwendahl, B., and Revang, Ø. (2003). 'Knowledge Development Through Client Interaction: A Comparative Study', *Organization Studies*, 24/6: 859–80.

Foucault, M. (1979). *Discipline and Punishment*. Harmondsworth: Penguin.

Foucault, M. (1980). *Power/Knowledge: Selected Interviews and Other Writings 1972–1977*. London: Harvester Wheatsheaf.

Fox, A. (1985). *Beyond Contract: Work, Power and Trust Relations*. London: Faber.

Fox, S. (2000). 'Practice, Foucault and Actor-Network Theory', *Journal of Management Studies*, 37/6: 853–68.

Frank, A., Ribeiro, J., and Echeveste, M. (2015). 'Factors Influencing Knowledge Transfer between NPD Teams: A Taxonomic Analysis Based on a Sociotechnical Approach', *R&D Management*, 45/1: 1–22.

French, J., and Raven, B. (1959). 'The Bases of Social Power', in D. Cartwright (ed.), *Studies in Social Power*. Ann Arbor: University of Michigan, pp. 150–67.

Frenkel, S., Korczynski, M., Donohue, L., and Shire, K. (1995). 'Re-constituting Work: Trends Towards Knowledge Work and Info-normative Control', *Work, Employment and Society*, 9/4: 773–96.

Friedman, V., Lipshitz, R., and Overmeer, W. (2001). 'Creating Conditions for Organizational Learning', in M. Dierkes, A. Bertoin Antal, J. Child, and I. Nonaka (eds), *Handbook of Organizational Learning and Knowledge*. Oxford: Oxford University Press, pp. 757–74.

Füller, J., Jawecki, G., and Mühlbacher, H. (2007). 'Innovation Creation by Online Basketball Communities', *Journal of Business Research*, 60/1: 60–71.

Gallaugher, J., and Ransbotham, S. (2010). 'Social Media and Customer Dialog Management at Starbucks', *MIS Quarterly Executive*, 9/4: 197–212

Gallie, D., White, M., Cheng, Y., and Tomlinson, M. (1998). *Restructuring the Employment Relationship*. Oxford: Clarendon Press.

Garud, R., and Kumaraswamy, A. (2005). 'Vicious and Virtuous Circles in the Management of Knowledge: The Case of Infosys Technologies', *MIS Quarterly*, 29/1: 9–33.

Garvey, B., and Williamson, B. (2002). *Beyond Knowledge Management: Dialogue, Creativity and the Corporate Curriculum*. Harlow: Financial Times/Prentice Hall.

Geertz, C. (1973). *The Interpretation of Cultures*. New York: Basic Books.

Gherardi, S. (2006). *Organizational Knowledge: The Texture of Workplace Learning*. Oxford: Blackwell.

Gherardi, S. (2009). 'Practice? It's a Matter of Taste!', *Management Learning*, 40/5: 535–50.

Gherardi, S., and Nicolini, D. (2002). 'Learning in a Constellation of Interconnected Practices: Canon or Dissonance?', *Journal of Management Studies*, 39/4: 419–36.

Gherardi, S., and Rodeschini, G. (2016). 'Caring as Collective Knowledgeable Doing: About Concern and Being Concerned', *Management Learning*, 47/3: 266–84.

Gherardi, S. and Strati, A. (2012). *Learning and Knowing in Practice-Based Studies*. Cheltenham: Edward Elgar.

Ghezzi, A., Gabelloni, D., Martini, A., and Natalicchio, A. (2017). 'Crowdsourcing: A Review and Suggestions for Future Research', *International Journal of Management Reviews*, from: http://onlinelibrary.wiley.com/doi/10.1111/ijmr.12135/abstract (accessed 15 June 2017).

Giauque, D., Resenterra, F., and Siggen, M. (2010). 'The Relationship Between HRM Practices and Organizational Commitment of Knowledge Workers. Facts Obtained from Swiss SMEs', *Human Resource Development International*, 13/3: 185–205.

Giboney, J. S., Brown, S. A., Lowry, P. B., and Nunamaker, J. F. (2015). 'User Acceptance of Knowledge-Based System Recommendations: Explanations, Arguments, and Fit', *Decision Support Systems*, 72: 1–10.

Gibson, C., and Birkinshaw, J. (2004). 'The Antecedents, Consequences, and Mediating Role of Organizational Ambidexterity', *Academy of Management Journal*, 47/2: 209–26.

Giddens, A. (1979). *Central Problems in Social Theory*. London: Macmillan.

Giddens, A. (1991). *Modernity and Self Identity: Self and Society in the Late Modern Age*. Cambridge: Polity Press.

Gilbert, E., Morabito, J., and Stohr, E. (2010). 'Knowledge Sharing and Decision Making in the Peace Corps', *Knowledge and Process Management*, 17/3: 128–44.

Gittelman, M., and Kogut, B. (2003). 'Does Good Science Lead to Valuable Knowledge? Biotechnology Firms and the Evolutionary Logic of Citation Patterns', *Management Science*, 49/4: 366–82.

Glazer, R. (1998). 'Measuring the Knower: Towards a Theory of Knowledge Equity', *California Management Review*, 40/3: 175–94.

Glisby, M., and Holden, N. (2003). 'Contextual Constraints in Knowledge Management Theory: The Cultural Embeddedness of Nonaka's Knowledge Creating Company', *Knowledge and Process Management*, 10/1: 29–36.

Goles, T., and Hirschheim, R. (2000). 'The Paradigm is Dead, the Paradigm is Dead . . . Long Live the Paradigm: The Legacy of Burrell and Morgan', *Omega*, 28/3: 249–68.

Goodall, K., and Roberts, J. (2003). 'Only Connect: Teamwork in the Multinational', *Journal of World Business*, 38/2: 150–64.

Gourlay, S. (2006). 'Conceptualizing Knowledge Creation: A Critique of Nonaka's Theory', *Journal of Management Studies*, 43/7: 1415–36.

Graham, A. B., and Pizzo, V. G. (1996). 'A Question of Balance: Case Studies in Strategic Knowledge Management', *European Management Journal*, 14/4: 338–46.

Grahle, C., and Hibbert, P. (2016). 'Everyday Creative Development Practices in Advertising', in K. Orr, S. Nutley, S. Russell, R. Bain, B. Hacking, and C. Moran (eds), *Knowledge and Practice in Business and Organizations*. London: Routledge, pp. 103–15.

Granovetter, M. (1973). 'The Strength of Weak Ties', *The American Journal of Sociology*, 78/6: 1360–80.

Grant, R. (1996). 'Towards a Knowledge Based Theory of the Firm', *Strategic Management Journal*, 17/Winter Special Issue: 109–22.

Grant, R. (2000). 'Shifts in the World Economy: The Drivers of Knowledge Management', in C. Despres and D. Chauvel (eds), *Knowledge Horizons: The Present and the Promise of Knowledge Management*. Oxford: Butterworth-Heinemann, pp. 27–54.

Gray, P., and Durcikova, A. (2005–6). 'The Role of Knowledge Repositories in Technical Support Environments: Speed versus Learning in User Performance', *Journal of Management Information Systems*, 22/3: 159–90.

Griffiths, D., and Moon, B. (2011). 'The State of Knowledge Management: A Survey Suggests Ways to Attain More Satisfied Users', *KM World*, 29 October, 20/10, http://www.kmworld.com/Articles/Editorial/Features/The-state-of-knowledge-management-A-survey-suggests-ways-to-attain-more-satisfied-users.-78481.aspx?PageNum=2 (accessed 29 October 2017).

Grimshaw, D., and Miozzo, M. (2009). 'New Human Resource Management Practices in Knowledge-Intensive Business Service Firms: The Case of Outsourcing with Staff Transfer', *Human Relations*, 62/10: 1521–50.

Güldenberg, S., and Helting, H. (2007). 'Bridging "The Great Divide": Nonaka's Synthesis of "Western" and "Eastern" Knowledge Concepts Reassessed', *Organization*, 14/1: 101–22.

Güldenberg, S., and Konrath, H. (2006). 'Bridging Leadership and Learning in Knowledge-based Organizations', in B. Renzl, K. Matzler, and H. Hinterhuber (eds), *The Future of Knowledge Management*. Basingstoke: Palgrave Macmillan, pp. 219–36.

Haas, A. (2015). 'Crowding at the Frontier: Boundary Spanners, Gatekeepers and Knowledge Brokers', *Journal of Knowledge Management*, 19/5: 1029–47.

Haas, M., and Hansen, M. (2007). 'Different Knowledge, Different Benefits: Towards a Productivity Perspective on Knowledge Sharing in Organizations', *Strategic Management Journal*, 28: 1133–53.

Hacker, J. (2017). 'Enterprise Social Networks—Platforms for Enabling and Understanding Knowledge Work?', in R. W. Helms, J. Cranefield, and J. van Reijsen (eds), *Social Knowledge Management in Action: Applications and Challenges*. Amsterdam: Springer International Publishing, pp. 17–37.

Hagel, J., and Armstrong, A. (1997). *Net Gain: Expanding Markets Through Virtual Communities*. Boston, MA: Harvard Business School Press.

Hales, C. (1993). *Managing Through Organization: The Management Process, Forms of Organisation and the Work of Managers*. London: Routledge.

Halme, K., Lindy, I., Piirainen, K. A., Salminen, V., and White, J. (2014). *Finland as a Knowledge Economy 2.0: Lessons on Policies and Governance. Directions in Development-Science, Technology, and Innovation*. Washington, DC: World Bank.

Han, T-S., Chiang, H-H., and Chang, A. (2010). 'Employee Participation in Decision Making, Psychological Ownership and Knowledge Sharing: Mediating Role of Organizational Commitment in Taiwanese High-Tech Organizations', *International Journal of Human Resource Management*, 21/12: 2218–33.

Handley, K., Sturdy, A., Fincham, R., and Clark, T. (2006). 'Within and Beyond Communities of Practice: Making Sense of Learning through Participation, Identity and Practice', *Journal of Management Studies*, 43/3: 641–53.

Hanneman, R., and Riddle, M. (2005). 'Introduction to Social Network Analysis', http://faculty.ucr.edu/~hanneman/nettext/ (accessed 3 November 2016).

Hansen, M. T. (2002). 'Knowledge Networks: Explaining Effective Knowledge Sharing in Multiunit Companies', *Organization Science*, 13/3: 232–48.

Hansen, M., Nohria, N., and Tierney, T. (1999), 'What's Your Strategy for Managing Knowledge?', *Harvard Business Review*, 77/2: 106.

Harris, L. C., and Ogbonna, E. O. (2002). 'The Unintended Consequences of Culture Interventions: A Study of Unexpected Outcomes', *British Journal of Management*, 13/1: 31–49.

Harrison, R., and Kessels, J. (2004). *Human Resource Development in a Knowledge Economy*. Basingstoke: Palgrave MacMillan.

Harrison, R., and Leitch, C. (2000). 'Learning and Organization in the Knowledge-Based Information Economy: Initial Findings from a Participatory Action Research Case Study', *British Journal of Management*, 11/2: 103–19.

Harryson, S., Dudkowski, R., and Stern, A. (2008). 'Transformation Networks in Innovation Alliances—The Development of Volvo C70', *Journal of Management Studies*, 45/4: 745–73.

Hartmann, A., and Doreé, A. (2015). 'Learning Between Projects: More than Sending Messages in a Bottle', *International Journal of Project Management*, 33/2: 341–51.

Harzing, A-W., Pudelko, M., and Reiche, S. (2016). 'The Bridging Role of Expatriates and Inpatriates in Knowledge Transfer in Multinational Corporations', *Human Resource Management*, 55/4: 679–95.

Hau, Y., Kim, B., and Lee, H. (2016). 'What Drives Employees to Share their Tacit Knowledge in Practice?', *Knowledge Management Research and Practice*, 14/3: 295–308.

Hayes, J. (2002). *The Theory and Practice of Change Management*. Basingstoke: Palgrave.

Hayes, N., and Walsham, G. (2000). 'Safe Enclaves, Political Enclaves and Knowledge Working', in C. Prichard, R. Hull, M. Chumer, and H. Willmott (eds), *Managing Knowledge: Critical Investigations of Work and Learning*. London: Macmillan.

He, Y., Lai, K., and Lu, Y. (2011). 'Linking Organizational Support to Employee Commitment: Evidence from Hotel Industry in China', *International Journal of Human Resource Management*, 22/1: 197–217.

He, Z., and Wong, P. (2004). 'Exploration vs. Exploitation: An Empirical Test of the Ambidexterity Hypothesis', *Organization Science*, 15/4: 481–94.

He, Z-L. and Wong, P-K. (2009). 'Knowledge Interaction with Manufacturing Clients and Innovation of Knowledge-Intensive Business Services Firms', *Innovation: Management, Policy and Practice*, 11/3: 264–78.

Hecker, A. (2012). 'Knowledge Beyond the Individual? Making Sense of a Notion of Collective Knowledge in Organization Theory', *Organization Studies*, 33/3: 423–45.

Heisig, P. (2009). 'Harmonisation of Knowledge Management—Comparing 160 KM Frameworks Around the Globe', *Journal of Knowledge Management*, 13/4: 4–31.

Heisig, P., Suraj, O., Kianto, A., Kemboi, C., Arrau, G., and Easa, N. (2016). 'Knowledge Management and Business Performance: Global Experts' Views on Future Research Needs', *Journal of Knowledge Management*, 20/6: 1169–98.

Heizmann, H. (2011). 'Knowledge Sharing in a Dispersed Network of HR Practice: Zooming in on Power/Knowledge Struggles', *Management Learning*, 42/4: 379–93.

Heizmann, H., and Olsson, M. (2015). 'Power Matters: The Importance of Foucault's Power/Knowledge as a Conceptual Lens in KM Research and Practice', *Journal of Knowledge Management*, 14/9: 756–69.

Helms, R. W. (2007). 'Redesigning Communities of Practice Using Knowledge Network Analysis', in A. S. Kazi, L. Wohlfart, and P. Wolf (eds), *Hands-On Knowledge Co-Creation and Sharing: Practical Methods and Techniques*. London: Knowledgeboard, pp. 251–74.

Helms, R. W. (2013). 'Social Network Services', in D. Straub and R. Welke (eds), *Wiley Encyclopedia of Management* (3rd edn). West Sussex: John Wiley and Sons Ltd.

Helms, R. W., and Booij, E. (2012). 'Reaching Out: Involving Users in Innovation Tasks through Social Media', *Proceedings of the 20th European Conference in Information Systems*. Barcelona: ECIS, paper 193.

Helms, R. W., and Buysrogge, C. M. (2006). 'Application of Knowledge Network Analysis to Identify Knowledge Sharing Bottlenecks at an Engineering Firm', in J. Ljungberg and M. Andersson (eds), *Proceedings of the 14th European Conference on Information Systems*. Gothenburg: ECIS.

Helms, R. W., and Werder, K. (2013). 'Who Reads Corporate Tweets? Network Analysis of Follower Communities', *Proceedings of the 19th Americas Conference on Information Systems*. Chicago, IL: AIS Library.

Helms, R. W., Diemer, D., and Lichtenstein, S. (2011). 'Exploring Barriers in Expertise Seeking: Why Don't They Ask an Expert?', *Proceedings of the 15th Pacific Asia Conference on Information Systems*. Brisbane: ECIS, paper 77.

Helms, R. W., Cranefield, J., and van Reijsen, J. (2017). *Social Knowledge Management in Action—Applications and Challenges*. Amsterdam: Springer International Publishing.

Hemetsberger, A., and Reinhardt, C. (2006). 'Learning and Knowledge-Building in Open-Source Communities: A Social-Experiential Approach', *Management Learning*, 37/2: 187–214.

Henttonen, K., Kianto, A., and Ritala, P. (2016). 'Knowledge Sharing and Individual Work Performance: An Empirical Study of a Public Sector Organisation', *Journal of Knowledge Management*, 20/4: 749–68.

Hindmarsh, J., and Pilnick, A. (2007). 'Knowing Bodies at Work: Embodiment and Ephemeral Teamwork in Anaesthesia', *Organization Studies*, 28/9: 1395–416.

Hinterhuber, H., and Stadler, C. (2006). 'Leadership and Strategy as Intangible Assets', in B. Renzl, K. Matzler, and H. Hinterhuber (eds), *The Future of Knowledge Management*. Basingstoke: Palgrave Macmillan, pp. 237–53.

Hislop, D. (2002a). 'Linking Human Resource Management and Knowledge Management: A Review and Research Agenda', *Employee Relations*, 25/2: 182–202.

Hislop, D. (2002b). 'Mission Impossible? Communicating and Sharing Knowledge via Information Technology', *Journal of Information Technology*, 17/3: 165–77.

Hislop, D. (2003). 'The Complex Relationship Between Communities of Practice and the Implementation of Technological Innovations', *International Journal of Innovation Management*, 7/2: 163–88.

Hislop, D. (2008). 'Conceptualizing Knowledge Work Utilizing Skill and Knowledge-Based Concepts: The Case of Some Consultants and Service Engineers', *Management Learning*, 39/5: 579–97.

Hislop, D. (2010). 'Knowledge Management as an Ephemeral Management Fashion?', *Journal of Knowledge Management*, 14/6: 779–90.

Hislop, D., Newell, S., Scarbrough, H., and Swan, J. (2000). 'Networks, Knowledge and Power: Decision Making, Politics and the Process of Innovation', *Technology Analysis and Strategic Management*, 12/3: 399–411.

Holsapple, C. W. (2005). 'The Inseparability of Modern Knowledge Management and Computer-Based Technology', *Journal of Knowledge Management*, 9/1: 42–52.

Holste, J., and Fields, D. (2010). 'Trust and Tacit Knowledge Sharing and Use', *Journal of Knowledge Management*, 14/1: 128–40.

Holten, A-M., Hancock, G., Perrson, R., Hansen, Å., and Høgh, A. (2016). 'Knowledge Hoarding: Antecedent or Consequent of Negative Acts? The Mediating Role of Trust and Justice', *Journal of Knowledge Management*, 20/2: 215–29.

Hong, J. (2012). 'Glocalizing Nonaka's Knowledge Creation Model: Issues and Challenges', *Management Learning*, 43/2: 199–215.

Hong, F., and Snell, R. (2008). 'Power Inequality in Cross-Cultural Learning: The Case of Japanese Transplants in China', *Asia Pacific Business Review*, 14/2: 253–73.

Hong, J., Heikkinen, J., and Blomqvist, K. (2010). 'Culture and Knowledge Co-creation in R&D Collaboration between MNCs and Chinese Universities', *Knowledge and Process Management*, 17/2: 62–73.

Hong, J. F. L., Snell, R. S., and Mak, C. (2016). 'Knowledge Assimilation at Foreign Subsidiaries of Japanese MNCs through Political Sensegiving and Sensemaking', *Organization Studies*, 37/9: 1297–321.

Hood, A., Bachrach, D., Zivnuska, S., and Bendoly, E. (2016), 'Mediating Effects of Psychological Safety in the Relationship between Team Affectivity and Transactive Memory Systems', *Journal of Organizational Behaviour*, 37/3: 416–35.

Horowitz, F., Heng, C., and Quazi, H. (2003). 'Finders, Keepers? Attracting, Motivating and Retaining Knowledge Workers', *Human Resource Management Journal*, 13/4: 23–44.

Howe, J. (2006). 'The Rise of Crowdsourcing', *Wired Magazine*, 14, http://www.wired.com/wired/archive/14.06/crowds_pr.html (accessed on 6 July 2017).

HR Magazine (2009). 'Leveraging HR and Knowledge Management in a Challenging Economy', *HR Magazine*, June.

Hsiao, R-L., Tsai, S., and Lee, C-F. (2006). 'The Problem of Embeddedness: Knowledge Transfer, Coordination and Reuse in Information Systems', *Organization Studies*, 27/9: 1289–317.

Hsiao, R-L., Tsai, D-H., and Lee, C-F. (2012). 'Collaborative Knowing: The Adaptive Nature of Cross-Boundary Spanning', *Journal of Management Studies*, 49/3: 463–91.

Hsu, M-H., and Chang, C-M. (2014). 'Examining Interpersonal Trust as a Facilitator and Uncertainty as an Inhibitor of Intra-Organisational Knowledge Sharing', *Information Systems Journal*, 24/2: 119–42.

Huang, H. C. (2009). 'Designing a Knowledge-Based System for Strategic Planning: A Balanced Scorecard

Perspective', *Expert Systems with Applications*, 36/1: 209–18.

Huang, Q., Davison, R., Liu, H., and Gu, J. (2008). 'The Impact of Leadership Style on Knowledge-Sharing Intentions in China', *Journal of Global Information Management*, 16: 67–91.

Huang, T-P. (2011). 'Comparing Motivating Work Characteristics, Job Satisfaction, and Turnover Intention of Knowledge Workers and Blue-Collar Workers and Testing a Structural Model of the Variables' Relationships in China and Japan', *International Journal of Human Resource Management*, 22/4: 924–44.

Huffaker, D. (2010). 'Dimensions of Leadership and Social Influence in Online Communities', *Human Communication Research*, 36/4: 593–617.

Hughes, J., Jewson, N., and Unwin, L. (2008). *Communities of Practice: Critical Perspectives*. London: Routledge.

Hume, C., and Hume, M. (2008). 'The Strategic Role of Knowledge Management in Nonprofit Organizations', *International Journal of Nonprofit and Voluntary Sector Marketing*, 13/2: 129–40.

Hunter, L., Beaumont, P., and Lee, M. (2002). 'Knowledge Management Practice in Scottish Law Firms', *Human Resource Management Journal*, 12/2: 4–21.

Huo, W., Cai, Z., Luo, J., Men, C., and Jia, R. (2016). 'Antecedents and Intervention Mechanisms: A Multi-Level Study of R&D Team's Knowledge Hiding Behavior', *Journal of Knowledge Management*, 20/5: 880–97.

Hustad, E., and Teigland, R. (2005). 'Taking a Differentiated View of Intra-Organizational Distributed Networks of Practice', *Communities and Technologies 2005*. Amsterdam: Springer Netherlands, pp. 239–61.

Hutchinson, V., and Quintas, P. (2008). 'Do SMEs do Knowledge Management? Or Simply Manage What they Know?', *International Small Business Journal*, 26/2: 131–54.

Hüttner, C., and Brem, A. (2017). 'Innovation in Business Education: The New Way of Learning at the Adidas Group Learning Campus', *International Journal of Innovation and Learning*, 21/3: 299–328.

Huzzard, T., and Ostergren, K. (2002). 'When Norms Collide: Learning Under Organizational Hypocrisy', *British Journal of Management*, 13: S47–59.

Hwang, E. H., Singh, P. V., Argote, L., Hwang, E. H., and Singh, P. V. (2015). 'Knowledge Sharing in Online Communities: Learning to Cross Geographic and Hierarchical Boundaries', *Organization Science*, 26/6: 1593–611.

Ichijo, K., and Nonaka, I. (2006). *Knowledge Creation and Management: New Challenges for Managers*. New York: Oxford University Press.

Inkpen, A. C., and Dinur, A. (1998). 'Knowledge Management Processes and International Joint Ventures', *Organization Science*, 9/4: 454–68.

Inkpen, A., and Pien, W. (2006). 'An Examination of Collaboration and Knowledge Transfer: Chinese-Singapore Suzhou Industrial Park', *Journal of Management Studies*, 43/4: 779–811.

Inkpen, A. C., and Tsang, E. W. (2005). 'Social Capital, Networks, and Knowledge Transfer', *Academy of Management Review*, 30/1: 146–65.

Introna, L., Hayes, N., and Dimitra, P. (2010). 'The Working Out of Modernization in the Public Sector: The Case of an E-Government Initiative in Greece', *International Journal of Public Administration*, 33/1: 11–25.

Iriberri, A., and Leroy, G. (2009). 'A Life-cycle Perspective on Online Community Success', *ACM Computing Surveys (CSUR)*, 41/2: 1–29.

Janowicz-Panjaitan, M., and Noorderhaven, N. (2009). 'Trust, Calculation, and Interorganizational Learning of Tacit Knowledge: An Organizational Roles Perspective', *Organization Studies*, 30/10: 1021–44.

Jarvenpaa, S., and Majchrzak, A. (2008). 'Knowledge Collaboration among Professionals Protecting National Security: Role of Transactive Memories in Ego-Centred Knowledge Networks', *Organization Science*, 19/2: 260–76.

Jasimuddin, S., Connell, N., and Klein, J. (2012). 'Knowledge Transfer Frameworks: An Extension Incorporating Knowledge Repositories and Knowledge Administration', *Information Systems Journal*, 22: 195–209.

Jasimuddin, S., Li, J., and Perdikis, N. (2015). 'Knowledge Recipients, Acquisition Mechanisms, and Knowledge Transfer at Japanese Subsidiaries: An Empirical Study in China', *Thunderbird International Business Review*, 57/6: 463–79.

Jeon, S., Kim, Y-G., and Koh, J. (2011). 'An Integrative Model for Knowledge Sharing in Communities-of-Practice', *Journal of Knowledge Management*, 15/2: 251–69.

Jonsson, A., and Kalling, T. (2007). 'Challenges to Knowledge Sharing Across National and Intra-Organizational Boundaries: Case Studies of IKEA and SCA Packaging', *Knowledge Management Research and Practice*, 5: 161–72.

Joo, B-K. (2010). 'Organizational Commitment for Knowledge Workers: The Roles of Perceived Organizational Learning Culture, Leader-Member Exchange Quality, and Turnover Intention', *Human Resource Development Quarterly*, 21/1: 69–85.

Joram, M. K., Harrison, B. K., and Joseph, K. N. (2017). 'A Knowledge-Based System for Life Insurance Underwriting', *International Journal of Information Technology and Computer Science*, 9/3: 40–49.

Jordan, J., and Jones, P. (1997). 'Assessing Your Company's Knowledge Management Style', *Long Range Planning*, 30/3: 322–98.

Judge, W., Witt, M., Zattoni, A., Talaulicar, T., Chen, J., Lewellyn, K., Hu, H., Shukla, D., Bell, R., Gabrielsson, J., Lopez, F., Yamak, S., Fassin, Y., McCarthy, D., Rivas, J-L., Fainshmidt, S., and Van Ees, H. (2015). 'Corporate Governance and IPO Underpricing in a Cross-National Sample: A Multilevel Knowledge-Based View', *Strategic Management Journal*, 36: 1174–85.

Kafentzis, K., Mentzas, G., Apostolou, D., and Georgolios, P. (2004). 'Knowledge Marketplaces: Strategic Issues and Business Models', *Journal of Knowledge Management*, 8/1: 130–46.

Kamoche, K., and Maguire, K. (2011). 'Pit-Sense: Appropriation of Practice-Based Knowledge in a UK Coalmine', *Human Relations*, 64/5: 725–44.

Kanawattanachai, P., and Yoo, Y. (2007). 'The Impact of Knowledge Coordination in Virtual Team Performance over Time', *MIS Quarterly*, 31/4: 783–808.

Kane, A., and Levina, N. (2017). 'Am I Still One of Them?' Bicultural Immigrant Managers Navigating Social Identity Threats When Spanning Global Boundaries', *Journal of Management Studies*, 54/4: 540–77.

Kane, G. C., Alavi, M., Labianca, G., and Borgatti, S. P. (2014). 'What's Different about Social Media Networks? A Framework and Research Agenda', *MIS Quarterly*, 38/1: 274–304.

Kang, S-C., and Snell, S. (2009). 'Intellectual Capital Architectures and Ambidextrous Learning: A Framework for Human Resource Management', *Journal of Management Studies*, 46/1: 65–92.

Kankanhalli, A., Tan, B., and Wei, K. (2005). 'Contributing Knowledge to Electronic Knowledge Repositories: An Empirical Investigation', *MIS Quarterly*, 29: 113–43.

Kanzler, S. (2010). 'Knowledge Sharing in Heterogeneous Collaborations—A Longitudinal Investigation of a Cross-Cultural Research Collaboration in Nanoscience', *Journal of Business Chemistry*, 7/1: 31–45.

Kaplan, A. M., and Haenlein, M. (2010). 'Users of the World, Unite! The Challenges and Opportunities of Social Media', *Business Horizons*, 53/1: 59–68.

Karkoulian, S., Halawi, L., and McCarthy, R. (2008). 'Knowledge Management, Formal and Informal Mentoring: An Empirical Investigation of Lebanese Banks', *The Learning Organization*, 15/5: 409–20.

Kärreman, D. (2010). 'The Power of Knowledge: Learning from "Learning by Knowledge-Intensive Firms"', *Journal of Management Studies*, 47/7: 1405–16.

Kase, R., Paauwe, J., and Zupan, N. (2009). 'HR Practices, Interpersonal Relations, and Intrafirm Knowledge Transfer in Knowledge Intensive Firms: A Social Network Perspective', *Human Resource Management*, 48/4: 615–39.

Kasper, H., Lehrer, M., Mühlbacher, J., and Müller, B. (2010). 'Thinning Knowledge: An Interpretive Field Study of Knowledge Sharing Practices of Firms in Three Multinational Contexts', *Journal of Management Inquiry*, 19/4: 367–81.

Kelly, S. (2008). 'Leadership: a Categorical Mistake', *Human Relations*, 61/6: 763–82.

Kets de Vries, M. (2005). 'Leadership Group Coaching in Action: The Zen of Creating High Performance Teams', *Academy of Management*, 19/1: 61–76.

Khan, Z., and Vorley, T. (2017). 'Big Data Text Analytics: An Enabler of Knowledge Management', *Journal of Knowledge Management*, 21/1: 18–34.

Khan, Z., Shenkar, O., and Lew, Y. (2015). 'Knowledge Transfer from International Joint Ventures to Local Suppliers in a Developing Economy', *Journal of International Business Studies*, 46: 656–75.

Khatri, N., Baveja, A., Agarwal, N., and Brown, G. (2010). 'HR and IT Capabilities and Complementarities in Knowledge Intensive Services', *International Journal of Human Resource Management*, 21/15: 2889–909.

Khodakarami, F., and Chan, Y. (2014). 'Exploring the Role of Customer Relationship Management (CRM) Systems in Customer Knowledge Creation', *Information and Management*, 51/1: 27–42.

Kietzmann, J. H., Hermkens, K., McCarthy, I. P., and Silvestre, B. S. (2011). 'Social Media? Get Serious! Understanding the Functional Building Blocks of Social Media', *Business Horizons*, 54/3: 241–51.

Kim, T. H., Lee, J-N., Chun, J. U., and Benbasat, I. (2014). 'Understanding the Effect of Knowledge Management Strategies on Knowledge Management Performance: A Contingency Perspective', *Information and Management*, 51/4: 398–416.

Kim, W., and Mauborgne, R. (1998). 'Procedural Justice, Strategic Decision Making, and the Knowledge Economy', *Strategic Management Journal*, 19/4: 323–38.

King, A. W., and Zeithaml, C. P. (2003). 'Measuring Organizational Knowledge: A Conceptual and Methodological Framework', *Strategic Management Journal*, 24/8: 763–72.

King, W., and Marks Jr, P. (2008). 'Motivating Knowledge Sharing Through a Knowledge Management System', *Omega*, 36: 131–46.

Klitmøller, A., and Lauring, J. (2013). 'When Global Virtual Teams Share Knowledge: Media Richness, Culture Difference and Language Commonality', *Journal of World Business*, 48: 398–406.

Knights, D., Murray, F., and Willmott, H. (1993). 'Networking as Knowledge Work: A Study of Strategic Inter-organizational Development in the Financial Service Industry', *Journal of Management Studies*, 30/6: 975–95.

Knol, P., Spruit, M., and Scheper, W. (2008). 'Web 2.0 Revealed—Business Model Innovation through Social Computing', *Proceedings of the Seventh AIS SIGeBIZ Workshop on e-Business*. London: WeB.

Kofman, F., and Senge, P. (1993). 'Communities of Commitment: The Heart of Learning Organizations', *Organizational Dynamics*, 22/2: 5–23.

Kogut, B., and Zander, U. (1996). 'What Do Firms Do? Coordination, Identity and Learning', *Organization Science*, 7/5: 502–18.

Kothari, A., Hovanec, N., Hastie, R., and Sibbald, S. (2011). 'Lessons from the Business Sector for Successful Knowledge Management in Healthcare: A Systemic Review', *Health Services Research*, 11: 173–84.

Kotlarsky, J., and Oshri, I. (2005). 'Social Ties, Knowledge Sharing and Successful Collaboration in Globally Distributed System Development Projects', *European Journal of Information Systems*, 14/1: 37–48.

Kotlarsky, J., Oshri, I., and Willcocks, L. (2007). 'Social Ties in Globally Distributed Software Teams: Beyond Face-to-Face Meetings', *Journal of Global Information Technology Management*, 10/4: 7–34.

Kotlarsky, J., Scarbrough, H., and Oshri, I. (2014). 'Coordinating Expertise Across Knowledge Boundaries in Offshore-Outsourcing Projects: The Role of Codification', *MIS Quarterly*, 38/2: 607–27.

KPMG (2000). *Knowledge Management Research Report*. London: KPMG Consulting.

KPMG (2003). *Insights from KPMG's European Knowledge Management Survey*. London: KPMG Consulting.

Krackhardt, D., and Hanson, J. R. (1993). 'Informal Networks: The Company Behind the Chart', *Harvard Business Review*, 71/4: 104–11.

Kumar, J., and Ganesh, L. (2011). 'Balancing Knowledge Strategy: Codification and Personalization during Product Development', *Journal of Knowledge Management*, 15/1: 118–35.

Kumar, K. (1995). *From Post-Industrial to Post-Modern Society: New Theories of the Contemporary World*. London: Blackwell.

Kunda, G. (1992). *Engineering Culture: Control and Commitment in a High-Tech Corporation*. Philadelphia: Temple University Press.

Kuo, R-Z., and Lee, G-G. (2011). 'Knowledge Management System Adoption: Exploring the Effects of Empowering Leadership, Task-Technology Fit and Compatibility', *Behaviour and Information Technology*, 30/1: 113–29.

Kwon, K., and Cho, D. (2016). 'How Transactive Memory Systems Relate to Organizational Innovation: The Mediating Role of Developmental Leadership', *Journal of Knowledge Management*, 20/5: 1025–44.

Kwong, T., Cox, M. D., Chong, K., Wong, W. L., and Nie, S. (2016). 'Assessing the Effect of Communities of Practice in Higher Education: The Case at Hong Kong Baptist University', *Learning Communities Journal*, 8/2: 171–98.

Lakemond, N., Bengtsson, L., Laursen, K., and Tell, F. (2016). 'Match and Manage: The Use of Knowledge Matching and Project Management to Integrate Knowledge in Collaborative Inbound Open Innovation', *Industrial and Corporate Change*, 25/2: 333–52.

Lam, A. (1997). 'Embedded Firms, Embedded Knowledge: Problems in Collaboration and Knowledge Transfer in Global Cooperative Ventures', *Organization Studies*, 18/6: 973–96.

Lam, W. (2005). 'Successful Knowledge Management Requires a Knowledge Culture: A Case Study', *Knowledge Management Research and Practice*, 3/4: 206–17.

LaPolombara, J. (2001). 'Power and Politics in Organizations: Public and Private Sector Comparisons', in M. Dierkes, A. Bertoin Antal, J. Child, and I. Nonaka (eds), *Handbook of Organizational Learning and Knowledge*. Oxford: Oxford University Press, pp. 557–81.

Lave, J., and Wenger, E. (1991). *Situated Learning: Legitimate Peripheral Participation*. Cambridge: Cambridge University Press.

Lee, K. C., Lee, S., and Kang, I. W. (2005). 'KMPI: Measuring Knowledge Management Performance', *Information & Management*, 42/3: 469–82.

Lee, L. (2011). 'The Effects of Challenge and Hindrance Stressors on Unlearning and NPD Success: The Moderating Role of Team Conflict', *African Journal of Business Management*, 5/5: 1843–56.

Lee, L., and Sukoco, B. (2011). 'Reflexivity, Stress, and Unlearning in the New Product Development Team: The Moderating Effect of Procedural Justice', *R&D Management*, 41/4: 410–23.

Lee, P., Gillespie, N., Mann, L., and Wearing, A. (2010). 'Leadership and Trust: Their Effects on Knowledge Sharing and Team Performance', *Management Learning*, 41/4: 473–91.

Leonard, D., and Sensiper, S. (1998). 'The Role of Tacit Knowledge in Group Innovation', *California Management Review*, 40/3: 112–32.

Leonardi, P. M. (2017). 'The Social Media Revolution: Sharing and Learning in the Age of Leaky Knowledge', *Information and Organization*, 27/1: 47–59.

Leonardi, P. M., and Treem, J. W. (2012). 'Knowledge Management Technology as a Stage for Strategic Self Presentation: Implications for Knowledge Sharing in Organizations'. *Information and Organization*, 22: 37–59.

Levin, D., and Cross, R. (2004). 'The Strength of Weak Ties You Can Trust: The Mediating Role of Trust in Effective Knowledge Transfer', *Management Science*, 50/11: 1477–90.

Levina, N., and Vaast, E. (2005). 'The Emergence of Boundary Spanning Competence in Practice: Implications for Implementation and Use of Information Systems', *MIS Quarterly*, 29/2: 335–63.

Levinthal, D., and March, J. (1993). 'The Myopia of Learning', *Strategic Management Journal*, 14/Special Issue: 95–113.

Levitt, B., and March, J. (1988). 'Organizational Learning', *Annual Review of Sociology*, 14: 319–40.

Levy, M. (2009). 'Web 2.0 Implications on Knowledge Management', *Journal of Knowledge Management*, 13/1: 120–34.

Li, J., Chang, X., and Ma, L. (2014). 'Meta-analytic Comparison on the Influencing Factors of Knowledge Transfer in Different Cultural Contexts', *Journal of Knowledge Management*, 18/2: 278–306.

Li, R., and Poon, S. (2011). 'Using Web 2.0 to Share Knowledge of Construction Safety: The Fable of Economic Animals', *IEA Economic Affairs*, March: 73–9.

Li, W. (2010). 'Virtual Knowledge Sharing in a Cross-Cultural Context', *Journal of Knowledge Management*, 14/1: 38–50.

Liao, L-F. (2008). 'Knowledge Sharing in R&D Departments: A Social Power and Social Exchange Theory Perspective', *International Journal of Human Resource Management*, 19/10, 1881–95.

Liao, S-H., Chang, W-J., Hu, D-C., and Yueh, Y-L. (2012). 'Relationships Among Organizational Culture, Knowledge Acquisition, Organizational Learning, and Organizational Innovation in Taiwan's Banking and Insurance Industries', *International Journal of Human Resource Management*, 23/1: 52–70.

Liebeskind, J. P. (1996). 'Knowledge, Strategy and the Theory of the Firm', *Strategic Management Journal*, 17: 93–107.

Lin, H-F. (2011). 'The Effect of Employee Motivation, Social Interaction, and Knowledge Management Strategy on KM Implementation Level', *Knowledge Management Research and Practice*, 9: 263–75.

Lin, S-W., and Lo, L. (2015). 'Mechanisms to Motivate Knowledge Sharing: Integrating the Reward Systems and Social Network Perspectives', *Journal of Knowledge Management*, 19/2: 212–35.

Littler, C., and Innes, D. (2003). 'Downsizing and Deknowledging the Firm', *Work, Employment and Society*, 17: 73–100.

Lloria, M. (2008). 'A Review of the Main Approaches to Knowledge Management', *Knowledge Management Research and Practice*, 6: 77–89.

López, S. P., Peón, J. M. M., and Ordás, C. J. V. (2004). 'Managing Knowledge: The Link Between Culture and Organizational Learning', *Journal of Knowledge Management*, 8/6: 93–104.

Lukes, S. (1974). *Power: A Radical Perspective*. London: Macmillan.

Luo, X., and Deng, L. (2009). 'Do Birds of a Feather Flock Higher? The Effects of Partner Similarity on Innovation in Strategic Alliances in Knowledge-Intensive Industries', *Journal of Management Studies*, 46/6: 1005–30.

Ma, W., and Chan, A. (2014). 'Knowledge Sharing and Social Media: Altruism, Perceived Online Attachment Motivation', *Computers in Human Behaviour*, 39/1: 51–8.

Mabey, C., and Zhao, S. (2017). 'Managing Five Paradoxes of Knowledge Exchange in Networked Organizations: New Priorities for HRM?', *Human Resource Management Journal*, 27/1: 39–57.

Machlup, F. (1962). *The Production and Distribution of Knowledge in the US*. Princeton, NJ: Princeton University Press.

Majchrzak, A., Cherbakov, L., and Ives, B. (2009). 'Harnessing the Power of the Crowds with Corporate Social Networking Tools: How IBM Does It', *MIS Quarterly Executive*, 8/2: 151–6.

Majchrzak, A., More, P., and Faraj, S. (2012). 'Transcending Knowledge Differences in Cross-Functional Teams', *Organization Science*, 23/4: 951–70.

Malhotra, N., Mossis, T., and Smets, M. (2010). 'New Career Models in UK Professional Service Firms: From Up-or-Out to Up-and-Going-Nowhere?', *International Journal of Human Resource Management*, 21/9: 1396–413.

Mandelson, P. (2009). *The Future of Universities in a Knowledge Economy*. London: Department for Business Innovation and Skills.

Mansell, R., and Steinmueller, W. (2000). *Mobilizing the Information Society: Strategies for Growth and Opportunity*. Oxford: Oxford University Press.

Mäntymäki, M., and Riemer, K. (2016). 'Enterprise Social Networking: A Knowledge Management Perspective',

International Journal of Information Management, 36/6: 1042–52.

Marabelli, M., and Newell, S. (2014). 'Knowing, Power and Materiality: A Critical Review and Reconceptualization of Absorptive Capacity', *International Journal of Management Reviews*, 16: 479–99.

March, J., and Simon, H. (1993). *Organizations* (2nd edn). Oxford: Blackwell.

Marin, A., Cordier, J., and Hameed, T. (2016). 'Reconciling Ambiguity with Interaction: Implementing Formal Knowledge Strategies in a Knowledge-Intensive Organization', *Journal of Knowledge Management*, 20/5: 959–79.

Mariscal, G., Marbán, Ó., and Fernández, C. (2010). 'A Survey of Data Mining and Knowledge Discovery Process Models and Methodologies', *The Knowledge Engineering Review*, 25/2: 137–66.

Markus, L. M. (2001). 'Toward a Theory of Knowledge Reuse: Types of Knowledge Reuse Situations and Factors in Reuse Success', *Journal of Management Information Systems*, 18/1: 57–93.

Marshall, N. (2014). 'Thinking, Saying and Doing in Collaborative Projects: What Can We Learn from Theories of Practice?', *Engineering Project Organization Journal*, 4/2–3: 107–22.

Marshall, N., and Brady, T. (2001). 'Knowledge Management and the Politics of Knowledge: Illustrations from Complex Product Systems', *European Journal of Information Systems*, 10/2: 99–112.

Marshall, N., and Rollinson, J. (2004). 'Maybe Bacon had a Point: The Politics of Collective Sensemaking', *British Journal of Management*, 15, Special Issue: s71–86.

Martins, E. C., and Martins, N. (2011). 'The Role of Organisational Factors in Combating Tacit Knowledge Loss in Organisations', *Southern African Business Review*, 15/1.

Martins, E., and Mayer, H. (2012). 'Organizational and Behavioural Factors that Influence Knowledge Retention', *Journal of Knowledge Management*, 16/1: 2012.

Mason, K., and Leek, S. (2008). 'Learning to Build a Supply Network: An Exploration of Dynamic Business Models', *Journal of Management Studies*, 45/4: 774–99.

Massingham, P. (2004). 'Linking Business Level Strategy with Activities and Knowledge Resources', *Journal of Knowledge Management*, 8/6: 50–62.

Massingham, P. (2008). 'Measuring the Impact of Knowledge Loss: More than Ripples on a Pond?', *Management Learning*, 39/5: 541–60.

Massingham, P. (2010). 'Managing Knowledge Transfer Between Parent Country Nationals (Australia) and Host Country Nationals (Asia)', *International Journal of Human Resource Management*, 21/9: 1414–35.

Mathew, J., and Ogbonna, E. (2011). 'Organisational Culture and Commitment: A Study of an Indian Software Organisation', *International Journal of Human Resource Management*, 20/3: 654–75.

Matschke, C., Moskaliuk, J., and Cress, U. (2012). 'Knowledge Exchange Using Web 2.0 Technologies in NGOs', *Journal of Knowledge Management*, 16/1: 159–76.

Matschke, C., Moskaliuk, J., Bokhorst, F., Schummer, T., and Cress, U. (2014). 'Motivational Factors of Information Exchange in Social Information Spaces', *Computers in Human Behaviour*, 36/4: 549–58.

Matson, E., and Prusak, L. (2010). 'Boosting the Productivity of Knowledge Workers', *McKinsey Quarterly*, 4: 93–6.

Matzkin, D. (2008). 'Knowledge Management in the Peruvian Non-Profit Sector', *Journal of Knowledge Management*, 12/4: 147–59.

Matzler, K., Renzl, B., Mooradian, T., von Krogh, G., and Mueller, J. (2011). 'Personality Traits, Affective Commitment, Documentation of Knowledge and Knowledge Sharing', *International Journal of Human Resource Management*, 22/2: 296–310.

McAdam, R., and McCreedy, S. (2000). 'A Critique of Knowledge Management: Using a Social Constructivist Model', *New Technology, Work and Employment*, 15/2: 155–68.

McAdam, R., Moffett, S., and Peng, J. (2012). 'Knowledge Sharing in Chinese Service Organizations: A Multi Case Cultural Perspective', *Journal of Knowledge Management*, 16/1: 129–47.

McAllister, D. J. (1995). 'Affect and Cognition Based Trust as Foundations for Interpersonal Cooperation in Organizations', *Academy of Management Journal*, 38/1: 24–59.

McClure Wasko, M., and Faraj, S. (2000). '"It Is What One Does": Why People Participate and Help Others in Electronic Communities of Practice', *The Journal of Strategic Information Systems*, 9/2: 155–73.

McDermott, R. (1999). 'Why Information Technology Inspired but Cannot Deliver Knowledge Management', *California Management Review*, 41/1: 103–17.

McDermott, R., and O'Dell, C. (2001). 'Overcoming Cultural Barriers to Knowledge Sharing', *Journal of Knowledge Management*, 5/1: 76–85.

McGivern, G., and Dopson, S. (2010). 'Inter-Epistemic Power and Transforming Knowledge Objects in a

Biomedical Network', *Organization Studies*, 31/12: 1667–86.

McKinlay, A. (2000). 'The Bearable Lightness of Control: Organisational Reflexivity and the Politics of Knowledge Management', in C. Prichard, R. Hull, M. Chumer, and H. Willmott (eds), *Managing Knowledge: Critical Investigations of Work and Learning*. London: Macmillan, 107–21.

McKinlay, A. (2002). 'The Limits of Knowledge Management', *New Technology, Work and Employment*, 17/2: 76–88.

McKinlay, A. (2005). 'Knowledge Management', in S. Ackroyd, R. Batt, and P. Thompson (eds), *The Oxford Handbook of Work and Organization*. Oxford: Oxford University Press, pp. 242–62.

McKinlay, A., and Starkey, K. (1998). *Foucault, Management and Organization Theory*. London: Sage.

McKinlay, A., Carter, C., Pezet, E., and Clegg, S. (2010). 'Using Foucault to Make Strategy', *Accounting, Auditing and Accountability Journal*, 23/8: 11012–31.

Mehra, A., Langer, N., Bapna, R., and Gopal, R. (2014). 'Estimating Returns to Training in the Knowledge Economy: A Firm-level Analysis of Small and Medium Enterprises', *MIS Quarterly*, 38/3: 757–71.

Mehrizi, M., and Bontis, N. (2009). 'A Cluster Analysis of the KM Field', *Management Decision*, 47/5: 792–805.

Mell, J., van Knippenberg, D., and van Ginkel, W. (2014). 'The Catalyst Effect: The Impact of Transactive Memory System Structure on Team Performance', *Academy of Management Journal*, 57/4: 1154–73.

Meroño-Cerdan, A., Lopez-Nicolas, C., and Sabater-Sànchez, R. (2007). 'Knowledge Management Strategy Diagnosis from KM Instruments Use', *Journal of Knowledge Management*, 11/2: 60–72.

Michailova, S., and Minbaeva, D. (2012). 'Organizational Values and Knowledge Sharing in Multinationals: The Danisco Case', *International Business Review*, 21: 59–70.

Milgram, S. (1967). 'The Small World Problem', *Psychology Today*, 1/61: 60–7.

Miller, K., McAdam, R., Moffett, S., Alexander, A., and Puthusserry, P. (2016). 'Knowledge Transfer in University Quadruple Helix Ecosystems: An Absorptive Capacity Perspective', *R&D Management*, 46/2: 383–98.

Milne, P. (2007). 'Motivation, Incentives and Organisational Culture', *Journal of Knowledge Management*, 11/6: 28–38.

Monks, K., Conway, E., Fu, N., Bailey, K., Kelly, G., and Hannon, E. (2016). 'Enhancing Knowledge Exchange and Combination through HR Practices: Reflexivity as a Translation Process', *Human Resource Management Journal*, 26/3: 304–20.

Mooradian, T., Renzl, B., and Matzler, K. (2006). 'Who Trusts? Personality Trust and Knowledge Sharing', *Management Learning*, 37/4: 523–40.

Moran, J. (2010). 'Doing More with Less: How a Multicompany Community of Practice Shares Knowledge and Saves Money', *Global Business and Organizational Excellence*, September/October: 50–6.

Mørk, B., Hoholm, T., Ellingsen, G., Edwin, B., and Aanestad, M. (2010). 'Challenging Expertise: On Power Relations Within and Across Communities of Practice in Medical Innovation', *Management Learning*, 41/5: 575–92.

Mørk, B., Hoholm, T., Ellingsen, G., Maaninen-Olsson, E., and Aanestad, M. (2012). 'Changing Practices Through Boundary Organizing: A Case from Medical R&D', *Human Relations*, 65/2: 263–88.

Morris, T. (2001). 'Asserting Property Rights: Knowledge Codification in the Professional Service Firm', *Human Relations*, 54/7: 819–38.

Morris, T., and Empson, L. (1998). 'Organization and Expertise: An Exploration of Knowledge Bases and the Management of Accounting and Consulting Firms', *Accounting, Organizations and Society*, 23/5–6: 609–24.

Motion, J., and Leitch, S. (2009). 'The Transformation Potential of Public Policy Discourse', *Organization Studies*, 30/10: 1046–61.

Mueller, J. (2015). 'Formal and Informal Practice of Knowledge Sharing Between Project Teams and Enacted Cultural Characteristics', *Project Management Journal*, 46/1: 53–68.

Mueller, J., Hutter, K., Fueller, J., and Matzler, K. (2011). 'Virtual Worlds as Knowledge Management Platform—A Practice Perspective', *Information Systems Journal*, 21/6: 479–501.

Nadler, D., and Tushman, M. (1990). 'Beyond the Charismatic Leader: Leadership and Organizational Change', *California Management Review*, Winter: 77–97.

Nag, R., and Gioia, D. (2012). 'From Common to Uncommon Knowledge: Foundations of Firm-Specific Use of Knowledge as a Resource', *Academy of Management Journal*, 55/2: 421–57.

Nahapiet, J., and Ghoshal, S. (1998). 'Social Capital, Intellectual Capital and the Organizational Advantage', *Academy of Management Review*, 23/2: 242–66.

Nayir, D., and Uzunçarsili, Ü. (2008). 'A Cultural Perspective on Knowledge Management: The Success Story of Sarkuysan Company', *Journal of Knowledge Management*, 12/2: 141–55.

Nebus, J. (2006). 'Collegial Information Building a Theory of Advice Network Networks: Generation', *Academy of Management Journal*, 31/3: 615–37.

Neef, D. (1999). 'Making the Case for Knowledge Management: The Bigger Picture', *Management Decision*, 37/1: 72–8.

Newell, S. (2015). 'Managing Knowledge and Managing Knowledge Work: What we Know and What the Future Holds', *Journal of Information Technology*, 30: 1–17.

Newell, S., David, G., and Chand, D. (2007). 'An Analysis of Trust Among Globally Distributed Work Teams in an Organizational Setting', *Knowledge and Process Management*, 14/3: 158–68.

Nguyen, H., and Mohamed, S. (2011). 'Leadership Behaviours, Organizational Culture and Knowledge Management Practices: An Empirical Investigation', *Journal of Management Development*, 30/2: 206–21.

Nicolini, D. (2007). 'Stretching Out and Expanding Medical Practices: The Case of Telemedicine', *Human Relations*, 60/6: 889–920.

Nicolini, D. (2011). 'Practice as the Site of Knowing: Insights from the Field of Telemedicine', *Organization Science*, 22/3: 602–20.

Nicolini, D. (2013). *Practice Theory, Work, and Organization: An Introduction*. Oxford: Oxford University Press.

Nieves, A., Quintana, A., and Osorio, J. (2016). 'Organizational Knowledge and Collaborative Human Resource Practices as Determinants of Innovation', *Knowledge Management: Research and Practice*, 14: 237–45.

Nishikawa, M. (2011). '(Re)defining Care Workers as Knowledge Workers', *Gender, Work and Organization*, 18/1: 113–36.

Nohlberg, M. (2009). 'Why Humans are the Weakest Link', in M. Gupta and R. Sharman (eds), *Social and Human Elements in Information Security: Emerging Trends and Countermeasures*. Hershey, PA: IGI Global, pp. 27–42.

Nonaka, I. (1991). 'The Knowledge-Creating Company', *Harvard Business Review*, November–December: 96–104.

Nonaka, I. (1994). 'A Dynamic Theory of Organizational Knowledge Creation', *Organization Science*, 5/1: 14–37.

Nonaka, I., and Hirose, A. (2015). 'Practical Strategy as a Co-creating Collective Narrative: A Perspective of Organizational Knowledge-Creation Theory', *Kindai Management Review*, 3: 9–24.

Nonaka, I., and Konno, N. (1998). 'The Concept of "Ba": Building a Foundation for Knowledge Creation', *California Management Review*, 40/3: 40–55.

Nonaka, I., and Peltokorpi, V. (2006). 'Objectivity and Subjectivity in Knowledge Management: A Review of 20 Top Articles', *Knowledge and Process Management*, 13/2: 73–82.

Nonaka, I., and Takeuchi, H. (1995). *The Knowledge Creating Company*. Oxford: Oxford University Press.

Nonaka, I., and Toyama, R. (2003). 'The Knowledge-Creating Theory Revisited: Knowledge Creation as a Synthesizing Process', *Knowledge Management Research & Practice*, 1/1: 2–10.

Nonaka, I., and Toyama, R. (2015). 'The Knowledge-Creating Theory Revisited: Knowledge Creation as a Synthesizing Process', *The Essentials of Knowledge Management*. London: Palgrave Macmillan, pp. 95–110.

Nonaka, I., and von Krogh, G. (2009). 'Tacit Knowledge and Knowledge Conversion: Controversy and Advancement in Organizational Knowledge Creation Theory', *Organization Science*, 20/3: 635–52.

Nonaka, I., Byosiere, P., Borucki, C., and Konno, N. (1994). 'Organizational Knowledge Creation Theory: A First Comprehensive Test', *International Business Review*, 3–4: 337–52.

Nonaka, I., Toyama, R., and Konno, N. (2000). 'SECI, "Ba" and Leadership: A Unified Model of Dynamic Knowledge Creation', *Long Range Planning*, 33/1: 5–34.

Nonaka, I., Toyama, R., and Hirata, T. (2008). *Managing Flow: A Process Theory of the Knowledge-Based Firm*. Basingstoke: Palgrave MacMillan.

Nonaka, I., von Krogh, G., and Voelpel, S. (2006). 'Organizational Knowledge Creation Theory: Evolutionary Paths and Future Advances', *Organization Studies*, 27/8: 1179–208.

Northouse, P. (2007). *Leadership: Theory and Practice* (4th edn). London: Sage.

NSTF (National Skills Task Force) (2000). *Skills for All: Research Report from the National Skills Task Force*. London: Department for Education and Employment.

Nystrom, P., and Starbuck, W. (2003). 'To Avoid Organizational Crises, Unlearn', in K. Starkey, S. Tempest, and A. McKinlay (eds), *How Organizations Learn: Managing the Search for Knowledge*. London: Thomson, 100–11.

Oborn, E., and Dawson, S. (2011). 'Knowledge and Practice in Multidisciplinary Teams: Struggle, Accommodation and Privilege', *Human Relations*, 63/12: 1835–57.

O'Dell, C., and Hubert, C. (2011). 'Building a Knowledge-Sharing Culture', *The Journal of Quality and Participation*, July: 22–6.

Olander, H., and Hurmelinna-Laukunnen, P. (2010). 'The Effects of HRM-Related Mechanisms on Communication in R&D Collaboration', *International Journal of Innovation Management*, 14/3: 415–33.

Olander, H., Hurmelinna-Laukunnen, P., and Mahonen J. (2009). 'What's Small Size Got to Do With It? Protection of Intellectual Assets in SMEs', *International Journal of Innovation Management*, 13/3: 349–70.

O'Leary, D. E. (1998). 'Enterprise Knowledge Management', *Computer*, 31/3: 54–61.

O'Leary, D. (2013). 'Driving Innovation and Knowledge Management Using Crowdsourcing', *Proceedings of the International Conference on Information Systems 2013*. Milan: ECIS.

Oltra, V. (2005). 'Knowledge Management Effectiveness Factors: The Role of HRM', *Journal of Knowledge Management*, 9/4: 70–86.

O'Neill, B., and Adya, M. (2007). 'Knowledge Sharing and the Psychological Contract: Managing Knowledge Workers Across Different Stages of Employment', *Journal of Managerial Psychology*, 22/4: 411–36.

Oostervink, N., Agterberg, M., and Huysman, M. (2016). 'Knowledge Sharing on Enterprise Social Media: Practices to Cope With Institutional Complexity', *Journal of Computer-Mediated Communication*, 21/2: 156–76.

Orlikowski, W. (2002). 'Knowing in Practice: Enacting a Collective Capability in Distributed Organizing', *Organization Science*, 13/3: 249–73.

Orr, J. (1990). 'Sharing Knowledge, Celebrating Identity: War Stories and Community Memory in a Service Culture', in D. Middleton and D. Edwards (eds), *Collective Remembering: Memory in a Society*. London: Sage.

Orr, J. (1996). *Talking about Machines: An Ethnography of a Modern Job*. Ithaca, NY: ILR Press.

Orr, K., Nutley, S., Russell, S., Bain, R., Hacking, B., and Moran, C. (2016). *Knowledge and Practice in Business and Organizations*. London: Routledge.

Oshri, I., Van Fenema, P. C., and Kotlarsky, J. (2008). 'Knowledge Transfer in Globally Distributed Teams: The Role of Transactive Memory', *Information Systems Journal*, 18/6: 593–616.

Osterloh, M., and Frey, B. (2000). 'Motivation, Knowledge Transfer, and Organizational Forms', *Organization Science*, 11/5: 538–50.

Otto, B. (2011). 'Organizing Data Governance: Findings from the Telecommunications Industry and Consequences for Large Service Providers', *Communications of AIS*, 29/3: 45–66.

Ozlati, S. (2015). 'The Moderating Effect of Trust on the Relationship Between Autonomy and Knowledge Sharing: A National Multi-Industry Survey of Knowledge Workers', *Knowledge and Process Management*, 22/3: 191–205.

Paasivaara, M., and Lassenius, C. (2014). 'Communities of Practice in a Large Distributed Agile Software Development Organization—Case Ericsson', *Information and Software Technology*, 56: 1556–77.

Pan, S., and Scarbrough, H. (1999). 'Knowledge Management in Practice: An Exploratory Case Study', *Technology Analysis and Strategic Management*, 11/3: 359–74.

Panahi, S., Watson, J., and Partridge, H. (2012). 'Social Media and Tacit Knowledge Sharing: Developing a Conceptual Model', *World Academy of Science, Engineering and Technology (WASET)*. Paris: WASET, pp. 1095–102.

Paraponaris, C., and Sigal, M. (2015). 'From Knowledge to Knowing, from Boundaries to Boundary Construction', *Journal of Knowledge Management*, 19/5: 881–99.

Paroutis, S., and Al Saleh, A. (2009). 'Determinants of Knowledge Sharing Using Web 2.0 Technologies', *Journal of Knowledge Management*, 13/4: 52–63.

Pawlovsky, P. (2001). 'The Treatment of Organizational learning in Management Science', in M. Dierkes, A. Bertoin Antal, J. Child, and I. Nonaka (eds), *Handbook of Organizational Learning and Knowledge*. Oxford: Oxford University Press, pp. 61–88.

Pedler, M., Burgoyne, J., and Boydell, T. (1997). *The Learning Company: A Strategy for Sustainable Development* (2nd edn). London: McGraw-Hill UK.

Peltokorpi, V. (2006). 'Knowledge Sharing in a Cross Cultural Context: Nordic Expatriates in Japan', *Knowledge Management Research and Practice*, 4: 138–48.

Peltokorpi, V., and Vaara, E. (2014). 'Knowledge Transfer in Multinational Corporations: Productive and Counterproductive Effects of Language-Sensitive Recruitment', *Journal of International Business Studies*, 45/5: 600–22.

Pinjani, P., and Palvia, P. (2013). 'Trust and Knowledge Sharing in Diverse Global Virtual Teams', *Information and Management*, 50/4: 144–53.

Polanyi, M. (1958). *Personal Knowledge*. Chicago: University of Chicago Press.

Polanyi, M. (1969). *Knowing and Being*. London: Routledge and Kegan Paul.

Polanyi, M. (1983). *The Tacit Dimension*. Gloucester, MA: Peter Smith.

Porter, C. E. (2004). 'A Typology of Virtual Communities: A Multi-disciplinary Foundation for Future Research', *Journal of Computer-Mediated Communication*, 10/1: art. 3.

Pozzebon, M., and Pinsonneault, A. (2012). 'The Dynamics of Client-Consultant Relationships: Exploring the Interplay of Power and Knowledge', *Journal of Information Technology*, 27/1: 35–56.

Preece, J. (2000). *Online Communities: Designing Usability and Supporting Sociability*. New York, NY: John Wiley and Sons Ltd.

Provera, B., Montefusco, A., and Canato, A. (2010). 'A "No Blame" Approach to Organizational Learning', *British Journal of Management*, 21: 1057–74.

Provost, F., and Fawcett, T. (2013). *Data Science for Business: What You Need to Know about Data Mining and Data-Analytic Thinking*. London: O'Reilly Media, Inc.

Quah, J. T., and Sriganesh, M. (2008). 'Real-time Credit Card Fraud Detection Using Computational Intelligence', *Expert Systems with Applications*, 35/4: 1721–32.

Rabinow, P. (1991). *The Foucault Reader*. London: Penguin Books.

Ragab, M., and Arisha, A. (2013). 'Knowledge Management and Measurement: A Critical Review', *Journal of Knowledge Management*, 17/6: 873–901.

Rai, K. (2011). 'Knowledge Management and Organizational Culture: A Theoretical Integrative Framework', *Journal of Knowledge Management*, 15/2: 779–801.

Raisch, S., Birkinshaw, J., Probst, G., and Tuckman, M. (2009). 'Organizational Ambidexterity: Balancing Exploitation and Exploration for Sustained Performance', *Organization Science*, 20/4: 685–95.

Ransbotham, S. (2016). 'Knowledge Entrepreneurship: Institutionalising Wiki-Based Knowledge-Management Processes in Competitive and Hierarchical Organisations', *Journal of Information Technology*, 31/2: 226–39.

Ravishankar, M., and Pan, S. (2008). 'The Influence of Organizational Identification on Organizational Knowledge Management (KM)', *Omega*, 36: 221–34.

Raz, A., and Fadlon, J. (2006). 'Managerial Culture, Workplace Culture and Situated Curricula in Organizational Learning', *Organization Studies*, 27/2: 165–82.

Razmerita, L., Kirchner, K., and Nabeth, T. (2014). 'Social Media in Organizations: Leveraging Personal and Collective Knowledge Processes', *Journal of Organizational Computing and Electronic Commerce*, 24: 74–93.

Razmerita, L., Kirchner, K., and Nielsen, P. (2016). 'What Factors Influence Knowledge Sharing in Organizations? A Social Dilemma Perspective of Social Media Communication', *Journal of Knowledge Management*, 20/6: 1225–46.

Reich, R. (1991). *The Work of Nations: Preparing Ourselves for 21st-Century Capitalism*. London: Simon and Schuster.

Reiche, S., Harzing, A-W., and Pudelko, M. (2015). 'Why and How does Shared Language Affect Subsidiary Knowledge Inflows? A Social Identity Perspective', *Journal of International Business Studies*, 46/5: 528–51.

Reijsen, J. van, and Helms, R. W. (2009). 'Revealing Knowledge Networks from Computer Mediated Communication in Organizations', in S. Newell, E. A. Whitley, J. Wareham, and L. Mathiassen (eds), *Proceedings of 17th European Conference on Information Systems*. Verona: ECIS, pp. 2503–515.

Renzl, B. (2008). 'Trust in Management and Knowledge Sharing: The Mediating Effects of Fear and Knowledge Documentation', *Omega*, 36: 206–20.

Rheingold, H. (1993). *The Virtual Community: Homesteading on the Electronic Frontier*. Reading, MA: Addison-Wesley Publishing.

Ribeiro, R., and Collins, H. (2007). 'The Bread-Making Machine: Tacit Knowledge and Two Types of Action', *Organization Studies*, 28/9: 1417–33.

Ribiere, V., and Sitar, A. (2003). 'Critical Role of Leadership in Nurturing a Knowledge-Supporting Culture', *Knowledge Management Research and Practice*, 1/1: 39–48.

Richtnér, A., Åhlström, P., and Goffin, K. (2014). '"Squeezing R&D": A Study of Organizational Slack and Knowledge Creation in NPD, Using the SECI Model', *Journal of Product Innovation Management*, 31/6: 1268–90.

Ridings, C. M., and Gefen, D. (2004). 'Virtual Community Attraction: Why People Hang Out Online', *Journal of Computer-Mediated Communication*, 10/1: art. 4.

Riemer, K., and Tavakoli, A. (2013). *The Role of Groups as Local Context in Large Enterprise Social Networks: A Case Study of Yammer at Deloitte Australia*. Report no. BIS WP2013, University of Sydney.

Riemer, K., Diederich, S., Richter, A., and Scifleet, P. (2011). 'Short Message Discussions: On the Conversational Nature of Microblogging in a Large Consultancy Organisation', *Proceedings of the Pacific Asia Conference on Information Systems*. Brisbane: CIS, paper 158.

Rifkin, J. (2000). *The End of Work: The Decline of the Global Workforce and the Dawn of the Post-Market Era*. London: Penguin.

Ripamonti, S., and Scaratti, G. (2011). 'Weak Knowledge for Strengthening Competencies: A Practice-based Approach in Assessment Management', *Management Learning*, 43/2: 183–97.

Ritala, P., Hurmelinna, H., Micahilova, S., and Husted, K. (2015). 'Knowledge Sharing, Knowledge Leaking and Relative Innovation', *Technovation*, 35: 22–31.

Rivera, G., and Cox, A. (2016). 'A Practice-Based Approach to Understanding Participation in Online

Communities', *Journal of Computer-Mediated Communication*, 21: 17–32.

Robert Jr, L., Dennis, A., and Hung, Y-T. (2009). 'Individual Swift Trust and Knowledge-Based Trust in Face-to-Face and Virtual Team Members', *Journal of Management Information Systems*, 26/2: 241–79.

Roberts, B. (2017). 'The Scaffolding Activities of International Returnee Executives: A Learning Based Perspective of Global Boundary Spanning', *Journal of Management Studies*, 54/4: 511–39.

Roberts, J. (2006). 'Limits to Communities of Practice', *Journal of Management Studies*, 43/3: 623–39.

Robertson, M., and O'Malley Hammersley, G. (2000), 'Knowledge Management Practices within a Knowledge-Intensive Firm: The Significance of the People Management Dimension', *Journal of European Industrial Training*, 24/2–4: 241–53.

Robertson, M., and Swan, J. (2003). '"Control—What Control?" Culture and Ambiguity within a Knowledge Intensive Firm', *Journal of Management Studies*, 40/4: 831–58.

Ron, N., Lipshitz, R., and Popper, M. (2006). 'How Organizations Learn: Post-flight Reviews in an F-16 Fighter Squadron', *Organization Studies*, 27/8: 1069–89.

Rosendaal, B. (2009) 'Sharing Knowledge, Being Different and Working as a Team', *Knowledge Management Research and Practice*, 7: 4–14.

Rosendaal, B., and Bijlsma-Frankema, K. (2015). 'Knowledge Sharing Within Teams: Enabling and Constraining Factors', *Knowledge Management Research and Practice*, 13/4: 215–47.

Ruggles, R. (1998). 'The State of the Notion: Knowledge Management in Practice', *California Management Review*, 40/3: 80–9.

Rushmer, R., and Davies, H. (2004). 'Unlearning in Healthcare: Nature, Importance and Painful Lessons', *Quality and Safety in Healthcare*, 13: 10–15.

Rutten, W., Blaas-Franken, J., and Martin, H. (2016). 'The Impact of (Low) Trust on Knowledge Sharing', *Journal of Knowledge Management*, 20/2: 199–214.

Sadler, P. (2001). 'Leadership and Organizational Learning', in M. Dierkes, A. Bertoin Antal, J. Child, and I. Nonaka (eds), *Handbook of Organizational Learning and Knowledge*. Oxford: Oxford University Press, pp. 415–27.

Saito, A., Umemoto, K., and Ikeda, M. (2007). 'A Strategy-Based Ontology of Knowledge Management Technologies', *Journal of Knowledge Management*, 11/1: 97–114.

Salaman, G. (2001). 'A Response to Snell: The Learning Organization: Fact or Fiction?', *Human Relations*, 54/3: 343–60.

Sanz-Valle, R., Naranjo-Valencia, J., Jiménez-Jiménez, D., and Perez-Caballero, L. (2011). 'Linking Organizational Learning with Technical Innovation and Organizational Culture', *Journal of Knowledge Management*, 15/6: 887–1015.

Sapsted, J., and Salter, A. (2004). 'Postcards from the Edge: Local Communities, Global Programs and Boundary Objects', *Organization Studies*, 25/9: 1515–34.

Scarbrough, H. (1998). 'Path(ological) Dependency? Core Competencies from an Organizational Perspective', *British Journal of Management*, 9/3: 219–32.

Scarbrough, H., and Swan, J. (2001). 'Explaining the Diffusion of Knowledge Management', *British Journal of Management*, 12/1: 3–12.

Scarbrough, H., Bresnan, M., Edelman, L., Laurent, S., Newell, S., and Swan, J. (2004). 'The Process of Project-Based Learning: An Exploratory Study', *Management Learning*, 35/4: 491–506.

Scarbrough, H., Swan, J., Laurent, S., Bresnen, M., Edelman, L., and Newell, S. (2004). 'Project-Based Learning and the Role of Learning Boundaries', *Organization Studies*, 25/9: 1579–600.

Scarso, E., and Bolisani, E. (2016). 'Factors Affecting the Use of Wiki to Manage Knowledge in a Small Company', *Journal of Knowledge Management*, 20/3: 423–43.

Scheepers, R., Venkitachalam, K., and Gibbs, M. R. (2004). 'Knowledge Strategy in Organizations: Refining the Model of Hansen, Nohria and Tierney', *Journal of Strategic Information Systems*, 13/3: 201–22.

Schein, E. (1996). 'Culture: The Missing Concept in Organization Studies', *Administrative Science Quarterly*, 41/2: 229–40.

Schenkel, A., and Teigland, R. (2008). 'Improved Organizational Performance through Communities of Practice', *Journal of Knowledge Management*, 12/1: 106–18.

Schmitt, A., Borzillo, S., and Probst, G. (2012). 'Don't Let Knowledge Walk Away: Knowledge Retention During Employee Downsizing', *Management Learning*, 43/1: 53–74.

Schultze, U., and Boland, R. (2000). 'Knowledge Management Technology and the Reproduction of Knowledge Work Practices', *Journal of Strategic Information Systems*, 9: 193–212.

Schultze, U., and Stabell, C. (2004). 'Knowing What You Don't Know: Discourse and Contradictions in Knowledge Management Research', *Journal of Management Studies*, 41/4: 549–73.

Seba, I., Rowley, J., and Delbridge, R. (2012). 'Knowledge Sharing in the Dubai Police Force', *Journal of Knowledge Management*, 16/1: 114–28.

Secundo, G., Magnier-Watanabe, R., and Heisig, P. (2015). 'Engineering Knowledge and Information Needs in Italy and Japan: Bridging the Gap between Theory and Practice', *Journal of Knowledge Management*, 19/6: 1310–34.

Senge, P. (1990). *The Fifth Discipline*. New York: Doubleday.

Serenko, A., and Bontis, N. (2013). 'The Intellectual Core and Impact of the Knowledge Management Academic Discipline', *Journal of Knowledge Management*, 17/1: 137–55.

Serenko, A., and Bontis, A. (2016). 'Understanding Counterproductive Knowledge Behavior: Antecedents and Consequences of Intra-Organizational Knowledge Hiding', *Journal of Knowledge Management*, 20/6: 1199–224.

Serenko, A., Bontis, N., Booker, L., Sadeddin, K., and Hardie, T. (2010). 'A Scientometric Analysis of Knowledge Management and Intellectual Capital Academic Literature (1994–2008)', *Journal of Knowledge Management*, 14/1: 3–23.

Sewell, G. (2005). 'Nice Work? Rethinking Managerial Control in an Era of Knowledge Work', *Organization*, 12/5: 685–704.

Shaw, M. J., Subramaniam, C., Tan, G. W., and Welge, M. E. (2001). 'Knowledge Management and Data Mining for Marketing', *Decision Support Systems*, 31/1: 127–37.

Shepherd, D., Patzelt, H., and Wolfe, M. (2011). 'Moving Forward from Project Failure: Negative Emotions, Affective Commitment, and Learning from the Experience', *Academy of Management Journal*, 54/6: 1229–59.

Shieh, C-J. (2011). 'Study on the Relations Among Customer Knowledge Managmeent, Learning Organization, and Organizational Performance', *The Service Industries Journal*, 31/5: 791–807.

Shipton, H. (2006). 'Confusion or Cohesion? Towards a Typology for Organizational Learning Research', *International Journal of Management Reviews*, 8/4: 233–52.

Shipton, H., and Sillince, J. (2012). 'Organizational Learning and Emotion: Constructing Collective Meaning in Support of Strategic Themes', *Management Learning*, 44/5: 493–510.

Shoemaker, M., and Zaheer, S. (2014). 'The Role of Language in Knowledge Transfer to Geographically Dispersed Manufacturing Operations', *Journal of International Management*, 20/1: 50–72.

Skeels, M. M., and Grudin, J. (2009). 'When Social Networks Cross Boundaries: A Case Study of Workplace Use of Facebook and LinkedIn', *Proceedings of the ACM 2009 International Conference on Supporting Group Work*. London: ACM, pp. 95–103.

Snell, R. (2001). 'Moral Foundations of the Learning Organization', *Human Relations*, 54/3: 319–42.

Spender, J. C. (1996). 'Organizational Knowledge, Learning and Memory: Three Concepts in Search of a Theory', *Journal of Organizational Change Management*, 9/1: 63–78.

Spender, J. C. (2003). 'Exploring Uncertainty and Emotion in the Knowledge-based Firm', *Information Technology and People*, 16/3: 266–88.

Spender, J. C., and Scherer, A. (2007). 'The Philosophical Foundations of Knowledge Management: Editors' Introduction', *Organization*, 14/1: 5–28.

Srivastava, A., Bartol, K., and Locke, E. (2006). 'Empowering Leadership in Management Teams: Effects on Knowledge Sharing, Efficacy, and Performance', *Academy of Management Journal*, 49/6: 1239–51.

Stamps, D. (2000). 'Communities of Practice: Learning is Social, Training is Irrelevant?', in E. Lesser, M. Fontaine, and J. Slusher (eds), *Knowledge and Communities*. Oxford: Butterworth-Heinemann, pp. 53–64.

Stanoevska-Slabeva, K., and Schmid, B. F. (2001). 'A Typology of Online Communities and Community Supporting Platforms', *Proceedings of the 34th Annual Hawaii International Conference on System Sciences*. Hawaii: IEEE Computer Society.

Star, S. (1989). 'The Structure of Ill-Structured Solutions: Boundary Objects and Heterogeneous Distributed Problem Solving', in M. Huhns and L. Gasser (eds), *Readings in Distributed Artificial Intelligence*. Menlo Park, CA: Morgan Kaufman.

Starbuck, W. (1992). 'Learning by Knowledge-Intensive Firms', *Journal of Management Studies*, 29: 713–40.

Starbuck, W. (1993). 'Keeping a Butterfly and an Elephant in a House of Cards: The Elements of Exceptional Success', *Journal of Management Studies*, 30/6: 885–921.

Starbuck, W. H. (1997). 'Learning by Knowledge-Intensive Firms', in L. Prusak (ed.), *Knowledge in Organizations*. Boston: Butterworth-Heinemann, pp. 147–75.

Starkey, K., Tempest, S., and McKinlay, A. (2003). *How Organizations Learn: Managing the Search for Knowledge*. London: Thomson Learning.

Steinmueller, W. (2000). 'Will New Information and Communication Technologies Improve the "Codification" of Knowledge?', *Industrial and Corporate Change*, 9/2: 361–76.

Stenius, M., Hankonen, N., Ravaja, N., and Haukkala, A. (2016). 'Why Share Expertise? A Closer Look at the Quality of Motivation to Share or Withhold Knowledge', *Journal of Knowledge Management*, 20/2: 181–98.

Stock, G., McFadden, K., and Gowen III, C. (2010). 'Organizational Culture, Knowledge Management, and Patient Safety in U.S. Hospitals', *QMJ*, 17/2: 7–26.

Storey, J., and Quintas, P. (2001). 'Knowledge Management and HRM', in J. Storey (ed.), *Human Resource Management: A Critical Text*. London: Thomson Learning, pp. 339–63.

Strati, A. (2007). 'Sensible Knowledge and Practice-based Learning', *Management Learning*, 38/1: 61–77.

Styhre, A. (2003). *Understanding Knowledge Management: Critical and Postmodern Perspectives*. Copenhagen: Liber, Copenhagen Business School.

Styhre, A., Josephson, P. E., and Knauseder, I. (2006). 'Organization Learning in Non-writing Communities: The Case of Construction Workers', *Management Learning*, 37/1: 83–100.

Su, Z., Ahlstrom, D., Li, J., and Cheng, D. (2013). 'Knowledge Creation Capability, Absorptive Capacity, and Product Innovativeness', *R&D Management*, 43/5: 473–85.

Sullivan, D., and Marvel, M. (2011). 'Knowledge Acquisition, Network Reliance, and Early-Stage Technology Venture Outcomes', *Journal of Management Studies*, 48/6: 1169–93.

Suppiah, V., and Sandhu, M. (2011). 'Organizational Culture's Influence on Tacit Knowledge-Sharing Behaviour', *Journal of Knowledge Management*, 15/3: 462–77.

Swan, J., Bresnen, M., Newell, S., and Robertson, M. (2007). 'The Object of Knowledge: The Role of Objects in Biomedical Innovation', *Human Relations*, 60/12: 1809–37.

Swart, J. (2011). 'That's Why it Matters: How Knowing Creates Value', *Management Learning*, 42/3: 319–32.

Swart, J., and Kinnie, N. (2003). 'Sharing Knowledge in Knowledge-Intensive Firms', *Human Resource Management Journal*, 13/2: 60–75.

Swart, J., and Kinnie, N. (2010). 'Organisational Learning, Knowledge Assets and HR Practices in Professional Service Firms', *Human Resource Management Journal*, 20/1: 64–79.

Swart, J., Kinnie, N., and Purcell, J. (2003). *People and Performance in Knowledge-Intensive Firms: A Comparison of Six Research and Technology Organizations*. London: CIPD.

Szulanski, G. (1996). 'Exploring Internal Stickiness: Impediments to the Transfer of Best Practice Within the Firm', *Strategic Management Journal*, 17/Winter Special Issue: 27–43.

Szulanski, G., Ringov, D., and Jensen, R. (2016). 'Overcoming Stickiness: How the Timing of Knowledge Transfer Methods Affects Transfer Difficulty', *Organization Science*, 27/2: 304–22.

Tallman, S., and Phene, A. (2007). 'Leveraging Knowledge Across Geographic Boundaries', *Organization Science*, 18/2: 252–60.

Tarekegn, A. N. (2016). 'Localized Knowledge Based System for Human Disease Diagnosis', *International Journal of Information Technology and Computer Science*, 8/3: 43–50.

Taskin, L., and Van Bunnen, G. (2015). 'Knowledge Management through the Development of Knowledge Repositories: Towards Work Degradation', *New Technology, Work and Employment*, 30/2: 158–72.

Tasselli, S. (2015). 'Social Networks and Inter-Professional Knowledge Sharing: The Case of Healthcare Professionals', *Organization Studies*, 36/7: 841–72.

Teece, D. J. (2000). 'Strategies for Managing Knowledge Assets: The Role of Firm Structure and Industrial Context', *Long Range Planning*, 33: 35–54.

Teo, T., Nishant, R., Goh, R., and Agarwal, S. (2011). 'Leveraging Collaborative Technologies to Build a Knowledge Sharing Culture at HP Analytics', *MIS Quarterly Executive*, 10/1: 1–18.

Thomas, J., Sussman, S., and Henderson, J. (2003). 'Understanding "Strategic Learning": Linking Organizational Learning, Knowledge Management and Sensemaking', *Organization Science*, 1/3: 331–45.

Thompson, M. (2005). 'Structural and Epistemic Parameters in Communities of Practice', *Organization Science*, 16/2: 151–64.

Thompson, P., Warhurst, C., and Callaghan, G. (2001). 'Ignorant Theory and Knowledgeable Workers: Interrogating the Connections Between Knowledge, Skills and Services', *Journal of Management Studies*, 38/7: 923–42.

Tong, J., and Mitra, A. (2009). 'Chinese Cultural Influences on Knowledge Management Practice', *Journal of Knowledge Management*, 13/3: 49–62.

Tooman, T., Akinci, C., and Davies, H. (2016). 'Understanding Knowledge and Knowing', in K. Orr, S. Nutley, S. Russell, R. Bain, B. Hacking, and C. Moran (eds), *Knowledge and Practice in Business and Organizations*. London: Routledge, pp. 17–29.

Tordoir, P. (1995). *The Professional Knowledge Economy: The Management and Integration of Professional Services in Business Organizations*. Amsterdam: Springer Science & Business Media.

Townley, B. (1994). *Reframing Human Resource Management: Power, Ethics and the Subject at Work*. London: Sage.

Tranfield, D., Duberley, J., Smith, S., Musson, G., and Stokes, P. (2000). 'Organisational Learning—It's Just Routine!', *Management Decision*, 38/4: 253–60.

Treem, J. W., and Leonardi, P. M. (2012). 'Social Media Use in Organizations: Exploring the Affordances of Visibility, Editability, Persistence, and Association', *Communication Yearbook*, 36: 143–89.

Trier, M., and Richter, A. (2014). 'The Deep Structure of Organizational Online Networking—An Actor-Oriented Case Study', *Information Systems Journal*, 25/5: 465–88.

Trowler, P., and Turner, G. (2002). 'Exploring the Hermeneutic Foundation of University Life: Deaf Academics in a Hybrid "Community of Practice"', *Higher Education*, 43: 227–56.

Trusson, C., Doherty, N., and Hislop, D. (2014). 'Knowledge Sharing Using IT Service Management Tools: Conflicting Discourses and Incompatible Practices', *Information Systems Journal*, 24/4: 347–71.

Tsang, E. (1997). 'Organizational Learning and the Learning Organization: A Dichotomy Between Prescriptive and Descriptive Research', *Human Relations*, 50/1: 73–89.

Tsang, E. (2008). 'Transferring Knowledge to Acquisition Joint Ventures: An Organizational Unlearning Perspective', *Management Learning*, 39/1: 5–20.

Tsang, E., and Zahra S. (2008). 'Organizational Unlearning', *Human Relations*, 61/10: 1435–62.

Tsoukas, H. (1996). 'The Firm as a Distributed Knowledge System: A Constructionist Approach', *Strategic Management Journal*, 17/Winter Special Issue: 11–25.

Tsoukas, H. (2000). 'What is Management? An Outline of a Metatheory', in S. Ackroyd and S. Fleetwood (eds), *Realist Perspectives on Management and Organisations*. London: Routledge, pp. 26–44.

Tsoukas, H. (2003). 'Do We Really Understand Tacit Knowledge?', in M. Easterby-Smith and M. Lyles (eds), *The Blackwell Handbook of Learning and Knowledge Management*. Malden: Blackwell, pp. 410–27.

Turner, N., and Lee-Kelley, L. (2012). 'Unpacking the Theory on Ambidexterity: An Illustrative Case on the Managerial Architectures, Mechanisms and Dynamics', *Management Learning*, 44/2: 179–96.

Tushman, M., and Nadler, D. (1986). 'Organizing for Innovation', *California Management Review*, 28/3: 74–92.

Uden, L., and He, W. (2017). 'How the Internet of Things Can Help Knowledge Management: A Case Study from the Automotive Domain', *Journal of Knowledge Management*, 21/1: 57–70.

Usoro, A., Sharratt, M., Tsui, E., and Shekar, S. (2007). 'Trust as an Antecedent to Knowledge Sharing in Virtual Communities of Practice', *Knowledge Management Research and Practice*, 5: 199–212.

Van den Hooff, B., Schouten, A., and Simonovski, S. (2012). 'What One Feels and What One Knows: The Influence of Emotions on Attitudes and Intentions towards Knowledge Sharing', *Journal of Knowledge Management*, 16/1: 148–58.

Van der Spek, R., and Hofer-Alfeis, J. (2002). 'The Knowledge Strategy Process', in C. W. Holsapple (ed.), *Handbook on Knowledge Management*. Heidelberg: Springer-Verlag, pp. 1–27.

Van der Velden, M. (2002). 'Knowledge Facts, Knowledge Fiction: The Role of ICT's in Knowledge Management for Development', *Journal of International Development*, 14: 25–37.

van Wijk, R., Jansen, J., and Lyles, M. (2008). 'Inter- and Intra-organizational Knowledge Transfer: A Meta-Analytic Review and Assessment of its Antecedents and Consequences', *Journal of Management Studies*, 45/4: 830–53.

Vera, D., and Crossan, M. (2004). 'Strategic Leadership and Organizational Learning', *Academy of Management Review*, 29/2: 222–40.

Verburg, R. M., and Andriessen, E. J. H. (2011). 'A Typology of Knowledge Sharing Networks in Practice', *Knowledge and Process Management*, 18/1: 34–44.

Vince, R. (2001). 'Power and Emotion in Organizational Learning', *Human Relations*, 54/10: 1325–51.

Vince, R., Sutcliffe, K., and Olivera, F. (2002). 'Organizational Learning: New Direction', *British Journal of Management*, 13: S1–6.

Voelpel, S., Dous, M., and Davenport, T. (2005). 'Five Steps to Creating a Global Knowledge-Sharing System: Siemens' ShareNet', *Academy of Management Executive*, 19/2: 9–23.

Vogt, K. (2016). 'The Post-industrial Society: From Utopia to Ideology', *Work, Employment and Society*, 30/2: 366–76.

Von Hayek, F. (1945). 'The Use of Knowledge in Society', *American Economic Review*, 25/4: 519–30.

Von Hippel, E. (1986). 'Lead Users: A Source of Novel Product Concepts', *Management Science*, 32/7: 791–805.

Von Krogh, G. (1998). 'Care in Knowledge Creation', *California Management Review*, 40/3: 133–53.

Von Krogh, G. (2012). 'How Does Social Software Change Knowledge Management? Toward a Strategic Research Agenda', *The Journal of Strategic Information Systems*, 21/2: 154–64.

Von Krogh, G., Ichijo, K., and Nonaka, I. (2000). *Enabling Knowledge Creation: How to Unlock the Mystery of Tacit Knowledge and Release the Power of Innovation*. Oxford: Oxford University Press.

Von Krogh, G., Nonaka, I., and Aben, M. (2001). 'Making the Most of Your Company's Knowledge: A Strategic Framework', *Long Range Planning*, 34/4: 421–39.

Von Krogh, G., Nonaka, I., and Rechsteiner, L. (2012). 'Leadership in Organizational Knowledge Creation', *Journal of Management Studies*, 49/1: 240–77.

Von Nordenflycht, A. (2010). 'What is a Professional Service Firm? Towards a Theory and a Taxonomy of Knowledge-Intensive Firms', *Academy of Management Review*, 35/1: 155–74.

Von Zedtwitz, M. (2002). 'Organizational Learning Through Post-Project Reviews in R&D', *R&D Management*, 32/3: 255–68.

Vuori, V., and Okkonen, J. (2012). 'Knowledge Sharing Motivational Factors of Using an Intra-organizational Social Media Platform', *Journal of Knowledge Management*, 16/4: 592–603.

Walby, S. (2011). 'Is the Knowledge Society Gendered?', *Gender, Work and Organization*, 18/1: 1–29.

Walsh, J., and Ungson, G. (1991). 'Organizational Memory', *Academy of Management Review*, 16/1: 57–91.

Walsham, G. (2001). 'Knowledge Management: The Benefits and Limitations of Computer Systems', *European Management Journal*, 19/6: 599–608.

Wang, H., He, J., and Mahoney, J. (2009). 'Firm-Specific Knowledge Resources and Competitive Advantage: The Role of Economic- and Relationship-Based Employee Governance Mechanisms', *Strategic Management Journal*, 30: 1265–85.

Wang, J. K., Asleigh, M., and Meyer, E. (2006). 'Knowledge Sharing and Team Trustworthiness', *Knowledge Management Research and Practice*, 4: 75–186.

Wang, Y., and Haggerty, N. (2009). 'Knowledge Transfer in Virtual Settings: The Role of Individual Virtual Competency', *Information Systems Journal*, 19/6: 571–93.

Ward, A. (2000). 'Getting Strategic Value from Constellations of Communities', *Strategy and Leadership*, 28/2: 4–9.

Warhurst, C., and Thompson, P. (2006). 'Mapping Knowledge in Work: Proxies or Practices', *Work, Employment and Society*, 20/4: 787–800.

Waring, J., and Currie, G. (2009). 'Managing Expert Knowledge: Organizational Challenges and Managerial Futures for the UK Medical Profession', *Organization Studies*, 30/7: 755–78.

Wasko, M., and Faraj, S. (2005). 'Why Should I Share? Examining Social Capital and Knowledge Contribution in Electronic Networks of Practice', *MIS Quarterly*, 29/1: 35–58.

Watson, H. J. (2014). 'Tutorial: Big Data Analytics. Concepts, Technologies, and Applications', *Communications of the Association for Information Systems*, 34/1: 1247–68.

Webster, F. (1996). *Theories of the Information Society*. London: Routledge.

Weick, K., and Westley, F. (1996). 'Organizational Learning: Affirming an Oxymoron', in S. Clegg, C. Nord, and W. Nord (eds), *Handbook of Organization Studies*. London: Sage, pp. 440–58.

Weir, D., and Hutchins, K. (2005). 'Cultural Embeddedness and Cultural Constraints: Knowledge Sharing in Chinese and Arab Cultures', *Knowledge and Process Management*, 12/2: 89–98.

Wenger, E. (1998). *Communities of Practice: Learning, Meaning and Identity*. Cambridge: Cambridge University Press.

Wenger, E., and Snyder, W. (2000). 'Communities of Practice: The Organizational Frontier', *Harvard Business Review*, 78/1: 139–46.

Wenger, E., McDermott, R., and Snyder, W. (2002). *Cultivating Communities of Practice*. Boston: Harvard Business School Press.

Werder, K., Helms, R. W., and Jansen, S. (2014). 'Social Media for Success: A Strategic Framework', in K. Siau, Q. Li, and X. Guo (eds), *Proceedings of the 18th Pacific Asia Conference on Information Systems 2014*. Chengdu: CIS.

Werr, A., and Stjernberg, T. (2003). 'Exploring Management Consulting Firms as Knowledge Systems', *Organization Studies*, 24/6: 881–908.

West, J., and Bogers, M. (2014). 'Leveraging External Sources of Innovation: A Review of Research on Open Innovation', *Journal of Product Innovation Management*, 31/4: 814–31.

Whittle, A., Mueller, F., Gilchrist, A., and Lenney, P. (2016). 'Sensemaking, Sense-Censoring and Strategic Inaction: The Discursive Enactment of Power and Politics in a Multinational Corporation', *Organization Studies*, 37/9: 1323–51.

Wiig, K. M. (1997). 'Knowledge Management: An Introduction and Perspective', *Journal of Knowledge Management*, 1/1: 6–14.

Wilcox King, A., and Zeithaml, C. P. (2003). 'Measuring Organizational Knowledge: A Conceptual and Methodological Framework', *Strategic Management Journal*, 24/8: 763–72.

Wilkinson, A., and Mellahi, K. (2005). 'Organizational Failure: Introduction to Special Issue', *Long Range Planning*, 38/3: 233–8.

Williams, C. (2011). 'Client-Vendor Knowledge Transfer in IS Offshore Outsourcing: Insights from a Survey of Indian Software Engineers', *Information Systems Journal*, 21: 335–56.

Wilson, T. (2002). 'The Nonsense of "Knowledge Management"', *Information Research*, 8/1: paper 144.

Wilson, J., and Elman, N. (1990). 'Organizational Benefits of Mentoring', *Academy of Management Executive*, 4/4: 88–94.

Windeck, D., Weber, J., and Strauss, E. (2015). 'Enrolling Managers to Accept the Business Partner: The Role of Boundary Objects', *Journal of Management Governance*, 19: 617–53.

Wong, P., Cheung, S., Yiu, R., and Hardie, M. (2012). 'The Unlearning Dimension of Organizational Learning in Construction Projects', *International Journal of Project Management*, 30/1: 94–104.

Wu, L-W., and Lin, J-R. (2013). 'Knowledge Sharing and Knowledge Effectiveness: Learning Orientation and Co-Production in the Contingency Model of Tacit Knowledge', *Journal of Business and Industrial Marketing*, 28/8: 672–86.

Yakhlef, A. (2010). 'The Corporeality of Practice-Based Learning', *Organization Studies*, 31/4: 409–30.

Yalabik, Z., Swart, J., Kinnie, N., and van Rossenber, Y. (2017). 'Multiple Foci of Commitment and Intention to Quit in Knowledge-Intensive Organizations (KIOs): What Makes Professionals Leave?', *International Journal of Human Resource Management*, 28/2: 417–47.

Yang, J-T. (2007). 'Knowledge Sharing: Investigating Appropriate Leadership Roles and Collaborative Culture', *Tourism Management*, 28: 530–43.

Yanow, D. (2004). 'Translating Local Knowledge at Organizational Peripheries', *British Journal of Management*, 15/Special Issue: S71–86.

Yeo, R., and Marquardt, M. (2015). 'To Share or Not to Share? Self-Perception and Knowledge Sharing Intent', *Knowledge Management Research and Practice*, 13: 311–28.

Yildiz, H., and Fey, C. (2010). 'Compatibility and Unlearning in Knowledge Transfer in Mergers and Acquisitions', *Scandinavian Journal of Management*, 26: 448–56.

Yli-Renko, H., Autio, E., and Sapienza, H. (2001). 'Social Capital, Knowledge Acquisition, and Knowledge Exploitation in Young Technology-Based Firms', *Strategic Management Journal*, 22: 587–613.

Youndt, M. A., Subramaniam, M., and Snell, S. A. (2004). 'Intellectual Capital Profiles: An Examination of Investments and Returns', *Journal of Management Studies*, 41: 335–62.

Yukl, G. (2008). *Leadership in Organizations* (6th edn). London: Pearson Education.

Zablith, F., Faraj, S., and Azad, B. (2016). 'Organizational Knowledge Generation: Lessons from Online Communities', *Business Process Management Journal*, 22/1: 33–55.

Zahra, S., and George, G. (2002). 'Absorptive Capacity: A Review, Reconceptualization and Extension', *Academy of Management Review*, 27/2: 185–203.

Zahra, S., Abdelgawad, S., and Tsang, E. (2011). 'Emerging Multinationals Venturing into Developed Economies: Implications for Learning, Unlearning, and Entrepreneurial Capability', *Journal of Management Inquiry*, 20/3: 323–30.

Zenger, T. R., and Lawrence, B. S. (1989). 'Organizational Demography: The Differential Effects of Age and Tenure Distributions on Technical Communication', *Academy of Management Journal*, 32: 353–76.

Zeynep, E., Schneider, A., and von Krogh, G. (2014). 'The Multifaceted Nature of Social Practices: A Review of the Perspectives on Practice-based Theory Building about Organizations', *European Management Journal*, 32: 712–22.

Zhang, J., Ackerman, M. S., and Adamic, L. (2007). 'Expertise Networks in Online Communities: Structure and Algorithms', *Proceedings of the 16th International Conference on World Wide Web*. Ann Arbor, MI: International World Wide Web Conferences, pp. 221–30.

Zhang, L., and Cheng, J. (2015). 'Effects of Knowledge Leadership on Knowledge Sharing in Engineering Project Design Teams: The Role of Social Capital', *Project Management Journal*, 46/5: 111–24.

Zhao, B. (2011). 'Learning from Errors: The Role of Context, Emotion, and Personality', *Journal of Organizational Behaviour*, 32: 435–63.

Zhao, Z., and Anand, J. (2013). 'Beyond Boundary Spanners: The "Collective Bridge" as an Efficient Interunit Structure for Transferring Collective Knowledge', *Strategic Management Journal*, 34: 1513–30.

Zhou, S., Siu, F., and Wang, M. (2010). 'Effects of Social Tie Content on Knowledge Transfer', *Journal of Knowledge Management*, 14/3: 449–63.

Zhuge, H. (2002). 'A Knowledge Flow Model for Peer-to-Peer Team Knowledge Sharing and Management', *Expert Systems with Applications*, 23/1: 23–30.

Zietsma, C., Winn, M., Branzei, O., and Vertinsky, I. (2002). 'The War of the Woods: Facilitators and Impediments of Organizational Learning Processes', *British Journal of Management*, 13: S61–74.

Zimmermann, A., and Ravishankar, M. (2014). 'Knowledge Transfer in IT Offshoring Relationships: The Role of Social Capital, Efficacy and Outcome Expectations', *Information Systems Journal*, 24: 167–202.

Zuboff, S. (1988). *In the Age of the Smart Machine: The Future of Work and Power*. Oxford: Heinemann Professional.

Index

The letters *t* and *f* following a page number denote tables and figures.

A

absorptive capacity 24, 28, 111, 122–3, 124–5
adhocracy 275, 276, 284
adidas 101–2
advertising industry 35
affect-based trust 186, 187, 225
algorithms 158
Alvesson and Kärreman, typology of knowledge management strategies 63–4
appropriating strategy 59
artifactual knowledge 22
autonomy, knowledge workers' 261

B

ba/shared space concept 111, 116, 123–4
Bell, Daniel 3–5, 7
big data 148, 157–8, 160
boundary types 226–7, 229, 230–1
boundary-spanners 228–9, 232
boundary-spanning knowledge processes 123, 208, 216–34
   and boundary objects 227, 229–31, 232
   brokers/brokering 208, 228, 232
   conflict in 220–1, 232
   and epistemological differences 222–4, 232
   facilitation of 227–31, 232
   importance of 218–19, 231–2
   and relationship management 228
   sense of identity and 220–2, 232
   and trust 224–6
Burbage Shakespeare company 250
bureaucratic (hierarchical) culture 275, 276, 284
business processes, and innovation 120
business strategy, and knowledge management 53–5

C

call centres 6
care workers 43–4, 74–5
cartographic approach 149*t*, 164
case studies and illustrations
   absorptive capacity 124-5
   adidas group learning campus 101–2
   advertising industry, collective character of knowledge and practice 35
   agile software development 213-14
   boundary-spanners in MNCs 228–9
   care home practices and collective knowledge 43–4
   centralizing knowledge management 65–6
   CERN 268–9
   coal mine risk assessment, disputed knowledge 242
   codification and personalization strategies, Indian manufacturing companies 62
   collective knowledge 43-4
   communities of practice 197, 206, 210–11, 213–14
   Danisco 284-5
   dock workers, Italy 36–7, 42
   Ericsson 213-14
   HRM practices 85-6
      and knowledge sharing 258, 259–60, 264, 268–9
   IT service firms as knowledge-intensive 70
   knowledge acquisition impact on task productivity 20
   knowledge assets 85-6
   knowledge creation
      and new product development 124–5
   knowledge creation theory and customer relationship management systems 115
   knowledge creation theory in Russia 119–20
   knowledge leakage 139–40

knowledge protection 141
knowledge repositories 154
knowledge sharing and functional diversity 225
knowledge sharing and high-involvement work practices 258
knowledge sharing and HRM practices 258, 259–60, 264, 268–9
knowledge sharing inhibiting factors 192–3
knowledge sharing and leadership 282, 283
knowledge sharing in MNCs 27–8, 56–7, 219, 221–2, 223–4, 228–9, 232–3, 260
knowledge sharing motivation 264
knowledge sharing and organizational culture 284–5
knowledge sharing in R&D via co-location 232–3
knowledge sharing and relationship conflict 183–4
knowledge sharing and resource-based power 240
knowledge sharing via Wiki 160-1
knowledge strategy frameworks 58–9
knowledge transfer, objective analysis 27-8
leadership 271–2, 282, 283
learning from errors 105–6
learning orientation 85–6
McKinsey's knowledge network 65–6
management consultants, ambiguous impact and output of some 77–8
Novartis cross-functional knowledge sharing 232–3
objective analysis of knowledge transfer 27-8
office equipment service engineers as knowledge workers 75–6

case studies and illustrations (*cont.*)
  online cross-organizational
    networks 40
  organizational culture 271–2,
    284–5
  organizational learning 107–8
  ParcelCo 192-3
  Pfizer knowledge workers 80–1
  power/knowledge in
    client-consultant
    relationships 247
  power/knowledge concept and
    knowledge management
    research 249–50
  professional service firms 85-6
  resource-based power and
    knowledge sharing 240
  sawmill workers, Italy, sensible
    knowledge 32
  small and medium-sized
    enterprises (SMEs) 55
  social media 168, 171–2
  team reflexivity and stress in new
    product development
    143-4
  telemedicine, practice-based
    perspective on 32–3
  time and discontinuities, role
    of 107–8
  transactive memory systems
    (TMSs) and knowledge
    sharing 165
  universities as learning
    organizations 99–100
  university knowledge transfer
    processes 123
  unlearning during change 132
  unlearning in joint
    ventures 127–8
  unlearning and team
    reflexivity 137, 143–4
  wiki-based knowledge
    management 160–1
  Yammer at Deloitte
    Australia 171-2
case-based systems 156
CERN 268–9
change
  communities of practice
    response to 211
  unlearning and processes
    of 131–3, 135
charismatic leadership 280, 281
China, Japanese subsidiaries
    in 103–4
clan culture 275
coaching 262–3
coal mine risk assessment, disputed
    knowledge 242

Coca-Cola 139–40, 170
codification of knowledge 27, 61,
    152, 159, 163, 246
codification knowledge
    management strategy
    60–1, 62, 152, 149t, 155,
    262, 263
codified knowledge *see* explicit/
    codified knowledge
coercive power 239, 240
cognitive-based trust 186, 187t, 225
collaborative knowing 34
collaborative working 261
    see also boundary-
      spanning knowledge
      processes;communities
      of practice
collective knowledge 21–3, 34,
    43–4
collectivism 189, 221
combination, of explicit
    knowledge 113–14, 115,
    119t
commoditization of knowledge 61
communities of practice 21, 31, 42,
    94, 167, 187, 188, 195–215,
    216, 217, 220
  blinkered and inward-
    looking 211–12
  critical perspectives on 209–12
  definition 196–7
  and formal work groups
    distinguished 196t
  group identity 199, 200
  intra-community knowledge
    processes 200
  and knowledge sharing 175–6,
    195, 198, 200, 208, 212
  management of 204–7
  online 201, 203–4
  origins, features, and
    dynamics 197–9
  power and conflict issues 209, 210
  types of 200–3
  visualizing and analysing
    207–9
community approach 63, 64f,
    149t, 170
competency traps 96, 126, 135
competitive advantage 17, 18
  and leadership 282
  resource-based theory of 78–9
competitive intelligence (CI) 248
complementary knowledge
    21–2, 23
conduit (transmitter–receiver)
    model of knowledge
    sharing 24–5, 27, 37, 41,
    152, 159, 164, 217

conflict 235, 241, 243–4
  boundary-spanning 220–1, 232
  and communities of
    practice 209–10
  and knowledge sharing 182–4,
    191, 220–1, 261
  and power/knowledge
    relationships 246–8
consensus perspective on social
    order 8, 236
constraints-based systems 156
constuctivist discourse
  on knowledge
    management 9f, 236
contextual knowledge 73, 74, 75
contingency model 57, 65
CRISP data mining model 158
critical discourse on knowledge
    management 9f, 236, 237,
    238–44
cross-cultural knowledge
    sharing 39, 56, 221
Crossan and Apaydin:
  multidimensional
    framework on
    innovation 110, 111,
    120–2, 123, 124
Crossan/Zietsma model
  of organizational
    learning 94–6, 96t, 107–8
crowd sourcing 163, 164, 169
crowd-based approach to
    ICT-based knowledge
    management 150t, 169–71
cultural diversity 55, 56
cultural embeddedness of
    knowledge 37–9, 118–19,
    221
cultural factors
  and approaches to training 221
  and differences in learning
    103–4
  see also national cultural
    factors;organizational
    culture;socio-cultural
    factors
customer relationship management
    (CRM) systems, and
    knowledge creation
    theory 115

D

Danisco 284–5
data analytics (data mining) 148,
    157–8
decision-making 33, 36–7, 101,
    182, 258, 261
defensive routines 135

Deloitte 171—2
dialogic discourse on knowledge
        management 9f, 236, 237,
        244—8
discourse, and power/knowledge
        claims 246
dissensus perspective on social
        order 8, 183, 235, 236—7,
        244, 246
dock workers, Italy 36—7, 42

E

embeddedness of knowledge
        cultural 37—9, 118—19, 221
        in practice 30, 31—3, 41
embodied knowledge 32, 34,
        35—7, 41, 51, 112, 177—8
emotions
        and knowledge sharing 179—80,
        185
        and learning 100, 105—7
        and unlearning 134
employment relationship
        and knowledge sharing 180—2,
        191
        and learning 97, 100—2
        power in 181, 235, 243—4
enacted blueprints 64, 149t
enterprise social networks
        (ESN) 150, 166
environmental knowledge
        intensity 60
epistemological differences,
        and knowledge sharing
        in boundary-spanning
        contexts 222—4, 232
epistemology 14
Ericsson 213
expanding strategy 59
expert knowledge 242
expert power 240, 241
expert systems see knowledge-based
        systems
expertise databases 166
expertise mapping 165—6
explicit/codified knowledge 15,
        16, 17, 18, 19—20, 24, 26,
        27—8, 33, 34, 36, 41, 61, 69,
        152, 242
        combination 113—14, 115, 119t
        internalization of 113, 114,
        115—16, 118, 119t
        leakage 138—9
        protection of 141, 142t
        sharing of 20, 25, 27, 28
        tacit—explicit dichotomy 19—20,
        21, 33, 112—13, 117—18
        and task productivity 20

extended library approach 63, 149t
externalization, of tacit
        knowledge 25—6, 113,
        114—15, 118—19

F

failure, admitting to, and learning/
        unlearning 134, 136
five-factor personality model 186,
        190—1, 259
forgetting 126
        accidental 129
        and technology
        development 130
        typology of 129, 130f
        unlearning as deliberate 128—31
        and unlearning
        distinguished 127
functional diversity, and knowledge
        sharing 225

G

gender issues 5
graph theory 208
group identity 256, 257, 274
        communities of practice 199,
        200
        and knowledge sharing 187—8

H

Hansen et al.: codification
        versus personalization
        framework 60—1, 62
hierarchical (bureaucratic)
        culture 275, 276, 284
hoard/share dilemma 177,
        178—80, 256
human capital 79
human resource management
        (HRM) practices 253,
        255—70
        coaching and mentoring 262—3
        importance to knowledge
        management 256—8
        job design 257, 260—1
        and knowledge sharing 256—65,
        268—9
        performance appraisal 258,
        260, 263
        recruitment and selection
        259—60
        reward systems 257, 258, 260,
        263—5
        and staff retention 265—7
        training and development 257,
        258, 261—2

I

ICTs and knowledge management 5,
        26, 49, 56, 147—9
        collaboration tools to facilitate
        knowledge sharing 150t,
        166—9
        crowd-based approach 150t,
        169—71
        exclusive camp 148
        identification camp 148
        network-based approach 149t,
        164—6
        objectivist perspectives
        on 151—62
        practice-based perspectives
        on 163—73
        process and domain model
        approach 149t, 155—7,
        159—60
        repository-based approach 149t,
        152—5, 159
        sensor-based approach 149t,
        157—8, 160
ideas competitions 170
identification-based loyalty 267
identity
        and boundary-spanning
        knowledge processes
        220—2, 232
        organizational 274
        see also group identity
illustrations see case studies and
        illustrations
immersion in practice 42
individual knowledge 20, 33, 34
individualism 189, 190, 207, 221
industrial society 3
informal knowledge
        management 55—6
information and communication
        technologies see ICTs
Infosys 154
innovation 79
        and absorptive capacity 24, 111,
        122—3
        and boundary-spanning
        knowledge processes 219
        and business processes 120
        Crossan and Apaydin's
        multidimensional framework
        on 110, 111, 120—2, 123, 124
        definition 110
        and knowledge processes 110,
        120—3
        and leadership 120
        managerial levers 120—1
        new product development 124—5
        open 121—3, 169
        and organizational culture 276

instrumental leadership 280, 281
instrumental-based loyalty 267
intellectual capital 79, 196, 248
    see also social capital
internalization, of explicit of
            knowledge 113, 114,
            115–16, 118
intuition 95f, 107–8
IT service firms 70

J

Japanese companies, subsidiaries in
            China 103–4
job design 257, 260–1
joint ventures 127–8, 226

K

Kim et al.: internal and
            external codification/
            personalization 60
knowledge 13–14, 49–50
    and action 112
    amplification of 114
    codification of 27, 61, 152, 159,
            163, 246
    collective 21–3, 34, 43–4
    commoditization of 61
    contestable nature of 39–40
    contextual 73, 74, 75
    culturally embedded nature
            of 37–9, 118–19, 221
    embeddedness in practice 30,
            31–3, 36
    embodiment in people 32, 34,
            35–7, 41, 51, 112, 177–8
    entitative character of 15–16,
            18, 31, 51, 152
    hiding 181
    individual–group/collective
            dichotomy 20–1, 33, 34
    institutionalization of 135–6
    legitimate 238, 242
    loss 265
        see also forgetting;knowledge
            leakage; unlearning
    as multidimensional and non-
            dichotomous 33–5
    objectivist perspective 8, 14,
            15–29, 43, 139, 198, 217
    practice-based perspective 8, 14,
            30–45, 75, 105, 112, 134,
            189, 195, 198, 217, 221, 227
    protection 140–2
    as a public good 178
    sensible 32
    socially constructed nature
            of 37–9

spill-over 169
tacit–explicit dichotomy 19–20,
            21, 33, 112–13, 117–18
    theoretical 3–4, 7, 69, 73, 74, 75
    thick and thin 56–7
    watering-down of 169
    see also explicit/codified
            knowledge;power/
            knowledge; tacit knowledge
knowledge conversion 111, 112,
            123
    SECI model 39, 111, 113–16,
            117–19, 157
knowledge creation 57, 59, 74, 78,
            79, 89
    and boundary-spanning
            knowledge processes 218,
            219
    informal 55
    and new product
            development 124–5
    and unlearning 128
    see also Nonaka's knowledge
            creation theory
knowledge domains 59, 219
knowledge economy *see* knowledge
            society
knowledge gaps, and knowledge
            transfer 223–4
knowledge integration/
            application 78, 79–80, 95f,
            108, 122
knowledge leakage 127, 137–40,
            143, 248, 265
knowledge management
    constructivist discourse 9f, 236
    contingency model 57, 65
    critical discourse 9f, 236, 237,
            238–44
    definitions of 49–51
    dialogic discourse 9f, 236, 237,
            244–8
    evaluation 51, 52t
    growth of interest in 1–2, 3
    key assumptions in literature 2–3
    lifecycle 50
    neo-functionalist discourse 8, 9,
            18, 236
    objectivist perspective on 25–6,
            51, 151–62
    organizational characteristics
            influencing 53–7
    practice-based perspective
            on 40–2, 51, 163–73
    processes 25–6
    rationale for 51, 52t
    theories underlying 51, 52t
knowledge management
            strategies 58

knowledge management strategy
            frameworks 60–4
    see also codification
            knowledge management
            strategy;personalization
            knowledge management
            strategy
knowledge processes 50, 51, 52t,
            59, 148
    and innovation 110, 120–3
    knowledge workers' willingness
            to participate in 82–4
    in knowledge-intensive firms 78,
            79–82
    see also knowledge creation;
            knowledge sharing/transfer
knowledge protection 126, 127
knowledge repository 26, 149t,
            152–5, 159
knowledge sharing/transfer 59,
            177–94
    in boundary-spanning contexts
            see boundary-spanning
            knowledge processes
    collaboration tools 150t, 166–9
    collective knowledge 23
    and communities of
            practice 175–6, 195, 198,
            200, 208, 212
    conduit (transmitter–receiver)
            model of 24–5, 27, 37, 41,
            152, 159, 164, 217
    and conflict 182–4, 191, 220–1,
            261
    cross-cultural 39, 56, 221
    culture 42, 274
    and emotions 179–80, 185
    and employment
            relationship 180–2, 191
    explicit knowledge 20, 25, 27, 28
    and functional diversity 225
    and group identity 187–8
    HRM practices and facilitation
            of 256–65, 268–9
    informal 55
    in joint ventures 127–8
    and knowledge gaps 223–4
    and language 221–2, 223, 260
    and leadership 282, 283, 284
    motivation 256–7, 263, 264
    multinationals 27–8, 56–7, 219,
            221–2, 223–4, 228–9, 260
    and national culture 188–90,
            192, 223
    objectivist perspective on 23–6
    and organizational culture
            284–5
    personality and attitude to
            190–1, 192, 259–60

and power 240
practice-based perspective
    on 40–2, 164
and procedural justice 182
share/hoard dilemma 177,
    178–80, 256
and social media 168–9, 180
tacit knowledge 20, 25, 28, 222,
    224, 263, 276
and trust 184–7, 187–8, 191–2,
    224–6, 240, 263
universities 123
wiki-based 160–1
willingness to share 154
knowledge society concept 3–6
critical evaluation of 6–8
gender and 5
and knowledge-intensive
    firms and knowledge
    workers 69–70, 84
knowledge strategy
    frameworks 58–60
knowledge work 50
and ambiguity 76–8
three-dimensional
    conceptualization of 73
knowledge workers 68–9
'all work is knowledge work'
    perspective 74–6, 84
autonomy 261
client-related knowledge 82, 84
as ideal employees 82–3, 84
inhibitions and conflicts 83–4
involvement in decision-
    making 258, 261
and knowledge processes 78,
    79–80
    willingness to participate
    in 82–4
    see also knowledge sharing/
    transfer
and knowledge society
    rhetoric 69–70, 84
loyalty 84, 255, 265–7
organizational commitment 256,
    257–8, 265
power of 243–4
productivity 73–4
professional knowledge work
    perspective 72–4, 75
recruitment and selection 259–60
retention of 84, 257, 261, 265–7
social capital 81–2, 84, 266
training and development 257,
    258, 261–2
turnover 84, 255, 265
knowledge-based systems 155–7
knowledge-based theory of the
    firm 17–18, 50

knowledge-intensity 6–7
knowledge-intensive firms 7
defining and characterizing 70–1
knowledge processes in 78–82
and knowledge society
    rhetoric 69–70
taxonomy of 71

L

labour market factors 7, 57, 84, 265
language
ambiguity/fluidity of
    meaning 37, 38
common, and shared sense of
    identity 221–2
competencies and skills 259, 260
and epistemological differences
    in boundary-spanning
    contexts 223
and knowledge sharing 221–2,
    223, 260
and power/knowledge
    claims 246
leadership 253, 271–2
behaviour-based
    perspective 279t
charismatic 280, 281
and competitive advantage 282
conceptualization of 278–81
contingency perspective 279t
and innovation 120
instrumental 280, 281
and knowledge management
    relationship 281–3
and knowledge sharing 282,
    283, 284
in learning organizations 100
and (micro-)management
    distinguished 280t
new leadership perspective 279t,
    280–1
strategic 280, 283
trait theory of 279
transactional 272, 280, 281
transformational 272, 280, 281,
    283, 284
learning 89, 91
ambidextrous 96
cultural differences in 103–4
emotional aspects of 100, 105–7
and employment
    relationship 97, 100–2
exploitation-based 95, 96
exploration-based 95, 96
from failure 134
group 93, 94, 95
individual 93, 94, 95

institutionalized 95–6
mechanisms and processes 92–3
project-based 93, 94
typologies 92, 93t
and unlearning, relationship
    between 131–2
see also learning organizations;
    organizational
    learning;unlearning
learning cultures 93
learning organizations 89, 92,
    96–107
definitions 99, 104
leadership in 100
politics and 100, 102–4
power issues 97, 100–5
sceptic/pessimistic camp 97,
    100–102
universities as 99–100
visionary/propagandists
    camp 97–100
learning orientations 85–6
legitimate knowledge 238, 242
legitimate power 239–40, 241
leveraging strategy 59
loyalty, knowledge workers' 84,
    255, 265–7

M

McKinsey 65–6
management consultants,
    ambiguous impact and
    output 77–8
market factors 57
market-based culture 275
memory
    loss 129, 130f
    organizational 94, 97
    see also forgetting;unlearning
mentoring 36, 119–20, 262–3
mind–body dichotomy 32, 34
model-based systems 156
motivation to participate in
    knowledge management
    activities
    HRM role in 256–7
    intrinsic and extrinsic
    motivation 257, 263, 264
multinational corporations
    (MNCs) 55
    boundary-spanning collaboration
    in 219, 228–9
    communities of practice 206, 213
    knowledge sharing within 27–8,
    56–7, 219, 221–2, 223–4,
    228–9, 232–3, 260
    power/knowledge
    relationships 247–8

N

national cultural factors 38–9,
    118–19, 221
    and knowledge sharing 188–90,
        192, 223
neo-functionalist discourse on
        knowledge management 8,
        9, 18, 236
network-based approach 149t,
    164–6
new product development
    and knowledge creation 124–5
    unlearning and team reflexivity
        in 143–4
Nike 170–1
Nonaka's knowledge creation
        theory 17, 20, 110–20,
        123–4
    ba/shared space concept 111,
        116, 123–4
    critique of 116–19
    epistemology of 112–13
    SECI model 39, 111, 113–16,
        117–19, 283
normative control approach 63–4
Novartis 232–3

O

objectivist perspective
    on knowledge 8, 14, 15–29, 43,
        139, 198, 217
    on knowledge management
        25–6, 51, 151–62
office equipment service
        engineers 75–6
oil exploration industry 147
online communities 201, 203–4
online cross-organizational
        networks 40
open innovation 121–3, 169
organizational capital 79
organizational commitment 256,
    257–8, 265
organizational culture 51, 52t, 253,
    271–2, 273–8, 284
    definition 273
    impact on knowledge
        management
        activities 273–6, 284
    and innovation 276
    and knowledge sharing 284–5
    management 277–8
    and organizational learning 276
    sub-cultures 278
    typology 274–6
organizational identity 274
organizational information systems
        maturity 60

organizational learning 91
    Crossan/Zietsma framework
        94–6, 96t, 107–8
    definition 94
    discontinuities 107–8
    dynamics of 94–6
    and organizational culture 276
    time factors 107, 108
organizational memory 94, 97
outsourcing 80, 84, 138, 169

P

performance appraisal
        systems 258, 260, 263
personality
    and knowledge sharing
        attitudes 190–1, 192,
        259–60
    and leadership 279
    and propensity to trust 186
personalization knowledge
        management strategy 60–3,
        149t, 150t, 262, 263
perspective making and taking 37,
        38, 41, 42, 105, 227–8
Pfizer knowledge workers 80–1
polarization of labour market 7
politics 182, 183, 243
    and learning organizations 100,
        102–4
    and power 240–2
positivism 16
post-industrial society concept
        3–6, 7
power 181, 182, 183, 235
    and communities of
        practice 209–10
    and employment
        relationship 181, 235,
        243–4
    and knowledge sharing 240
    of knowledge workers 243–4
    and learning organizations 97,
        100–5
    legitimate 239–40, 241
    and politics 240–2
    resource-based perspective 237,
        238–44, 246, 248
power distance 189
power/knowledge 39, 102–3, 184,
        235, 236, 237, 238–40,
        244–9
    conceptualizing 245–6
    and conflict across organizational
        boundaries 246–8
    importance in knowledge
        management
        research 249–50

practice 30
    embeddedness of knowledge
        in 30, 31–3, 36
    immersion in 42
    indeterminacy of 36–7
    see also communities of practice
practice-based perspective
    on knowledge 8, 14, 30–45, 75,
        105, 112, 134, 189, 195, 198,
        217, 221, 227
    on knowledge management
        40–2, 51, 163–73
pragmatic boundaries 226, 227,
        230t, 231
probing strategy 59, 60, 66
procedural justice 182, 265
product design 170–1
productivity, knowledge
        workers' 73–4
professional service firms 70, 71
    learning orientations 85–6
project-based learning 93, 94, 129
public goods 178, 191

R

recruitment and selection 259–60
reference power 240
repository-based approach 26,
        149t, 152–5, 159
retention of workers 84, 257, 261,
        265–7
reward power 239, 240
reward systems 257, 258, 260,
        263–5
rule-based systems 156
Russia, and knowledge creation
        theory 119–20

S

SECI model of knowledge creation/
        conversion 39, 111,
        113–16, 117–19, 157, 283
semantic boundaries 226–7,
        230–1
sensible knowledge 32
service sector 3, 5, 6, 7
share/hoard dilemma 177,
        178–80, 256
shared knowledge 21, 22t
shared space see ba/shared space
        concept
skill(s)
    categories of 73
    intensity 5
small and medium-sized
        enterprises (SMEs) 54–5,
        56, 160–1, 271–2

social capital 79, 80, 81–2, 84,
    196, 266
social construction of
    knowledge 37–9
social identity theory 221
social media 140, 148, 163, 164,
    166, 167, 168–9, 171–2,
    180, 203
social network analysis 207–9
social order
    consensus-based perspective
        8, 236
    dissensus-based perspective 8,
        183, 235, 236–7, 244, 246
socialization, tacit knowledge 113,
    114, 115, 116, 117, 118, 119
socio-cultural factors 175–6,
    177–94
    conflict, ubiquity of 182–4, 191
    employment relationship
        180–2, 191
    group identity 187–8
    national culture 188–90, 192
    personality 190–1
    share/hoard dilemma 177,
        178–80
    trust 184–7, 191–2
spatial school 150t, 166–7
staff see knowledge workers
strategic leadership 280, 283
strategic school 150t, 169
structural holes theory 208
symbolic analysts 69, 72
syntactic boundaries 226, 227t, 230
system-based approach 149t, 157

T

tacit knowledge 7, 15, 16–17, 18,
    19–20, 27, 33, 34, 36, 61,
    74, 75, 78, 177–8, 242
    externalization of 25–6, 113,
        114–15, 118–19
    leakage 138–9
    protection 141, 142t
    sharing of 20, 25, 28, 222, 224,
        263, 276

socialization 113, 114, 115, 116,
    117, 118, 119
tacit–explicit dichotomy 19–20,
    21, 33, 112–13, 117–18
    and task productivity 20
task productivity, tacit/explicit
    knowledge and 20
teams
    reflexivity, and attitude to
        unlearning 137, 143–4
    transactive memory systems
        (TMSs) and knowledge
        sharing in 165
technology
    and knowledge leakage 138,
        140
    and unintentional forgetting 130
    see also ICTs
technology-organization-
    environment (TOE)
    framework 60
telemedicine, practice-based
    perspective on 32–3
theoretical knowledge 3–4, 7, 69,
    73, 74, 75
time factors, organizational
    learning 107, 108
training and development 92, 93,
    257, 258, 261–2
    cultural differences in 221
transactional leadership 272, 280,
    281
transactive memory systems
    (TMSs) 163, 164, 165
transformational leadership 272,
    280, 281, 283, 284
transmitter–receiver model see
    conduit model
trust 82, 123, 184–7, 256–7, 282
    and boundary-spanning
        knowledge processes
        224–6
    definition 185
    and knowledge sharing 184–7,
        187–8, 191–2, 224–6,
        240, 263
    and organizational culture 274

personality and propensity
    to 186
types of 186, 187
truth claims, legitimation of 246
turnover, staff 84, 255, 265

U

universities
    knowledge transfer 123
    as learning organizations
        99–100
unlearning 89, 126–7, 143
    and change relationship 131–3,
        135
    as deliberate forgetting 128–31
    and forgetting distinguished 127
    individual-level antecedents
        of 133, 134–5
    in joint ventures 127–8
    and knowledge creation 128
    and learning, relationship
        between 131–2
    organizational-level antecedents
        of 133, 135–7
    and team reflexivity 137, 143–4
    types of 133

V

Von Krogh et al.: knowledge
    strategy framework 58–9

W

weak tie theory 204, 208
Web 2.0 technologies 167, 262
Wikipedia 169
wikis 160–1, 164–5
William Bethwey and Associates,
    Australia 141
workflow management
    systems 155

Y

Yammer 168, 171–2